BRITAIN AND JAPAN
1859–1991

BRITAIN AND JAPAN
1859–1991

Themes and Personalities

Edited by Sir Hugh Cortazzi and
Gordon Daniels

Published on the occasion
of the centenary of the
Japan Society
1891–1991

London and New York

First published 1991
by Routledge
11 New Fetter Lane, London EC4P 4EE

Simultaneously published in the USA and Canada
by Routledge
a division of Routledge, Chapman and Hall, Inc.
29 West 35th Street, New York, NY 10001

Typeset in Garamond by
Falcon Typographic Art Ltd, Edinburgh & London
Printed and bound in Great Britain by
Biddles Ltd, Guildford and King's Lynn

British Library Cataloguing in Publication Data

Britain and Japan 1859–1991
I. Title   II. Cortazzi, Hugh, 1924–
III. Daniels, Gordon

ISBN 0–415–05966–6

Library of Congress Cataloging in Publication Data
has been applied for

ISBN 0–415–05966–6

CONTENTS

CONTENTS

CONTENTS

FIGURES

CONTRIBUTORS

Louis Allen Formerly of the School of Modern European Languages, Durham University, United Kingdom

Helen Ballhatchet Department of Economics, Keio University, Toyko, Japan

Carmen Blacker Japan Research Centre, University of Cambridge, United Kingdom

Richard Bowring Japan Research Centre, University of Cambridge, United Kingdom

Roger Buckley International Christian University, Osawa, Japan

John Clark Department of Far Eastern Art, Australian National University, Canberra, Australia

Sir Hugh Cortazzi Chairman of the Japan Society, and a former British Ambassador to Japan

Gordon Daniels Department of History, University of Sheffield, United Kingdom

Dallas Finn Specialist in Meiji architecture, Bethesda, Maryland, USA

Haruko Fukuda The Nikko Securities Co. (Europe) Ltd, London, United Kingdom

Valerie Hamilton Scottish Centre for Japanese Studies, University of Stirling, United Kingdom

Phillip Harries Queen's College, University of Oxford, United Kingdom

Colin Holmes Department of History, University of Sheffield, United Kingdom

Janet Hunter Department of Economic History, London School of Economics and Political Science, United Kingdom

A. H. Ion Department of History, Royal Military College of Canada, Ontario, Canada

P. F. Kornicki Japan Research Centre, University of Cambridge, United Kingdom

Sarah Metzger-Court Japanese Section, University of Birmingham, United Kingdom

Ian Nish Department of International History, London School of Economics and Political Science, United Kingdom

Jon Pardoe Manor House, Ville du Roi, St Peter Port, Guernsey, Channel Islands

Brian Powell Keble College, University of Oxford, United Kingdom

Dennis Smith Department of History, University of Ulster, Coleraine, United Kingdom

FOREWORD

Sir Hugh Cortazzi

The Japan Society (originally called the Japan Society of London) was started in September 1891 when a preparatory committee was formed. A small sum was set aside some years ago by the Council of the Society to celebrate the Society's centenary in 1991/2.

When proposals for a Japan Festival in the United Kingdom in the autumn of 1991 which would mark the Society's centenary took shape, the Council agreed to use the bulk of its centenary fund to produce a commemorative volume. The Council decided that the book should contain a history of the Society, but that the bulk of the work should be devoted to personalities who had been prominent in Anglo-Japanese relations since the establishment of modern diplomatic links in 1859. Approaches were made to scholars in Britain, Japan, Canada, Australia and the United States to contribute essays on various personalities in whom they had a particular interest. The Council wish to record their sincere thanks to the contributors.

A major problem was to select the personalities to be included. In principle, it was decided that personalities who had been the subject of recent monographs or whose contributions to Anglo-Japanese relations were already well known should not for the most part be covered in the book.

An attempt was also made in the commissioning of articles to choose individuals who are in one way or another representative of major aspects of Anglo-Japanese relations. Even so, there are many omissions, and if we had more space and more time we could have presented a fuller picture.

Why are there so few Japanese personalities covered in this book? One reason is that, despite the extent of British influence in the second half of the nineteenth century and the Anglo-Japanese Alliance of 1902 and its successors, Britain for Japan was just one of a number of major western powers.

Three essays cover the formative period of Anglo-Japanese relations in the final years of the Shogunate. A further ten illustrate developments in the Meiji period and when Britain exerted a major influence on Japan's modernization and the Anglo-Japanese Alliance became a central feature of British and Japanese diplomacy. Anglo-Japanese relations in the Taisho period are sketched in four studies which outline the ending of the Alliance and the broadening of links in the fields of literature and religious studies. The final essays in this collection analyse aspects of cultural relations in the Showa period and the impact of war on postwar Anglo-Japanese relations. Since the war the United States had not only replaced Britain as the dominant power in Japanese foreign relations but her universities have come to dominate Japanese studies in the western world.

Selective though the book is, it does, I think, demonstrate the wide variety of personalities, British and Japanese, who have contributed over the last hundred years or more to the relations between our two countries.

The book ends with a brief chronology of Anglo-Japanese relations since 1859. It is not possible in a short introduction to give a comprehensive survey of these years, but a brief overview setting the personalities covered in this book into context may be helpful.

INTRODUCTION

Sir Hugh Cortazzi and Gordon Daniels

Admiral James Stirling concluded the first British treaty with Japan in 1854. This was very limited in scope. Lord Elgin's mission in 1858 opened the way to the establishment of diplomatic and consular relations in 1859 when Rutherford Alcock arrived and established a British legation in the temple of Tozenji in Shinagawa, then a suburb of Edo. The next nine years, up to the Meiji Restoration in 1868, were dangerous ones for the diplomats and the traders who established themselves in the treaty ports, notably in Yokohama, which had a frontier-town atmosphere. Attacks and assassinations were frequent, and the British responded with gunboat diplomacy. Kagoshima was bombarded in retaliation for the murder of a British merchant at Namamugi on the Tokaido in 1862. In 1864 the British took the lead in bombarding Shimonoseki with the aim of keeping open the straits to the Inland Sea.

Charles Wirgman was a British artist who arrived soon after the reopening of Japan to the west and stayed on in Meiji Japan. He captured in his sketches the Yokohama scene. John Clarke in his essay on Wirgman notes that, 'Despite its limitations Wirgman's work has always remained as the first significant body of drawings and paintings by a western artist working in Japan'.

W.G. Aston and Ernest Satow were two of the first members of the Japan Consular Service to master the language and culture of the country. Their task, without dictionaries, manuals and grammars, was a formidable one. Aston's contribution to Japanese studies was significant but he is inevitably overshadowed by Satow as a diplomat if not as a scholar. Satow's account of his years in Japan in *A Diplomat in Japan* (1921) is one of the most exciting and fascinating diplomatic memoirs ever written. Thanks in part at least to the contacts which Satow established with young Japanese samurai from the outer fiefs, Sir Harry Parkes, the British minister, was not identified with the Tokugawa Shogunate in its decline and fall as was his French rival Leon Roches. This put the British in a relatively strong position for the post-Restoration period. Peter Kornicki's essays on Aston and Satow underline their contribution to the development of Anglo-Japanese relations in the second half of the nineteenth century.

The years from 1868 to 1882 were ones in which Britain often succeeded in exercising a major influence on Japan, supplanting the United States who in the 1860s had been involved in a destructive civil war. The French had supported the losing side in the Japanese civil war and were themselves defeated by the Prussians in the Franco-Prussian war of 1870–1. In terms of 'man years' just under half of the foreign employees, the *o-yatoi gaikokujin*, were British. But the Japanese were always careful to ensure that no country had a monopoly of influence and power. The Imperial Japanese Navy was trained by the British, but the army looked first to the French and then to the Germans. The British provided teachers of engineering and mathematics, but the Japanese turned to Germany for education in medicine. In matters of law, French influence was strong.

The Japanese authorities found Sir Harry Parkes difficult and arrogant, but they often respected him. The British were seen by the Japanese as the main obstacle to the revision of the unequal treaties of 1858, while the United States often seemed sympathetic to Japanese aspirations. The 1880s also saw a reaction to the cult of western customs and attitudes. From the beginning the Japanese had been determined to dispense as quickly as possible with their western tutors, and in the 1880s ths pace quickened. All these factors led to a decline in British influence, especially in the latter part of this period.

One of the British *yatoi* was Josiah Conder, who inspired much of the architecture of Meiji Japan. While many other foreign employees of the Meiji government were sent home in the 1880s, Conder was asked to stay on. His most famous building, the Rokumeikan was designed to advance the cause of Treaty Revision by providing a setting for western style entertainments. However as a tool of diplomacy its effectiveness remains doubted.

The Reverend Walter Weston is remembered in Japan not as a missionary and clergyman but as a mountaineer who introduced mountaineering and the appreciation of mountain scenery to millions of Japanese. A.H. Ion concludes that Weston's contribution must be regarded as 'one of the significant lasting legacies of British influence upon Japan in the the late nineteenth and twentieth centuries'.

Baba Tatsui is, as Helen Ballhatchet comments, 'interesting as a case study of the young western-educated Meiji intellectual'. He studied in Britain and was much influenced by British political thought, although he was critical as well as complimentary about Victorian Britain.

Sir Francis Taylor Piggott came to Japan as a legal adviser to Ito Hirobumi and was one of the last *yatoi*. He, and especially his son Major General F.S.G. Piggott, were devoted friends of Japan and staunch supporters of the

Japan Society. Indeed, Sir Francis was one of the founders of the Society and his son was one of the prime movers in re-establishing the Society after the end of the Second World War. Carmen Blacker gives a sympathetic account of their contribution to Anglo-Japanese relations.

Basil Hall Chamberlain was also a *yatoi* but is remembered more as a scholar of Japanese language and culture. Richard Bowring concludes his essay with Chamberlain's own words: 'I confess that patriotism, anywhere, is a thing altogether distasteful to my mind; for I was born cosmopolitan, began to travel and to learn foreign languages at the age of two and a half, and now feel at home in no country but an amused guest in all.'

Janet Hunter's essay on 'British Training for Japanese Engineers: The Case of Kikuchi Kyozo' is in fact a tribute to the educational work of Henry Dyer. His students, as she points out, 'played a crucial role in providing scarce skills for industries of strategic importance' for Japan.

Agreement was finally reached with Britain in 1894 on revision of the unequal treaties. The new arrangements did not come into force until 1899, but the Japanese felt that they were approaching a position of equality. Their victory in the Sino-Japanese war of 1894–5 came as a surprise to most people in the west. The British were impressed and did not associate themselves with the Triple intervention by France, Russia and Germany which humiliated the Japanese and left a deep feeling of resentment in Japan.

Ian Nish has charted the history of the Anglo-Japanese Alliance in earlier works and here contributes an account of the efforts of Hayashi Tadasu in London which led one British diplomat to describe him as 'the prime mover, if not the creator of the alliance'. Ian Nish concludes that Hayashi combined 'a desire for national progress with a sensitivity to internationalism'.

The Japanese victory in the Russo-Japanese War led to pacans of praise in Britain, for Japanese bravery, patriotism, modernity and national organizations. Indeed by 1907 Tokyo Imperial University was so well established that it provided a temporary base for Marie Stopes' scientific research.

But as Carmen Blacker points out in her account of Marie Stopes' connections with Japan, the most important single factor was her unconsummated love affair with a Japanese professor recorded in *Love Letters of a Japanese* and published anonymously in 1911. However she also developed a deep interest in the Noh and produced some of the first English translations of Noh plays. She read a paper to the Society on Japanese fossils in 1910 and was the first woman to take the chair at a lecture meeting. This was a meeting addressed by Arthur Waley on the Noh.

In the years btween 1905 and 1914 some British intellectuals saw Japan as a possible model for a reformed and strengthened British Empire. Against this background Sydney and Beatrice Webb visited Japan during their world tour in 1911–12. As Colin Holmes points out in his essay, the Webbs developed a very favourable view of Japan during their visit. Despite some criticisms, they emphasized that Japan was 'so civilized a country' and believed that Japan was 'still the land of the Rising Sun'. However by 1937 Beatrice Webb was disillusioned and wrote: 'Since the Great War she has been an evil influence in the world, intensely imperialist, militarist, insincere in her religious faith, reactionary in her political and economic doctrine. Japan has, in fact, "lost her head", and I think her soul.'

In the 1920s Anglo-Japanese relations began to deteriorate following the ending of the Anglo-Japanese Alliance, but during this decade, in the light of the efforts which some Japanese were making to develop a more democratic form of government for Japan, it was still possible for observers to believe that Japan could be a force for good in the world. After the beginning of the Manchurian 'Incident' and the rise of expansioned influence, Japan became increasingly unpopular in Britain. However the emotional ties which stemmed from the earlier alliance continued to influence some aspects of Japanese society. Malcolm Kennedy was one of these. He started as an army language officer, later joined the Rising Sun Oil Company of Japan and afterwards became Reuters correspondent in Japan. His book *The Problem of Japan*, published in 1935, sought, John Pardoe notes, 'to explain and to some extent justify Japanese action in Manchuria'.

Sir Charles Eliot, British ambassador to Japan from 1919 to 1925, was another supporter of the Japanese position in China in the 1920s, but he died (in 1931) before the aggressive character of Japanese policies was clearly demonstrated. Dennis Smith records that Eliot urged the Foreign Office to accept his view that 'British and Japanese interests in China did not conflict and that Britain should pursue policies in tandem with Japan rather than with the United States'. His account of 'Japanese Buddhism' was probably his greatest contribution to British understanding of Japan.

Admiral Yamanashi Katsunoshin was a Meiji figure who survived into the post-war world. As a naval cadet in 1895, he was steeped in the traditions of the Royal Navy. In 1900 he came to Britain to oversee the construction of the *Mikasa*, which became the flagship of The Japanese Navy. In the rest of his naval career, as Haruko Fukuda points out in her essay on Yamanashi, he played an important role in relations with Britain until his resignation as vice-minister for the navy in 1930. But this was not the end of the admiral's career, as he was appointed in 1939 to take charge of the education of the Crown Prince Akihito, now emperor of Japan. Six years later, in the aftermath of the war, he played a key role in suggesting the Emperor's renunciation of his 'divinity':

No book devoted to personalities in Anglo-Japanese relations would be complete without a tribute to Arthur Waley. Philip Harries reminds us that Waley 'made some of Japan's greatest literature available in English as classics in their own right', and 'For many who today pursue the study of Japan in many walks of life, he was the first inspiration and the model of humane, sensitive scholarship to which to aspire'.

A parallel Japanese figure was Tsubouchi Shōyō, who between 1909 and 1930 translated the whole of Shakespeare into Japanese. As Brian Powell notes, his translations 'had a rhythm and sonority that would not have been out of place on the *kabuki* stage'. Brian Powell also brings out Tsubouchi Shōyō's interest in western pageants as a device for developing new forms of popular drama.

William Plomer lived for nearly thirty years after the Second World War, but the Japan which he experienced and about which he wrote was Japan before the Second World War. Plomer was a homosexual who felt at home in Japan. He was a sensitive writer and poet and is certainly one of the better imaginative writers who were inspired by Japan. Louis Allen concludes with this quotation of what Japan meant to Plomer:

> Civilization has many dialects but speaks one language, and its Japanese voice will always be present to my ear, like the pure and liquid notes of the bamboo flute in those tropical evenings on the Indian Ocean when I heard it the first time, speaking of things far more important than war, trade and empires – of unworldliness, lucidity and love.

The Second World War left a legacy of bitterness in Anglo-Japanese relations which has not yet finally disappeared. But there have been many who in different ways have tried to bridge the gaps in our relations with Japan. This collection discusses three individuals who were active before the war but who continued to contribute to understanding between our two countries in the years following the Second World War.

The first of these is Professor G.C. Allen, who did so much to explain and recount Japan's economic development and to outline the background to Japan's economic miracle. Sarah Metzger-Court in her account of Allen's long association with Japan notes that in his speech accepting the Japan Foundation Award in 1980:

> he was able to sweep his audience through nearly sixty years of their own modern history in a single sentence. 'Since I first set foot in your country and remarked on the *daikon* drying on the pine trees in the neighbourhood of Nagoya, Japan has been transformed from an agricultural society with a fringe of modern industry to one of the most progressive and admired countries in the world.'

Our penultimate essay is by Roger Buckley on Sir Esler Dening, the first British ambassador to Japan after the war and a distinguished former member of the Japan Consular Service. Dening's time as ambassador to Japan from 1951 to 1957 was a difficult one in Anglo-Japanese relations. British resentment against and suspicions of Japan were still strong, and Dening, who had worked in Japan and in Japanese occupied Manchuria and Korea before the war, had justifiable doubts about the Japanese pre-war politicians who controlled the governments of post-war Japan. But he noted that 'just disliking the Japanese may prove an expensive luxury' and that 'if their outlook is materialistic and their policy governed by self-interest, I do not know that this differs very much from other nations with whom we have close relations'.

Finally, Sir George Sansom's career is analysed in an essay which outlines his diplomatic and scholarly activities before, during and after the Pacific War. Sansom's diplomatic experiences in Washington, and his final years at Columbia and Stanford vividly illustrate America's emergence as the major force in Japan's foreign relations and as the centre of Japanese studies in the west. As Gordon Daniels points out his greatest achievements were those of a historian who combined courage, humanity and scholarly refinement.

CONVENTIONS

Throughout the book Japanese names appear in the style of that language; that is, surname first and given name second.

1

THE JAPAN SOCIETY:
A HUNDRED-YEAR HISTORY

Sir Hugh Cortazzi

When I undertook to prepare a history of the Society for its centenary I did not realize what a wealth of material I would find. First, there are the *Transactions and Proceedings* up to the Second World War and the *Bulletins* and *Proceedings* in the post-war period. Second, there are six large volumes covering the minutes of the Council's meetings up to 1966. Third, and possibly the most fascinating, were some large volumes of cuttings about the Society, its personalities and its activities in the years up to 1914. It was not an easy task to select from this mass of material. I have tried to make my selection and the account of the Society as objective and balanced as possible but, as an amateur historian, I found some of the earlier material particularly interesting and I have accordingly written a good deal more about the early years of the Society than about the post-war period. I have also included some material which only concerns the Society's activities marginally, because some of it seemed to me amusing. I hope that these items will add an element of interest to the account of the Society's activities over a hundred years which otherwise would inevitably make turgid reading.

ORIGINS AND EARLY ACTIVITIES OF THE JAPAN SOCIETY

The Japan Society was founded during the International Congress of Orientalists held in London in 1891. At a meeting of the Japanese Section of the Congress on 9 September 1891 in the library of the Incorporated Law Society, with Professor L. de Rosny of Paris in the chair, Mr Arthur Diosy, one of the honorary secretaries of the Section:

> explained a scheme, which he had prepared several years ago, for the establishment in London of a society for the encouragement of Japanese studies and for the purpose of bringing together all those in

1

the United Kingdom, and throughout the world, interested in Japanese matters.

This proposal was warmly supported by other members of the Section, and a resolution proposed by Diosy and seconded by Mr Daigoro Goh, chancellor of the Imperial Japanese Consulate General in London, was passed unanimously calling on Messrs Diosy and Goh as honorary secretaries *pro tem* to take preliminary steps to establish a society. The Society's objectives were stated to be 'the encouragement of the study of the Japanese Language, Literature, History and Folk-Lore, of Japanese Art, Science and Industries, of the Social Life and Economic Condition of the Japanese People, past and present, and of all Japanese matters'.

Diosy and Goh 'obtained the valuable co-operation' of Mr (later Sir) Francis T. Piggott, who had been Legal Adviser to the Japanese cabinet and proceeded to form an organizing council. Three meetings of this Council were held at the Royal Society of Arts in John Street, Adelphi. The first took place on 8 December 1891 with the acting Japanese Consul-General in the chair. There were 124 original members and two corresponding members. Professor William Anderson FRCS was elected as the first chairman.[1]

F.T. Piggott became vice-chairman. Diosy and Goh were confirmed as honorary secretaries. Among the members of the first Council were Mr Lasenby Liberty of Liberty's department store in Regent Street, Mr (later Sir) Alfred East, painter, and Mr M. B. Huish, whose book *Japan and Its Art* had been first published in 1888. The Japanese minister, Viscount Kawase, became the first president, and vice-presidents included Lord Brassey (the Railway magnate); Lord de Saumarez, who had been in the British Legation in Tokyo; Sir E.J. Reed MP, whose book *Japan, Its History, Traditions and Religions with the Narrative of a Visit in 1879* had been published in two volumes in 1880; Mr (later Sir) Ernest Satow; and the Hon. P.H. Le Poer Trench, who had been British minister in Tokyo in succession to Sir Harry Parkes. The Council's offices were at 20 Hanover Square in London, and annual subscriptions were set at one guinea for ordinary members and half a guinea for corresponding members. A nucleus of a library was formed.

The inaugural meeting of the Society was held at the Royal Society of Arts on 29 April 1892. After an address from the president, a lecture was delivered by Mr T. Shidachi of Tokyo on 'Ju-Jitsu, The Ancient Art of Self-Defence by Sleight of Body':

> Mr Shidachi illustrated his lecture by practical demonstrations, with the assistance of Mr Daigoro Goh, *Hon. Secretary*. Several modes of defeating an assailant were shown, the Lecturer repeatedly throwing Mr Goh over his head, apparently with the greatest ease.

Other lectures in the first series were on 'the Uses of Bamboo in Japan', 'Some Japanese Industrial Art Workers' (Crape Printers), 'The Naturalistic Art of

Japan' and 'The Genealogy of the Miochin Family, Armourers, Swordsmiths and Artists in Iron'.

The first annual dinner of the Society was held on Thursday 23 June 1892 in the Whitehall Rooms of the Hotel Metropole, Whitehall Place, London. The price of a ticket including wines was one guinea (Fig. 1.1). There were many toasts in addition to the loyal toasts to the Queen and the Emperor. One toast, 'Success to the Japan Society', coupled with the name of Mr Arthur Diosy, 'to whom the Society owes so very much – indeed, its foundation', was proposed by Sir J.J. Trevor Lawrence Bart., MP. 'The toast was received with great cheering, the Band playing *Miya Sama*, as arranged by Sir Arthur Sullivan. The toast to the Royal Navy was inevitably followed by the band playing *Rule Britannia* and that to the British army by *The British Grenadiers!*' After dinner the company adjourned to the Victoria Room. 'The scene was a brilliant one, many Members and Guests wearing Orders and Medals, and the dresses of several of the Ladies being of Japanese brocade and embroidered silks. Eighteen Japanese were present, amongst them one Lady.'

On 1 November 1892 Viscount Kawase wrote to the chairman, Professor Anderson, conveying the 'approbative greetings, coupled with the hope for its continued prosperity' of His Majesty the Emperor of Japan on the foundation of the Society. A cheque for 100 guineas as a present from the Emperor to the Society was enclosed.

In the review of the first session prepared on 31 August 1892 the honorary secretaries summed up the work of the Society under three headings: 'Encouragement of Research, Dissemination of Information and Stimulation of a Demand for Information'. They noted that 'Attempts were made from various quarters to involve the Society in the discussion of political and religious questions of a controversial nature. They were all politely, but firmly, resisted.'

A number of honorary members were soon elected to the Society. They included scholars such as W.G. Aston; Captain F. Brinkley; Basil Hall Chamberlain; John Gubbins, then Japanese secretary to the British Legation at Tokyo; John Milne, Professor of Mining and Engineering at Tokyo Imperial University; Kakuzo Okakura, Principal of the Tokyo College of Fine Arts and author of *The Book of Tea* (1906); Professor J.J. Rein of the University of Bonn and author of *Japan, Travels and Researches* (published in English by Hodder & Stoughton, London 1884) and *Industries of Japan* (published in English by Hodder & Stoughton, London 1884 and 1889); and Lieutenant Julien Viaud of the French Navy (i.e. Pierre Loti, author of *Madame Chrysanthème*).

In addition to the library, the Society established its own 'museum' with the object of forming 'a Collection of such specimens of Japanese Works of Art and Industry, and of the Natural Products of Japan, as are not, usually found in Public or Private Collections, and which may serve to illustrate various phases of Japanese Life, Manners and Customs'. The first catalogue

The Japan Society,
LONDON.

FIRST
ANNUAL DINNER.

THE PRESIDENT,

HIS EXCELLENCY the JAPANESE MINISTER

VISCOUNT KAWASÉ,

IN THE CHAIR.

THURSDAY, 23RD JUNE, 1892

WHITEHALL ROOMS:
HÔTEL METHOPOLE,
LONDON.

Menu Du Diner.

Hors d'Oeuvres variés.

POTAGES.
Consommé Tachibana Himé.
Purée Portugaise à la Mendez Pinto.
—o—
DRY SHERRY.

POISSONS
Saumon, Sauce Hollandaise à la Deshima.
Blanchaille à la Urashima et à la Onigashima.
—o—
NIERSTEINER.

ENTRÉES.
Tournedos à la Ushiwaka.
Aspic de Foies Gras à la Katata-no Ruku-Gan.

Sorbet Moskovite.

MAX SUTAINE & CO., EXTRA QUALITY, EX. DRY 1884.

RÔTS.
Selle de Pré Salé à la Broche.
Jambon Braisé au Madière.
—o—
PIPER HEIDSIECK, BRUT 1834.

Petits Pois au Beurre.
Pommes de Terre Satsuma.
Cailles Rôties sur Tokonoma.
Salade Nana Kusa.
—o—
BORDEAUX CHATEAU BÉCHEVILLE.

ENTREMETS.
Turban à la Futami-ga Ura.
Japonaise de Fraises au Champagne à la Nikko.

LIQUEURS.

Filet de "Bloater" à la Will Adams
Glacé.
Bombe Fuji-Yama.
Gâteaux Shojo.

Dessert.   Café Noir.

COCKBURN'S OLD BOTTLED PORT.

TOASTS:
"THE QUEEN"
"THE EMPEROR OF JAPAN."
"THE JAPAN SOCIETY."

Figure 1.1   Menu of the first annual dinner of the Japan Society

was reproduced in the second volume of the *Transactions and Proceedings*. The list of objects in the catalogue does not suggest that the Society had acquired any great treasures.

The Daily Graphic, dated Monday 6 June 1892, reported on a 'Japanese Night' dinner of 'The Sette of Odd Volumes' presided over by His Oddship Dr William Morrell. Many of those present were apparently members of the Japan Society, including Messrs Diosy, Piggott and Huish. In response to a toast, the Japanese naval attaché responded 'in his own tongue'. Oscar Wilde, who was a guest, 'was called upon to respond for himself, an opportunity of which he made the most, prefacing his remarks by assuring the Sette that it was the one subject that had engrossed his attention from his earliest recollection'. *The Graphic* recorded that 'The menu of the evening, presented by brother Huish, suggested the gathering of a kindred society in Japan, discussing an apology for English art!'

Another Japanese evening involving members of the Japan Society was the 1895 annual banquet of the London Thirteen Club on 13 March that year. Thirteen items of music included the Japanese national anthem played by Mr Pougher's 'Bijou' orchestra. They also played the *Mazurka Japonaise* '*Mousme*', *Cho-Cho-Tombo* and *Miya Sama*. The menu card was brief:

As a knowledge of what is to come dulls the edge of appetite, the list of dishes is withheld. Everyone is at liberty to ask the waiters for a full description of the goods the gods provide, and reject one or all of the proferred dishes. One glass of *saqui* will be served out to each guest; if, which is highly improbable, a second is desired, it will not be withheld.

The inauguration of the Society and its first meetings were generally the subject of favourable comments in the press of the time, but some ironic comments were inevitable. *The Umpire* of 4 June 1893 started an article on the subject as follows:

The latest society for the minding of somebody else's business is a Japan Society which has just been formed in London with the object of setting matters right in Japan. We have hitherto been very much in the habit of regarding the territory of the Mikado as a sort of great museum or wholesale manufactory whence we get innumerable quaint and artistic articles at a remarkably cheap rate. But now that we have a Japan Society, this deplorable ignorance is to be done away with, and we shall be expected to shudder as each phase of unsound political and social life is laid bare, and the 'unaccustomed brine' will be expected to flow at the recountal of the wrongs of the Japs.[2]

The Society continued during the next few years to hold regular lectures on a variety of subjects with a high proportion on aspects of Japanese art, but there were also lectures on such diverse subjects as mountaineering in Japan, Japanese railways, Japanese pastimes and amusements.

One lecture given by Mr F.H. Balfour of 26 June 1894 on the subject of 'Court and Society in Japan' contained some condescending comments. He noted that

> the emperor is a good and thoroughly honest man, with a large amount of common sense; but happily for Japan, he has no ambition to pose as a genius, and he can be on occasion, extremely tenacious. His great passion is for horses and military reviews; he is always reviewing this or the other garrison, and takes the very keenest interest in the army. He is also a keen critic of ladies' dresses, and it may interest some present to hear that His Majesty detests the present fashion of sleeves puffed out at the shoulders. He says they are like angels' wings and altogether ridiculous.

Another of Balfour's comments was:

> By your side in a railway carriage, or at a dinner-table, or in a smoking-room, you have a pleasant well-dressed gentleman, who reads his paper, and drinks his champagne, and smokes his cigarette just like anybody else; he is not particularly brilliant, but he has probably taken a degree at Cambridge, and knows something about ecclesiastical architecture, and remembers a ballet he once saw at the Alhambra; essentially a man of the 19th century, AD. And then you think to yourself – Now, five-and-twenty years ago, that man would have been invisible; if ever he went out of doors he would have been carried in a close-shut chair, and accompanied by a great cavalcade of formidable armed men; and if I, meeting him, had not got out of the way, or abstained from going on my knees and head before him, his retainers would have cut me down with their swords, he knowing or caring nothing whatever about it.

Balfour deplored the globe trotters' delight in the *musume*, whom he described as a

> plump, dimpled little person, much given to giggling and squirming, and characterized by a primitiveness, an innocence (to put it mildly) in her demeanour towards the other sex which was frequently misunderstood'. He went on to describe 'Society which is composed of ladies who, in all essential respects, are the counterparts of their European sisters. The stately Marchioness Nabeshima, formerly Ambassadress at Rome, who gives delightful balls; the beautiful Countess Toda, formerly Ambassadress at Vienna, and generally considered the belle of Tokyo; the homely, but gracious and kindly Countess Saigo, one of the very best women in Japan; good old Viscountess Hijikata, in her everlasting black silks; the pious and charitable Princess Mori and Princess Sanjo, so constant in their attendance at the great Hongwanji'

He declared: 'one meets the Imperial Family everywhere. . . . They dance with immense spirit, and their frocks and jewels are, as might be expected, much criticized and admired.'

A lecture on 'Japanese Shipping' by Francis Elgar in May 1895 led to an exchange which seems to have become fairly heated. Mr Martell, chief surveyor of Lloyd's Register of Shipping, commented that Japan would soon become 'a difficult competitor'. After drawing attention to the development of Japanese shipbuilding and steel production, he said that he had been told that the Japanese could make a ship of between 3,000 and 4,000 tons for something like £4,000 less than it would cost in Britain. This irritated the naval architect Sir E.J. Reed. But Captain Inglis, who had been naval adviser to The Japanese Navy agreed with Martell that 'we had better beware of Japan'. The chairman, Mr Takakaki Kato, the Japanese minister in London, thanked Dr Elgar 'for the sympathetic way in which he had dealt with the aspirations of the Japanese people'.

On 23 February 1898 Mr Noel E. Buxton read a paper on 'Mountaineering in Japan'. Ernest Satow, who was in the audience, is recorded as having said that the great charm of mountaineering in Japan was that 'there were no crowds of tourists, with guides all over the place, and one did not cut one's feet, when climbing the mountains, with broken champagne bottles'.

On 8 November 1899 Arthur Diosy, then vice-chairman of the Society, whose book *The New Far East* had been published in 1898, gave 'Some Account of My Recent Visit to Japan'. He spoke with enthusiasm about the new Japan and the Japanese he met:

> I do not suppose that many of you realize what a grand thing it is to be a member of the Japan Society; you would not realize it until you go out to Japan. I found that in remote hamlets the Japan Society's 'passport' was a more potent document than that issued from the Foreign Office in Downing Street, and I found that the mere mention of the words 'Rondon Nippon Kiokwai,' meaning 'the London Japan Society', brought every Policeman smartly up to the salute, and caused every Village Headman to double up in the most graceful and profound Japanese bow. . . . Everything that could be done by a body corporate, or by individuals, was done at once for the travelling Member of the Japan Society. That is because the Japanese know that ours is a Society composed of their friends, and there is no nation in the world whose heart goes out more warmly to the people who love them than the Japanese. . . . I am sure it would have warmed your hearts if you could have heard the words in which His Majesty the Emperor deigned to express himself about the work of this Society when I had the honour of being received in farewell audience, a few days before I left Japan.

Diosy declared: 'If the navy is a miracle, the army is a marvel.' He admired such things as Japanese prisons' and the great copper-mine at Ashio. He

7

thought that 'we were just about a quarter of a century behind Japan in applied electricity'. He concluded that Japan was 'a thoroughly sound country'.

Diosy had been much pleased by a garden party given in honour of himself and his wife at Shinjuku Gardens by 'the Old Country Club', a Japanese Society consising of Japanese who had resided in Britain.[3] The chairman, Professor Anderson, commented that 'It was not to be wondered at that Mr Diosy felt at home in Japan, for he really was at home in that country. The explanation might be that Mr Diosy, in a previous state of existence, had been a Japanese.'

Mr Arthur Diosy, of part Hungarian origin, had been made an honorary Commander of the Order of the Rising Sun in 1895. The Society's scrap books are full of cuttings about his doings, his speeches and his knowledge of Japan. *To-Day*, dated 20 June 1896, for instance, recorded an interview with Diosy under the heading 'How "The Geisha" was "Japanned"'. Diosy had been selected to advise on the production of the popular musical *The Geisha*, by Mr George Edwardes, because he 'probably knows more about Japan and the Japanese than any other man in England; in addition to which he is the founder and Vice-Chairman of the Society'. The first thing he did 'was to supply Mr Edwardes with an accurate description of the Japanese girl, her physical characteristics and ways, more especially, of course, those of the Geisha'.

> The choice was so carefully made, that it may safely be said there are not thirty European women in existence who look so thoroughly Japanese as the ladies taking Japanese parts in 'The Geisha'. . . . A Japanese gentleman, who attended some of the rehearsals, came up and spoke to Miss Colette, thinking she must be a native.

Diosy became chairman of the Society in 1901 following the death of Professor Anderson and remained chairman until 1904, when he was replaced by Mr Charles Holme, who had been honorary secretary of the Society. Diosy's penchant for flamboyant self-promotion led after his retirement as chairman to a resolution of the Council on 2 November 1904 criticising advertisements declaring him to be 'the Founder of the Society, and also as the Vice-President of the Society, distinctions which he only shares in common with some other members of the Society'. The resolution also noted that 'neither Mr Diosy nor the Japan Society are entitled to take credit for the welcome Treaty of Alliance [The Anglo-Japanese Alliance of 1902] which was so happily concluded by those great statesmen who represented England and Japan'. The passing of this resolution led Mr Diosy to send a telegram on 5 January resigning from the Council. The tiff was patched up and Arthur Diosy continued to play a prominent part in the work of the Society in future years (Fig. 1.2).

Annual dinners on the lines of the inaugural dinner were held at the

Figure 1.2 Arthur Diosy

A JAPANESE DINN

The second annual dinner of the Japan Society was held on Tuesday in the Whitehall Rooms of the Hôtel Métropole. The president of the society, the Japanese Minister, Viscount Kawasé, and the Viscountess received the guests upon arrival. About two hundred and forty sat down to dinner. The artistic menu bore upon the fly-leaf a delightful little sketch, apparently drawn by a Japanese

WHAT OUR ARTIST EXPECTED TO SEE.
(*A Sketch made before going to the dinner.*)

artist. The dishes were all given Japanese names, but proved to be familiar friends in disguise. The following announcement was made to the guests :—
"The dinner committee of the council regret to announce that, owing to neglect on the part of a forwarding agent in Japan, the bamboo baskets (*Take-Kago*) and the Kioto confectionery (*Hi-Gwashi*) have not arrived in time for dinner. They will be

THE JAPANESE MINISTER, VISCOUNT KAWASÉ, PROPOSING THE HEALTH OF THE QUEEN.

distributed on arrival to members and guests who attend the dinner." While dinner was in progress the Bijou Orchestra, under the conductorship of Mr. J. Pougher, played a selection of music, among the pieces being several Japanese melodies. The president and Viscountess Kawasé sat side by side in the centre of the chief table ; while upon the Viscountess's right were Sir Trevor Lawrence, Bart., Professor Church, F.R.S., and Mr. Cock, Q.C., and upon the Viscount's left Lady Lawrence, and Professors Ander-

' DRINKING THE EMPEROR OF JAPAN'S HEALTH IN SAKÉ.

son and Roberts-Austen. The Japanese Minister proposed the health of the Queen, and Sir Trevor Lawrence that of the Emperor of Japan. The latter was drunk in *saké*, the national wine—a drink which is not likely to become popular in England. "The Japan Society" was proposed by Professor Anderson, and "The President" by Dr. Elgar.

Figure 1.3 'A Japanese Dinn' (*St James Budget*, 30 June 1893)

Metropole Hotel. The second annual dinner provoked some amusing sketches in 'St James Budget' under the heading 'A Japanese Dinn' (Fig. 1.3).

One of the speakers at the third annual dinner of the Society on 21 May 1894 was Sir Edwin Arnold, the author and poet who was married to a Japanese lady. He declared that the Japanese were 'the Greeks of Asia' and lavished praises on Japan and the Japanese. This provoked *Punch* to produce a cartoon of 'Sir Edwin Mikarnoldo' with the subtitle 'A Real Good Jap saluting the Rising Sun' (Fig. 1.4).

At the seventh annual dinner on 12 May 1898 the toast to the Society was proposed by the Earl Spencer, who had just returned from a visit with Countess Spencer to Japan. As a former First Lord of the Admiralty he had naturally been interested in The Japanese Navy. In Tokyo 'he had to speak at a great dinner when he addressed about three hundred Japanese, who did not understand him, and about twenty Englishmen, who, he hoped, did understand him'.

The Society was involved in July and August 1893 with the 'Cornwall Fisheries Exhibition' at Truro. The Society forwarded from their library 'a book of stencil reproductions' and an original plate consisting of two leaves cut separately. According to the *Cornwall Gazette* for 3 August 1893 the Japanese exhibits 'which were supposed to be among the most attractive . . . although despatched from London four or five days before the exhibition opened, did not arrive until the end of the week'. At the 'One and All' Dinner for the exhibition Mr Goh, honorary secretary of the Society, who 'has a Japanese accent but speaks English well . . . made a capital humorous speech'. He noted that

> Both countries were largely dependent on fish, and had skilful fisher-men and brave sailors. He had been particularly struck by the similarity between Japan and the county of Cornwall on account of its extensive coast, and tin and copper being its chief minerals. . . . The English people did not eat as much fish as the Japanese, and if the traditional belief was true that fish was good for the brain, the Japanese had good chance of becoming the cleverer nation of the two. (Laughter and applause.)

In its early years the Lord Mayors of London tended to be closely involved with the Society. In 1894, according to *The Daily Graphic*, one of the most successful of the receptions given by Sir George and Lady Tyler, the Lord Mayor and Lady Mayoress, was that in July 1894 to meet the Japanese Minister (Viscount Aoki) and other members of the Japan Society. *The Daily Telegraph* for 25 July 1894 recorded that 'A collection of art metal work, including sword mounts, arrow wings, keys, and locks, was supplemented by some exquisite embroideries.' The 'Bijou' Orchestra played a selection of music which included *Mazurka Japonaise*, entitled *Mousme* by Ganne, and *Miyako-Dori* [sic] (a) *Sayonara* and (b) *Honen Uta*.

FANCY PORTRAIT.

SIR EDWIN MIKARNOLDO.
A Real Good Jap saluting the Rising Sun.

[" We admire the secret of that delicate artistic gift . . . which makes you the Greeks
of Asia. . . . It is impossible that a splendid future should not lie before the Empire of
the Rising Sun."—*Extract from Speech made by Sir Edwin Arnold at the Japanese Society
Banquet at the Hôtel Métropole, Monday, May* 21.]

Figure 1.4   Sir Edwin Arnold (*Punch*, 2 June 1984)

The Society's scrap books contain other references to exhibitions. There is
for instance an invitation to the Horniman Museum from Mr F.J. Horniman,
a member of the Society, to meet the Japanese minister and members of the
Society on 26 October 1894. There is also an invitation to a private view
at the Goupil Gallery at 5 Regent Street, Waterloo Place, London, to an
exhibition of 'A Connoisseur's Treasures being paintings and Drawings by

Mr J.M. Whistler, Sir E. Burne-Jones, Bt, Mr G.F. Watts, RA, D.G. Rossetti, Mr Albert Legros, Albert Moore and others together with Rare Artistic examples of . . . Japanese Bronzes.'

Exhibitions also played a part in the regular annual *Conversazione* organized by the Society. For instance, the *Conversazione* held at the premises of the Royal Institute of Painters in Water Colours in Piccadilly on 26 January 1898 featured an exhibition of Japanese embroideries and brocades lent by members of the Society. The *Conversazione* was from 9 pm to 11.30 pm. 'Evening Dress' was specified. There was a 'Bijou band' and refreshments were served. Tickets cost five shillings.

The Society was involved in collecting money for relief of sufferers in Japan from the tidal wave that struck the north-east coast of Japan in June 1896. A total of £3,872 8s 4d was handed over and distributed by the Governors of Aomori, Iwate and Miyagi prefectures.

In its first decade the Society had got off to a good start. By 1 August 1897 the number of members had risen to 803. The average attendance at the first three lectures was 166 and seems to have remained high throughout the first decade as an average attendance at lectures of 200 was recorded in 1905.

THE SOCIETY IN THE HEYDAY OF ANGLO-JAPANESE RELATIONS, 1902–14

The Society prospered in the climate engendered by the Anglo-Japanese Alliance of 1902 and its members joined in the general admiration of Japanese exploits in the Russo-Japanese War of 1904–5. The culmination for the Society was the Japan–British Exhibition at Shepherds Bush in 1910.

At the seventy-first ordinary meeting of the Society on 13 January 1904 Arthur Diosy, the chairman, opened the proceedings with a few words about the crisis in the Far East: 'The nation in which we are all so deeply interested will come out of the ordeal with credit to itself; the Japanese people will quit themselves like men, as they have always done before.' The paper which followed these remarks was somewhat ironically on 'The Bringing up of Japanese Girls' by Mr Chukuro Kadono, a member of the Council.

At the next meeting, on 10 February 1904, the chair was taken by Mr Charles Holme, the honorary secretary, who pointed out that 'current politics are wisely excluded' from the scope of the Society's work. He added that the Society was receiving 'a very large number of letters from British officers desirous of joining the Japanese forces' but said that these should be directed to the representatives of the Imperial Japanese Government in Britain. The Society would, however, be considering whether it would be possible to 'do something, from a purely humanitarian motive, for the succour of the sick and wounded'. The Society duly issued an appeal for funds for the relief of the sick and wounded in the war to be handed over through the president, Viscount Hayashi, to the Red Cross Society of Japan.

At the thirteenth annual dinner in May 1904, which was addressed by the Japanese politician Baron Kencho Suematsu, Viscount Hayashi expressed appreciation of the 'handsome manner' in which members of the Japan Society and others had contributed to the Red Cross Fund. *'Tit-Bits'* for 8 October 1904 recorded that more than £20,000 had been handed to Viscountess Hayashi for the Fund of which she was the English head. Some £3,000 had been collected by the Japan Society.

On 13 December 1905 Mr Alfred Stead read a eulogistic paper on 'Japanese Patriotism'. Mr Stead began as follows:

> A spirit of fervent patriotism has always been one of the most highly prized treasures of the Japanese nation. In Japan patriotism is the corner stone of the national existence, it is the flame illuminating every heart from palace to farmer's hut, and providing the motive power for all national action.

He also heaped praise on the Japanese army and navy, declaring that their traditions 'are the finest and the most potent ones which teach love of country and loyalty to the emperor – there is no fetish-worship of buttons and shoulder-straps'. According to the report in the *Transactions*, members of the audience who spoke after the paper were equally uncritical. A visitor suggested that the British should study Bushido. A member called on his fellow countrymen to follow the Japanese example declaring: 'We think too much of our rights and too little of our duties. The time is coming when the individual must help the State.' Another member asked: 'How can we aspire to be equal to a nation which lives at the fountain of life? The Japanese have everything that a man can think and pray and hope for. We in England should have a little more chrysanthemum and rather less football.' Yet another member contrasted unfavourably the attitude of the two parliaments: 'During the Boer War every sum of money voted in parliament was subject to much criticism, question and opposition'. The vote of thanks proposed by the Right Honourable Lord Strathcona and Mount Royal, one of the Society's vice-presidents, was 'carried with applause'.

The next lecture on 10 January 1906 was on 'The Red Cross Society in Japan' by Miss Ethel McCaul. She ended her paper with these words: 'O Japan! you have allowed all nations to see the purity of your soul, which is as perfect as the petals of the cherry blossom. May we, who have witnessed your life-struggle, learn some of the lofty lessons you have so humbly laid before us.'

The Society was much involved in these years with visiting Japanese princes and statesman. Marquis (later Prince) Hirobumi Ito was in London in January 1902.[4] On 3 January of that year he received a delegation from the Society at his hotel. Viscount Hayashi, the Japanese minister, presented to Ito Sir Laurence Alma-Tadema, vice-president of the Society,[5] and Mr Arthur Diosy, the chairman. According to the *Standard* of 4 January, Ito, speaking in Japanese, which was interpreted into English by Hayashi, expressed his appreciation of the great work which the Society had done in promoting and cementing friendly relations between Japan and Great Britain. He later replied 'in excellent English' to the greetings of the Society conveyed by Diosy. He thanked the officers of the Society, declared his delight at the increase in its membership and expressed 'the hope that all good Britons would join' the Society.

In May 1902 Count Masayoshi Matsukata, former prime minister and finance minister, and Countess Matsukata visited London. They attended the eleventh annual dinner of the Society at the Metropole Hotel. The Lord Mayor, Sir Albert Rollitt, Bt, in proposing a toast to the Japanese minister (according to the *Islington Gazette* of 15 May 1902) declared that the minister

> ably represented the Emperor of Japan, the 123rd Sovereign of his dynasty, the first one being contemporary with Nebuchadnezzar, reigning in the palmy days of Greece, about the time when Romulus and Remus were skipping over the rising walls of ancient Rome, and when the English nation itself was growing somewhere on the Elbe – was in fact being made in Germany.

The coronation of Edward VII brought other Japanese notables to London in July 1902. The emperor was represented by Prince Akihito Komatsu, his brother. On 14 July the Japan Society entertained at a garden party at the Botanical Gardens in Regents Park Rear Admiral Ijuin and officers of the Japanese naval squadron which had escorted the prince to Britain. This consisted of the *Asama* and the *Takasago*. The band of the *Asama* played selections of European and Japanese music. The Viscountess Hayashi wore, according to the *Pall Mall Gazette* of 15 July, 'a most graceful dress of grey crepe de chine, knife pleated, trimmed with lace, a white chiffon ruffle and large white hat, while round the yoke of her bodice was a lovely wreath of pale pink flowers in crepe, evidently of Japanese manufacture.' The band played several Japanese airs which were 'pathetic and haunting, reminding those present of the weird strains which pervaded that delightful little play, *Madame Butterfly*, melodies which seem to have no stereotyped beginning and no conventional end'. Many papers carried a photograph of the very tall figure of Sir Alfred Gaselee, late commander-in-chief in China, in full dress uniform with sword and white handlebar moustache talking to a tiny Japanese officer (Fig. 1.5).

The garden party was followed by a visit to Portsmouth by Viscount Hayashi who among others was accompanied by Arthur Diosy. The mayor of Portsmouth also gave a garden party at which the band of the *Asama* performed. *The Daily Telegraph* of 16 August 1902 commented: 'One has frequently remarked the close resemblance between the English Jack Tar and his new ally the sturdy Jap.'

Figure 1.5   Sir Alfred Gaselee talking to a Japanese officer at the Japan Society's
garden party, July 1902

The Japan Society was again entertained at the Mansion House in April
1903 by the Lord Mayor and Lady Mayoress Sir Marcus and Lady Samuel.
Sir Marcus Samuel (later Lord Bearsted), the founder of Marcus Samuel &
Company, merchants and merchant bankers, and of the Shell Oil Company,
had had a long-standing business relationship with Japan and was a friend
of Viscount Hayashi. An exhibition of bonsai and flower arrangements was
given in the long gallery and a programme of music was supplied by the
Viennese White Band under the direction of a Herr Wurm.

16

In January 1904 Diosy, the chairman of the Society, embroiled himself in a controversy with the famous actor Mr Beerbohm Tree. According to the *Daily Mirror* of 18 January 1904, in a speech at the 'Playgoers Club' on the subject of 'The Japanese Stage', Diosy criticized the play *The Darling of the Gods* as hopelessly un-Japanese.

> It smells of the carpenter's glue. . . . The play is, I imagine, the outcome of a long railway journey taken by Mr Luther Long and Mr Belasco. They made a hasty purchase at the car bookstalls of Japanese illustrated books, and Long scanned the letterpress while Belasco glanced at the pictures. . . . The exclamations are Chinese, the invocations of the heroine absurd, and one little cry instead of meaning something very sweet means really – the opposite of heaven. . . . To sum up, Mr Tree has done his best to give real Japan and hopelessly failed, as all western stage managers will.

In a long letter published in *The Daily Paper* on 20 January 1904 Beerbohm Tree commented ironically on Diosy's criticisms: 'I think that Mr Diosy did his Sabbath-breaking of a butterfly with a somewhat western crudeness for one who appears to have travelled in Japan.' Tree pointed out that the play was not intended to be realistic. The authors had

> merely sought to write a play which shall hold an audience entertained and enthralled for three hours, while my modest endeavour has been to create the necessary illusion, taking every care to create upon the stage that make-believe of reality which has drawn from many of those who are familiar with Japanese life the assurance that the sense of that life is vividly reproduced upon the stage.

He then quoted a Mr Koike, Second Secretary of the Japanese Legation, in support of his views. Tree might have added that the programme for *The Darling of the Gods* was illustrated by none other than the Japanese artist Yoshio Markino.

In 1905 the Japan Society organized an exhibition of Japanese arms and armour at the premises of the Royal Society of Painters in Watercolours in Waterloo Place. The exhibition lasted for three weeks from 30 June 1905. The *Evening Standard* and *St James's Gazette* commented that the exhibition was 'a very interesting one, and in a sense timely, since it consists of the arms and armour of the wonderful country which has made such marvellous changes in its methods and life and assimilated with such extraordinary adaptability Western customs'. The paper noted also the aesthetic aspects of the exhibits 'for the Japanese, in their crafts as well as their arts, adorn everything they touch. Most exquisite is the bronze work in breastplates, head-gear, and leg pieces, some of them elaborately inlaid with silver.'

Among the exhibits were pieces from the collection at Windsor Castle including a suit of armour belonging to George III 'decorated with raised peonies in gold'. Also included were two Court swords presented to Queen Victoria by the emperor on the occasion of the Golden Jubilee in 1887. A number of colour prints illustrating the use of the armour formed part of the display. There were also 'models of the equipment of the Japanese soldier, in the useful uniform of khaki and black cloth trimmed with the conventional red' and 'a case showing the rations, of all sorts of dried vegetables, with tins of fish and other comestibles served out to the soldiers'. The catalogue included contributions from art experts such as M.B. Huish and Edward F. Strange.

King Edward VII visited the exhibition on 29 June 1905. He was received by His Imperial Highness Prince Arisugawa, who was visiting London at the time; by Viscount Hayashi, the Japanese minister and president of the Japan Society; Mr Charles Holme, the chairman of the Council; and the exhibition committee.

Prince Takehito Arisugawa and Princess Arisugawa [Arisugawe],[6] who were received at Victoria Station by the Prince of Wales and the Duke of Connaught, were driven to Buckingham Palace with an escort of Life Guards and were there received by King Edward VII and Queen Alexandra. They stayed at St James's Palace, dined at Buckingham Palace and were entertained to lunch at the Mansion House, where at the close of his speech he read a telegram from the emperor 'desiring him to confer the Order of Commander of the Rising Sun on the Lord Mayor'. This action 'elicited hearty plaudits from the assembled guests'.

The Japan Society gave a garden party in honour of their Imperial Highnesses at the Botanical Gardens in Regent's Park on 27 June 1905. There were nearly 2,000 guests at the party, including the famous actress Ellen Terry. According to a report in *The Lady*, the imperial visitors only stayed half an hour 'so that late-comers arrived to meet with disappointment, but a solatium was afforded by an exceedingly interesting demonstration of "Ju-jitsu"'.

In March 1906 a Mansion House Fund was established for the relief of suffering caused by a famine in north-east Japan following the failure of the rice and silk crops. This was launched with a donation of £1,000 from Sir Marcus Samuel and partners. More than one million people were reported to be on the brink of starvation. The Japan Society, which according to the *Pall Mall Gazette*, then had some fourteen hundred members, also issued an appeal which brought 'a prompt and generous response, Lord Strathcona and Mount Royal having sent £100'. By 13 March £11,000 had been handed over from various sources to Viscount Hayashi, who had now been promoted to ambassador, the status of the Japanese Legation having been raised to that of an embassy.

On 9 March 1906 the ambassador was entertained to a farewell lunch at the Mansion House. On 11 March he was the guest of the officers and Council of the Japan Society at a private dinner at the Metropole

Hotel. The members of the Society were able to say their farewells to their president at a *Conversazione* on the evening of the 12th; nearly 800 guests were present on this occasion. Among those who saw the ambassador off was Lord Lansdowne, who had been foreign secretary at the time of the signature of the first Anglo-Japanese Alliance in 1902. According to the *Daily Mail* of 21 March Viscount Hayashi made the following comments to their correspondent at Southampton:

> Our desire has always been to know more of England. For this reason we study English works far more than those of other European countries. We know as much as we can of England. I wish that a similar desire were evinced on this side to know more of Japan's conditions and aspirations.

This is a sentiment still shared by the Japan Society.

After Viscount Hayashi had departed, London was visited by 600 Japanese blue-jackets ('Togo's 600' as *The Daily Telegraph* of 27 March 1906 described them) who had come to Britain to man two battleships built for the Japanese Navy at British shipyards. These were the *Katori*, built at Barrow in Furness, and the *Kashima*, built at the Armstrong works at Elswick. Twenty-eight officers, including Captain Sakamoto of the *Katori* and Captain Ijichi of the *Kashima* were entertained to lunch at the Mansion House on 26 March. (Mr C. Holme, chairman of the Council of the Society, was one of the Lord Mayor's guests.)

Three hundred Japanese sailors visited St Paul's Cathedral and paid their respects at Nelson's tomb. They went on through welcoming crowds to Westminster Abbey where, according to *The Globe* of 26 March 1906, after their officers had arrived, they marched up the nave three abreast. The men appeared to be most interested in the Coronation Chair. In the Poet's Corner, 'the men eagerly flocked round the grave of Irving, whose fame appeared to have reached each of them'. *The Tribune* reported that at 12 o'clock

> the visitors adjourned to the Caxton Hall, where a substantial dinner of whiting, roast beef, roast mutton, vegetable, plum pudding, and lager beer was served, the party being reinforced by several of our own sailors from HMS *Pembroke*, who were formerly stationed off Japan, and who drank the health of the Mikado with as much enthusiasm as the Japanese displayed in drinking to King Edward. [According to *The Daily Telegraph* the lunch was provided by the Japanese community in London] ... The drive from Caxton Hall to the Marble Arch was memorable for the wild scenes of enthusiasm it evoked, despite the occasional showers of rain, hail and sleet. There was one continuous volume of cheers from Queen Anne's-gate, through Birdcage-walk, Constitution-hill, and Hyde Park Corner.

They then attended a performance at the Coliseum, where the first part of the programme 'somewhat puzzled the guests, but they rapturously applauded a clever troupe of Japanese acrobats, and went almost frantic with delight as the arrival of the Iyo Maru and pictures of the late fight with Russia were displayed on the bioscope'.

According to the *Morning Post* for 5 December 1906, the Japan Society took part in a deputation which called on the Prime Minister Sir Henry Campbell-Bannerman to urge 'the appointment of a Departmental Committee to consider generally and in detail the present allocation of grants by the several Government Departments for the purpose of instruction in Oriental languages'. From this initiative grew the School of Oriental and African studies in the University of London.

On 6 May 1907 Prince Fushimi, head of one of the senior princely families, arrived in England to express to King Edward VII the acknowledgements of the emperor of Japan for the mission which the king had sent to Tokyo in 1906 to convey the Order of the Garter to the Emperor Meiji. According to *The Daily Telegraph* the Prince was

> accorded a great public welcome. . . . The Prince of Wales welcomed Prince Fushimi on his arrival at Victoria, and the Duke of Connaught, Prince Arthur of Connaught (to whom the King entrusted the Garter Mission to Japan), the Duke of Fife, the Duke of Argyll, the Prime Minister, the Foreign Secretary, the Home Secretary, Earl Roberts, and Admiral of the Fleet Sir E. Seymour formed part of a brilliant company present at the railway station to receive the Prince.

The Prince of Wales, 'who was in the uniform of an admiral, wore the pink and cerise sash of the Order of the Chrysanthemum'. When the Japanese prince appeared on the platform with the Prince of Wales, the guard of honour presented arms and the band of the Irish Guards played the Japanese national anthem. The cortège on its way to Buckingham Palace was 'welcomed in a thoroughly British fashion by a mass of people'. At Buckingham Palace the Prince was greeted by the King in the uniform of a British field marshal and a full guard of honour of Scots Guards.

Prince Fushimi stayed at York House, which was decorated with roses and lilies. The apartment prepared for him was adorned with cherry blossom. 'Credit for this must be given to the Japan Society.' The Society apparently experienced some difficulty in obtaining the blooms, which 'came from some well-known nurseries in Sussex'. The prince received a civic welcome at the Guildhall, and a luncheon was given in his honour at the Mansion House. Among the many dinners he attended were banquets given by Sir Edward Grey at the Foreign Office and by the prime minister, Sir Henry Campbell-Bannerman, at 10 Downing Street. On 15 May he was the guest of honour at the Japan Society's annual dinner at the Hotel Metropole presided over by the new Japanese ambassador Baron Komura. The prince's health was proposed by Lord Redesdale (A.B. Mitford), who had accompanied Prince Arthur of Connaught on the Garter Mission the previous year and had served with the British Legation in Edo (later Tokyo) between 1866 and 1870). The prince replied in Japanese. At the conclusion of his state visit he visited Cambridge, Elswick to see the Armstrong works (where the *Kashima* had been built), Edinburgh, Glasgow, Barrow-in-Furness (where the *Mikasa*, Togo's flagship, and the *Katori* had been built) and Liverpool and Portsmouth.

The Japan Society had heard a lecture in 1904 by Mr Arthur Diosy about William Adams, the first Englishman in Japan. In December 1907 William Crewdson, who had become chairman of the Council of the Society, addressed letters to British newspapers calling for subscriptions to a fund to repair the grave of William Adams near Yokosuka. This followed a lecture to the Society by Lord Redesdale entitled 'Three Hundred Years Ago', that is, when William Adams was in Japan.[7]

The guest of honour of the Society at its seventeenth annual dinner on 20 May 1908 was Sir Edward Grey, the foreign secretary, who spoke warmly of the Anglo-Japanese Alliance.

In 1909 the Society were once again hosts to another Japanese imperial prince and princess. They were Prince Morimasa Nashimoto, a cousin of the emperor, and Princess Nashimoto, who were on a private visit to London. The Society gave a garden party at the Botanical Gardens in Regent's Park on 8 June 1909. According to *The Standard*,

> delightful weather prevailed. . . . The Gardens were profusely deco-
> rated with the Japanese and English flags. . . . A large bank of lilies
> of the valley and scarlet carnations, showing the national colours
> of Japan, completed the scheme of decoration. . . . Her Imperial
> Highness was dressed charmingly in a gown of thick cream silk
> crepe with a woven pattern. Over this a three-quarter coat of cream
> lace was worn, and a long boa of cream ostrich feathers. Her hat was
> of cream chiffon wreathed with pink roses and white jasmine. The
> *Morning Post* reported that Sir Arthur and Lady Conan Doyle were
> among the guests. The prince and princess had lunch with the king
> and queen, and the king conferred on the prince the order of a Grand
> Commander of the Royal Victorian Order.

The Japan Society played a significant part in the preparations for the Japan–British Exhibition in 1910. At a preparatory committee meeting at the Mansion House on 22 December 1909 the Lord Mayor 'gave his hearty support to the great undertaking'. Prince Arthur of Connaught had agreed to become honorary president of the Council for the exhibition, and the Duke of Norfolk would be the president. The committee, on a proposal from Mr Wilson Crewdson, chairman of the Japan Society, recorded its appreciation of the excellent progress which had been made.[8]

The Japan Society contributed to the exhibition a display of objects illustrating the growth of commercial relations and friendship between Britain and Japan. This section was intended to form a 'bridge' between the British and Japanese parts of the exhibition.[9] The items displayed included two suits of armour lent by King Edward VII from Windsor Castle, a suit of armour from the Tower of London, two spears and eleven swords presented to Queen Victoria and the Duke of Edinburgh (on his visit to Japan in 1869). There was also a series of documents relating to the early trading of the East India Company with Japan, and especially the voyages of Will Adams. These were lent by the secretary of state for India. A collection of books, dictionaries, grammars and photographs was lent by the Imperial University of Tokyo. There were in addition some items from private collections including portraits of Sir Rutherford Alcock, the first British minister to Japan from 1859 and of his successor Sir Harry Parkes who arrived in 1865 as well as models of two ships of the early seventeenth century, similar to those in which William Adams's voyages were made. A Mr Shigeta Shiga sent a portion of the timbers of the English brig, the *Beagle*, which had taken part in the Crimean war and had been the ship on which Charles Darwin made his famous voyage. It had been sold to the Satsuma clan and renamed the *Kenko*. The relic had on it a painting of the *Beagle* and the signature of Admiral Heihachiro Togo.

The intention was that the exhibition at Shepherd's Bush would be opened by the Prince of Wales, accompanied by the Princess of Wales, on 12 May 1910. A ceremony was to be held on the Grand Plaza in front of the Palace of Fine Arts. Their highnesses were then to view the *tableaux* of British dress and to pass on to the Japan Society's exhibit before looking at the twelve *tableaux* which the Japanese government had provided and which represented epochs in Japanese history. Thereafter they were to view 'the Japanese Gardens' and visit other exhibition palaces. The death of King Edward VII in early May 1910, however, led to the cancellation of the official opening and the exhibition was opened informally on 14 May. The newspapers of the time were full of praise for the exhibition. *The Referee* of 15 May commented that

grand as is the display in the British arts and industries, interest will be centred in the Japs themselves and in their works and doings generally. The Japanese aim is to be artistic in all things – everywhere and all the time. The untravelled visitor will stand long and stare long at the quaintness and the beauty of the temples; the houses, the shops, the gates, and other structures they have set up. A stroll among the beauties that have been provided in front of the grand panorama on the left of the Wood-lane entrance must on no account be missed. It will afford a multitude of delights for the eye, with rockeries and rustic bridges over picturesquely-placed ponds, and by trees and plants and flowers that seem to suggest fairy land. This is just the place for lovers' meetings, and for the quiet rest after the bustle and excitement by the Flip Flap, and the Mountain and Scenic Railways, and the Wiggle Woggle, and the Witching Waves which stand just where they did.

One of the livery companies which took part in the exhibition was the Worshipful Company of Fanmakers, who hoped to revive British interest in the buying of fans. Prince Arthur of Connaught was delighted to find a replica of a tea-house in which the tea ceremony had been demonstrated to him during the Garter Mission to Japan. The Japanese wrestlers who gave two performances a day also attracted much attention.[10] All in all the Japanese parts of the exhibition seem to have been more popular than the purely British exhibits.

Among visitors to the exhibition in July 1910 were Japanese sailors from the Japanese cruiser *Ikoma*. The Japan Society for its part invited the officers, led by Captain Shoji in command of the *Ikoma*, to a *Conversazione* in the Whitehall rooms at the Hotel Metropole. Some 800 attended the party. According to 'The Queen' of 30 July, the programme included 'some excellent musical selections, together with some interesting exhibitions . . . of Japanese top-spinning and conjuring'.

Prince Yorihito Higashi-Fushimi and Princess Higashi-Fushimi represented the emperor at the coronation of King George V.[11] The prince and princess were guests of honour at the Society's annual dinner at the Hotel Metropole on 29 June 1911. The princess, according to the *Belfast Evening Telegraph* of 3 July 1911,

> wore magnificent jewels, a high dog collar of pearls, a necklace and broad diamond straps on her sleeves, and a high tiara of diamonds, with enormous emeralds in its shamrock leaves, while across her low bodice was the riband of an Order, her hair being softly dressed in the becoming Japanese style, so well calculated to show off jewels.

The prince in his speech stressed the valuable services of the Society in promoting friendship between the two countries.

Admiral Heihachiro Togo and General Maresuke Nogi, heroes of the Russo-Japanese war, were among the company on this occasion. Admiral Sir Archibald Douglas, who had been responsible for organizing and operating the first modern naval training establishment in Japan, proposed a toast to their health. In his speech Admiral Douglas referred to the Japanese Admiral as 'the silent Togo'. The *Belfast Evening Telegraph* commented that it was 'said of him that, like Bismarck, he can be silent in six languages'. Togo's 'few words' in reply, while General Nogi stood, were 'loudly cheered'.

In November of that year Sir Joseph Dimsdale, Bt, who had been Lord Mayor of London from 1901 to 1902, was elected to succeed Mr Crewdson as chairman of the Council. He led a delegation which on 12 January 1912 presented to the Japanese chargé d'affaires a book containing copies of the documents which the Society had shown at the exhibition in 1910, for His Majesty the Emperor. Sir Joseph did not hold the office of chairman for long as he died in August of that year.

The death of the Emperor Meiji and the official mourning which lasted until 30 July 1913 led to the cancellation of the annual dinner in 1913. The death of the Empress Dowager in 1913 caused the cancellation of the dinner in 1914.

The Society gained its first royal patron in January 1913, when Prince Arthur of Connaught, who had represented the king at the emperor's funeral, accepted the Society's invitation to become their patron. After the end of the First World War on 22 November 1918, a letter was sent to Admiral Prince Yorihito Higashi-Fushimi asking him if he too would be an honorary patron of the society. His Imperial Highness duly accepted.

Throughout the twelve years from 1912 to 1924 the Society maintained a full programme of lectures. Many of these continued to be devoted to aspects of Japanese art and were by well-known experts, such as Laurence Binyon, Edward F. Strange and Henri L. Joly. A wide range of other topics historical, literary and social, were also covered.

H.J. Edwards, Dean of Peterhouse, Cambridge, spoke on 11 January 1905 on 'Japanese Undergraduates at Cambridge University'. One of the first Japanese undergraduates at Cambridge was registered as Dairoku Yasuyuki Kikuchi, who entered St John's College in 1873 from University College School. He became nineteenth wrangler in 1877. He went on to become Professor of Mathematics at Tokyo University, later president of the University, minister of education and a member of the House of Peers. While at the college he apparently proposed in the college debating society the motion 'That the conduct of Englishmen in Japan is unworthy of their nationality'. Another undergraduate at St John's was (Baron) Kencho Suematsu. The Japanese Club at Cambridge University was founded by Manjiro Inagaki, a student at Gonville and Caius College from 1886. The chief object of the club was apparently 'to study the training and character of the English Gentleman'. Two successive Japanese ministers to the Court of St James, Viscounts Kawase and Aoki, were presidents of the club. Mr Edwards urged that a chair for the study of Japanese culture should be established 'in the near future'. Alas this had to wait for nearly eighty years until 1984 when funds were provided through the Japanese Federation of Economic Organizations (Keidanren) largely from Tokyo Electric Power Company.

On 10 March 1910 Marie Stopes who was to become famous for her work on birth control gave a lecture on 'The Value and Interest of Japanese Fossils'. On 14 December 1910 a paper by Mr F.H. Trevithick on 'Japan's Railway System' was read on his behalf. Trevithick who had been attached to the Railway Department in Japan between 1876 and 1897 and had revisited Japan in 1907 was one of the leading British railway engineers who served in

Japan. On 15 March 1911 Mr Horace F. Cheshire spoke on 'The Japanese Game of Go'. He saw 'no reason why the game should not be played very generally in Europe'. After the lecture a demonstration game of Go was then played on the blackboard by two Japanese professors and a Miss Utagawa gave a selection of *koto* music.

THE SOCIETY DURING THE FIRST WORLD WAR

The outbreak of the First World War on 4 August 1914 led to a reduction in membership of the Society through resignations and deaths. A number of members were killed in action.

The Society also faced some financial difficulties. At the Council meeting on 12 October 1914 the honorary treasurer explained

> his inability, in consequence of the war, to realize (without considerable loss) any of the Investments of the Society. He was accordingly authorized to borrow temporarily on the security of the Japanese Government Bonds held by the Society, such a sum as the Bankers would lend at the rate of interest charged by the Bank of England with a minimum of 5 per cent per annum.

The Society's balance sheet dated 31 December 1914 recorded total assets of £1,164 10s 9d of which Japanese Government Bonds were valued at £274 14s 11d. Annual expenditure and income for the year ending 31 December 1914 came to £865 10s 6d. In 1916 the Society received a generous donation of £100 from the Marquis Maeda.[12]

The war inevitably curtailed the activities of the Society. In particular there were very few social events, although the honorary secretary's report for the year 1915–16 recorded that on 16 November 1915 the Japanese ambassador had entertained the vice-presidents, officers and Council to lunch 'in honour of the Coronation of His Imperial Majesty the Emperor of Japan' (Taishō Tenno). The honorary secretary also noted in the same report that, 'In spite of the war, Ordinary Meetings of the Society have been held each month during the Session, although it was considered advisable to hold them in the afternoon instead of the evening, owing to the lighting regulations, and the darkness of the streets.' Two joint meetings of the Japan and China Societies had been held.

Some of the Society's lectures dealt with the Japanese part in the First World War. On 21 January 1915 the Society heard a paper by William Blane on 'Tsingtao' which had been taken from the Germans by the Japanese. This provided Arthur Diosy with the opportunity to heap praise on the 'yeoman service that Japan had rendered the good cause by what she has done in the Far East'. A stop had been put to the 'German dream of preponderance in the Far East'.

On 12 January 1916 the Society heard an account by Dr J. Suzuki of 'The Japanese Red Cross Mission to England'. The Mission arrived at Netley on 31 January 1915, and Dr Suzuki and his colleague Dr Oshima looked after various huts of the Irish Hospital. Dr Suzuki reported that 'between February 1 and December 31, 1915, for 334 days two of us looked after 661 patients, mostly in the Irish section, while our sisters, under the English medical officers in other huts, had the honour of taking care of 1,892 patients'. The Mission had originally been sent to Britain for six months but were ordered to stay to the end of the year. They arrived with a feeling of anxiety, 'for we could neither speak English fluently, nor were we all acquainted with the English customs and manners'. But they managed and on their departure Drs Suzuki and Oshima were made honorary Companions of the Order of St Michael and St George (CMG).

Arthur Diosy who had just spent six months' voluntary service as staff-lecturer, under the auspices of the YMCA, with HM naval and military forces in the Mediterranean and Egyptian war areas, spoke on 27 June 1917 on 'Japan's Part in the War, 1914–1917'. Having regaled the Society with an account of his war exploits, he spoke about the fall of Tsingtao and the role played by The Japanese Navy. He praised in particular the escorts which had been provided for contingents of ANZAC forces. He also declared, 'Japan has done something more wonderful . . . something so fantastic that it is almost like a fairy-tale. Japan has lent us money! – £35,000,000 sterling were placed at the disposal of the British Treasury.' Arthur Diosy was in the chair on 30 April 1919 when Commander G. Nakashima of the Imperial Japanese Navy read a paper, 'The Japanese Navy in the Great War'. In this he dealt briefly with the capture of Tsingtao, operations in the Indian Ocean, in the East Sea [sic] and China Sea, in the Pacific, on the western coast of America, in the Mediterranean and in Siberian waters.

Many of the Lectures were, however, on more general themes. Admiral the Honourable Sir Edmund Fremantle on 13 February 1918 gave his 'Reminiscences of Japan'. He recalled his first visit in 1855 and his first view of Hakodate. He noted that while they had been allowed 'considerable freedom' ashore in Hakodate, 'the Japanese looked upon us with some suspicion and we were generally escorted at a respectable distance by armed retainers with two swords'. He also described how in 1894, at the beginning of the Sino-Japanese War, he nearly caused an international incident by saluting the flag of Admiral Miyoji Ito in his flagship *Matsushima*. 'It was this innocent salute which caused great indignation in Japan, where I was accused of firing guns to give warning to the Chinese of the approaching Fleet.'

Another lecture of reminiscences was one given on 13 December 1916 entitled 'Twenty Years of Japan' by Robert P. Porter, who had been on the editorial staff of *The Times* (he was killed in a motoring accident in March 1917). The following anecdote seems worth repeating:

One evening whilst I was sitting on the veranda of the Yaami Hotel [a hotel near the Chionin temple in Kyoto much used by British visitors in the nineteenth century], contemplating the ancient city stretched forth in the valley below, a Japanese gentleman who was sitting next to me said rather abruptly:

'Porter, what an inconvenient man you are!'

'Why?' I inquired.

'You require so much more than we Japanese to keep you comfortable. Here, for example, you are paying 3 yen (6 shillings) per day, and I am only paying 75 sen or about 1s 6d of your money. I am just as comfortable and happy as you are. To be sure you have tables and chairs and washstands and pitchers and a bedstead and a sofa, and goodness knows what, in your rooms. I have nothing of the sort. A nice clean tatami and a quilt is good enough bed for me. Then you give so much more trouble at your meals, with your tables and chairs and crockery and glassware and knives and forks and spoons and mustard and pepper pots. Then you are crowded together in one room. My meals are served on a tray in my room by a pretty maid who kneels before me while I eat, and chats and makes herself interesting, looking after my every want at the same time. Then you cart a lot of unnecessary luggage around. The hotel furnishes me a satisfactory dressing-gown and a nice clean night-robe, and a new toothbrush in a paper bag, as well as what I use as a knife and fork similarly encased. No; say what you like, you Europeans are inconvenient people. You do not go along the line of least resistance. You make too much effort to live. It costs you too much in worry and anxiety, in flesh and blood, and grey matter as well.'

The chair was to have been taken at Mr Porter's lecture by Viscount Chinda, the Japanese ambassador and president of the Society, but he was unable to be present and a secretary read a message from him. In this the ambassador paid tribute to the work of the Society and expressed his hope that the Society would continue to contribute to knowledge in Britain about Japan. He noted

how very little is known here, after all, concerning Japan. I venture to submit that you in England do not know one-tenth as much about us as we do about you, let it be said without reproach. . . . With you to study our language, for instance, is merely a matter of choice and convenience; with us the acquisition of the English tongue is an important matter of interest, if not of absolute necessity

Mr Wilson Crewdson, who had been honorary secretary of the Society and chairman, wrote a paper for the Society's meeting on 22 March 1916 on 'Japanese Leather'. Mr Crewdson, who was doing hospital work in France, was unable to read the paper himself. Mr H.L. Joly, the editor, inserted into the record some very harsh criticism of the paper. His comments began: 'Mr Crewdson's paper could have been of more value if it had consisted merely of translations from the sources named, and if the author had not jumped into a pitfall and evolved an untenable theory from that accident.' He accordingly recorded his 'protest' against 'the assertion . . . that fine leather was printed from blocks in 834'.

Mr W.L. Hildburgh gave another of his lectures on aspects of magic in Japan. On 12 April 1916 he spoke on 'Some Japanese Minor Magical or Religious Practices connected with Travelling'. Sir George James Frazer (1854–1941), author of *The Golden Bough*, was in the audience. He found the paper 'most interesting' and noted some parallels in other cultures.

THE SOCIETY IN THE 'INDIAN SUMMER' OF ANGLO-JAPANESE RELATIONS, 1918–30

Following the end of the war the Society revived its social programme and membership grew again after the wartime decline, but numbers never reached pre-war levels. In 1923, for instance, the honorary secretary recorded that there were then 658 members. Of these 158 were corresponding members, 29 were honorary, 22 were life and 449 were ordinary members. In 1926 the numbers had risen to 709, but they had fallen slightly by November 1930, when the total membership was 674.

The Council were dismayed to receive a letter dated 8 May 1919 from Knight, Frank & Rutley, the Society's landlords at 20 Hanover Square, informing the honorary secretary that the lease for the office which they had used since the 1890s would not be renewed as it was required by the partners to accommodate staff returning from the army and because of the volume of their business. Eventually the Society found alternative office space at 22 Russell Square, but continued to use a hall at 20 Hanover Square for lectures.

The Society had to make do on a restricted budget. Expenditure in 1920 amounted to £1,305 13s 8d; this was only covered by a generous donation of £600 from Japanese friends of the Society among the Japanese business community. In 1921 the Society received a donation of £500 from the Japanese Crown Prince (later the Emperor Shōwa), who visited London that year. In 1929 expenditure was restricted to £886 10s 5d, and even to cover this the Society needed the donations of £202 2s recorded in the accounts. The value of the Society's investments on 31 December 1929 was put at a mere £765 9s 1d. Not surprisingly the Council were very careful about costs. The minutes for the Council's meeting on 20 October 1919 refer to a letter from Claridges Hotel stating that the charge for hiring a room for the Society's evening reception on 3 December 1919 at 9 pm would amount to 15 guineas. Refreshments would cost 7s 6d per head. These were to consist of tea, coffee, chocolate, cake, bread and butter, ices, and so on. Floral decorations would be extra. The Council decided to issue one ticket to each member and to charge 7s 6d for additional tickets. When discussing the 1922 dinner to be held at the Metropole Hotel, the chairman of the Council submitted menus at 17s 6d and a guinea per head without wine. The Council accepted the 17s 6d menu, 'provided that the Hotel reduced the price to 15/6'. The String band of the Grenadier Guards was engaged for this occasion at a cost of £15 'from 7 to 10.30 pm'. For the 1924 dinner the dinner committee accepted an 'amended menu at 12/6'; members were to be charged 15 shillings but would have to pay £1 1s for their guests. Salaries in those days were low. In 1920 the assistant secretary received £3 15s per week, income tax being paid. The Council agreed on 18 October 1920 to pay him an extra £1 per week, but Mr Brice was to pay his own income tax. In 1921 the Council also agreed to a special payment of £10 to Mr Brice as a gratuity to mark 'the Council's appreciation of his industry in carrying out the arrangements for the dinner in honour of the Crown Prince and of their satisfaction with the manner in which everything had been done'.

In the 1920s the Society was much involved with members of the Japanese Imperial House and of the British Royal Family and managed to achieve imperial and royal patronage of the highest distinction.

The high point for the Society was the visit of the Japanese Crown Prince Hirohito (later the Emperor Shōwa). On 13 May 1921 Professor Joseph H. Longford, the chairman of the Council, led a delegation which was received by the Crown Prince at Chesterfield House, where they presented an address of welcome 'engrossed on vellum with beautifully illuminated borders of rose, thistle and shamrock by H.R. Ball, and sumptuously bound in blue crushed morocco'. The address reminded the Crown Prince of the support given to the Society in 1892 by the Emperor Meiji and assured him that 'we shall continue, unceasingly and untiringly, our efforts in furtherance of the sacred trust of bringing the two Nations into a still closer Alliance through the sure ties of mutual sympathy and good understanding'. The Crown Prince in his reply declared that it was his 'fervent wish that it [the Society] may continue in the prosperity and success befitting its exalted aspirations'. On 26 May a banquet was given in the Crown Prince's honour by the Society at the Hotel Cecil. The Crown Prince was accompanied by Prince Kanin. The dinner was also attended by the Duke of York (who in 1937 became King George VI). In proposing the Crown Prince's health Professor Longford told how fifty-two years earlier (1869) he had been present as a junior member of the staff of the British Legation in Tokyo when the Duke of Edinburgh, son of Queen Victoria, had been received by the young Emperor Meiji. In his reply (in Japanese) the Crown Prince reiterated his appreciation of the work of the Society and drank a toast to 'the prosperity of Great Britain . . . and . . . the continued success of the Japan Society of London'.

The Emperor Shōwa always looked back with nostalgia on his visit to

Britain in 1921. He had left Japan in March 1921 on the *Katori*, which had been built in Britain and the *Kashima*, also built in Britain, accompanied the party. In Cairo the prince attended a garden party given by Field Marshal Allenby. At Malta he visited the theatre and heard a performance of Verdi's *Otello*. At Buckingham Palace he encountered British royal informality. On the first morning of his stay (according to Leonard Moseley's *Hirohito, Emperor of Japan*) King George V suddenly walked into Hirohito's suite at breakfast time. To the horror of the Japanese equerries he was only half dressed, wearing trousers, braces, carpet slippers and an open shirt, and he walked straight up to the Prince and slapped him on the back. 'I hope, me boy,' he said, 'that everyone is giving you everything you want while you are here. If there is anything you need, just ask. I'll never forget how your grandfather treated me and my brother when we were in Yokohama. I've always wanted to repay his kindness.' He chuckled. 'No geishas here, though, I'm afraid. Her Majesty would never allow it.'[13]

The Crown Prince is reported to have found Lord Curzon 'an amiable and affable host' when he attended a banquet given by the foreign secretary at Carlton House Terrace. Pavlova performed on this occasion *Le Mort du Cygne*.

Both the Crown Prince and the Prince of Wales, who had himself visited Japan in 1921, became patrons of the Society, as did the Duke of York and Prince Kanin. When Prince Hirohito became emperor in 1926 it was, however, decided that it would no longer be appropriate for him to remain a patron.

The Prince of Wales (later King Edward VIII), who made an official visit to Japan in 1922, was the guest of honour at the Society's dinner on 4 June 1923. He spoke briefly about his recent visit to Japan and praised the beautiful sights he had seen. He also reiterated his thanks for the warm welcome which had been given him. The annual dinner on 30 June 1925 was honoured by the presence of the Duke of York and Prince Asuka, who also became a patron of the Society and who was accompanied by Princess Asuka. The duke in his speech referred to the expected arrival of Prince Chichibu, the younger brother of the Crown Prince, who had by then become Prince Regent. Sir Austen Chamberlain, the foreign secretary, proposed the toast on this occasion to the president, the Japanese ambassador.

Prince Chichibu duly became a patron of the Society and was the guest of honour at the Society's annual dinner on 28 January 1926. Mr Charles Sale, the chairman of the Council, proposed the toast to the Prince, who 'replied in English and in the clearest of voices'. The Society decided to make a presentation to Prince Chichibu in 1928 on the occasion of his marriage to Setsuko, the daughter of Mr Tsuneo Matsudaira, the Japanese ambassador. This was a silver statuette of a skier made by the Goldsmiths & Silversmiths Company, which had been displayed and approved at the Annual General Meeting on 28 June 1928 (Fig. 1.6). A paper by Prince Chichibu entitled

Figure 1.6   The Japan Society's gift to Prince Chichibu in 1928

'A Climb in the Japanese Alps' was read to the Society on 25 April 1929 by the Reverend Walter Weston. This paper was an English translation, with the technical details omitted, of an article written for a magazine entitled *Chikaki Mikaki* (literally, 'Near the August Enclosure'), which was a journal circulating among the imperial princes of Japan.

The guest of honour at the Society's annual dinner on 28 June 1927 was Prince George, who became Duke of Kent in 1934. In his speech he recalled with pleasure his two visits to Japan. On 14 March 1929 the Society gave a banquet to the Duke of Gloucester, the third son of King George V, shortly before his departure for Japan to present the Insignia of the Order of the Garter to the Emperor Shōwa. In his speech the Duke stressed the 'personal friendship which has long flourished between the Imperial Family of Japan and my own Royal House'. He was looking forward to seeing 'not least that visible embodiment of Japan's magnificent patriotism, her glorious Army and Navy – that Navy which gave us such welcome help during the desperate days of the War'. The Society's guests on 8 July 1930 were Prince Takamatsu, the second younger brother of the Emperor Showa, and Princess Takamatsu. The toast to the prince and princess was proposed by Prince Arthur of Connaught. Prince Takamatsu replying in Japanese declared that the emperor and his brother Prince Chichibu as well as he himself were 'profoundly interested' in the activities of the Society. Prince Takamatsu also became a patron of the Society.

'A Solemn Service of Prayer and Recollection' for the late Emperor Taishō was held in Westminster Abbey on 9 February 1927 'on the suggestion of the Japanese Christian Union and under the auspices of the Japan Society'. The king was represented at this service by Prince Arthur of Connaught. An address in Japanese, followed by special prayers in Japanese, was given by the Bishop of Southampton who had previously been bishop in south Tokyo. On 10 February 1927 Mr Baldwin, the prime minister, proposed in the House of Commons that an address be presented to the king conveying 'the deep regret' of the House on learning of the death of the emperor. Mr Ramsay MacDonald and Mr Lloyd George associated themselves with the address. But there was a note of warning in Mr MacDonald's speech: '*Despite deep-seated differences*, we have many things in common' (emphasis added).

The great earthquake of 1923 caused much loss of life and property in Yokohama and Tokyo. The Society responded by opening a relief fund. This was done jointly with the Nihonjinkai, the Society of Japanese residents in London. By 24 October donations of £8,686 5s 3d had been collected.

An exhibition of *ukiyoe* was organized by the Society on 29 April 1925 at 3 Cavendish Square, the offices of the Nihonjinkai. The exhibition consisted of 138 prints from the collections of nine members of the Society. It was attended by 153 members and guests. It cost £1 5s 3d to mount the exhibition! This sum was spent on 'Push pins and reinforcing tabs for hanging the exhibits; conveyance of the exhibits to and from Cavendish Square; and tips to the domestic staff of the Nihonjinkai'.

In 1928 following discussions between Sir John Tilley, the British ambassador to Japan, and Mr Charles Sale, the chairman of the Council, a Shakespeare Medal was instituted. This was to consist of a gold medal and was to be given for an essay in English dealing with the language, literature, art, history or institutions of England. The first of these medals was handed to Dr Onozuka, president of Tokyo Imperial University, by the Duke of Gloucester during his mission in June 1929.

Although ladies had lectured to the Society on a number of occasions, the first time the chair was taken by a lady was on 25 April 1920. Dr Marie Stopes, who had herself written on the Noh, took the chair at a meeting addressed by Arthur Waley on 'The Noh: Some Translations'. On 5 December 1922 the Council agreed a resolution that it was 'to the interest of the Society that lady members should be invited to serve on the Council'. The Baroness D'Anethan and Lady Arnold were then invited to join the Council. The Dowager Lady Swaythling later joined it.

The controversy over the question of who founded the Society was reopened in 1930 by a paper delivered on 27 March 1930 by Mr F.J. Peplow, a member of the Council, on 'The Transactions of the Japan Society: A

Retrospect'. In this he declared that 'The origin of the Society was due to Arthur Diosy'. At the Council meeting on 13 November 1930, Colonel F.S.G. Piggott (later Major General), son of the late Sir Francis Piggott, referred to letters which he had received, 'demurring' from Mr Peplow's statement. These letters argued that the 'inception' of the Society had been due to Sir Francis Piggott. The controversy rumbled on until November 1931 when the Council, after much debate, no doubt fairly heated at times, agreed a draft addendum to Mr Peplow's original article as 'a fair reconciliation of the two points of view'.

The Council in 1930 became involved in lengthy debate about the correct romanization of Japanese place names. The Council did not like the new romanization, the so-called *kokusiki*, which the Japanese authorities had begun to adopt in place of the Hepburn system. A memorandum on the subject was prepared by Mr Koop and approved at the meeting of the Council on 12 March 1931. The Japanese ambassador in his capacity as president of the Society had previously agreed to submit it to the appropriate authorities in Japan.

There were many scholarly lectures to the Society during these years. In particular the Society were indebted to [Latin professor] Charles Boxer for a number of papers relating to the Portuguese in Japan in the sixteenth and seventeenth centuries. The *Transactions* also carried lengthy historical accounts from Mr R.A. Ponsonby Fane, a corresponding member of the Society, about Kyoto and the Imperial Family.

Some lectures were of a more general interest. On 21 January 1925 the Society heard a talk given by Colonel the Master of Sempill, late Acting Captain in the Imperial Japanese Navy. His subject was 'The British Aviation Mission in Japan'. After a brief account of aviation in Japan during which the speaker reminded the audience that the first aeroplane was flown in Japan by Captain Hino of the Japanese army in December, 1910, he explained that in 1921 the Japanese authorities had requested Great Britain to assist in the reorganization, equipment and training of their naval air service. The mission consisted of eighteen officers and twelve warrant officers, Second Class:

> The work was divided into four principal Sections: Flying, Technical, Armament, and Photography. The Central Training Station of the Naval Air Service was set up on the shores of Lake Kasumi-ga-ura and the site was approved by the British advance party, who arrived in April 1921. The mission were provided with very comfortable quarters, including a billiard-room containing two full-size English billiard-tables.

The speaker commented on the Japanese trainees: 'Their courage and determination to carry out orders under any conditions are most noticeable. They have in general no very great interest for mechanical contrivances, which have, of course, only recently been imported into Japan.' The mission remained in Japan for three years. The Master of Sempill expected that a service of airships might soon be established between London and Tokyo enabling the journey to be covered in four days. The airship would need to be not less than 700 feet long. 'The speed would be about 70 miles an hour and each stage some 2,000 miles.'

A lecture on 20 January 1926 with the Master of Sempill in the chair provided an interesting follow-up to his account of the aviation mission. The speaker on this occasion was Mr Ryunosuke Shimatani and his subject, 'The recent aeroplane flight from Tokyo to London'. This venture, which was backed by the *Asahi* newspaper, 'one of the few newspapers in the world that has its own air transport service', involved two machines (French Breguet 19A2 with 400 hp Lorraine-Dietrich engines) and cost some £40,000, to which the Japanese government had promised to contribute £2,200. The Soviet authorities had been difficult, although 'great kindness was met with on the whole from the Russian people and local officials, and especially from those in the villages, who from ignorance and lack of newspapers knew little and cared less about political affairs since 1917'. The provision of supplies on route had presented real problems. One temporary landing place had to be prepared by the *Asahi* itself. The two planes 'had been christened by the Prince Regent's father-in-law, Prince Kuni, under the names *Hatsukaze* and *Kochikaze*'. Their longest hop was from Harbin to Chita. They left Harbin at 5 am and reached Chita at 2.30 pm, covering '1,300 kilometers in nine and a half hours, an average speed of about 137 km per hour'. 'The flight from Chita to Moscow was much slowed down owing to continual bad weather, dense clouds and thunderstorms meeting them at every turn.' 'Moscow was reached on 23 August 1925, thirty days from the start, and a total distance of 9,656 kilometres.' Engine trouble with the *Hatsukaze* caused further delays. However, 'on October 12 they left Paris for Croydon, but owing to fog they lost their way and one of them had to come down at Farnborough, the other making a forced landing at Cove village.'

The Japanese business community, which seems in recent years to have become *obsessed* by golf, should be interested in the paper by Mr Chozo Ito on 'Golf in Japan', which was read to the Society in an English translation on 28 April 1927. According to Mr Ito, 'The first golf club established in Japan was the Kobe club, which has its links on the top of Rokko-zan.' The development of these links was 'due to the enterprise of two Britons, Mr A.H. Groom and Dr Thornicraft, who also have the credit of founding this the first golf club in Japan. The ground of nine holes was leased in August of 1902, and in October of the same year four holes were ready.' When the club was officially inaugurated on 27 February 1903 there were 135 members, mostly foreign residents in Osaka and Kobe. The greens at the Rokko-zan course in those days were sand. The course was a very windy one and the author said that on one of these greens a player had 'the grand record of twenty-four putts . . . the rule being that if the player does not hole out in one from the edge of the green the ball must be played back to the edge again'. The next club founded was the Yokohama Golf Club. In 1913 a club was organized at Komazawa by some members of the Tokyo Club. This course was extended to eighteen holes in 1926. It was on this course that the Prince of Wales (Edward VIII) played with the Crown Prince (the Emperor Shōwa). Mr Ito declared that there were about 2,500 golfers in Japan, including many distinguished Japanese. The Imperial Household had a private golf course in Shinjuku Gardens. In those days all clubs and balls had to be imported. Mr Ito considered that 'the comparatively short stature of the Japanese does not offer any great disadvantage in the matter of golf'.[14]

A lecture on 11 May 1923 by Professor Heiji Hishinuma on 'The main features of the Japanese Problem' aroused some controversy. The Professor said that there were signs of democracy everywhere in Japan. He hoped that in twenty years time 'the world will look on Japan as one of the foremost progressive democratic nations'. He defended the growth of militarism in Japan, but did not deny that 'Japanese militarism has sometimes gone beyond the limits of self-defence'. He noted that 'The majority of the nation are against this system, and have for many years been putting forth efforts to abolish it.' In the Professor's view the most serious problem for Japan was that of 'surplus population'. 'Naturally Japan casts her eyes upon the vast and very thinly populated continents like North and South America, Canada, Australia and Siberia. She will not want to conquer these, but simply to send her surplus population'. He then criticized racial prejudice and discrimination, which he thought was 'the most war-breeding element'. Professor Longford, ex-chairman and a vice-president of the Society, in supporting the vote of thanks commented:

The Lecturer complains of the injustice shown to his people in other countries in which Japanese immigrants are not welcomed. I fail to see where the injustice comes in. . . . It is not just for him to complain that European and American nations show unwillingness to receive Japanese labouring people on equal terms, when the Japanese themselves will not receive Chinese or Koreans

Professor Longford also criticized the lecturer's reading of history: 'To say, however, that the rise of militarism was the effect of Christian propaganda, is to go back on the whole history of the country.'

The 'Indian Summer' in Anglo-Japanese relations was coming to an end as the hopes of the 1920s for democracy in Japan were dimmed and Japanese militarism grew in strength and influence. Some members of the Society had perhaps begun to see the dangers.

THE SOCIETY DECLINES AS ANGLO-JAPANESE RELATIONS DETERIORATE, 1931–41

The Society's objectives were educational and cultural, but apart from the regular lectures and occasional exhibitions, the Society's activities were mainly social. It had generally tried to avoid any involvement in controversial matters of a political or religious nature. But it was difficult for members of a Society devoted to the promotion of understanding of Japanese affairs from taking a pro-Japanese position on some controversial topics. Members of the Society had demonstrated their support for Japan in the Russo-Japanese War: in this case they were merely reflecting general British opinion. In the 1930s opinion in Britain was hostile towards Japanese actions in Manchuria and China, and the pro-Japanese sentiments of members of the Society at this time were out of line with public sentiment in Britain. But although the Society provided an occasional forum for propagandist statements in favour of the Japanese position, it was generally careful to avoid becoming a friendship society devoted to expounding the Japanese position, and attempts by some members, led by Brigadier (later Major General) F.S.G. Piggott, to push the Society into a more political pro-Japanese position were resisted.

On 9 March 1932 Brigadier Piggott urged the Council to organize an early dinner 'with a view to showing sympathy with Japan at the present juncture of affairs'. This suggestion 'met with general approval' and a committee was formed to try to organize a dinner. Piggott also

> expressed his pleasure at the recent letter in *The Times*, signed, *inter alia*, by several Members of the Society, in reply to that of Viscount Cecil on the 18th February. With reference to the latter, he moved that the name of Sir Charles Addis, by whom the latter [letter] had also been signed, should be removed from the list of those about to be submitted to H.E. the President for consideration for the honour of appointment as Vice-Presidents. This was unanimously approved. The Chairman remarked, that, in accordance with an unwritten law, Members of the Society as such, did not intervene in political discussions in the press. For that reason, no concerted action had been taken at the present juncture of affairs.

The dinner in fact had to be postponed.

The Society continued to give its support for exhibitions and major efforts were put into a display of Festival Dolls and Models from 2 to 9 December 1932. In view of the success of the exhibition it was extended from 9 December 1932 to 31 January 1933, although less interest was shown in the exhibition in this second period. Under the patronage of Princess Arthur of Connaught and the presidency of Mrs Matsudaira, the wife of the Japanese ambassador, the display consisted of some 400 items consisting of 'beautiful dolls and their appurtenances', sent from Japan as a gift to the Society, organized by Viscountess Motono and collected from ladies who had graduated from the Peeresses School. It was put on at the Arlington Gallery, 22 Old Bond Street. Among the 5,000 visitors in November 1932 were the queen, the Princess Royal, the Duchess of York, Princess Elizabeth of York (Queen Elizabeth II) and Princess Alice, Countess of Athlone. A number of the dolls were given to the Cheyne Hospital for children, which also received the profits of the first week's opening amounting to nearly £90. Other dolls were given to the YWCA and the Girls' Public Day School Trust for exhibition. 'A number of the more interesting models, too, were presented to the Victoria and Albert Museum and certain provincial museums for permanent display.'

Manchuria featured in two lectures. On 19 January 1933 Lieutenant Colonel St Clair Smallwood spoke on 'Manchuria, Land of Promise'. Brigadier Piggott commented on 'the wonderful way in which the country had been opened up'. 'We must realize', he said, 'what Manchuria means to Japan, and it will help us to do so if we bear in mind the ceremonies for the souls of those fallen in battle, at the Yasukuni shrine at the top of Kudan Hill in Tokyo, which resemble closely our Armistice Day celebrations in this country'. A paper entitled 'Second Thoughts on the Lytton Report' was read to the Society on 23 March 1933. Mr E.M. Gull, the author, was critical of the recommendations in the report declaring that

> the whole reasoning of the Report precludes action on the lines now advocated by Lord Lytton.... Clearly the argument for sanctions automatically becomes dependent upon the nature of the compromise suggested. That is a matter both of opinion and expediency. And in substituting that ground for the clear ground of principle the Lytton Commission's Report has, in my view, given the case for sanctions away completely and irretrievably.

Some members of the Council felt that this lecture was political and should not be printed, but their views were not accepted by the majority on the Council.

On 11 February 1932 the grand old man of Japanese parliamentary institutions, Mr Yukio Ozaki, addressed the meeting on 'Constitutional Government in Japan'. He made some cogent comments on the political system as it had evolved in Japan under the Meiji Constitution:

> If you examine the fate of twenty Cabinets after the first party Cabinet was formed by the Marquis Okuma in 1898 you will find hardly one of them has risen or fallen as the result of a general election. Four of them fell by the death of the Prime Minister (two assassinated and

two dying a natural death); another four by internal dissensions; three by intrigues; another three by riots; one as a result of an attempt on the life of the Prince Regent (the present Emperor); five from unknown causes; and only one as the result of a general election, which was conducted under unusual circumstances. Why is it that deaths, riots, or internal dissensions become the predominant causes of Cabinet changes in Japan, whilst a general election has almost no effect? Simply because the party in power can always command a majority, if it appeals to the nation. Why does the majority of voters always support the party in power? Because the common Japanese are power-worshippers even now.

One story which Mr Ozaki told his audience concerned a Japanese prime minister from one of the two clans who remained dominant until 1898 (Satsuma and Choshu) and who filled the post twice between 1885 and 1898 despite the fact that he was

rather slow and dull, and when the Emperor asked him anything he was often unable to answer. Even if he could reply he generally played for safety by saying, 'I shall make careful investigation and offer humble answers to your Majesty the next time.' One day the Emperor asked him how many children he had. He carefully counted from one to more than a dozen, then stopped and said: 'After a careful investigation, I shall answer your Majesty's . . .', to the great amusement of the Emperor.

Mr Ozaki explained that 'bureaucracy and militarism took the place of clan supremacy'. He pointed out that 'Out of twenty-two Cabinets since 1898 eighteen were presided over by bureaucratic ex-officials; and even of the remaining four, the Prime Ministers in three instances had been in the government service for a long time as bureaucrats.' Mr Ozaki was highly critical of the rule by which the ministers for the army and navy had to be generals or admirals on the active list. He also noted the 'distorted interpretation of the Constitution' by which 'the Emperor's prerogative as Commander-in-Chief of the Army and Navy was excluded from the sphere of the Prime Minister's advice and responsibility'.

His prognostication for the future was that 'After complete failure in both politics and economics, in the near future, owing to the mental isolation of self-satisfaction and pride, the whole of Japan is sure to wake up for the sake of saving herself from destruction, and a second reformation will come.'

After the lecture Brigadier F.S.G. Piggott in moving the vote of thanks said that the original drafts of the Meiji Constitution, 'which had been amongst his late father's most treasured possessions should be presented to the Society on this occasion'.

In March 1933 Mrs Basil Taylour, who had written a book about Japanese gardens, wrote to the secretary suggesting that 'a memorial expressing sympathy with Japan and her cause should be prepared for general signature and eventual presentation to the ambassador'. It was urged by some members that to do this would be 'an infringement of the Society's rule whereby politics are barred from the purview of its activities'. Nevertheless, the Council unanimously approved a resolution that the chairman, Mr Charles Sale, should 'call officially on the ambassador to convey to him the sympathy of the Council and Members with Japan at this juncture of Affairs'. The letter which the chairman presented when he called was inserted in the minutes of the Council's meeting on 4 May 1933. It recorded the condemnation by the Council

of the unfair discrimination shewn by the League of Nations in its attitude towards Japan; the satisfaction with which the Members have followed the success of the measures adopted by Japan for the suppression of brigandage and for the establishment of law and order throughout the State of Manchukuo; and finally its respect and admiration of the stand taken by Mr Matsuoka, the Delegate of the Japanese Government, in the interests of peace and humanity and justice during the recent assembly at Geneva.

At a lunch on 14 March 1933 for Mr Yosuke Matsuoka (1880–1946), the Japanese Delegate to the League of Nations, Mr Sale, in proposing a toast to the Society's guest, had spoken warmly of the 'blessings' brought to Manchukuo by 'the establishment of law and order, with the suppression of brigandage and of anarchy, with a just taxation, a sound currency and a good administration'.

In October 1935 the Council, under the acting chairmanship of Major General Piggott (he had been promoted in June 1935), considered a proposal for 'the formation, under the aegis of the Society, of an Anglo-Japanese Association for the promotion of friendly relations and co-operation between the peoples of the two countries by active political means'. After some discussion the word 'political' was deleted from the proposal, and it was agreed that the memorandum should be circulated to all members of the Council. At the next meeting of the Council on 7 November 1935, under the acting chairmanship of Mr T.R. Haslam, this proposal was debated at length. The secretary reported that Mr Charles Sale, the chairman, was opposed to the proposal as it 'would involve the Society in much correspondence and many complications'. Eventually, on the suggestion of Major General Piggott, who argued strongly for further action by the Society, the Council agreed, with only the acting chairman voting against, that there was 'room for further development in the Society's activities' in promoting mutual understanding and good feeling and called on the chairman and vice-chairmen to examine the possibilities. As the memorandum made clear,

39

Piggott wanted the Society to be involved in advocating and encouraging political and economic co-operation, as well as promoting personal relations leading to 'a frank and useful interchange of intelligence'. The organization would also 'make all possible use of the Press, supplying authoritative articles and information'. The new organization would be a political branch of the Society.

At the subsequent Council meeting on 11 December 1935 the secretary reported that Mr Sale had discussed the proposal with Sir Edward Crowe, vice-chairman. They had concluded that the proposal 'did not come within the sphere of the Society's activities; nor would funds be forthcoming to meet the necessary additional expenditure'. This conclusion was accepted by the Council. Sir Francis Lindley, who had been British ambassador at Tokyo and who succeeded Mr Charles Sale as chairman, was more diplomatic and cautious and on occasions reiterated that the Society was not a political one. Piggott clearly found it difficult to appreciate the true nature of Japanese actions in the Far East. In a lecture to the Society on 5 March 1940 he spoke of the 'warm and generous heart of Japan' which he had even found 'in somewhat unexpected quarters; in the army at Shanghai, the Japanese community at Tientsin, the Japanese Embassy and commander-in-chief's headquarters at Peking, at Dairen, Mukden, Hsinking and Harbin'. As late as 16 April 1941 Piggott, who was blinded by his emotional attachment to Japan, referred at a Council meeting to 'the transient political disagreement that unfortunately existed'.

Despite the apolitical character of the Society, Japanese notables made use of Society occasions to promote the Japanese line. Viscount Ishii, Japan's special envoy to Europe, for instance, at a dinner in his honour on 17 February 1938 took the opportunity to affirm that 'Japan has no territorial ambitions in China' and spoke of Japan's efforts to 'promote the welfare of the Chinese people'. Mr Mamoru Shigemitsu (1887–1957), then Japanese ambassador in London, declared at the dinner in his honour on 18 January 1939 that 'friendship with China, more than anything else, is what we desire'.

Attendance at lectures fell and the Society's membership declined after 1937, when there were 638 members. In March 1939 membership was down to 567 and by December 1941 it was only 511.

The Prince of Wales and the Duke of York on becoming King Edward VIII and King George VI respectively gave up their patronage of the Society in accordance with the precedent set when Crown Prince Hirohito ceased to be a patron on his accession. Only one British patron, the Duke of Gloucester, remained after Prince Arthur of Connaught died in 1938. Four Japanese princes, namely Princes Chichibu, Takamatsu, Kanin and Asaka, continued as patrons up to the outbreak of the war with Japan in 1941.

Prince and Princess Chichibu revisited Britain for the coronation of King George VI in 1937. The Society gave a party on 9 June 1937 for the Prince and Princess in the garden at Grove House belonging to Mr and Mrs Sigismund Goetze. This stood on high ground above the Regent's Canal and ran for a quarter of a mile along the banks. Unfortunately it rained from four o'clock until six and Prince Chichibu was unable to be present 'owing to indisposition', but was 'ably represented by the Princess, who was most gracious and charming'.

The Society continued to have difficulties in finding funds to meet expenditure despite the Society's limited costs. A special finance committee was set up in 1937 with Viscount Hisaakira Kano, of the Yokohama Specie Bank and an active vice-chairman of the Society, in the chair. It recommended, *inter alia*, the organization of monthly city lunches with speakers, who would talk for about twenty minutes, at a cost not to exceed 5 shillings per head. Light entertainments with special features, 'such as a singer, dancer, etc., with the object of stimulating interest in the Society', should also be organized. Donations should be sought from vice-presidents and members of the Council to wipe out the deficit, and increased charges should be made for dinners to cover costs. These recommendations were generally accepted. The city lunches in particular, with the vigorous backing of Viscount Kano, seem to have been very successful. One 'light entertainment with a special feature' organized by the Society was a demonstration of dancing by Miss Chieko Kagawa at the Rembrandt Hotel SW7 on 16 April 1937.

A number of donations were received which helped to keep the Society going. Annual subscriptions were also raised to £1 5s for ordinary members. Nevertheless a deficit of £126 11s 8d occurred in 1939, and there was a deficit of £105 10s 11d in 1940. The Society's assets at that time amounted to £1,072 6s 3d. On 3 May 1934 the Council considered a suggestion that the Society should seek the establishment of 'a fund for the provision of a permanent home for the Society by donations from Members and firms interested in Trade with Japan'. But nothing came of this idea, and temporary premises continued to be used as offices and for meetings. In the 1937/8 session the Society's offices were removed from 22 Russell Square to 10 Grosvenor Place.

The usual dinners presided over by the president, the Japanese ambassador, were held. Mrs Haruko Ichikawa, has left a description of a dinner given in honour of Sir Francis Lindley, British ambassador to Japan.[15] She noted that 'England is a country of antique formality in everything'. The 'big waiter' who stood bolt upright behind Ambassador Matsudaira's chair looked 'as if he had swallowed a straight stick' and 'so serious that if Charlie Chaplin had brought in Harold Lloyd on his shoulders, he would not smile'. She noted how he struck the table hard with a wooden hammer first for grace and then for each of the toasts. 'Every time the toast was given, he rose with his shout.' There were nine toasts in all:

> and thus they awkwardly stood up and sat down nine times. . . . Although they did their utmost to avoid it, the scraping of the chairs made a strident noise because there were many people, but this also formed part of the etiquette. In China they call a most polite salute 'a kowtowing three and nine times', and this Chinese etiquette seems to me to have some similarity to that of England.

In 1935 the annual dinner, or banquet as the *Transactions* called it, was held in honour of the president, Mr Tsuneo Matsudaira, and his wife, who were returning to Japan. The guest of honour on this occasion was Sir Samuel Hoare, the British foreign secretary. Presents of silver salvers made by Messrs Wakely and Wheeler were given to the Matsudairas' son (Ichiro) and daughter (Masako) on the occasion of their weddings. Masako married Mr Yoshitomo Tokugawa.[16]

Mr Tsuneo Matsudaira was succeeded as Japanese ambassador and president of the Society by Mr Shigeru Yoshida (1878–1967). He was accompanied by his wife and his daughter Kazuko. When they left, a silver salver was presented by the Society to the Ambassador and another smaller one to Kazuko on her forthcoming marriage to Mr Takakichi Aso. Mrs Kazuko Aso addressed the Society on 'The Japanese Woman' on 26 May 1938.[17]

Contacts were maintained with the Japan–British Society in Tokyo and the chairman, Mr Charles Sale, used the inauguration of a telephone service between Britain and Japan on 13 March 1935 to send the Council's greetings to the chairman and Council of the Japan–British Society in Tokyo and asked that their 'respectful good wishes should be communicated also to the president and vice-presidents, and in particular to the Patron of the Society, His Imperial Highness Prince Chichibu'. A congratulatory message was also sent to the Japan Society in the Kansai when it was formed in 1935.

The lecture programme was maintained and the Society continued to be indebted to professor Charles Boxer and R. Ponsonby Fane for scholarly contributions. Sir Percival David, to whom Britain owes the magnificent collection of Chinese ceramics in the galleries of the Percival David Foundation spoke to the Society about the Shosoin on 23 October 1930. A paper by Mr E.V. Gatenby on 'The Influence of Japan on English Literature' was read on 25 February 1937 by the honorary editor as the professor was unable to be present. There were as usual many carefully researched papers on aspects of Japanese art. Japanese scholars whose papers were read to the Society included one by the eminent art historian Professor Yukio Yashiro, who lectured on 17 October 1935 on 'Scroll Paintings of the Far East'. A paper entitled 'The Foundation of Buddhist Culture in Japan' by Dr M. Anesaki, an expert on Japanese religion, was read to the Society by Colonel Somerville on 23 May 1940.

Although war with Japan began in December 1941 it was not until a Council Meeting on 1 April 1942 that it was decided formally to suspend the activities of the Society. At this meeting the Council agreed to end the lease on the Society's offices, to store the library and to cease publication of the *Transactions*. No subscriptions would be accepted until further notice. But the Society would 'remain in being unless some unexpected event makes a change of policy desirable. Names of members will be kept on the books.'

THE SOCIETY REVIVES AS JAPAN RECOVERS FROM DEFEAT, 1949–70

It was not until 1949, four years after the end of the Second World War, that the Society was revived. In the immediate post-war years feelings against Japan, particularly among ex-prisoners of war, were strong and the pre-war leaders of the Society were wise not to rush into a revival of a society devoted to extending knowledge of an ex-enemy country. Before the war the Society had been primarily a cultural and educational organization, and although on occasions it and leading members of it had been outspokenly and enthusiastically supportive of the Japanese cause (e.g. in the Russo-Japanese War and in relation to Manchuria), attempts to turn it into a politically motivated friendship society had been resisted.

When the Society was revived the emphasis on culture and scholarship weakened and under the leadership of Sir Robert Craigie, the last British ambassador to Japan before the war who became chairman, and Major General Piggott, who became vice-chairman and on Craigie's retirement in 1958 chairman, the Society became more overtly political and supportive of Japan. The first objective of the new constitution adopted in 1958 was declared to be the 'promotion of mutual understanding and good feeling between the British and Japanese peoples'. The encouragement of the study of Japan, as defined in the first constitution, took second place both in the constitution and in practice. Where General Piggott had failed before the war, he got his way after the war. The Japanese authorities were appreciative. Sir Robert Craigie, Lord Hankey, Sir Edward Crowe and General Piggott, who were the four leading personalities in the Society after the war, were awarded Japanese honours (First Class) in a ceremony at the Japanese Embassy on 24 January 1955. Sir Robert Craigie and Lord Hankey received the Order of the Rising Sun and Sir Edward Crowe and General Piggott the Order of the Sacred Treasure.

The Society was revived at an Extraordinary General Meeting held at the Royal Society of Arts in John Adam Street on 28 September 1949. Sir Francis Lindley, who had been the last chairman before the war, took the chair initially, but announced that because of his age he wished to resign. The meeting then elected Sir Robert Craigie as chairman and Major General Piggott and Colonel George Sale as vice-chairmen. As diplomatic relations had not yet been resumed with Japan, the office of president was left vacant.

The first meeting of the new Council was held on 23 November 1949 at the Royal Society of Arts. Including seventy-two life members, the membership of the revived Society then totalled 199. The executive committee met for the first time on 14 December 1949 and Colonel Marsden was appointed secretary to the Society. When they met again on 17 January 1950 the value of the Society's investments, partly in Japanese government stock and partly in Metropolitan Water Board Stock, were estimated at £407.

The first number of the new bulletin of the Society appeared in June 1950. It consisted of eight pages of news about the Society and its members. The first regular post-war meeting of the Society was held on 16 January 1950, when a paper entitled 'Japan – Past and Present' was read by the Society's chairman, Sir Robert Craigie, with Major General Piggott in the chair. In the early post-war issues of the bulletin, lectures were not printed in full and only abstracts were given.

In 1950 the Japan Association was formed to look after British trade interests in Japan, with Sir Edward Crowe, vice-president of the Society, as its first president. Membership of the Japan Association has grown over subsequent years to over 200 companies involved in business with Japan.

The Society warmly welcomed the signature on 8 September 1951 at San Francisco of the Peace Treaty with Japan. On 30 August that year a Japanese agency under Mr Koichiro Asakai was opened in London and a reception was given in honour of members of the agency on 23 October at the Criterion-in-Piccadilly. The coming into force of the Peace Treaty on 28 April 1952 was followed by an Anglo-Japanese occasion on 29 April 1952 when Mr Asakai entertained guests to mark the emperor's birthday. Bulletin Number 7 of June 1952 reported that 'The names of the English guests stood for old associations, old acquaintance (and "old lang syne"), old co-operation, old confidence. . . . Everyone belonged to the Japan Society and included the Chairman and both Vice-Chairmen of the Council, five Vice-Presidents and four Members of the Council.'

At the Annual General Meeting on 12 June 1952 the former Japanese vice-presidents, namely Mr Shigeru Yoshida, Viscount Hisaakira Kano (titles had been abolished in post-war Japan, but the Society at this time insisted on continuing to use them), and Prince Shimazu were re-elected. Lord Hankey proposed that Mr Mamoru Shigemitsu, who had been the last Japanese Ambassador before the war, should also be elected a vice-president. The proposal was carried 'with an outburst of applause'.

The Society's bulletins contain many enthusiastic and friendly references to Mr Mamoru Shigemitsu (1887–1957), who had been convicted at the Tokyo War Crimes Tribunal and sentenced to seven years imprisonment. He was released on 21 November 1950. He served as foreign minister during and at the end of the war and again between December 1954 and

December 1956. He visited London in that capacity in August 1956. Lord Hankey, General Piggott and others considered that Mr Shigemitsu had been wrongly convicted and argued strongly in his favour.

Bulletin Number 8 of October 1952 carried favourable comments on General Masaharu Honma, who had been executed as a war criminal in Manila in February 1946. Before the war Honma had been military attaché in London, a member of the Council and a friend of General Piggott. Whatever the merits of the case, the arguments used by the prosecution were not mentioned. The death on 22 August 1952 of Baron Kiichiro Hiranuma, another convicted war criminal, was the subject of a somewhat bland obituary which referred to him as an 'old statesman' with a 'distinguished past'.

The Society was involved in these years in the entertainment of many important Japanese visitors, including prime ministers and foreign ministers. But the highlight for the Society was the visit in 1953 of the Crown Prince (Akihito) to attend the coronation of Queen Elizabeth II. An enthusiastic account of the visit is contained in Bulletin Number 10 of June 1953. General Piggott and the late Mr David Symon, then Third Secretary in the British Embassy, were attached to his suite. The Crown Prince was the guest of honour of the Society at its first post-war dinner on 4 May 1953 at the Hyde Park Hotel. Over 200 attended the dinner. Sir Robert Craigie, the chairman, proposed a toast to the Crown Prince and asked Mr Edmund Blunden to recite the poem of welcome he had composed for the prince. One verse reads:

> – Prince, pilgrim, envoy, dwell
> Among us happily as in your own
> Japan; you will find those here who tell
> Their love with few words, but their love is known.

The prince replied briefly with a toast to the Society. 'Everyone was impressed by the Prince's confident bearing, and clearly spoken words, and H.I.H. received an ovation on resuming his seat.' General Piggott had the honour of entertaining the Crown Prince at his home at Cranleigh and was clearly deeply moved by the whole visit.

The opening lecture of the 1953/4 season on 29 September 1953 was given by Mr Hitoshi Ashida, who had been for a short time Japanese Prime Minister in 1948. He spoke on 'Japan Today'. General Piggott in introducing Mr Ashida expressed his pleasure at the announcement the previous day that two of the Society's vice-presidents, Mr Yoshida and Mr Shigemitsu, had reached agreement about the rearming of Japan and creation of an 'army'.

The visit to Britain in October 1954 of Mr Shigeru Yoshida, a vice-president of the Society and the first by a serving Japanese prime minister, was marked by a joint reception by the Japan Society and the Japan Association at the Hyde Park Hotel on 26 October and was attended by over 300 guests. Mr Yoshida spoke warmly of the efforts of the Society and the Association to 'repair and restore the British–Japan friendship broken by the war'. He noted that following the 'ascendance of the military clique in our country, British–Japan relations began to deteriorate until, finally, under the dictatorship of a minority, our nation was driven into a reckless and ruinous war'.

Mr Nobusuke Kishi, who had been a member of General Tojo's war cabinet, visited London as Japanese prime minister in July 1959. A joint reception by the Japan Society, Japan Association and the Japanese Chamber of Commerce was given at the Savoy Hotel on 15 July with some 350 guests present. After speeches had been given by the heads of the three organizations, Mr Kishi noted that the history of the Society was 'virtually the history of Anglo-Japanese relations'. He also expressed his admiration of those 'who strove against tremendous odds to revive it in the difficult days immediately after the War'.

In 1962 the Society had the pleasure of entertaining Princess Chichibu, who following the death of her husband had become patron of the Japan–British Society in Japan. She came to Britain in July 1962 to repay the visit made by Princess Alexandra of Kent to Japan in the previous autumn. Princess Alexandra's visit to Japan had been the first visit by a member of the British Royal Family after the war. Princess Chichibu, as the elder daughter of Ambassador Tsuneo Matsudaira, a former president of the Society, was well known to many members of the Society. A garden party was given in her honour at the Hurlingham Club on 26 July by the Society, acting together with the Japan Association and the Nippon Club. 'Unfortunately the occasion was marred by continuous rain so that the party had to be held indoors. This led to considerable congestion, since there was a record attendance of more than 560 members and guests.'

When Mr Hayato Ikeda, the then Japanese prime minister, came to London in November 1962 to sign the new Treaty of Commerce and Navigation, which had been the subject of many years negotiation, the Japan Society joined with the Japan Association and the Japanese Chamber of Commerce to give a joint reception at the Kensington Palace Hotel on 14 November.

On 2 November 1965 the Society acting on its own gave a reception at the Hyde Park Hotel in honour of Prince Hitachi, the emperor's younger brother, and Princess Hitachi, who were on a European tour following their marriage.

For the seventy-fifth anniversary of the Society Princess Chichibu was invited to revisit London. She was the guest of honour at the Anniversary Banquet of the Society at the Savoy Hotel on 30 January 1967. Sir Norman Roberts, the chairman, in proposing the health of the Princess quoted from Mr Arthur Diosy's speech at the inaugural banquet in June 1892: 'If the Japan Society succeeds, in the course of years, in twisting only one more silken thread into the red cord between the hearts of the people of Japan and the hearts of the people in Britain, then, I think, our Society will not have existed in vain.' Princess Chichibu presented the Society with a silver vase duly inscribed to the Society on its seventy-fifth anniversary and dated January 1967. In her reply, in which she proposed a toast to the Society, she reminded her audience that she had been born in Walton-on-Thames when her father had been attached to the Japanese Embassy in London. She brought greetings from the Japan–British Society in Tokyo and their wish to co-operate in strengthening the bonds of friendship and promoting deeper understanding.

During these years membership steadily increased. In 1956 a total of 657 members were recorded. In 1964/5 the total reached 1,004 and on 11 December 1962 the president, the Japanese ambassador, Mr Katsumi Ohno, and Mrs Ohno gave a dinner at the Hyde Park Hotel to celebrate the passing of the one-thousand mark. Unfortunately in the following year the numbers dropped to 907 as a result of a scrutiny of the membership list to weed out those who had not paid their subscriptions, but the total in 1970 was again over a thousand. The number of members attending lectures was low, although it was noted in 1965 that attendances of between fifty and sixty had been achieved that session. The system of corporate membership was instituted in 1958. Until this was agreed the Society's finances were under constant strain. For instance, the reception for Mr Kishi caused a deficit of £200. Without generous donations the Society could not have survived. Mr Yoshida on his visit gave the Society £150, Ambassador Matsumoto £100, Ambassador Nishi £200 and in 1956 the accounts record a donation of £400 from the Japanese Embassy.

The Council spent much time discussing the problem of finding premises which it could afford to rent. The library remained in store until 1957 and was not fully operational until 1959 when new headquarters were obtained in Carey Street off Chancery Lane. These were opened by Ambassador Katsumi Ohno, president of the Society, on 30 April 1959. But these arrangements turned out to be only temporary. In 1965 the Japanese Embassy offered the Society space at 9 Grosvenor Square. The Council decided that they wished to keep the headquarters of the Society separate, but in 1966 accepted the Embassy's offer to provide space for the library.

In 1956 an attempt was made to get the Society to change its name from 'The Japan Society of London' to its current name 'The Japan Society', but General Piggott adamantly refused to contemplate any change while he was alive.

In these years the Society had a number of committees. In 1959, for instance, in addition to the Executive Committee, there were separate Social, Programme, Library, House, Entertainment, Publications, Finance and Garden Committees. The Garden Committee led to the establishment in 1961 of the Bonsaikai (which eventually separated from the Society in 1988). There was also a stamp group and in 1964 an ikebana group. There were two separate art circles. From the reports published in the bulletins it would seem that the art circles were active bodies working within the Society. For instance, an exhibition of Japanese works of art belonging to members of the Society was organized at the premises of the Oriental Ceramics Society from 18 to 30 October 1958. Among objects shown were sword blades from the collection of General (later Field Marshal) Sir Francis Festing. In 1958 an Anglo-Japanese Parliamentary Group was organized under the chairmanship of Mr (later Sir) Julian Ridsdale, who was to become chairman of the Society. A group of younger people, Japanese and British, was formed in 1959 called the Wakatakekai ('Young Bamboos'). In 1962 arrangements were made for the merger of this group in which Mr Shijuro Ogata of the Bank of Japan, Mr (now Professor) Keith Thurley and Mr M. Isherwood were active members. The chairman in 1962 was John Gettrup. In 1962 the group organized three dances among other social events. The Otomodachi-kai, an informal group of English and Japanese ladies, was organized in December 1961 on the initiative of Mrs (later Lady) de la Mare and Mrs Cheke, who were closely associated with the Society.

In 1959 a typhoon caused serious damage in Japan. In October that year the chairman of the Society launched an appeal which resulted in donations of £2,440 14s 1d.

Although the bulletins in post-war years contain fewer contributions to scholarship on Japan and many lectures were of ephemeral interest, the lecture programme remained a significant part of the Society's activities. One of the first post-war lectures to the Society was one on 9 October 1950 by Edmund Blunden on 'The Japanese Poem'.

Mr F. Ashton Gwatkin, better known as 'John Paris', author of a series of novels (including *Kimono*) with a Japanese setting, gave a number of lectures. His first, entitled 'A Japanese Dog', was given on 14 November 1950. Another lecture which attracted a large audience, entitled 'Tales of Old Japan', was given on 5 October 1955. It dealt with the life and work of A.B. Mitford (later Lord Redesdale). A third, on 6 November 1962, under the chairmanship of Mr Sacheverell Sitwell, who had written a book about his visit to Japan entitled *Bridge of the Brocade Sash*, was devoted to 'Pierre Loti and Japan'. On 17 November 1966 he gave a talk on 'The Life and Times of John Paris'.

Professor A.L. Sadler lectured to the Society on 1 December 1953 on 'Tokugawa Tsunayoshi: the Eccentric Shogun'. Geoffrey Hudson, Fellow of All Souls, gave his first lecture to the Society on 3 March 1953 on the 'first' Japanese Emperor Jimmu Tenno. Richard Storry (later Professor), a member of the Council, spoke on 10 April 1956 on the theme 'Sazae San – The Creation of Hasegawa Machiko the Cartoonist' and showed many examples of these amusing and satirical cartoons. E.B. Ceadel of Cambridge University lectured on 8 January 1957 on 'Early Japanese Poetry, Spirit and Technique'. Father Michael Cooper, SJ, who became editor of Sophia University's *Monumenta Nipponica*, lectured, with Professor Charles Boxer

48

in the chair, on 8 December 1966 on the subject of 'Joao Rodrigues and Japan'. (His book '*Rodrigues the Interpreter: An Early Jesuit in Japan and China*' was published in 1974.) An example of Japanese scholarship was the lecture on 10 March 1970 by Mr H. Yamanouchi, who spoke on 'The Romantic Spirit in Modern Japanese Literature'.

Sir Esler Dening, former ambassador to Japan and chairman of the Council, gave a talk on 14 January 1969 entitled 'Reminiscences of the Meiji and Taishō Periods, 1875–1925'. Sir Esler reminded his audience that Sir Ernest Satow, who was British minister in Tokyo from 1894 to 1900, was the first plenipotentiary to speak the language of the country: 'He was also the last until, fifty-two years later, I myself was appointed ambassador to Japan'. There were, of course, many able men in the Japan consular service who had a good knowledge of Japanese, but before the Second World War they were not considered eligible for 'diplomatic' posts. Sir Esler ended his talk with a note of realism:

> I myself am not by temperament a dweller on the past, and I have no nostalgia for it. I prefer the present, with all its problems, and as far as Anglo-Japanese relations are concerned, I think they rest on far healthier foundations today than they ever did in the days about which I have been talking. It is in that direction that I hope they will continue.

It was good advice.

ANGLO-JAPANESE RELATIONS MATURE, 1971–91

During the last twenty years relations between the Imperial and Royal families have grown closer. The Society, in support of the developing relationship, organized various functions which were honoured by the presence of members of the two families.

For the Society the most significant Imperial occasion was the visit of the Emperor Shōwa and the Empress Nagako to London in September 1971. A joint reception with the Nippon Club, the Japan Association and the Japanese Chamber of Commerce was held in honour of Their Majesties at Claridges on 7 October 1971. When Their Majesties arrived at the Hotel, leading representatives of the four organizations were presented to them. They then entered the ballroom, where they were greeted by a fanfare from four trumpeters of the Life Guards. After the emperor and empress had taken their seats on a dais Sir Norman Brain, the chairman of the Society, gave a short speech of welcome in English and Japanese. In his brief reply in Japanese the emperor noted the deepening friendship between our two countries and declared: 'These happy developments owe much to the efforts you are constantly exerting.' The reception was well covered by press and television.

On 18 December 1973 the Society gave a reception at the Banqueting House in Whitehall in honour of the Duke and Duchess of Kent, who had just returned from a visit to Japan. Another reception was given at the Banqueting House on 14 June 1974 in honour once more of Princess Chichibu, who was on another visit to Britain. The Prince of Wales was the guest of honour on this occasion. On 11 February 1975 the Society, with the three other organizations, held a reception at St James's Palace in honour of the visit which the Queen and the Duke of Edinburgh were making to Japan that year. The Duke of Edinburgh also attended the reception.

While she was in Japan in 1975 the Queen invited the Crown Prince Akihito and the Crown Princess Michiko to be her guests at Windsor Castle during Ascot week 1976. Their stay at Windsor was followed by an official visit to Britain as the guests of the government. On this occasion a reception was held by the Society and other organizations in their honour at St James's Palace. Princess Alexandra and her husband also graced the occasion. Mr (later Sir) Julian Ridsale, as chairman of the Society, received the guests. The Crown Prince and Princess returned to London in July 1981 to attend the wedding of the Prince and Princess of Wales. On 30 July, the day after the wedding, Their Imperial Highnesses honoured the Society by attending a reception given by the Society at the Dorchester Hotel. Over 600 members and guests attended this reception. The Crown Prince responded to a short speech of welcome from Mr Dudley Cheke, chairman of the Society. In this he welcomed the Great Japan Exhibition due to begin that autumn at the Royal Academy and stressed his hope that the Society would continue to work for mutual understanding and friendship.

The Great Japan Exhibition provided a further opportunity for a visit by Princess Chichibu, who together with Princess Alexandra, performed the opening ceremony. This visit enabled Her Imperial Highness to attend the Ninetieth Anniversary dinner of the Society at the Intercontinental Hotel on 23 October 1981, when Sir Hugh Casson, president of the Royal Academy, as guest speaker gave a witty speech.

His Imperial Highness Prince Naruhito, Hiro no Miya, now the Crown Prince, came to Britain in 1983 to study at Merton College Oxford. His Imperial Highness honoured the Society's annual dinner on 17 October 1984. Sir John Pilcher, as chairman of the Society, expressed the Society's good wishes for the prince's stay and studies. A farewell party for his imperial Highness was given jointly with other Anglo-Japanese organizations at the Banqueting House on 17 September 1985. The lead was as usual taken by the Society, which also undertook the organization of the party. Sir Hugh Cortazzi, the chairman of the Society, on behalf of the Society, presented the prince with an antique print of Merton College as a souvenir of his studies at Oxford.

In 1985 the Society once again secured royal patronage. Her Royal Highness Princess Margaret, at the request of the Queen, graciously agreed to become our patron. A reception in her honour was given on 23 April 1986 at the Banqueting House in Whitehall.

Prince Naruhito, Hiro no Miya, was followed at Oxford by his younger brother Prince Fumihito, Aya no Miya, in 1988. A reception was given in his honour in the Ballroom of the Japanese Embassy in Piccadilly on 4 October 1989.

Owing to the serious illness of the Shōwa Emperor the Society decided to postpone its annual dinner in 1988. The Society heard with deep regret of the death of the Emperor Shōwa in January 1989 and expressed its condolences to the Imperial Family, the Japanese government and people. The Society, not being a political organization, took no official part in the unfortunate controversy, which preceded and followed the emperor's demise, about his wartime role and the question of representation at the funeral.

The Society also took the lead in arranging receptions for other Japanese leaders who visited Britain in these years. These included four Japanese prime ministers. Mr Kakuei Tanaka was guest of honour at a joint reception at the Savoy Hotel on 2 October 1973. Mr Zenko Suzuki was also entertained at the Savoy Hotel at a joint reception on 16 June 1981. On the occasion of his visit Mr Suzuki gave the Society a generous donation of 1 million yen (then about £2,500). A joint reception for Mr Yasuhiro Nakasone was given at the Intercontinental Hotel on Sunday 10 June 1984. In his speech on this occasion Mr Nakasone spoke in warm terms about Sir Ernest Satow, a former vice-president of the Society, and his contribution to the modernization of Japan after the Meiji Restoration. Mr Nakasone said that he had visited Prince Hiro at Oxford and recorded that when he met the Prince of Wales at dinner, Prince Charles had told him that 'the British Royal Family considers Prince Hiro as one of their members'. On 3 May 1988 the Society arranged a joint reception at the Banqueting Hall for Mr Noboru Takeshita. Sir Hugh Cortazzi, chairman of the Society, told the Japanese prime minister about the plans for a Japan Festival in the autumn of 1991, which would mark the centenary of the Society. Mr Takeshita in his response and in his speech at the Lord Mayor's luncheon referred to the importance which he and the Japanese government attached to the development of cultural relations between the two countries.

The Society continued to operate in these years on a restricted budget and depended largely for its work on the freely given efforts of its officers and members. Major efforts were made to strengthen the Society's finances by recruiting increased numbers of corporate members both Japanese and British. Without their support the Society would probably have foundered; certainly corporate subscriptions made it possible to keep individual subscriptions at a reasonable level. In 1988 the Society benefited greatly from a generous donation of 5 million yen (now about £20,000) from the Buddhist organization Soka Gakkai through its UK branch NS(UK). This donation was made on the initiative of the honorary chairman Mr Daisaku Ikeda and two further donations of 5 million yen were promised and received. The

Society did not yet, however, have adequate funds to establish permanent offices and accommodation for its valuable library. The Japanese Embassy kindly agreed to continue to provide space for the library in its new buildings in Piccadilly.

Between 1986 and 1988 a number of amendments to the Society's Constitution were agreed. Following the retirement of Sir Robert Craigie as chairman the Society had instituted a rule limiting the Chairman to a term of three years at any one stretch. (Sir John Pilcher served as chairman for two separate periods of three years.) An amendment agreed in 1988 provided that the chairman and members of the Council, subject to annual election, could serve without time limits on length of office.

The name of the Society was finally altered to 'The Japan Society' from 'The Japan Society of London'. Of greater significance was the decision to rewrite the Society's objectives, underlining its charitable status and purposes. It was agreed that the Society had three main objectives:

(a) To promote the study of Japan and its people in all their aspects, traditional and modern, and to make the results of such study more accessible to the general public.
(b) To promote the study of Britain and its culture by Japanese people and to further educational exchanges between Britain and Japan.
(c) To maintain in England a central institution for the collection, provision, maintenance and diffusion of information and knowledge upon all such matters aforesaid.

The Council thought that it was an important function of the Society to try to do more to integrate the Japanese community into British life. It also wanted to do more for younger members and welcomed the efforts of the William Adams Society (Anjinkai), the group established by former British teachers in Japan. It has to be admitted, however, that the efforts of the Society in these respects met with at best limited success in these years.

The Society's lecture programme has been maintained and extended. In addition to various general lectures about aspects of modern Japan, the Society has been fortunate in securing the co-operation of the growing community of British scholars of Japanese who have spoken to the Society on various aspects of Japanese history and culture. Among the numerous scholars who have spared the time to address the Society in these and earlier post-war years, in many cases more than once, have been Professors F.J. Daniels, C.J. Dunn, P.G. O'Neill. Richard Storry, W.G. Beasley, Ian Nish, Arthur Stockwin and Ian Gow. The Society owes a particular debt of gratitude to Dr Carmen Blacker, who in addition to giving a number of lectures to the Society, acted as the first editor after the war. Other British academics who have lectured to the Society include Dr Douglas

Mills, formerly of Cambridge University, Louis Allen, formerly of Durham University, and Dr Gordon Daniels of Sheffield University. Among the non-academic lecturers who have been staunch supporters of the Society and lectured more than once, mention must be made of the late Sir Vere Redman, Sir John Figgess and Mr Soame Jenyns. A number of the Society's presidents, including Mr Tadao Kato, have also spoken to the Society.

The Society welcomed the formation of the UK–Japan 2000 Group in 1985. Some members of the Society belong to the Group and take part in its annual high-level conferences. At the annual dinner of the Society on 22 November 1986 at the House of Commons (sponsored by Sir Julian Ridsdale MP, a vice-president and former chairman of the Society) the Right Honourable Patrick Jenkin MP (now Lord Jenkin of Roding), then the UK chairman of the Group, was the Society's guest of honour.

The formation of the British Association of Japanese Studies (BAJS) was also welcomed by the Society, which has always favoured an expansion of Japanese studies in Britain. The publication in 1989 of *Japan Forum*, the journal of the BAJS, provided a new and significant regular publication in Britain devoted to scholarship on Japan. A number of members of the Society, including the chairman Sir Hugh Cortazzi, belong to the Association.

The council did all they could to support and promote the 1991 Japan Festival in the United Kingdom which marked the Society's centenary in 1991. The society was greatly honoured by the evening reception given by the Lord Mayor and corporation of London at Guildhall on 17 September 1991 in the presence of the Crown Prince of Japan to mark the Society's centenary and the opening of the Japan Festival.

The Council have been working with their limited resources to advance the educational objectives of the Society. They have been determined to maintain the Society as an independent non-political organization devoted to the promotion of Anglo-Japanese understanding.

Unfortunately the Society's efforts to win greater involvement in its activities by the large and growing Japanese community have so far met with limited success. The Wakatakekai founded in the 1960s has sadly ceased to function and the Society accordingly does little for its younger members.

The Society, if it is to develop and play a more significant role in promoting better Anglo-Japanese understanding, needs a firmer financial base. It has survived for too long on a pitifully small budget. It still has no permanent headquarters where its offices and library can be combined under one roof. It remains almost totally dependent on the services freely given by its officers and members and has no full-time paid staff. To work effectively the Society needs an adequate capital endowment.

2

CHARLES WIRGMAN (1835–1891)

John Clark

Charles Wirgman was one of those engaging, eccentric, polyglot personalities who adventured around the Far East in the second half of the nineteenth century. Many deserved their reputation as semi-criminals out for quick money, but Wirgman, though probably never rich, has nowhere left an image of such avariciousness. He was correspondent of the *Illustrated London News* in Japan in the 1860s, where he arrived in April 1861, and was a vital eye-witness observer of the opening of the country. Active in the treaty port press, he founded his own satirical review, the *Japan Punch*, in Yokohama in May 1862. He contributed in part to the development of Meiji oil painting by training Goseda Yoshimatsu, and Takahashi Yuichi, and indirectly contributing to that of several others.

This brief survey of Wirgman's life will discuss some of his early experiences and character traits, his work as a journalist and communicator of images of Japan, the way he appeared on the stage of treaty port life and his role as a mediator between Japanese and western painting.[1]

EARLY LIFE AND PERSONALITY

Wirgman was the first son of Ferdinand Charles Wirgman (1806–57), from a family of successful silversmiths which had originally come to England from Sweden in the early eighteenth century. Later the family married into French emigré Protestant families, and it was in France that Wirgman's father probably studied veterinary science for a while in the 1830s. Although one cannot be certain, Charles Wirgman was probably born in London, but his family's continental connections meant that he must have spent a large part of his youth in France and Germany.

His sister Clara (1841–1905) married into a French family called Thevenard, and Charles certainly spent time drawing in Paris during the years 1852 to 1855, probably through an informal arrangement with a painter's studio which was common among the higher middle class of his time. Wirgman was also linked to both the German-speaking world and the British military through his uncle, Theodore (1809–84), who served in the Austrian cavalry, and later fought in the British army in both the Crimean War and the Indian Mutiny.

Nothing certain is known of Charles's education, only its results. What he may have learnt in a Paris atelier is not clear. His later work almost continuously declares a lack of interest in formal academic control, his hand is that of a Constantin Guys, the drawing technique that of a military draughtsman, the eye interested in characterizing gesture not manifesting it. His oil painting seems to have been begun later in life after some period of residence in Japan, and was barely competent, again indicating a lack of professional training.

His language skills may have been acquired by osmosis as part of his social milieu. His friend Rudolf Lindau knew him to be nearly bilingual in French and German, and fluent in Italian and Dutch. He knew Latin and Greek, was able to write in Spanish, Portuguese, and quote literary tags in Russian, Scottish Gaelic and Arabic. He later definitely acquired interpreter-level competence in spoken Japanese, although one cannot be sure how good his written Japanese became.[2] He also had a certain knowledge of Chinese.

In later material for the *Japan Punch* much of this skill appears in a kind of deadpan humour which may quote tags in as many languages as there are lines on a page – in the original, including non-roman scripts. One may argue that this is evidence for a Joycean imagination before its time. But his cross-linguistic punning mentality speaks more of the small boy playing with the baubles of knowledge rather than forging its vessels. Such trivialization of complex and hard-won language ability may have been an acquired English private-school habit. Or it may have been a defence against serious thought, possibly exemplified for him in the family by his grandfather, Thomas (1771–1840), translator of German philosophy and correspondent of Madame de Staël.

As good social company as Wirgman was, in the attestation of many contemporary witnesses, there was an element of bravado and almost forced eccentricity in his personality which was evident in his wearing of Japanese clothes, in going about in the street without tie or waistcoat or in riding a cow through the streets of Yokohama, *pour épater les étrangers et les indigènes*. He could play the *shamisen* and may well have attempted unsuccessfully to have his liaison with a Japanese woman recognized as a marriage by the British Consulate. He had genuine affection for Japan and the Japanese which went beyond mere exoticism and treaty port opportunism: 'There are some countries one gets tired of but Japan is as fresh today as it was the first time Punch saw it and charms as much' (from *Sketchbook*, 1876–7). This agreeable unconventionality was mixed with perhaps manic courage and fits of depression. One cannot doubt his bravery, in walking about unarmed at a time when foreigners were often in peril of their lives – during the attack on the British Legation of July 1861, and while travelling with Satow in June 1867. From time to time he also indicates emotional instability through mention of his continual but ineffectual attempts to leave Japan. Lindau records that he only left briefly when recalled by the *Illustrated London News (ILN)* in 1862, after which he returned apparently on a whim and on borrowed funds from a returning British diplomat whom he had casually met in Hyde Park. He also returned to Europe for a few months in 1887, possibly for medical attention, and returned to Japan apparently ill, to die at the German Hospital in Yokohama on 8 February 1891.

His jocular tales in the *Japan Punch* sometimes speak of amorous failure as does the single surviving letter to his brother in 1878, which refers to someone he loves in Rome. As statements of his *weltanschauung* there only remain the pages of the *Japan Punch*, and among his relatives there survives a handwritten draft of material for the *Japan Punch* (possibly from 1884) which sarcastically mimicks the style of Sir Walter Scott, which ends, 'No man can escape his stomach, quoth he, as with cheerful glee he felt his morbid symptoms leave him, and on his wall all men he had painted the Legend as a warning that man at his birth is Radically Good. Bile alone make him Evil.' [*sic*]

CORRESPONDENT AND EYE-WITNESS

Wirgman's first report for the *ILN* is from Malta on 3 March 1857. He was proceeding to the Far East to cover the developing crisis with China which was to develop into the 'Arrow' War, after Chinese seizure of a lorcha of the name on 8 October 1856. We do not know how he came to go. But his father died in February 1857, and this event possibly connected with an introduction via his uncle, may have provided the opportunity to leave England for a while. *ILN* records did not survive the Second World War, but the journal must have anticipated the Arrow War because Wirgman left England before Palmerston's March re-election, the departure of Lord Elgin for China in April and the news of the outbreak of the Indian Independence War (Mutiny) at Meerut on 10 May 1857.

It is possible that Wirgman originally went to the Far East in a private capacity with a trader such as Robert Jardine whom he was with in the Philippines in July 1857, and had originally been contracted to do some traveller's reports – so popular at the time in the *ILN*. It was only at the end of 1857 that Wirgman was in the Hong Kong/Canton area, and he does not seem to have covered the first limited hostilities in northern China, which ended in the Treaty of Tainjin in July 1858. It was the failure of the second British attack on the Taku forts in June 1859 which provoked full-scale military action in northern China that ended with the Anglo-Chinese Treaty of October 1860.

It was this campaign that Wirgman was to cover as a fully-fledged *ILN* correspondent, together with the British photographer Felice Beato who now is thought to have originally come from Corfu. Such experience and proven skill in the northern China campaign of 1859–60 may have led to Wirgman being selected to send reports from Japan, where he probably arrived in late April 1861.

In principle, Japan had been opened to foreign intercourse by Perry in 1854 and by subsequent foreign pressures, but in practice it was the opening of Yokohama to foreign residence and trade in June 1859 which transformed Japan's position. This date marked the beginning of a transitional period in Japan's domestic and foreign politics which was symbolically completed with the move of the Emperor Meiji to Tokyo in 1868. In reality this period of transition ended in 1877 with the defeat of Satsuma forces in the Rebellion of that year. In many respects the new Japan only reached its final form with the Meiji Constitution of 1889. Wirgman was to be a principal witness, of this thirty-year period of change in Japanese history of which he left a significant visual record, within the conventions of its genre.

Wirgman seemed to have been interested in certain categories of Japanese experience. There were his drawings of particular events, sometimes done on the spot, sometimes reconstructed from memory or from a photograph, which document the historical action closest to him and which was thought important for his readers in the *ILN*. This category to some extent overlapped with his drawings made on travels around Japan, many of which were done purely for personal notes. However, some of these appeared in the *ILN* or were bought by foreign residents. Wirgman was also interested in Japanese types, such as the warrior, or the serving girl, and even the artist. Interspersed among these may be found portraits and, some time in the 1870s, drawings were worked-up into oil paintings to order.

In the early 1870s his work for the *ILN* came to an end, although a single surviving letter indicates that he received payments from the publishers in 1878, and it is possible to connect his name with some work which appeared in the *ILN* as late as January 1887. Certainly his byline of 'Special Artist and Correspondent' seems valid no longer than August 1868, and it would appear that by 1872 Régamey was doing work in London from photographs sent from Japan. Japan was itself reported from by the famous *ILN* reporter Simpson in August 1873. Wirgman's *Sketchbook of Japan* was published in Yokohama in March or April 1884 and various sources indicate that these litho-reproductions were of drawings from ten or twelve years earlier.

TREATY PORT LIFE

Wirgman quickly became a figure who was prominent in the life of the newly opened treaty port of Yokohama, and among the foreign community general. Very soon after his arrival in September 1861, he made himself available to take a visiting officer with antiquarian interest to see the Japanese artist who worked for P.F. von Siebold, of whom Wirgman made a portrait sketch in December of that year.

Wirgman had established the *Japan Punch* in May 1862 on a loan from Lindau, and this ran intermittently until 1873 with regular monthly publication thereafter until March 1887. The magazine was originally printed on woodblock but was, from December 1883, litho-printed, lithography having largely begun in Japan in 1874. This was a semi-satirical illustrated magazine which caricatured the prominent figures of the foreign community in Yokohama, normally under transparent pseudonyms. Wirgman also went into partnership with Beato from 1865 to 1867, and their price list survives with Beato's photographs on one side and Wirgman drawings on the other. From 1867 there also survives a record of Wirgman's works being purchased by the Chief Justice in Shanghai, and one may expect that in addition to his journalistic activities Wirgman was a regular port of call for visiting foreigners seeking souvenir drawings.

It is not clear that Beato and Wirgman were always in favour with the British authorities, and there is a hint from Beato photographs of Wirgman drawings in Leiden that in 1864 they were both in danger of being put in the British Yokohama jail. But in February 1876, when Parkes acceded to Japanese pressure and forbade foreigners publishing newspapers in Japanese, he did not extend this to English-language media, especially to the *Japan Punch* in which he was regularly pilloried; so one may conclude that by that time Wirgman's journal had become an untouchable local institution.

Wirgman also worked as an interpreter from time to time and, in known cases, for the British Legation in June 1870 and June 1872. Some Japanese sources have at times stated he was thought to be a British spy, but there is no evidence for this, either in Japanese or British sources. Wirgman must have occasionally been involved in trade deals on his own account, and the *Japan Punch* is full of insider references to current trading deals or financial failures in the foreign business community. In February 1870 he was even said to have been involved in securing a railway contract, which if true may indicate one source of his income.

His sketching and journalistic activities meant that Wirgman's drawings had two functions: one was as a kind of famous local product in Yokohama which would appear in the *ILN* and as illustrations to books published in London and Paris. The other was as a social currency, his engagement in the production, or the sale and exchange of, which secured his place and not merely a part of his economic security, in a community whose members were frequently changing. As social currency their sale and exchange also served as markers of identity in a community which was otherwise only linked by trade or various social clubs. Wirgman, a skilled amateur at best, was thus kept in touch with a changing cycle of patrons and visitors, including artists, to whom his work might otherwise mean little or remain at best a curiosity. Wirgman's role was as an artistic mediator in two directions: from Japan to Europe and vice versa.

Wirgman's images formed part of the basic stock of European illustrations of Japan for about ten years from the early 1860s to early 1870s (Figs. 2.1 and 2.2). But he was also important in mediating contacts with visiting European artists and Japan. When Bird and Baldwin were murdered in November 1865, he was out sketching with the French naval illustrator Roussin, alongside whose work some of Wirgman's drawings would appear in Humbert's *Le Japon Illustré* of 1870. When Guimet and his illustrator Régamey – who had already done illustrations for the *ILN* in London – arrived in Yokohama in August 1876, they went to Enoshima the next day with Wirgman. In the same year Frank Dillon, a British illustrator did work in Japan, and was almost certainly known to Wirgman. In October 1878 a portrait of Wirgman was done in Yokohama by an unidentified American painter. Such anecdotal evidence taken together suggests that into the late 1870s Wirgman was a regular contact in the Yokohama community for foreign artists or illustrators visiting Japan, with whom he would go sketching or whom he would introduce to Japanese artists.

Wirgman must also have been a mediator between the foreign community, especially diplomats, and Japanese artists. He was an inveterate companion of the young Satow from just after his arrival in Japan in September 1862. During a later posting to Uruguay in 1891, Satow thought it worth mentioning in his diary that he had been visited by the 'younger brother of my old friend Charles', nine months after Wirgman's death.

Satow and Wirgman were so familiar they went to a Shinagawa brothel together in April 1867. In March 1872 they went to a *shogakai*, an art exhibition at the equivalent of a commercial gallery, in which painting and poetry scrolls were for sale and at which some artists did rapid compositions together in a convivial atmosphere. Wirgman had already illustrated such a meeting in the *ILN* in January 1865. There can be little doubt that Wirgman who was known as an artist, fluent in Japanese, and the social intimate of diplomats. He introduced some diplomats to Japanese art circles.

I have already noted Wirgman's visit in September 1861 to a Japanese artist who worked for von Siebold. But Wirgman was also engaged through the *Japan Punch* in activities which brought him into contact with Japanese printing craftsmen, through whom his reputation and contacts must have spread among artists both in Yokohama and Edo. As the *Japan Punch* was printed by woodblock from 1862 until 1883 he would have required Japanese block-cutters for this. As early as May 1864 the *ILN* had received sketches which included those of a woodblock carver, and this very image, very similar to a woodblock printed book of Yokohama views in the British Museum, is stylistically close to the work of Goseda Horyu I, an artist whose son, Goseda Yoshimatsu, Wirgman was to teach from 1865. One can only suppose that by this date Wirgman was already in close contact with a number of Japanese artists.

Goseda Yoshimatsu (1855–1915) was to become the first Japanese artist

Figure 2.1

Figure 2.2

to exhibit at a Paris Salon in 1881, and became Wirgman's pupil when he was aged 12. By 1873 Wirgman was reported as praising Yoshimatsu as a more talented artist than himself, and indeed some works from this time are hardly distinguishable between them. By 1874 it was recorded that Yoshimatsu had moved to Tokyo, and from 1876 he studied for a while with the Italian Fontanesi at the newly established Tokyo Technical Art School. But some links with Wirgman must have been maintained, for just prior to Yoshimatsu's departure for Europe in July 1880 he visited Wirgman twice in Yokohama, as it was Japanese etiquette to visit a teacher before a long journey away from home. Yoshimatsu also probably sent something to London – on his behalf – from Paris in November 1880, and was in England at the same time as Wirgman could have been in 1887.

His more significant connection, though perhaps not of the same stylistic import as that with Yoshimatsu, was that with Takahashi Yuichi (1828–94). Yuichi had been an official of the Bureau for the Study of Western Books since 1862 (from 1864 he was in the Painting Bureau of the Development Office) – so when he was taken to see Wirgman after a chance encounter with Beato in August 1866, he was an influential if minor official. How much Wirgman actually taught Yuichi is doubtful, and one source indicates that initial instruction in oil painting was given by Mrs Schoyer, the wife of an American businessman. In general their relations, at least in the second half of the 1860s, must have been close and in 1869 and 1870 Yuichi unsuccessfully attempted to gain permission for Wirgman to live with him in Tokyo, then off-limits to foreigners. What is more likely is that for a brief period Wirgman served as a role model of what a foreign artist could be and probably provided technical advice about pigments or showed painting manuals to Yuichi. These were to arrive from Japanese sources in some numbers in 1866 and 1874.

Wirgman was also significant as a stylistic source for a notion of visual realism because of his friendship with the photographer Beato and the photographic nature of some of his own compositions. Some of his figures are placed in the mid-ground of a picture plane as if posed for a contemporary photograph of a 'Japanese type'. There are also several drawings of groups by Wirgman where the figures are strung out parallel to the picture plane without artful rearrangement in perspective, and these phenomena reappear in some of Yuichi's work.

Wirgman died in 1891, and was to be followed by his Japanese wife Kane in 1897 and their son Ichiro, himself married but childless, in 1922. However, his reputation and his importance were never eclipsed by the later and much richer growth of Japanese oil painting. His work was exhibited in the retrospective of Japanese oil painting by members of Yuichi's studio in 1893. There was probably an exhibition in 1904 in

Yokohama, and there were other retrospectives in Tokyo in 1937 and Yokohama in 1970.

Despite its limitations, Wirgman's work has always remained as the first significant body of drawings and paintings by a western artist working in Japan and with which Japanese were in contact. He is also one of the few western artists to be buried there.

3

WILLIAM GEORGE ASTON
(1841–1911)

P.F. Kornicki

Both to their contemporaries and to several generations of successors, Aston, Satow and Chamberlain had no equals as scholars of Japan. While Satow and Chamberlain had distinguished public careers, however, one as a diplomat and the other as a professor at Tokyo University, Aston remained in the humbler ranks of the consular service until forced by persistent ill health to retire at the early age of 48. The survival of diaries and letters have enriched our knowledge of the private lives of Satow and Chamberlain, while that of Aston seems destined to remain beyond our reach. On the other hand, it is Aston's writings that have stood the passage of time best, that are still in print almost a hundred years after they were written and that are still extensively quoted and referred to. This is perhaps not so much an irony of fate as the token of a life given up less to a public persona than to scholarship. But the result is that he remains a shadowy figure.

The story of Aston's early years and his career in the consular service is soon told. Aston was born near Londonderry in 1841. In the early 1850s his father, who was a preacher in the Unitarian Church of Ireland, moved to the village of Saintfield to establish a school. Aston grew up in Saintfield and taught in his father's school before matriculating at Queen's College, Belfast, in 1859. His university career was distinguished: he took his BA in 1862 and was gold medallist in classics, and was then awarded a Senior Scholarship in modern languages and modern history for his MA, which he took in 1863. He was, in short, a scholarship boy from the provinces who made good and acquired on the way a thorough if conventional education in classical and modern philology. He had none of Chamberlain's cosmopolitan upbringing or of Satow's more adventurous education, but he was able to expand his intellectual horizons in Japan and in 1882 his old university recognized his achievements as a scholar when it conferred on him an honorary doctorate of literature.

In the summer of 1864 Aston passed the competitive examination for entry to the Consular Service and was appointed Student Interpreter at the British Legation in Edo, where his task was to learn Japanese for the conduct of consular and diplomatic business. In that same year he first made the acquaintance of Kido Takayoshi and other discontented samurai who were later to play an important part in the Meiji Restoration of 1868 and the politics of the new Meiji government. These contacts gave him a good understanding of the political undercurrents in the turbulent years preceding the fall of the Tokugawa shogunate, and the advice of Aston and his contemporary at the Legation, Ernest Satow, was instrumental in ensuring that British policy was well-informed and reponsive during the years of confrontation between the shogunate and its opponents. In the summer of 1867, for example, Aston was on board HMS *Serpent*, first of all in the Shimonoseki Straits reporting on the understanding between Satsuma and Chōshū before moving on to the west coast of Japan in search of a site for an open port on the Japan Sea coast.

In 1870 he was appointed Interpreter and Translator to the Legation and in that capacity was in attendance on the Iwakura Mission during its stay in Britain from August to December 1872: the Mission, which included several senior government ministers, spent the best part of two years examining the constituents of a successfully developed and industralized society in the United States and a number of European countries. In *Macmillan's Magazine* in that year Aston published an account of Japan for the occasion: 'the most important embassy that has ever left the shores of Great Japan is now in England, and the moment therefore appears fitting to inquire into the course of events which led to its despatch, and into the present position of the country whence it comes'.[1] Aston made no secret of his sympathy with the desire of Kido and others in the new government to centralize and direct the economic development of Japan, but his reaction to the social changes he had already witnessed in Japan and to the wave of enthusiasm for all things western was bemusement, and he was lost for an explanation: it had all taken place 'by magic'. Aston saw some dangers lying ahead, caused both by the extremely rapid pace of change and by the destabling effect of a leadership composed of revolutionaries, but he saw the visit of the Embassy as a 'golden opportunity' for Kido and the others: 'They can examine our factories, our machinery, and all the various industries for which we are famous, and they can thus learn the source of England's greatness.'[2] There are several strands to Aston's thought here. On the one hand, there is little doubt that Aston was genuinely enthusiastic about Japan's progress and genuinely concerned that it did not lead to instability. On the other hand, his patriotism, and more importantly his loyalty to his own culture, injected a note of condescension into his writing that is apparent here: in the same piece he argued that it was too early to end the extraterritorial privileges enjoyed by British subjects in Japan, as some were advocating, for the new Meiji law codes were untried and it was therefore premature to entrust British subjects to the uncertain mercy of the Japanese courts.

Also in 1872 Aston was one of the founder members of the Asiatic Society of Japan. The Society held regular meetings and published its *Transactions*, and these were a forum along with its German equivalent for enquiry into the history and culture of Japan. Among the other founder members were Brinkley, Dickins, Griffis, Gubbins, Satow and Summers, all of whom were to write extensively on Japan in the years ahead. Aston served as president of the Society from 1888 to 1889 and was a regular contributor to the *Transactions*: to the first issue he contributed an account of Russian activities in the islands to the north of Japan drawn from manuscript copies of the private correspondence of Japanese officials on duty at Hakodate, and in the issue that appeared just before his death he contributed a short piece correcting an earlier contributor's attempt to locate Takamagahara, the legendary dwelling place of the gods, somewhere in Japan.[3] In 1875 Aston was appointed assistant Japanese secretary at the Legation in Tokyo, and amongst his other tasks at this time were the arrangements for a substantial Japanese presence at the Intercolonial Exhibition held in Melbourne towards the end of the year. In the early 1880s he served several spells as acting consul at Hiogo (Kōbe) and then in 1882 he was appointed consul at Nagasaki.

In August 1882 Aston accompanied Vice-Admiral Willes and his squadron to Korea for negotiations on a trade treaty. The new treaty was closely modelled on the recent American treaty and was signed later that year; but following representations from Sir Harry Parkes, the British minister in Tokyo, about the difficulties it would impose on British traders in Korea, the British government refused to ratify it. In 1883 Parkes and Aston drafted a revised version, and in October Aston met up with Parkes in Korea for further negotiations, which resulted in the Treaty of Friendship and Commerce between Her Majesty Queen Victoria and His Majesty the King of Korea, which was signed at Hanyang (Seoul) in November 1883. In 1884 he was provisionally appointed Consul-General for Korea and took up residence in the house he had selected in 1883 as the best site for a British Legation. The accommodation proved unsatisfactory in the cold winters and difficult to defend from attacks, and at one stage he was compelled to take refuge in the American Legation. It was a difficult year for Aston: he struggled to compile a summary of Korea's foreign trade for the use of British merchants thinking of establishing trading links with Korea, but found that the Japanese consuls had done a better job of gathering statistics than the fledgling Korean customs service; he was not sanguine about the prospects for British traders, and although he did his best to assist Jardine Matheson & Company in their mining and other ventures in Korea, they found the returns insufficient to justify remaining and pulled out of Korea. As the year drew to a close Aston became increasingly convinced that the tension between conservative and reformist elements in the Korean government would only be resolved by a violent clash between the two. In this he was right and in early 1885 was forced by ill health to return to Japan. The dramatic story behind his return to Japan was told after his death by J.C. Hall (1844–1921), one of Aston's sucessors as student interpreter at the Legation:

> In December of that year he [Aston] was one of the guests at the notorious Post-Office dinner when the hosts, led by Kim Ok Kiun, left the table and betook themselves to the work of assassinating their rivals in the government. The guests dispersed in confusion, each finding his way home as best he could. The exposure to the frosty night air brought on a pulmonary attack which nearly cost Aston his life.[4]

It was thanks to Count Inoue [Kaoru], the Japanese foreign minister, who happened to be in Korea at the time, that Aston was able to return speedily to Japan and to expert medical care, and although he planned to return to Korea he proved too unwell to do so.

In 1886 he was appointed Japanese secretary in Tokyo, but chronic trouble with his lungs got the better of him and he retired on a pension in 1889. He first spent some time recuperating in Switzerland and then moved to Beer in Devon, where he spent the rest of his life. The remaining twenty-two years of that life, right up to the time of his death in November 1911, saw the publication of his most important works on Japan. Of his private life during all this time and before, all we know is that he married Janet Smith of Belfast in 1871 and that she died childless in 1908. It seems from Satow's letters that she was an accomplished pianist and from Aston's letters to Sir Harry Parkes that she performed the supremely difficult role of diplomatic spouse in Korea with distinction. During Aston's subsequent illness she was both nurse and amanuensis. Aston dictated his view of recent political upheavals in several letters she wrote for him to Sir Harry. Of the rest, of his political views, of his beliefs, of his friendships and even of his views of Japan, we can only make inferences from his writings. Just as he was a profoundly textual scholar, so he has left us only texts to work on.

His first task in Japan was learning the language and for that he was as well prepared as Satow or Chamberlain. Like both of them he excelled in this and rapidly acquired an enviable mastery of the spoken and written forms of the language. How he accomplished this in the absence of reliable grammars is less clear in Aston's case than it is in Satow's. He may have made use at first of one of several exploratory grammars published in the 1860s for the burgeoning market of foreigners resident in Japan, though it is unlikely that he would have found their attempts to apply European grammatical categories to Japanese very helpful. It appears that one of his principal teachers of classical Japanese and Japanese linguistics was Hori Hidenari (1819–87), a long-forgotten student of the Kokugaku (Nativist) school of learning who published several dozens of books concerning the Japanese language and the spiritual values of Japan. If this is the case, however, it is surprising that not one of these books is now to be found in the collection of Aston's books in Cambridge University Library. At any rate, by 1870 he was sufficiently proficient in spoken Japanese to be able to manage interpreting tasks with ease: in that year, when Sir Harry Parkes, then British minister in Tokyo, and his wife visited Wakayama, Aston interpreted for Lady Parkes in her chats with the former *daimyō*. In the same year some of his translations from speeches made in the forerunner of the Japanese Diet were printed in the Foreign Office Blue Books (Confidential Prints).

Aston's earliest publications were closely connected with his mastery of the language. In 1869 he published *A Short Grammar of the Japanese Spoken Language*, which met an immediate need: further editions of it appeared in 1871, 1873 and 1888, and in 1873 a translation of it into French by a French consular official was published in Yokohama. The differences between these four editions reveal fundamental changes not only in the level of Aston's understanding of the language but also in the social setting of language in Meiji Japan. In the first three editions he states that, 'an uneducated Japanese has no word for, nor much idea of, any shorter period of time than one European hour. It is impossible to make him understand what is meant by "five minutes" or "a quarter of an hour"', and that educated speakers use *bunji* or the English word 'minute' to refer to a minute of time; in the fourth edition he states that Japan had now completely gone over to the European system of reckoning time and that the word for minute was *fun*, as it still is now.[5] In all four editions he warns readers against the error of using honorifics when addressing servants or coolies, but his injunction against the use of Malay words in the misapprehension that they are Japanese words is omitted from the fourth edition, which can be taken as an indication of the decline of the pidgin Japanese used in earlier days by the expatriate community. His treatment of the two particles that tax the understanding of students of the language also underwent substantial changes.

In the first edition he describes *wa* as a 'sort of definite article',[6] and *ga* as 'sometimes an indefinite article',[6] definitions that are so unhelpful as to be demoralizing to the student: as an analyst of the language he was still very much in the dark and at the stage of trying to tie Japanese to the procrustean bed of European grammatical terminology. But in the third edition he arrived at a much better understanding: *wa* is 'a distinctive or separative particle' and it 'has the force of isolating or singling out one object from among a number, or of opposing one thing to another', and *ga* 'often follows nouns in the nominative case'; in the fourth edition these definitions are amplified still further with more examples.[7] The Preface to the first three editions stated that, 'this book is intended for the use of merchants and others who wish to acquire a colloquial knowledge of the Japanese language', and it was therefore an attempt to fulfil a practical end and as such in keeping with his commercial responsibilities as a member of the consular service.[8]

The fourth edition, however, has a different preface which points out that the work has been almost entirely rewritten and that, 'more exclusive attention has been paid in it to the Tokio dialect, which now bids fair to become the language of the upper classes of Japan generally'.[9] Among the new material in the book was a warning that categories such as 'noun' and 'verb' were only of limited use for describing the Japanese language because of its fundamental differences from European languages. It is on this work that Aston's reputation as a linguist rests. It was an epoch-making work in that it marked the end of the period in which westerners sought to understand and analyse the Japanese language in terms of the grammar and categories of European languages and constituted the first serious attempt to grasp the internal logic of the Japanese language. As such it remained influential until the end of the century and beyond and set the pattern for subsequent grammars of Japanese, including that of Chamberlain.

Aston's *Grammar of the Japanese Written Language with a Short Chrestomathy* was equally successful, being first published in 1872 and then appearing in subsequent editions in 1877 and 1904. In it he gives a historical and analytical account of the syntax of the classical Japanese written language and appends, for the student to practice upon, a selection of texts reproduced from block-printed Japanese books and notices. It was a more scholarly work and Aston describes it himself as a 'treatise' containing 'the results of a first study of some of the principal works of native writers on Japanese Grammar'.[10] These works, which are listed in an appendix, form an awesome collection of difficult texts; many have now been reprinted in modern annotated editions, but Aston had to work through them in the raw, in the original block-printed editions. As late as 1907 Chamberlain was still recommending it as 'an admirably lucid work embodying all the best results obtained by the native school of grammarians'.[11]

It should be mentioned at this stage that although Aston can be described as a British japanologist, he was by no means as limited in his mental horizons as that term might suggest. In the first place, he took pains to keep himself abreast of European writing on Japan in French and German. In 1871–2 he published several reviews of French translations of Japanese works in which he painstakingly identified errors of interpretation. Regarding *Anthologie japonaise* by Leon de Rosny (1837–1916), appointed the first professor of Japanese at the Ecole des langues orientales in Paris in 1868, Aston admired 'the capital essay on Japanese poetry which forms the introduction', but found de Rosny's philological standards wanting: the translations were 'far from attaining to that degree of accuracy which the student requires'; 'the few grammatical remarks which are ventured upon are rarely correct'; and Aston rightly queries the use of the word 'professeur' to translate the Japanese word *oiran*, which refers to a class of courtesan![12] In the second place, Aston was a scholar of Korean and other languages as well as of Japanese. In 1876 Aston had been one of a party which visited the Loochoo Islands, now known as Okinawa and a part of Japan; the following year he visited Hokkaido. As a result of these two trips he wrote in 1879 an account of the Loochooan and Ainu languages, concluding that the former was 'merely a dialect of Japanese

... and contains words which are obsolete in the modern language' and that the latter was quite unrelated to Japanese or Korean.[13] Aston begun his much more serious studies of Korean some time in the 1870s, probably using the manuscript manuals which had been prepared in the 1830s by the Japanese interpreters resident in Pusan in southern Korea; Aston's own copies of these manuals are kept today in the Institute of Oriental Studies in Leningrad. By 1878 he had already acquired some Korean books as well as a collection of Japanese books concerning Korea, and between 1878 and 1883 he wrote an extensive account, making use of Korean as well as Japanese sources, of Hideyoshi's invasion of Korea in the closing years of the sixteenth century.[14] Satow and Chamberlain were also making efforts to learn Korean by this time, and like Aston had Korean nationals resident in Japan as private teachers, but it appears from Satow's letters that it was Aston who made the most progress and achieved fluency in the spoken language by 1881. Aston was clearly well prepared, therefore, for his negotiations with the Korean authorities in 1882 and for his residence there as consul-general later. Of his visit in 1882 he wrote, 'At all the places visited I conversed with large numbers of Coreans, and found them invariably friendly, though sometimes inclined to be unpleasantly familiar. Their desire for information knew no bounds.'[15] He wrote several other articles on Korean literature and language, but his principal achievement in this area was his article, published in 1879 in the *Journal of the Royal Asiatic Society*, comparing the Japanese and Korean languages. This article, in which Aston was the first to demonstrate that the two languages were linguistically related, has been described as a 'breakthrough to the first scientific comparison' of the two languages, and in 1976 the German scholar of Japanese and Korean Bruno Lewin stated that, 'Aston's arguments for the kinship of the two languages are still worthy of consideration even today.'[16]

Although all of Aston's work was based on the most rigorous of philological foundations, in a sense his work in the area of linguistics was a preparation for the literary, religious and anthropological studies with which he occupied himself after his retirement. His earliest published work concerning Japanese literature was a partial translation and summary of the *Tosa nikki*, which he published in 1875.[17] Here, however, his interests were still predominantly philological: his notes touch on such matters as the light which *Tosa nikki* can cast on the nature of colloquial speech in the Heian period, and finally he recommends it as a work with which to begin the study of Japanese classical literature.

Aston is best known today for the three major works of his later life, of which the first was his translation of the *Nihon shoki* (Chronicles of Japan), or *Nihongi*, as he referred to it, which was first published in London by the Japan Society in 1896. It is still the standard translation in English, which is perhaps not surprising given the difficult Chinese, and to a lesser extent Japanese, of the *Nihon shoki* and the later commentaries, and it is still regularly cited. It is indicative of the areas to which his interests were turning and of the audience for whom he was to write more and more, that he declared in the Preface that his object was 'to make accessible to European scholars the very considerable store of material for the study of mythology, folk-lore, early civilization, and manners and customs which it contains'.[18]

Aston's second major work was *A History of Japanese Literature*, which was first published in 1899. This too was a remarkably successful work: it was reprinted several times in England in Aston's own lifetime, and in the United States was reprinted no less than nine times between 1899 and 1937. In the bibliographical note appended to this work Aston acknowledges his 'very considerable obligations' to Mikami Sanji and Takatsu Kuwasaburō's *Nippon bungakushi* (History of Japanese literature) which had appeared in 1890 and had been the first work of its kind to be published in Japan.[19] Aston's own copy of this work is preserved in the Aston Collection in Cambridge University Library and the extensive annotations testify to its usefulness to Aston. But Aston was no slave to it. First, Mikami and Takatsu have nothing whatever to say on the subject of Japanese literature since 1868, whereas Aston devotes his final section to the political novels, new-style poetry and other works written in the years since he first reached Japan. It was this section too which was omitted when Aston's work was translated into Japanese in 1908. One of the works he describes in detail in this section is Tsubouchi Shōyō's popular novel, *Tōsei shosei katagi* (The characters of students today), which was serialized in 1885–6 and then published in book form. It appears from Aston's own copy of this work that he bought and read it soon after its publication. He wrote a note in it to the effect that the dialogue was full of vulgar student slang and was not to be imitated, but that did not stop him from using two extracts in the fourth edition of his *A Grammar of Japanese Spoken Language*, which differed from the earlier editions in appending a collection of transliterated passages from works of colloquial fiction. In *A History of Japanese Literature*, Aston describes it as a 'realistic novel', and says that 'it is well written, and contains some graphic and humorous sketches of modern student life viewed from the seamy side, but has little plot, portraiture of character, or dramatic incident'.[20] He gives much less space to Tsubouchi's theoretical work, *Shōsetsu shinzui* (The essence of the novel), which was far less influential at the time than modern scholarship would have us believe, and thus better reflects the climate of opinion in the 1880s.

Second, Aston's emphasis and judgement differ from those of Mikami and Takatsu, and this is nowhere more apparent than in the section dealing with *ninjōbon*, a romantic genre of fiction popular in the 1830s. Mikami and Takatsu took the view that these works, many of which were set in the demi-monde, were morally exceptionable, but, while recognizing that 'the society into which they introduce the reader is far from select, and the morality sadly defective', Aston's overall estimation of their worth was high: 'The great service rendered by Shunsui and his fellow-composers of Ninjōbon was to recall the attention of writers and readers of fiction to human nature as the proper subject of the novelist's art. Since the time of Murasaki no Shikibu this branch of study had been sadly neglected in Japan.'[21] There are good grounds for supposing that Aston's appreciation of *ninjōbon* and conviction that they represented a literary path worth following were shared by writers and readers in the 1880s, although not by literary scholars. It is only in the last twenty years that *ninjōbon* have been seriously studied in Japan.

Aston's overall estimation of Japanese literature is guarded. Morality is throughout an important consideration, and this prevents him from dealing with Saikaku and his works at any length: 'the very titles of some of them are too gross for quotation'.[22] He had a clear notion of what poetry should be and found Japanese efforts in this direction seriously wanting; he is impatient with classical court poetry and confidently asserts that, 'it would be absurd to put forward any serious claim on behalf of Haikai [haiku] to an important position in literature', though he is prepared to grant that 'it is difficult to see how more could be made of it than Bashō has done'.[23] That is not to say that he sees no merit in any of the Japanese literature he read, but it is true that, although extraordinarily well read in Japanese literature, he tended to see the works of his own literary tradition as norms. On the author of *The Tale of Genji*, for example, he has this to say: 'None, however, but an extreme Japanophile (the species is not altogether unknown) will go so far as to place Murasaki no Shikibu on a level with Fielding, Thackeray, Victor Hugo, Dumas, and Cervantes.'[24]

The last of Aston's major works was *Shinto (The Way of the Gods)*, which was published in 1905. The writing of this book sprang partly from Aston's long-standing interest in early Japanese history and partly from a new interest in anthropology and the study of religion, stimulated in part by his reading of Frazer's *The Golden Bough* and Tylor's *Primitive Culture*. In the Preface he wrote that it was 'intended, primarily and chiefly, as a repertory of the more significant facts of Shinto for the use of scientific students of religion'.[25] He also wrote a number of articles between 1900 and 1911 for *Man, Folk-Lore* and the *Journal of the Anthropological Institute of Great Britain and Ireland*, which evince his desire to bring Japanese evidence into debates about the origin of language, primitive religion and other matters. In 1902 he wrote an article attacking the use by 'our most eminent anthropologists', by whom he meant Frazer in particular, of Kaempfer's *History of Japan* as an authority on Japanese religion. He knew no Japanese and 'his ignorance is colossal', wrote Aston, who referred anthropologists instead to some of Satow's articles written in the 1870s and 1880s.[26] He set himself the task of providing an accurate and textually based study of Japanese religion that engaged issues of interest to scholars of the phenomenology of religion, and in this respect one of his greatest contributions, apart from his book on Shinto, was the series of articles he wrote for James Hastings's *Encyclopedia of Religion and Ethics*, encompassing the art and architecture of Shinto, fetishism, adoption and several other subjects.

Aston's *Shinto* is a work based on philological study of the texts rather than on folklore, popular religion or religious practice *per se*: the first chapter is telling in this respect, for it is concerned solely with 'Materials for the Study of Shinto'. As such, it cannot escape the charge that it attempts to see Shinto as a scripturally based and organized religion like Christianity and Islam. As a result, it is not surprising that Aston finds Shinto 'decidely rudimentary in character': 'its polytheism, the want of a Supreme Deity, the comparative absence of images and of a moral code, its feeble personifications and hesitating grasp of the conception of spirit, the practical non-recognition of a future state, and the general absence of a deep, earnest faith – all stamp it as perhaps the least developed of religions which have an adequate literary record'.[27] Although Aston goes on to acknowledge that Shinto 'is not a primitive cult', he is primarily concerned with historical Shinto. Of Shinto in the Japan that he knew at first hand he is dismissive: 'The official cult of the present day . . . has little vitality. . . . A rudimentary religion of this kind is quite inadequate for the spiritual sustenance of a nation which in these latter days has raised itself to so high a pitch of enlightenment and civilization.' And he concludes, mistakenly, 'as a national religion, Shinto is almost extinct'.[28] Inevitably, therefore, his writing on Shinto has long since been superseded.

In most of his writing Aston was almost entirely dependent on his personal library of Japanese books. Like his colleague Satow, Aston was an inveterate collector of books. He and Satow often went book-hunting together in Japan, and even had copies made of rare manuscripts in each other's possession. In later years Satow gave away a great many of his books, some to Chamberlain but the greater part to Aston in 1892 in order to provide Aston with the materials for his research after his retirement to England. In 1911 Aston offered, with Satow's approval, his collection of Japanese books to Cambridge University. He died before the arrangements could be completed, but they were bought from his executors shortly afterwards for £250, which the University rightly considered a very moderate sum. This collection, which contains many rare and unique items, forms an important part of Aston's legacy to his successors in the field of Japanese studies in Britain, but it only contains a small part of his collection of Korean books: the remainder went, at some unknown date between 1900 and 1911, to the Asiatic Museum in St Petersburg and are now preserved in the Academy of Sciences in Leningrad.

Aston's standing with his contemporaries was high. The great French orientalist Henri Cordier wrote in his obituary notice that, 'Aston formait avec Basil Hall Chamberlain et Ernest Mason Satow ce triumvirat de japonisants qui n'ont pas leur egal dans les autre pays.'[29] It was the view of Haga Yaichi (1867–1927), perhaps the most distinguished literary scholar of his day, that Aston's published work on Japanese literature had done much to create the favourable climate for Anglo-Japanese relations that resulted in the Anglo-Japanese Alliance concluded in 1902. Much later one of Aston's successors as diplomat-cum-scholar, Sir George Sansom, observed in an address at the School of Oriental and African Studies in London: 'I have noticed that some young students are inclined to dismiss Aston and his judgements as old-fashioned, what they call Victorian'; but he continued to look up to Aston and Satow, for 'their work in their several fields of study was voluminous, accurate and penetrating. It still remains valuable, and I doubt whether it will be excelled.'[30]

From the perspective of the 1990s, three aspects of Aston's work must strike every student of Japan very forcefully. First, Aston worked before the Japanese publishing industry began to produce its flood of secondary literature, annotated editions or even simple movable-type reprints of works of classical literature. He worked therefore sometimes from manuscripts but mostly from block-printed texts, each reproducing a different calligraphic hand and each posing difficulties of decipherment. The philological difficulties he and his contemporaries had to surmount gave them an opportunity for careful textual study as a basis for their future studies. Second, there is Aston's concern not to bury himself as a japanologist but to bring Japan into general debate about language, religion and literature, to take part in a universal, rather than a local, discourse. It is this that drove him to present papers at meetings of the British Association for the Advancement of Science and at the Anthropological Institute and to contribute papers to, and engage in debates in, a variety of journals. Third, there is his conscious membership of a European community of scholars. For de Rosny, it is true, he did not have much respect, perhaps because de Rosny never set foot in Japan and Aston was something of a purist in such matters, but he had very different views about other French writers and German writers, and in particular about Dr Karl Florenz (1865–1939). Before becoming the first professor of Japanese studies at the University of Hamburg, Florenz had resided in Japan as Professor of Philology and German Literature at the Imperial University and had published his own translation of the *Nihon shoki* into German and his own *History of Japanese Literature* in German (1906). Aston frequently acknowledges his debts to Florenz's work, which covered as many different fields as did his own. In each of these respects, his philological mastery, his intellectual breadth and his use of European scholarship, Aston pursued a course that many of his successors have deviated from. As a scholar he had his weaknesses, of course: some of his early ventures in Japanese linguistics were ill-conceived, such as his speculations on Japanese affinity with Aryan languages in 1874 and his attempt to rearrange the order of the Korean alphabet smacks of cultural imperialism, a charge which perhaps few writers on Japan in the nineteenth century can escape entirely. But he passes the acid test: his translation of the *Nihon shoki* and his *A History of Japanese Literature* are still in use, more than ninety years after they were written. No scholar could hope for more.

FURTHER READING

Dictionary of National Biography, Second Supplement 1 (1912) 67–8.

Grace Fox, *Britain and Japan: 1858–1883*, Oxford University Press, 1969.

Toshio Yokoyama, *Japan in the Victorian Mind: A Study of Sterotyped Images of a Nation, 1850–80*, Basingstoke: Macmillan, 1987.

N. Hayashi and P.F. Kornicki, *Early Japanese Books in Cambridge University Library: The Aston, Satow and von Siebold Collections*, Cambridge University Press, 1990.

4

ERNEST MASON SATOW
(1843–1929)

P.F. Kornicki

Ernest Satow was a celebrity, the first of the old Japan hands to win the public recognition of a knighthood, membership of the Privy Council, honorary degrees from Oxford and Cambridge, and a caricature in *Vanity Fair*. He was not unaware that he had a place in history, for in 1921 he published an autobiography covering his early years in Japan which takes some liberties with the historical record and suggests that Satow's own views were more influential than they in fact were. On his death he donated to the Public Record Office the extensive diaries and private correspondence that he had carefully preserved over the years. In Japan he is still a celebrity, partly because of the recent serialization in the *Asahi shinbun* of a detailed biography, and partly because of the high regard in which he continues to be held as a book-collector and scholar and as an intimate associate of men who led the Restoration movement and controlled the course of Japanese politics up to the end of the century and beyond.

Satow was born in north London to a family with a cosmopolitan flavour. His father was a Swedish merchant who had travelled extensively and finally moved from Riga in Latvia to London in 1825. Perhaps it was from him that Satow inherited his interest in foreign countries and his aptitude for foreign languages. He was undoubtedly quick at his books, for he entered University College, London, in 1859 at the age of 16 and graduated just two years later; when he reached Japan on 8 September 1862 he was not yet 20. While a student at London University, he is said to have attended some of the lectures of James Summers, who was Professor of Chinese at King's College and who launched several short-lived periodicals for the study of the cultures of Japan and China, though he did not set foot in Japan until 1873. Satow claims in his autobiography that his interest was first drawn to Japan by a copy of the account of Lord Elgin's mission to China and Japan which his brother had borrowed from the famous Mudie's Circulating Library. At any rate, Satow came first in the examination for student interpreters to serve in the Consular Service in the Far East and opted for Japan. It was believed at the time that a knowledge of Chinese was a prerequisite for the study of Japanese and so Satow was first sent to the Legation at Peking, where he not only learnt some written and spoken Chinese but also made a start on the study of Manchu. After a few months in Peking he was summoned to take up his duties in Japan.

Satow had left England without any of the few books that had by then been published on the Japanese language and found that those that were to be had in Japan were of little use. After he had insisted that his first task was to learn the language, his superiors allowed him the mornings free of routine consular tasks, such as copying out despatches, in order to work on the language, but gave him no teacher. After a couple of unsatisfactory months he induced the chargé d'affaires to pay for lessons from the Reverend Samuel R. Brown, an American missionary who had just published a work entitled *Colloquial Japanese*, and to pay for the cost of hiring a native teacher. At first it was Brown's lessons that proved more useful, for none of the Japanese teachers knew any English and they did not have an educated understanding of their own language. But then Satow secured the services of a doctor from Wakayama, Takaoka Kaname by name, who 'used to write a short letter in the running-hand, and after copying it out in square character, explain to me its meaning'[1]. After this Satow used to make a translation into English and practise reading the two Japanese versions until he had mastered the whole letter. It was a laborious procedure, but effective as a training in reading handwritten documents. Satow had a succession of other teachers and also took lessons from calligraphy masters: at first he made the mistake of learning a tradesmen's writing style, but after the Restoration of 1868 he took lessons from Takasai Tanzan, described by Satow as one of the best half-dozen teachers in Tokyo, and his written Japanese improved markedly in appearance. Cambridge University Library contains some of the notebooks which he used when first reading Japanese texts and some catalogues of his Japanese books which he compiled much later, and the transformation from the awkward, wooden characters most foreigners are condemned to repeat, to the confident, elegant script of the catalogues is remarkable.

In 1864 Satow had the satisfaction of being appointed interpreter to Admiral Küper on his flagship for the punitive expedition to the Shimonoseki Straits. The domain authorities in Chōshū had been vigorous in their pursuit of an anti-foreign policy and had closed the Straits to foreign shipping. Immediately, two domain samurai, Itō Hirobumi and Inoue Kaoru, who had both participated in the attack on the British Legation in 1861 and who were later to distinguish themselves in government, returned from England, where they were studying to try to persuade their superiors in the domain of the folly of continuing to resist the foreign presence. Satow met them and asked them to convey to the *daimyō* the determination of the foreign powers to keep the Straits open and to ensure that Chōshū observed the treaties; with the help of one of his Japanese teachers he translated a message to that effect in Japanese and then put them ashore, well knowing that they had imperilled their lives by fraternizing with the enemy. As it happened they were not executed, but their mission was unsuccessful and as a result Satow saw action. The squadron bombarded the Chōshū shore batteries until they fell silent, and then a strong force of British, French and Dutch troops landed to take the batteries; Satow was detailed to accompany them in case an intepreter was needed and so came under fire. The landing was successful and the batteries were destroyed, and Itō then came back to Satow to state that the *daimyō* acknowledged his defeat and now wished to sue for peace. This episode marked the beginning of Satow's acquaintance with Itō, an acquaintance that was to prove very useful to both of them in the late 1890s, when Satow was British envoy in Tokyo (1895–1900) and Itō was prime minister (1892–6 and January to June 1898).

Satow's services during the Chōshū expedition made his superiors realize, for the first time, the importance of having someone on hand who could communicate in Japanese without difficulty. Accordingly, early in 1865 he was promoted to the rank of Interpreter at the Consulate in Yokohama and was freed from all other duties. His language abilities were soon put to the test when he had to interrogate a Japanese prisoner prior to witnessing his execution: this was one of the supposed murderers of Lieutenant Bird and Major Baldwin, two members of the Legation Guard who had been hacked to death as they were leaving Kamakura in November 1864. Later in 1865 Satow acted as the interpreter for Sir Harry Parkes, the British minister in Japan, and Léon Roches, his French counterpart, during the fraught negotiations in Osaka over the emperor's ratification of the treaties which the shogun had signed with the foreign powers. The crucial document acceding to the demands of Parkes and Roches was delivered at half past two in the morning, and Satow was immediately summoned to read it out and to make a translation: 'it was a proud moment for me', he wrote, 'when I displayed my knowledge of written Japanese in the presence of the French minister, whose interpreter even could not read a document without the assistance of his teacher'.[2]

Satow was also becoming involved in political journalism at this time. Following the successful conclusion of the negotiations at Osaka, he wrote an anonymous editorial for the *Japan Times* in which he declared that, 'Japan is now for the first time really and legitimately open to foreign trade' and argued that the power of the shogun 'was a shadow and his title a mockery' compared with that of the emperor.[3] In the following year, 1866, Satow published three articles in the *Japan Times* on English policy towards Japan, which were subsequently translated into Japanese, printed and sold on the streets of Kyoto and Osaka. The extensive conversations he had had with the leading *daimyō* of western Japan and their retainers had already convinced him that the western powers were wrong to deal exclusively with the shogun and that the real rulers of Japan were the emperor and a body he called the Confederate Daimyo. The shogun, he argued, had overstepped his authority and was powerless to enforce compliance with the treaties in areas of Japan outside his direct control. So the line he took in these articles was one which was sympathetic to the opponents of the shogunate.

Following the Yokohama fire of 1866, which destroyed his house, Satow moved to a house in Edo. As he described it, 'there was an upper storey where I had my bedroom and apartments for the entertainment of Japanese guests and three staircases provided means of escape in case of attack from the midnight murderer'.[4] Satow's matter-of-fact acceptance of danger reflected the very real possibility of attack by fanatical members of the anti-foreign party. In 1867 Satow travelled from Osaka to Edo overland in the company of Charles Wirgman, an artist working for the *Illustrated London News*. On the way, they were attacked one night as they slept in an inn, and it was only thanks to the cool bravery of Satow's Japanese retainer, Noguchi, that they all escaped with their lives. Again in 1868, when Satow was in the party accompanying the British minister, Sir Harry Parkes, to his first audience with the young Emperor Meiji in Kyoto, two samurai set upon them with swords. Having missed Parkes, one slashed at Satow only to injure his horse instead: as Parkes coolly remarked, this was 'sensation diplomacy',[5] but it did have the effect of provoking an imperial proclamation calling for an end to anti-foreign sentiment.

On 1 January 1868 Satow became the Japanese Secretary to the British Legation, a position he was to hold for some sixteen years and one which made him responsible for all dealings with the Japanese government. It was in 1868 that the anti-shogunate movement came to a head and through-out the year Satow maintained close contact with Itō and other Japanese acquaintances from the domains. As a result he had an exceptionally clear understanding of the strength of feeling against the shogun. He had already concluded that the use of the expression 'His Majesty' in the treaties to refer to the shogun was mistaken and had established to his own satisfaction that the shogun was subordinate to the emperor. There was no doubt where his own sympathies lay. In reports that he wrote for Parkes he referred to the shogun as the emperor's 'rebellious vassal' – but the claim later made by Satow and others that he had swayed Parkes against the shogun and had enabled Britain to support the victorious side does not stand up to close examination. As late as January 1868, when Parkes and Satow were very much afraid that the confrontation between supporters of emperor and shogun would result in civil war, Parkes was considering how he might mediate between the two parties and was unwilling to commit himself to either side. With the advantage of hindsight, it may seem inevitable that the Restoration forces would not only triumph but also establish a stable form of government, but at the time this did not appear at all certain. In fact Parkes maintained a cautious neutrality until the result of the conflict was no longer in doubt.

Early in 1869 Satow sailed for England for his first home leave since setting foot in Japan. Before leaving he received a gift from the Japanese foreign minister with a letter; 'during your period of service in this country,' he wrote, 'you have spoken our language with extreme facility, and the great services you have rendered to Japan have come to the knowledge of His Majesty'.[6] Satow had lived through a momentous period in the history of Japan, and he wrote much later that, 'those years from 1862 to 1869 were the most interesting portion of my life; then I lived, now I seem to vegetate'. The changes that were still to take place in the years between 1869 and 1884, when he was returning from Japan, were also far-reaching, but it was the earlier period that dominated his memories of Japan, and in later life when he wrote his memoirs, *A Diplomat in Japan*, he drew the narrative to an end with his return to England in 1869.

Satow had been under fire several times and had been fully involved in the intricate diplomatic problems of the 1860s, but he had also begun to train himself as a scholar and he was probably the first foreigner to become a serious and well-informed collector of Japanese books. As a bibliographer he was an expert, and as a collector insatiable. There were Japanese bookshops in Yokohama, but they were forbidden to sell maps or *bukan* (lists of *daimyō* and officials) to foreigners. Satow solved this problem by having his teachers buy materials for him and in this way he managed to acquire a number of manuscripts, including copies of official papers, that were too sensitive to be published or to pass the inspection of the censors. In the Yokohama fire of November 1866 he lost many of his Chinese and European books as well as the notes on Chinese and Manchu which he had made in Peking. In 1868, however, when he was one of the first foreigners to visit Kyoto for several hundred years, he made it his business to head for the bookshops. In the 1880s he was spending large sums of money on early Japanese books, including books printed with movable type in the early seventeenth century and racy fictional works of the later seventeenth century.

He was also buying what Korean books he could find in Japan and sending further sums of money to Korea, presumably by way of his Korean teachers, which were unobtainable in Japan. Like Aston and Chamberlain, who are the subjects of separate chapters in this book, he had made efforts to learn Korean in the 1870s and 1880s and had engaged a Korean teacher as well as making use of a manuscript grammar of Korean prepared by Aston. He and Aston often went book-hunting together in Kyoto and Osaka. In 1882 he wrote to Aston: 'the booksellers say that 1,200 yen would secure all there is in Japan of rare editions. I have spent 600 or 700, and so must have about half.'[7] He was clearly exaggerating, but there can be no doubt that his collection was the best ever assembled by a westerner. In later years he gave away or lent large quantities of his Japanese books, to Chamberlain, to Aston and to other former colleagues from his Japan days, and his books are now to be found in London, Cambridge, Bristol, Manchester, Tokyo and several other locations: they carry impressions of the Japanese ex-libris stamp he had made in Japan, and many of them are unique copies of works that have not survived in Japan.

He was no passive collector, for his bibliographical researches on the books in his collection resulted in several articles on the history of printing in Japan and Korea. In fact, he was the first person to establish that movable-type printing in Korea was older than the books that came from Gutenberg's press – by more than a hundred years. He also published, in 1888, a detailed bibliographic study of the Jesuit Mission Press in Japan. This press had printed a number of doctrinal works, together with several works of European and Japanese literature, both in romanized form and in Japanese script, in the late sixteenth and early seventeenth centuries. He owned none of these books himself, for most of these works had survived in only one or two copies, and his researches, which established for the first time the extent of the Jesuits' printing operations in Japan, took him to private and public libraries all over Europe.

In 1884 Satow made the move that was to accelerate his career as a diplomat: he moved to Siam, now Thailand, to take up the position of consul-general in Bangkok. As soon as he arrived he wrote, 'my student days are now at an end',[8] but he continued to buy books voraciously, to study and to write. In 1885 he wrote an article on contacts between Japan and Siam in the seventeenth century, and in 1886 he published a lengthy 'Essay towards a bibliography of Siam', in which many of the items described came from his own personal library and were later to be donated to the Bodleian Library, Oxford.[9] His style as a diplomat differed from that of the irascible Sir Harry Parkes, and although he found the 'corruption in the native courts, endless delays, equivocation and falseness on the part of native officials' exhausting to deal with, he considered that, 'when one is angry it is very important to be more polite than usual and to have an air of regret at having to remonstrate'.[10] His diplomacy was effective and there were fears in Britain that France's wars in Indo-China might spread into Siam. So in 1885 Satow was promoted to the rank of Minister, which signalled a shift from the more humdrum duties of the consular service to the status and responsibilities of the diplomatic service.

While in Bangkok Satow suffered badly from the climate, and in 1887 he asked to be transferred, and returned to England. During the lengthy period of leave that followed, he completed the legal studies which he had begun earlier and qualified as a barrister; he travelled in Italy, Spain and Portugal in search of books printed by the Jesuits in Japan; and he became a convinced Christian: he was confirmed by the Bishop of London at St Paul's in October 1888.

In that year he was appointed minister at Montevideo in Uruguay. During his four years there he was still accompanied by his Japanese servant, Saburō, who had followed him from Japan to Bangkok. In 1893 he proceeded to

Tangier as envoy to Morocco, where in the midst of a succession crisis following the Sultan's death he led the diplomatic community in recognizing the heir rather than a rival known as 'the one-eyed decapitator'. His tact gained him the admiration of the Foreign Office, which wrote, 'you seem to have managed to get your colleagues to work together – a thing which I believe is unprecedented at Tangier'.[11]

After his success in Morocco, which earned him his knighthood, he went on to fill the positions of envoy in Tokyo (1895–1900) and Peking (1900–6). As the head of British missions in Japan and China he fulfilled duties now undertaken by ambassadors, but in more eurocentric days, these states were not regarded as important enough to justify ambassadorial representation. Thus the status and title of ambassador eluded him. His final appointment was as British member of the Court of Arbitration in The Hague, after which he retired to Devon. Satow never married, but there are passages in his diaries that allude to his relationships with Japanese women, and others that have been discreetly papered over. It appears that for much of his time in Japan he had a common-law wife and that he had at least two children.

Satow's appointment as envoy to Japan in 1895 was itself a significant act. In the previous years the foreign secretary, Lord Kimberley, had signed a new treaty with Japan which transformed Anglo-Japanese relations by renouncing the principle of extraterritoriality and making Britons subject to Japanese courts in place of consular jurisdiction. Kimberley was eager for Japan to strengthen its armed forces and hoped for the development of a warm relationship between Britain and Japan, explicitly in order to prevent Russia acquiring a warm-water port on the Pacific. For such purposes no better envoy than Satow could have been imagined, for not only did he have command of the language but among Japanese government leaders of the day were men whom he had known thirty years earlier when they were radical samurai. Satow reached Japan soon after Japan's victory in the Sino-Japanese War and the subsequent intervention of Russia, France and Germany, which forced Japan to renounce some of its gains in the war. The British government was in the midst of a domestic political crisis and in no position to come to Japan's assistance. The general election of July 1895 precipitated a change of government and Lord Salisbury, who now held the offices of prime minister and foreign secretary, was much more sceptical about Japan's capability and reliability than Kimberley had been. Salisbury overestimated Britain's strength in the Far East and saw no need of an ally to help counter Russian expansion. In this he was mistaken, as became only too apparent in the winter of 1897/8 when Britain was powerless to prevent Russia annexing Port Arthur, one of the war gains which Japan had been forced to abandon earlier. Thus the tsar acquired a fortified warm-water port. 'I am convinced,' Satow had already written to Salisbury, 'that the Japanese are ambitious of being a great naval and military power and they are confidently persuaded that they possess the necessary gifts', and he became convinced too that Japan was preparing to challenge the Russian position in the Far East.[12]

Before taking up his position in Peking, Satow returned to England in 1900 for consultations with the Foreign Office and a spell of leave. He was aware that Russian designs on Korea, Manchuria and China were perceived as threatening by the Japanese government, but he believed that Japan would certainly take no action before 1903, by which time her army and navy would have reached their full strength. Even then Japan would only act with Britain's support. During the summer news reached London of the Boxer Rebellion in China, of the dramatic siege of the British Legation and the international relief force. Satow's leave was therefore cut short and in August he set out for Peking.

In Peking Satow's first and most onerous task was to conduct the negotiations between the Chinese authorities and the representatives of the western powers over an indemnity and guarantees for the safety of diplomatic representatives and foreign nationals resident in Peking. Subsequently he followed the growth of Russian activities in Manchuria, which alarmed both Britain and Japan and created the atmosphere in which the Anglo-Japanese Alliance (1902) was conceived. The negotiations took place in London, between the foreign secretary and the Japanese Ambassador, Hayashi, and Satow was not directly involved, but his reports on the fortifications at Port Arthur and the growth of Russian armaments there strengthened convictions in London that war between Japan and Russia was imminent. Satow was not alone in being surprised by the Japanese successes in the Russo-Japanese War, and after the fall of Port Arthur he wrote that, 'they have achieved a wonderful exploit in forcing the surrender of a place so strongly defended by nature and art, when it was still provided with fuels, food and ammunition'.[13] After the terrible losses of the war, from which the European powers learnt so little, Satow had no confidence that lasting peace would follow: 'I give the world', he wrote, 'ten years peace in this part of the world. During that time Japan will recoup her losses and be ready to begin again.'[14] As it happened, less than ten years were to elapse before the outbreak of the First World War.

Throughout his long life Satow read widely and deeply and he wrote on a variety of subjects. His first published writings were two pieces he contributed to James Summers' short-lived journal, *The Chinese and Japanese Repository*, in 1865. One was a description of the various styles of Japanese writing and the other was a translation of the diary of a member of the Japanese mission to Europe of 1862–3. In the early 1870s he had several pieces in Summers' next short-lived journal, *The Phoenix*, and by that time he was contributing regularly to the *Japan Herald* and the *Japan Times*. These contributions included political commentary on current events, accounts of trips made in Japan, and serialized translations of Japanese texts: his translation of *Kinsei shiryaku*, a history of Japan from 1853 to 1869, which he published as a book in 1873, first appeared in this way. He later revised his travel pieces to compile *A Handbook for Travellers in Central and Northern Japan*, which was first published in 1881 and over several editions was the globe-trotter's guide to Japan. He was one of the founder members of the Asiatic Society of Japan and contributed a variety of pieces to the published *Transactions*: some were of an antiquarian nature, such as his articles on the introduction of tobacco to Japan and the use of the fire-drill in Japan, but there were also several important works of scholarship among them, particularly his studies of Shinto and of printing in Japan and Korea.

Unlike Aston and Chamberlain he never made an attempt to compile a grammar of the Japanese language. The nearest he came to doing so was a curious book published in Yokohama in 1873 with the title, *Kuaiwa-hen, Twenty-five Exercises in the Yedo Colloquial*. This consists of sentences in romanized Japanese accompanied by a separate volume of commentary, and it appears that Satow first prepared this work for A.B. Mitford, later Lord Redesdale, when he was posted to Japan in 1866 and wanted to learn some Japanese. He lent it out in manuscript to a number of eager students before deciding to have it printed, and it seems to have enjoyed some success, for a second edition and a French translation were published in due course. He adopted Aston's system of transliteration and made extensive use throughout of Aston's *A Short Grammar of the Japanese Spoken Language*. How useful purchasers really found *Kuaiwa-hen* is difficult to gauge; Satow confessed in the Preface that 'all allusions to Japanese manners and customs which have since become things of the past have been left untouched', which suggests that he saw it as much as a record of patterns of speech as a tool for learning the language.[15] A few years later he joined with a member of the Japanese Foreign Ministry to compile *An English–Japanese Dictionary of the Spoken Language*, which was published in 1876. Here too Satow is explicit about his debt to Aston and follows Aston's system for classifying the conjugations of Japanese verbs. This dictionary underwent a number of revisions over the years, and was still in use during the Second World War, albeit in a much expanded and altered form.

After 1900 Satow wrote very little about Japan, although in 1909 he did write a section on Japan for the *Cambridge Modern History*. The major work of his later years betrayed very little of his knowledge of East Asia: this was his monumental *Guide to Diplomatic Practice*. This was first published during the First World War, in 1917, and at least three further editions were published subsequently, each embodying substantial revisions. Much more than a manual of procedures, it is embued with a feeling for the evolution of European traditions of diplomacy and of the privileges and functions of diplomats. It is immensely rich in its historical and international coverage, and reveals Satow's familiarity with most of the languages of Europe. Japan, of course, had no part to play in the evolution of European diplomacy and was a newcomer to the world of international diplomacy, and it is therefore only to be expected that Japan would not feature prominently in such a work. Nevertheless, it does come as a surprise to find that even in the sections on monarchies and precedence among nations Satow hardly troubles to mention Japan at all. The result is a book which presents diplomacy as a ritual enacted by the great European powers. Part of the blame for this must be attributed to the scholarly, historical approach underlying the book, which is also one of its strengths, but it also suggests that Satow failed to grasp the meaning of Japan's rise to prominence, even after the shock of Japan's victory in the Russo-Japanese War, and failed to appreciate the changing nature of international society in the twentieth century. It was not that he was no longer interested in Japan, but that Japan did not disturb his world view.

Satow's published writings have now all been superseded and are rarely cited. His private papers, which are preserved in the Public Record Office, are disappointingly discreet and betray little in the way of judgements of policy or personality. Nevertheless, they continue to be pored over by historians, for, like John Reed's account of the Russian Revolution in *Ten Days that Shook the World*, they are unique as a record of a non-participant's view of the relatively peaceful Japanese revolution of the 1860s.

FURTHER READING

Bernard M. Allen, *The Rt. Hon. Sir Ernest Mason Satow G.C.M.G: A Memoir*, London: Kegan, Paul, Trench, Trübner & Co., 1933.

Gordon Daniels, 'The British Role in the Meiji Restoration: A Re-interpretive Note', *Modern Asian Studies*, 2 (1968), 291–313.

Grace Fox, *Britain and Japan, 1858–1883*, Oxford University Press, 1969.

N. Hayashi and P.F. Kornicki, *Early Japanese Books in Cambridge University Library: A Catalogue of the Aston, Satow and von Siebold Collections*, Cambridge University Press, 1990.

George Alexander Lensen, *Korea and Manchuria Between Russia and Japan, 1895–1904*, Tallahassee: Florida State University Press, 1966.

E.M. Satow, *A Diplomat in Japan*, London: Seeley, Service & Co., 1921; reprinted 1968.

Nobutoshi Hagihara: *Tōi Gake* Tokyo: Ashai Shinbunsha, 1980,

5

JOSIAH CONDER (1852–1920) AND MEIJI ARCHITECTURE

Dallas Finn

In 1876 a young architect in Buckingham Street signed a contract with the Japanese government agreeing to teach western-style architecture in the newly created Engineering College in Tokyo, and also to serve as an architect for the Ministry of Public Works. While we do not know precisely why Josiah Conder made this commitment, we do know why the Japanese government was so eager to hire western technical experts at this time.

The leaders of the new Meiji regime, established in 1868, were convinced westernizers. Their inclinations in this direction had only recently been reinforced by a prestigious mission to the United States and Europe led by Prince Iwakura Tomomi. After the prince and his colleagues had scrutinized Great Britain from Clydesdale shipbuilding to Yorkshire mining to Midlands iron and textile plants to – a favourite – the Enfield rifle factory, the government concluded, though it was loath to follow any one western model, that, in general, British technology was the best to emulate.

This conclusion was enthusiastically supported by Queen Victoria's envoy in Tokyo, the forceful Sir Harry Parkes. He not only convinced the Japanese that they needed Britons to build their lighthouses, their railroads and their navy, he also assisted in procuring a British faculty for a proposed engineering college. As a result, a British engineer erected a red-brick building for the college, one of the first in Tokyo, and in 1873 it opened with a faculty drawn largely from recent graduates of Glasgow University. The school's director, Henry Dyer, seems to have favoured a mixture of talent, however, and he may have been indirectly responsible for the appointment of an architect who had studied at the South Kensington School of Art.

We can only surmise why Josiah Conder – who had just received an award from the Royal Institute of British Architects and had trained with two prominent Victorian architects, G.E. Street and, William Burges, and was excellently placed to do well at home – decided to go to Japan. Quite possibly, since Japanese contracts with foreign workers were deliberately short term, Conder thought his stay would be brief. He surely thought it would be interesting for he was caught up in the enthusiasm for 'the East' that suffused the Pre-Raphaelite environment in which he worked. While Burges was dedicated to reviving Gothic architecture, he was also endlessly intrigued by the obscure and the exotic: Moorish, Byzantine, Islamic, Moghul. Already one of his former pupils had contrived a successful colonial architectural style for India, something called 'Anglo-Indian-Gothic'.[1]

Burges himself had taken up the challenge of combining east and west by proposing (unsuccessfully) a Gothic-Oriental design for an art school in Bombay. His enthusiasm also spread to Japan, its fine papers, ceramics, lacquer, even furniture (photographs of his quarters show he prized a *tansu* chest). Concerned with all forms of design and decoration, he worked Japanese *netsuke* into his hand-wrought inkstands and ewers.[2] It is not hard to imagine that Conder, influenced by his virtuoso teacher, regarded Japan with an admiration that other Britons going there – engineers, traders, missionaries, diplomats – might not have felt. Unfortunately, in this case as in so many other intriguing junctures in his long career, Conder did not leave letters or personal reminiscences. We can only understand him in terms of his context, his buildings and what others said about him.

Soon after his arrival in early 1877, Conder set to work simultaneously teaching and, as a high priority, planning new buildings for the government. Not only did the Japanese leaders need western buildings for the numerous western institutions which they were introducing, they wanted western architecture in order to show the outside world that Japan – smarting from the western treaties permitting extraterritoriality – was a 'civilized' nation. Conder was not the only western or, for that matter, British architect employed to make this point, though perhaps he made it most effectively and persistently.

It soon developed that, while Conder was a good architect, he was an even better teacher. His technique was to train his students in all the current western styles of architecture and to do so on the job. As a result, young Satachi Shichijirō would work on the Moorish-Gothic art museum in Ueno (1881) while Watanabe Yuzuru helped build the Venetian-Gothic exhibition hall for Hokkaido products in central Tokyo (1882). In 1885 Katayama Tokuma assisted Conder in building the first two western palaces in Japan, one in Renaissance-revival style for Prince Arisugawa and a French Gothic one for Prince Kitashirakawa. Tatsuno Kingo, the top-ranking graduate of Conder's first class (a total of four) in 1879, was put in even closer contact with mid-Victorian architecture by being sent to London to work in Burge's office. Although the talented Tsumaki Raiko did not graduate from the Engineering College but went off to study abroad, he too was a Conder pupil. In time, these students became Japan's major western-style architects. Thus Conder in his kindly, eclectic way set the seal of British Victorian architecture on the first generation of western-style Japanese architects.

We can judge how well liked and diplomatic Conder must have been by

what happened to him – or, rather, what did not happen to him – after
1881. At this point almost all foreign employees of the government were
dismissed. In many cases they had done their short-term job and in almost
all cases their high salaries were more than the impoverished government
could afford. Conder's contracts, however, were continuously renewed. In
1881 he received an appointment to work on buildings for the imperial
household and Inoue Kaoru, the foreign minister, called on him to design
a government entertainment house, something in the manner of an elegant
British club, where government officials could meet with foreigners and each
other in a thoroughly western way. By this time Conder must have felt quite
acclimatized to Japan for in 1880 he married a Japanese woman.

When Inoue and Conder sat down to discuss the details of the proposed
entertainment house, later to be called the 'Rokumeikan' (Hall of the Cry
of the Deer) after a Chinese poem celebrating friendship with strangers, the
foreign minister expressed his misgivings about the style of some of Conder's
earlier buildings. They did not seem quite western enough. Little did Inoue
know that the 'Saracenic' Ueno Museum and the 'Venetian' Hokkaido
Products Hall were as British as William Burges. In the Ueno Art Museum
with its Islamic towers and Moorish arches, Conder was reflecting Burges's
Bombay Art School and the Anglo-Indian-Gothic notions of his teacher's
pupil Sir William Emerson. The elegant little Hokkaido Products Hall set
by the river at Eitaibashi was strikingly similar to Burges's proposal for a
speech hall at Harrow.[3] No matter. Conder designed what was to be his
most famous building (though hardly his best) in the Renaissance-revival
style which the Japanese preferred.

The Rokumeikan proved sensational after it opened in 1883, probably not
so much for its architecture as for what went on there. The activities involved
western-style parties, banquets, billiards, charity bazaars and even – this was
the shocker – ballroom dancing. It was chiefly, members of the Japanese
political and social élite who used the completely western-style building with
its salons, games rooms, dining and ball rooms; but on occasions like the
annual emperor's birthday ball the government invited scores of foreigners,
western diplomats, traders, even missionaries. One casual visitor was the
French writer, Pierre Loti, who was more impressed by the young Japanese
women, the food, the flowers and the music than by Conder's building. He
declared that the gas-lit, white-painted, brick building with its two stories of
arched verandas and mansard roof reminded him of a provincial casino.[4]

Disapproval came from more important quarters. When Inoue failed to
negotiate an acceptable treaty with the western powers on extraterritoriality
in 1887, he was accused of pandering to the west. The Rokumeikan became a
symbol of official frivolity and the futility of aping foreign ways. In the wake
of Inoue's resignation and the fall of the cabinet, the government quickly sold
the building to the peers for a private club. Actually, Conder's Rokumeikan
was a good and useful building, there were no western hotels, clubs or

auditoriums in Tokyo and no place where western guests of the government could stay except in the embarrassing treaty ports. It survived one earthquake in the 1890s (Conder repaired it and made it a bit more Second Empire) and the great earthquake in 1923. It was casually torn down in 1941 but not before it had long been a favourite lodging for famous westerners and an infectious model for rich Japanese. It was the first of Conder's 'Renaissance villas', a style he was to repeat many times.

Conder's position as the major architectural influence on the government changed radically by the mid-1880s for two reasons. First, the Public Works Ministry was abolished and the Engineering College became part of an expanded Tokyo University. For a short time Conder stayed on as a member of the architectural department, but Tatsuno assumed the role of dean. Apparently, Conder considered these developments predictable and normal. In any case, even after 1888 when he left the university to open his own architectural firm in Tokyo, he did not leave the government which, indeed, continued to treat him well. In 1884 the emperor honoured him with the Order of the Rising Sun (fourth class) and after the demise of the Works Ministry he was made an adviser to its bureaucratic successor.

The second reason for the waning of Conder and the primacy of British architecture was the Meiji government's embrace of things German. The dominant political leader of the era, Itō Hirobumi, who had once sailed to England on a merchantman and knew it better than any other foreign country, still considered Germany a better model for the constitution and representative government Japan was about to adopt. Shortly before his fall, foreign minister Inoue, embittered, perhaps, at Britain's opposition to treaty revision, cancelled a request to the Japanese envoy in London to look for British architects to build structures for the new constitutional Japan: a parliament, a justice ministry and a high court. Instead, the government turned to Germany, where it engaged the Berlin firm of Ende and Boeckmann.

When Wilhelm Boeckmann arrived in 1886 to sign the contract with the government, he stayed at the Rokumeikan, which he found 'a very good building', and he soon found Conder, who took him on sightseeing trips to Japanese temples and drank beer with him, 'a lively, fine colleague'.[5] Before his return to Berlin he even made sure that the Japanese invited Conder to his farewell banquet at which the Japanese celebrated their new architectural alliance with Germany. Conder seems not to have minded this development either. In fact, he took advantage of it, to visit England the next year in the course of escorting two of his former students, Tsumaki Raiko and Kawai Kozo, to Berlin for further study.

Now Conder had an opportunity to reinforce his connections with British architectural circles, a tie he had maintained despite his distance from London. As early as 1878, for instance, he submitted a paper on Japanese temples, probably the first professional treatment to appear in England, to the Royal Institute of British Architects, of which he was then an associate. In 1884 he published a description of his new Gothic-style Law and Literature Building for Tokyo University in *The Builder* and the RIBA named him a fellow. On his trip to London in 1887 he gave a lecture on Japanese architecture at the RIBA, which had recently published his *Notes* on this esoteric subject. Already in 1883 Conder had persuaded his former students, Japan's pioneer western architects, to found an architectural association similar to the RIBA. From that point on, like its British counterpart, it began to publish reports on new structures. It remains to this day the primary organization for Japanese architects, the Kenchikugakkai.

Meanwhile, back in Japan, the Germans were busy with their plans for new government buildings and for boulevards, plazas and heroic statues to reshape Tokyo along the lines of Wilhelmine Berlin. Only a small part of these proposals materialized, notably the extremely well-built brick Justice Ministry and the High Court. The plans for the Diet Building (the Japanese avoided using the word 'parliament') provoked a great controversy, and in the end the Germans designed and helped the Japanese erect what was only a temporary structure.

Amusingly, the Germans faced the same resistence which Conder had previously encountered when they proposed making their buildings more 'Oriental'. Conder, of course, had thought that Islamic-style buildings, being suited to masonry as Japanese wooden structures were not, might bridge the gap between east and west. Ende went further. He submitted drawings to the Japanese cabinet showing tile temple roofs, Japanese gables and pagoda-like towers resting on otherwise conventionally western foundations. Outraged, the Japanese insisted on *echt* western architecture. The Germans were forced to redesign. Costs soared. Finally, the Yamagata cabinet cut short their contract and the Germans went home.

At this point the government summoned Conder back and asked him to fill the unfinished site in Kasumigaseki next to the High Court and the Justice Ministry. Here, in 1894 he erected the Navy Ministry, a massive red-brick Renaissance-revival building with mansard roofs, less expensive but not too different in style from its German neighbours. In the same year the emperor bestowed the Order of the Sacred Treasure on this long and faithful architect. The Navy Ministry was, however, the last official building to be designed by Conder or by any foreigner.

Conder could not have been too dismayed by this development. He had already effectively retired from government in 1890. If he could no longer look to a future in government work, he had the satisfaction of seeing his students take over major official commissions. By 1895 Tatsuno, unaided, had built the neo-classical Bank of Japan, and Katayama, charged with royal architecture, had finished the Baroque Nara Museum and the Second-Empire Kyoto Museum. In any case, Conder no longer needed government work. Not only was he much sought after by the foreign community to build legations (he designed them for the Germans, the Austrians and the Italians as well as the British) and clubs and churches, he found new business in the burgeoning world of Japanese business.

In particular, Conder found congenial patrons in the family that founded Mitsubishi in the early Meiji period, the Iwasakis. More than anything else this association catapulted Conder into commercial building and then, probably even more to his satisfaction, into luxurious domestic architecture. This juncture was, in a sense, Conder's mid-life crisis and a very remunerative and pleasant one it turned out to be. Where he had once hobnobbed with political leaders, he now came to know the economic movers and shakers. To a man, and in this they were not much different from their aggrandizing political counterparts, these successful Japanese wanted to be surrounded by an aura of Britishness.

Nowhere was this more apparent than in the style of buildings Mitsubishi contemplated for its unprecedented development of the Marunouchi section of central Tokyo. Here, on over a hundred empty acres the company planned to build not only its own headquarters but blocks of rental office buildings. Their style was to suggest Victorian London, and in 1890 Iwasaki Yanosuke called on Conder to produce this effect. It was so successful, at least in Japanese eyes, that when the project was finished in 1905 people called Marunouchi 'Londontown', or as the company seemed to prefer, 'Lombard Street'.

In 1895 Conder finished the first and most important building, Mitsubishi No. 1, a red brick three-storey structure trimmed with white stone in his favourite 'French Renaissance' style with tall mansard roofs spiked with decorative iron cresting. (French Renaissance also graced the real Lombard Street.) Thereafter, Conder's favourite pupil, the quiet, gentlemanly Sone Tatsuzo, took over the Mitsubishi project, becoming, thanks to Conder, the in-house architect for the company. (Mitsubishi tore it all down after the Pacific War.)

If Yanosuke sought out Conder for the office it may have been because he already knew him at home. In 1889 Conder had built the first of three mansions for the Iwasaki family, some of his most interesting buildings, of which two remain. In the course of their construction between 1889 and 1908 Conder's style gradually moved away from Burgesian mid-Victorianism into a kind of early twentieth-century classicism. The red-brick Kiyomizu Mansion, the first Iwasaki house, east of the Sumida river in Fukagawa, was lost in the 1923 earthquake, so we only know it from Conder's plans, old photographs and descriptions by foreigners like the Baroness d'Anethan, the English wife of the Belgian ambassador.[6] Evidently its basic style was Tudor, emphasized in its pediment trimmed with stone balls, but it had a staircase tower with an Islamic roof. British imports prevailed: outside, in lacy cast-iron balconies and a blue slate roof, inside, in walls and ceilings of Lincrusta Waltona and, according to the admiring Mary d'Anethan, paintings by Leighton and Millais and furniture from the London firm of Maple & Co.

It was too bad, she noted, that no-one seemed to use the place. The reason was that even as late as 1912 most wealthy Japanese preferred to live in Japanese-style houses and keep their western-style ones for entertainment. The Iwasakis, of course, had a number of both.

In 1896 Conder built his second Iwasaki house, the wooden Kayacho mansion in Bunkyo ward, for Hisaya, the third head of Mitsubishi, son of the founder, Yataró. Hisaya was genuinely Anglo-American in his leanings. He had studied finance at the Wharton School of the University of Pennsylvania and two of his brothers studied at Cambridge. Conder built him an extremely eclectic house blending American clapboards with French Renaissance pilasters, dormers, parapets and a tower on the front and in back, overlooking the garden, a two-storey loggia in his Italian villa style. Inside are echoes of the Rokumeikan in the elaborately carved main staircase ('Jacobean') and of Conder's early taste for the 'Saracenic'. Though the furniture and many details have been lost, the house still stands, exhibiting such unmistakable signs of the Victorian gentleman's house as a smoking room with Moorish decorations, coal-burning fireplaces with Gothic-revival tile surrounds, even a separate rustic cottage for billiards. All the chandeliers and metalwork were British.

Some people feel Conder's best house was the third Iwasaki mansion built in Shinagawa in 1908, now called Kaitōkaku and used by Mitsubishi as a company club. Here, due to Conder's adjustment to new styles and particularly to the demands of his patron, in this case the second head of Mitsubishi, Yataro's younger brother, Yanosuke, Conder deserted his romantic eclecticism for a kind of classic restraint. (Yanosuke actually took Conder's plans with him to England for other architects to examine.) The interior with its splendid woods, art collection, English fittings including a Turkish bath imported from Ashton & Green was lost during the war and has been completely changed. The original exterior remains, magisterial, even a bit austere, with a very restrained two-floor loggia over the garden and granite-covered walls in a quiet Renaissance style that Conder called 'Jacobean'. Gone is any hint of the Islamic, though there is a square, unromantic tower on the east side. Unfortunately, Yanosuke died just as the mansion was completed, but his son Koyata, another Cambridge graduate, lived on here in the style of an Edwardian gentleman for more than twenty years.

Yanosuke did not desert his favourite architect even in death for before he died he commissioned Conder to create a special tomb in western Tokyo. This imposing stone mausoleum (1910) took the form of a Greek cross with a dome and vaults over each of its four wings. Conder was in great demand for tombs and also designed one for the British ambassador, Sir Claude MacDonald, who played an important role in framing the Anglo-Japanese alliance and died at his post.

In all, Conder designed some seventy major buildings from Tokyo to

Nagasaki. He produced a number of country villas for elder statesmen and *zaibatsu*, but he was also often engaged by foreigners, and his range of styles was prodigious. In 1905 he built a house for himself that was a very good symbol of his own life, part British half-timbering, part Japanese. His religious architecture was extremely varied: Old English Gothic, a proposed 'Japan Revival' church for the Unitarians (they decided against it), the famous still-standing Russian Orthodox cathedral (Nicolaidō, 1891) in Byzantine style.

Of his late buildings, perhaps the most appealing surviving one is neither the Shimazu House (a somewhat more graceful version of Kaitokaku) or the gloomy Furukawa House of 1917 (his last major residence), but the Mitsui Club of 1913. In this stone-clad brick building Conder's restrained late style is balanced by his innately decorative and romantic outlook. Like Kaitokaku it has a steel frame and truss, but its mood looks back to the Rokumeikan. It is, however, a much better Rokumeikan. At the back, its curving, two-storey loggia, overlooking a fountain and a wide garden, has arches, balustrades, pilasters and a central cartouche done in an elegant Baroque manner. Inside, attention to detail is equally impressive: a two-storey main hall under a stained-glass dome (shades of Burges and his cartoonist for English church windows, H.W. Lonsdale), a monumental turning staircase, arched doorways and dentile mouldings, Ionic pilasters on the first floor, Corinthian on the second.

Conder should also be remembered for his early efforts to interpret Japanese culture to the English-reading western world. One book described traditional painting, specifically the work of Conder's own teacher Kawanabe Kyosai. Another, *Flowers of Japan and the Art of Floral Arrangement*, first published in 1891 in Japan and later in London, introduced *ikebana*. His *Landscape Gardening in Japan*, which grew from one of his papers for the Asiatic Society of Japan, has been republished many times since it first appeared in Yokohama in 1893.

Conder's own work, after his death in Tokyo in 1920, was memorialized in a handsome volume edited by Baron Furuichi Koi and numbers of Conder students, including Sone. Filled with colour drawings of his principal buildings, this *Collection of the Posthumous Works of Josiah Conder* came out in a limited edition in Tokyo in 1931. Though the designs for the Rokumeikan have been lost, Kyoto University holds a large number of other original plans and elevations which have now been published.[7]

Conder has a quiet grave beside his wife at Gokokuji, a Buddhist temple not far from Tokyo University. There, in front of the engineering department, he has been honoured by a life-sized statue which was carefully hidden during the wartime scrap metal driver. It shows a handsome man with a moustache looking rather more serious than Conder, a devotee of amateur theatricals and convival parties in his rose garden, might have been in life. Still, the Japanese sculptor remembered to put a bronze cigar in his hand.

6

MOUNTAIN HIGH AND VALLEY LOW: WALTER WESTON (1861–1940) AND JAPAN

A.H. Ion

Every year on the first weekend in June, the climbing season in the Japanese Northern Alps is begun by a festival named after Walter Weston (1861–1940), the leading western pioneer of mountain climbing as a popular leisure sport in Japan. That this Anglican clergyman is remembered in this way points to the durability of sports in cross-cultural relations, a durability resulting from the fact that they normally pose neither a direct intellectual challenge to the indigenous culture nor are subject to the whims of fashion to the same degree as foreign intellectual ideas. Even so, while Japan has indigenized hundreds of sports from abroad (as well as exporting to the outside world a number of her own traditional sports), Weston is virtually unique in his identification as an individual westerner with the emergence of a sport in Japan. Beyond his fame as a pioneer mountaineer in the Japan Alps, Weston's chief legacy lies in the image of an Alpine Japan and its people that he projected in his writings.

Japan helped satisfy the two dominant themes in Weston's life: his Christian sense of service to others and his love of the mountains and mountain people. But he did not live in Japan for all his working life; his career there covered three separate periods: 1888–95, 1902–5 and 1911–15. Importantly, though, between his times in Japan, Weston wrote extensively about Japan to an English audience. In all, he wrote four books in the twenty years from 1896 to 1926, three of which were written after Weston had finally left Japan.[1] Weston was also a 'Society man' and was an active member of the Japan Society of London, the Alpine Club of Great Britain and the Royal Geographical Society. In his later life, he served on the Councils of both the Japan Society and the Royal Geographical Society. He made good use of these societies, for he not only faithfully attended most of their meetings in his later years but also presented papers before them which included some of the material that would later appear in his books.

In his writings, Weston provides interesting observations about Japan and the Japanese which bespeak a deep affection for them. He brought a knowledge of things Japanese, especially of Alpine Japan, to an audience that otherwise might have remained ignorant of an important aspect of a foreign culture. What makes Weston's opinions and insights attractive and valuable is that his experiences provided him with a unique perspective from which to comment upon changing Japan. In exploring his views about Japan and attempting to understand what appealed or did not appeal to him one is investigating the personalized foundations of Anglo-Japanese goodwill during an important period of close and warm relations between Britain and Japan. But it is particularly important to consider Weston's efforts in the light of what inspired them, if a proper understanding of the significance of his work is to be achieved.

Before turning to Weston's views about Japan, it is important to consider Weston briefly in the context of his own career and the broad pattern of Anglo-Japanese cultural relations. Walter Weston was born in Derby in 1861. He was educated at Derby School and at Clare and Ridley Hall, Cambridge, before taking Holy Orders in 1885.[2] He made his first visits to the Swiss Alps in 1878 and 1883, and proved his ability as an Alpine climber in 1886 and again in 1887 when, together with his older brother, he scaled the Matterhorn and other peaks.[3] He belonged to the second generation of English Alpine climbers; it was after all only in 1865 that the Matterhorn was first conquered and the pioneers of Alpine climbing as a leisure sport such as Edward Whymper (1840–1911), Douglas W. Freshfield (1845–1934) and Sir William M. Conway (1856–1937) were not only alive but still actively climbing at this time. Mountaineering was an amateur sport for these pioneers, who had the money and opportunity to climb in Switzerland, the Canadian Rockies, the Andes and even further afield. One explanation of how he could afford to indulge in this expensive sport might be that his father was a Derby factory owner.[4]

However, Swiss holidays came to an end for a time in 1888, when Weston gave up his curacy in Reading in order to become a missionary in Japan under the auspices of the Church Missionary Society. He was first posted to Kumamoto in Kyushu diocese.[5] But in the same year he moved to Kobe to take charge of St Andrew's Church, Kobe, and while he helped at the CMS Theological School in Osaka,[6] his chief work was catering to the needs of the British community in Kobe. He also served as the chaplain to the Seamen's Mission in Kobe, and one lasting result was his warm support for Missions for Seamen, which continued to his death in 1940.[7] Indeed, after he left Japan for the first time in 1895, Weston initially became the curate of the Seamen's Mission in London before becoming the curate at Christ's Church, Wimbledon, in 1897. His experiences in Japan were not forgotten, however, for the climbs and explorations that he had made in the Japanese Alps during his summer holidays from 1891 to 1894 came to form the basis for his first book on Japan, which was published by John Murray in 1896. Once established in Wimbledon, Weston was to remain in England for a further five years, but he did resume his climbing in the Swiss Alps, which included finding a route up the Eiger.[8] His exploits in Switzerland during the 1890s helped raise his reputation as a climber among English Alpinists and gave authority to his speeches and writings about Japan.

Weston's climbing did not end with his marriage in 1902 to the second daughter of Sir Francis Fox of Osmaston Manor, Derbyshire, who was a distinguished engineer. The Fox family also maintained a house in Wimbledon, and this, combined with common links to Derbyshire and a mutual love of nature, led to a happy marriage. Considerably younger than her husband, Frances Weston (1872–1937) matched him in her interest both in mountain climbing and in Christian work.[9] Their honeymoon was spent climbing in the Canadian Rockies.

However, Japan called again in 1902, when Weston agreed to take charge of St Andrew's, Yokohama. He was responsible for the construction of a fine new church building for St Andrew's which was dedicated in March 1905.[10] It was a church building, according to a latter priest-in-charge, that 'for beauty and convenience is second to none in the diocese'.[11] While its construction was supported by a grant from the Society for the Propagation of the Gospel in Foreign Parts's Marriot Bequest, Weston's skill as a fund-raiser was also clearly important. It was fortunate for the new church that the British community in Yokohama gave generous support to the building fund.[12] Likewise, it was perhaps also helpful that both Weston and his wife came from wealthy backgrounds. Unfortunately, St Andrew's was one of the many churches that were destroyed during the 1923 Kanto earthquake.

The fact that Weston was able to see a church built was testament to his Christian zeal. However, Yokohama was an extremely difficult city in which to undertake evangelistic work among the Japanese. H.B. Walton, who was priest-in-charge at St Andrew's in 1908, wrote that 'Yokohama has been the happy hunting ground of every form of heresy and quack religion; and here if anywhere the Church would need to present God's Truth in strength and power. And, last but not least; the materialistic tone and temper of the place make it confessedly a very difficult field.'[13] Nevertheless, although there were some twenty-five ordained Anglican clergy and as many women missionaries in the city, only one Anglican missionary and a Japanese catechist were assigned to evangelistic work among the Japanese community. During his time at St Andrew's, Weston's work was further hampered by the difficulty of finding a capable catechist to assist him. In April 1904 Weston reported that 'at present, however, the work is every [sic] seriously handicapped through the want of a native catechist or clergymen, since after more than a year under a lethargic *DENDOSHI* (catechist) we have now been without one at all for nearly 3 months', and he went on to say that 'Hopes have been raised from time to time without fulfilment, and at the time of writing it is not known what or when provision will be made to enable aggressive work to be prosecuted in [a] way worthy of the Seikokwai in Yokohama.'[14] No provision was forthcoming. Weston was clearly hard-working, and he was greatly helped by his wife who participated in the work among women. But given the difficulties of evangelistic work among the Japanese in Yokohama, it was not surprising that ill-health forced him to return to England in 1905.

Weston was in Japan first and foremost to do Christian work, and he worked hard. The three years that he spent at St Andrew's, Yokohama, were without doubt the most arduous years of his Christian career in Japan. However, in the summer he and his wife did have some opportunities, to explore the Japanese Alps. Climbing in the Japan Alps was a relaxation and escape from a very demanding life in the city. Others were also beginning to enjoy climbing for pleasure and sport in the Japan Alps, and this led to the formation of the Japanese Alpine Club in 1906. Even though Weston had returned to England by this time, he became an active publicist for it in Britain. He was the first foreign honorary member of the club and his wife was one of its first members.

In 1911 another opportunity to work in Japan arose. Now Weston was in charge of the English congregation of Christ Church, Yokohama. This was much less demanding than working in a Japanese parish. Once again, the summers were spent exploring and climbing in the Japan Alps. It was during this time that Weston undertook some of the most physically demanding climbs of all the many he undertook in Japan. By 1911 his mountaineering exploits were also becoming known in Japan, for he was asked to give public lectures under the auspices of the Japanese Alpine Club and also invited to speak in schools.[15]

Regardless of his growing fame, in 1915 Weston left Japan for the last time, and returned to London to help in the Missions to Seamen. He also became a University Extension Lecturer and Lecturer for the Gilchrist Educational Trust.[16] He was becoming recognized as an authority on Japan. In May 1915 Douglas Freshfield, one of the pioneer English Alpinists and president of the Royal Geographical Society, noted about Weston after a paper on exploration in the Northern Japanese Alps that 'he has, in fact made himself an apostle of mountaineering in the European sense of the word, in Japan'. Freshfield argued that Weston had done this because Weston had

> discovered that the Japanese were very much wanting in physical sports. They have their wrestling and single-stick, but they have no cricket and no golf, nothing to replace the outdoor sports in which an Englishman passes his leisure. He therefore tried to instil into them a passion for mountain climbing for its own sake, and in this he has been singularly successful.[17]

In 1917 Weston received the Back Grant from the Royal Geographical

Society 'in respect of his travels and explorations among the little-known Highlands of Japan'.[18] On this occasion, Douglas Freshfield noted that Weston had not only 'proved to the Japanese that mountaineering, which they have for centuries practised as a religious duty, might also be treated as a sport', but also had helped edit the new *Murray's Guide to Japan*.[19] This latter publication was important for western travellers to Japan, including the peripatetic Freshfield himself, who had visited Japan a few years before. It was in the eleven years after 1915 that Weston was at his most prolific in writing about Japan.

Weston's writings and ideas about Japan were not formed in isolation from the literary trends that existed within the resident British community. In fact, Weston should be considered in the tradition of the scholar-missionaries who contributed so much to Japanese studies during the late nineteenth and early twentieth centuries.[20] With respect to this latter point, Weston was not a scholar of the calibre of, say, Arthur Lloyd, one of the early pioneers in the study of traditional Japanese Buddhism and also the author of a very fine and detailed study of everyday Japan.[21] However, Weston shared a common approach to Japan with Lloyd and other British missionary writers. Professor Cyril Powles, in his study of British Anglican missionaries in Meiji Japan, has argued that these missionaries 'belonged to a status society which had enjoyed a long history. They loved tradition and the things of the past. They loved Japan for laying hold on the very things that were disappearing in their own country'.[22] In 1909 Lloyd pointed out in regards to Japan's development over the previous forty years that:

> Organisations, machinery, institutions, systems, have been renewed or changed, but the essence has been left untouched as far as possible. In law, in commerce, in military arts and sciences, in education, in religion, the constant effort and determination of Japan has been to make everything material and tangible as perfect as possible, but to preserve the SAKE OF national spirit untouched, in legal arrangements, in ways of doing business, in the carrying on of war, in the education of children, in the worship of God, and, more than all, in social life.[23]

In general, Weston would have agreed. But his favourite Japan was rural, not urban. In 1925 he wrote:

> It is only in rural Japan that we gain an insight into the most character-istic features of the life of the people, and the real strength of national organization. The most attractive aspects of the national character cannot fully be appreciated until one passes from the Westernized ways of the great cities and of the beaten tracks to the country-side with the fields and farms of one of the most intelligent, diligent, and friendly peasantry in the world.[24]

Weston's Alpine explorations in Japan reflected a search for the naturalness and purity both in nature and in man which was disappearing under the pressures of industrialization and modernization in urban centres. Among the country folk, particularly those of the mountain regions, Weston commented that

> There is something in the open and communistic character of the daily life and toil of these people, a result of their close and open contact with nature and its operations, that seems to render them all the more natural and considerate, and that promotes resourcefulness and readiness to help one another. Here you find human nature most unsophisticated and unspoilt, and adorned with an inborn simplicity and a native courtesy which still justify, in its truest sense, the old title KUNSHI NO KOKU, 'The country of Gentlemen'.[25]

As an English gentleman himself, this idea of rural Japan as 'KUNSHI NO KOKU' was obviously attractive to Weston, for it is a theme that appears in all his writings.

While Weston's books were in keeping with the practice of fellow British Anglican missionaries to write about a Japan off the beaten track, his writings do transcend the confines of missionary literature on Japan. In describing Japanese customs and manners, Weston was also part of another tradition. As he noted in a paper read at the Royal Geographical Society in December 1895:

> Books have been written containing observations extending over all imaginable periods of time, varying from 'Nine Years in Nippon' to 'Three Weeks in Japan'. Indeed, one may scarcely look forward to the Ultima Thule, of the downward limit, being reached till the publication of the remarkable work with which residents in Japan have been threatened by their globe-trotting visitors – 'Five Minutes in Japan,' in two volumes.[26]

This was an obvious play on Basil Hall Chamberlain's opinion of Japan, that 'as for books of travel, there is literally no end to the making of them'.[27] Chamberlain was a friend.[28] The author of the famous Things Japanese also aided Weston in a practical way as he helped arrange with Kelly Walsh (the book agents and publishers) the marketing of The Japanese Alps in Japan and the Far East.[29] Moreover, an account of a journey that Chamberlain had made in 1881 when he was the first European visitor to explore the Hayakawa valley was the stimulus which first induced Weston to turn his attention to the Japanese Alps. In 1903 Weston had the pleasure of following, in reverse, the route Chamberlain had taken through this valley.[30] Sir Ernest Satow was another who had made an early journey, among the 'Snow Mountains' of the Hida-Shinshū region, and later became Weston's friend.[31] The mountains were a bond that linked Weston to famous Britons such as Sir Rutherford Alcock, who made the first recorded ascent of Fuji by a European in 1860, or Lady Parkes, who in 1867 had the distinction of being the first European woman to climb to the top of the same mountain.[32] But not all Weston's old-Japan-hand friends were mountain climbers; one of them, Sir Claude Macdonald, admitted that 'the most terrible obstacle I had ever tackled was the Camp Hill at Yokohama, which any one who has been to Yokohama will know is about as formidable as Primrose Hill'.[33]

There were other western residents who shared Weston's love of the mountains. One of these was H.J. Hamilton, a Canadian Anglican missionary stationed at Nagoya, who had climbed in the Canadian Rockies and accompanied Weston on his trip to the Japan Alps in 1894.[34] Hamilton was also a photographer, and provided some of the pictures that illustrated *The Japanese Alps*. Indeed, the photographs of mountains, valleys and people which illustrate all Weston's books add considerably to their value as a record of past era. Another missionary mountaineer was W.H. Murray Walton, who came out to Japan the year Weston returned home for the last time. He followed in Weston's footsteps by climbing virtually all the major peaks in the Japanese Alps as well as in other parts of the Japanese empire between 1915 and 1930. But missionaries were not the only ones interested in climbing. Weston held that Kobe was 'the home of a most sporting colony of British and other residents',[35] among whom were not only some keen golfers but also some who climbed in the golf off-season.[36] Chief among these was H.E. Daunt, a long-term resident in Japan and editor of the magazine *Inaka*, who after carefully reading Weston's *The Japanese Alps* retraced his footsteps.[37] While Daunt and other British residents climbed the same mountains as Weston soon after his exploits, and climbed much more extensively than he ever did, Weston still remains the most famous foreign mountaineer of all.

For after all, as Shiga Shigetaka (Juko) of the Japanese Alpine Club wrote in 1918 in his foreword to Weston's *The Playground of the Far East*, it was 'through the energetic and enterprising spirit of our intrepid climber, that is, Rev. Weston, [that the] so-called "Japanese Alps" have become known world-wide, and by the influences of his ardent exploitation the Nippon Sangaku-Kwai, or "Japanese Alpine Club," had been founded some twelve years ago'.[38] Weston was able to capture a special place in the hearts of Japanese mountaineers. One reason why Weston was liked must simply have been that he gave his Japanese friends full credit for their own achievements. He applauded their efforts to make mountaineering a recreational sport. In 1918 he wrote in appreciation of the Japanese Alpine Club that

> the strides made by mountaineering, as a recreation, in Japan have reflected the national upwards progress of the nation itself in those many spheres of modern material civilisation which it has set itself to achieve. The Japanese have, through many centuries of their history, shown true mountain lovers. Now the educated youth of the nation have begun to cultivate – and that with immense activity and success – the pursuit of a closer and wider acquaintance with all that the

mountains have to bestow on them in satisfying the tastes of men of every type.[39]

Flattering though this statement might be to the Japanese, there is reason to believe that the feelings expressed here were genuine. At an individual level, when his friend Omori Funakichi, Professor of Seismology in the Imperial University of Tokyo, died, Weston wrote an obituary stressing his very considerable achievements.[40] This was an unsolicited gesture but characteristic of a man who sincerely appreciated the Japanese who loved the mountains and went out of his way to say so.

Weston's first acquaintance with the mountains of central Japan had come with a trip that he took with H.W. Belcher in the summer of 1891. The starting point for his explorations was Karuizawa, then relatively newly discovered by foreigners and unspoilt. Over the next three years, with different western friends as company, Weston climbed in all parts of the Japanese Alps. During his final summer visit in 1894, he traversed the whole of the range north to south. He wrote:

> By doing so, and climbing the chief peaks I had not hitherto ascended, I hoped to gain a truer conception of the main features of the chain as a whole. The issue proved the experiment a great success. It put one in a position to fully appreciate the value of such a work as Sir William Conway's splendid volume on his travels along 'The Alps from end to end', and enabled me to realize that an 'excentric' mountaineer is not necessarily an eccentric one.[41]

There was a certain scientific approach to his explorations, and a thoroughness in the careful noting of heights, geographic characteristics of mountains and the types of flowers and trees on their sides and summits which made *The Japanese Alps* more than 'a record of four years' holiday wanderings in the high mountain regions of Central Japan'.[42] In fact, Weston was obviously trying to provide as complete a picture of the Japanese Alps as Conway had of the Swiss Alps. Indeed, the Swiss Alps were never far from Weston's imagination when he was in the Japanese Alps. This is seen in the following description of a view of the southern Alps which he came across during his first trip with Belcher:

> Coming unexpectedly as the prospect did, we were almost startled by its magnificence. The whole of the central and southern part of the chain rose up before us westwards like a great barrier between the broad plain of Matsumoto that lay at our feet, and the lonely province of Hida beyond. Snow-seamed ridges and noble peaks of 10,000 feet and more in height stand up in sharp outline against the opalescent sky of the dying day. Yarigatake, the 'Spear Peak', the Matterhorn of Japan; Jonendake, with its graceful triangular form, that recalls in miniature the Weisshorn, queen of the Pennine Alps; and further southward the

massive double-topped Norikura, the 'Saddle mountain', each arrests the eye with a characteristic profile.[43]

As the above quotation indicates, Weston's talent as a writer lay in his descriptive ability to create powerful images of mountains and their peoples. The disadvantage of the Japanese Alps that he saw between 1891 and 1894 was that they lacked the height, the glaciers and the landscape of pastoral life of the European mountains. The mountaineering, which Weston accomplished during this first period in the Japanese Alps, was not an 1890s version of the roped climber up sheer precipices associated with modern expeditions to the Himalayas, but rather was more akin to hiking. The Japanese mountains were not challenging to climb; indeed parties of religious pilgrims had been climbing virtually all of them for centuries. There was only one mountain, 'Ho-wo-zan, the miniature Aiguille du Geant of the Southern Japanese Alps',[44] that Weston could claim to be the first to have scaled. This was during a later expedition in 1904, when he reached its needle summit after a hair-raising almost vertical climb, or as he understated it, 'a strenuous scramble'.[45] But while the mountains themselves might only be two-thirds the scale of those of Switzerland, they were still beautiful. Weston claimed that 'the picturesqueness of their valleys, and the magnificence of the dark and silent forests that clothe their massive flanks, surpass anything I have met with in European Alpine wanderings.[46]

It was not only the splendour of the scenery but also the atmosphere of the mountains which appealed to him. As he noted in 1915, 'in those regions I have during the last twenty years explored and attempted to describe, you find yourself transported back nearly one thousand years, with human nature, and, for the most part, human ways, still what they were before the Normans invaded England'.[47] Weston's deep knowledge of the Japanese Alps might have led one to hope that he might have had an exotic choice of favourite mountain; however, it was Mount Fuji that he treasured the most. He climbed Fuji some nine times. Approaching the mountain by a variety of routes, Weston was always impressed by its majesty. In 1915 he wrote:

There is one spot above all others (in every sense) where those far-sundered centuries meet – the loftiest height in the land of the Rising Sun, the summit of Fuji San. By the side of the most sacred shrine on that most sacred summit, at a height of nearly 12,400 feet, where there is worshipped one of Japan's most august divinities, there stands a post-office, from which the summer tourist sends his picture post-cards for a halfpenny to the remotest regions of the empire. There, outside the most modern of meteorological stations, you may find nearly every summer morning at early dawn the shivering form of some aged pilgrim, who has at length gained the loftiest goal of his heart's desire – to be able from the eastern edge of the crater lip, to clap his wrinkled hands in invocation and bow his head in humble adoration to the Rising Sun.[48]

It is this juxtaposition of new and old which Weston liked. By far, however, he preferred the old to the new.

One of the major inconveniences to the mountaineer in the Japanese Alps was the common Japanese flea. Of all the hardships that Weston suffered in his explorations of the Japanese Alps, it was probably fleas which caused him the greatest physical irritation. Staying as he did in *ryokan* or *onsen* in the valleys or in hunters' huts in the mountains, his nights were often spent awake fighting off fleas. He was also disturbed by the noise of other guests, whose propensity for all-hours-jollifications sometimes denied him what opportunities for sleep the fleas allowed. For a different reason, he did not like staying in inns where other Europeans had stayed – it meant that the Japanese innkeepers would attempt to over-charge him. In part, this was the result of the lack of politeness and courtesy of many westerners in their dealings with Japanese hoteliers.[49] But Weston did like mountain *onsen*, even the most primitive ones, and he found the parboiling practices of the Japanese at hot-springs mildly amusing. Yet he thoroughly approved of the bathing habits of the Japanese and felt that cleanliness was one of the prime things that set the Japanese apart from (and, by inference, above) other East Asian peoples.[50]

While Weston had no qualms about staying in remote *onsen*, he was a British explorer in the Japanese Alps. He climbed in hob-nailed boots and Norfolk jacket and brought along his Keating's Insect Powder and Jeyes fluid against fleas, and his Burroughs Wellcome 'Alpine Case' against cuts and illnesses, as well as some western food. He found some Japanese food, especially *sakana tempura* much to his taste, but at the end of a day's work he also liked his Halford's curried fowl perhaps washed down by some De Jongh's cocoa. One reason for taking such food with him on climbs was, as he said, 'the man who is able to subsist entirely on the scanty resources of an out-of-the-way hamlet is a rarity, and even if he is able to, it is a question whether it is wise to do so'.[51] There was much poverty in the mountains, and often wholesome food was not readily available, so the European climber had to be prepared. Weston and his companions would normally engage porters to carry their equipment and provisions, and also to carry them, so that their British feet would not get wet when streams had to be forded. As well as porters, Weston would also hire guides from among mountain hunters. He was well aware that even though the mountains might not be hazardous to climb, it was dangerous to be lost or caught in bad weather without a knowledgeable local Japanese.

The hunters, who acted as his guides, were people whom westerners would normally never meet. Of all the many hunters Weston came to know over the course of his trips to the mountains, his favourite was Kamonji Kamijo, who guided him on a number of climbs in the Yari region of the Northern Alps. In 1912, when Weston returned to climb in this area after an absence of eighteen years, he re-employed Kamonji. About their reunion, Weston wrote that:

103

It was soon plain that eighteen years had not lessened the limits of the familiar expansive smile, nor had the weird cackle which with him does duty for a laugh lost aught of its infectious humour. Though the build and gait and nimbleness at times suggest an entirely Simian ancestry, for in them he resembles nothing more than a wholly benevolent gorilla, yet Kamonji is never anything but a man.[52]

To celebrate their reunion, they decided 'to try the first ascent of the highest peak of the whole Hodaka group from Kamikochi direct by a route he had once partly worked out when stalking a bear some seventeen years ago, but which he had not actually accomplished in its entirety'.[53] Kamonji was a simple tough old man who, like Weston, got great pleasure from sharing a new adventure with good friends.

As a writer, Weston was at his finest when he described the mountains, the hunters, and the ways of the mountain folk whom he came to know. However, he also generalized from his experiences about some of the characteristics of the Japanese. His opinions, to some extent, reflected Japan's contemporary circumstances.

By coincidence, in each of the three periods during which he explored the Japanese Alps, Japan was at war: first against China, then against Russia and lastly against Germany. *Playground of the Far East* was written during the First World War and included a chapter on the making of the soldier. At this time, Weston saw nothing sinister about the Japanese military. Likewise, he saw nothing wrong in the patriotism of the Japanese. His sympathy towards the army might well have been influenced by the fact that it was one of the most enthusiastic groups when it came to mountain climbing. In 1924 he wrote that he believed 'the sturdiest fighting men in the whole of the Japanese army are drawn from the peasant classes – hardy, stolid, and entirely unafflicted with nerves. Most of these come from the hill country, where their daily occupations and surroundings have left a permanent impress on their habits and their character.'[54] Be that as it may, the army also played a significant role in Japanese politics. Yet, as late as 1926, Weston remained sympathetic to the military and accepted without question that 'the main bulwark against radical tendencies, officially styled "dangerous thought", is set up by the Army and Navy, with their system of *seishin kyoiku* (spiritual education) and its far-reaching propaganda, which inculcates the truest forms of loyalty and patriotism'.[55]

This opinion perhaps reflected that fact that Weston was gradually losing touch with the current atmosphere in Japan, for by 1926 the army was not as popular as it had been during the Russo-Japanese or First World Wars when Weston had lived in Yokohama. There was also another important change in terms of Weston's writings. In his two books written in the 1920s *Wayfarer in Unfamiliar Japan* (1925) and *Japan* (1926), he was not writing primarily about mountains and adding chapters on topical subjects (as was the case with

Playground of the Far East, but he was writing books of a more general nature on modern Japan. This was not so much a problem in *Unfamiliar Japan* for it was clearly directed towards an audience whose interest in Japan had been stimulated by the 1923 Kanto earthquake. The book's core was the byways of Japan off the beaten track, but not exclusively the Japanese Alps. To this he could add a detailed account of the devastation of the Gifu earthquake of 1891 as well as providing information about the tragedy of 1923. The current trends within modern Japan were secondary to the concerns raised by the Kanto earthquake. But, in the later *Japan*, Weston could not avoid dealing with contemporary political and social events.

In dealing with political issues in *Japan*, Weston's conservative inclinations came to the fore, and in hindsight his understanding of these issues would appear to be flawed. In 1926 he wrote:

> There are signs that the former fine spirit of self-sacrifice of the individual for the sake of the nation and the Emperor are in danger of becoming things of the past. Owing to the flood of cheap Russian literature and to the increasing contact between some classes of Japanese Labour and Soviet Russia, radical, if not revolutionary, thought is making its mark on the minds of the extreme sections of the proletariat. The spread of industrialism and commercialism among a people hitherto largely agricultural tends to deaden the finer qualities of the community as a whole.[56]

As later became apparent it was not from the Left but from the Right that the political danger emanated. The finer qualities of the community, which he felt were being destroyed, were obviously those traditional values which had made Japan the '*kunshi no koku*'. He also saw a deterioration of the moral ideas of the Japanese working classes, a deterioration coming not only from a flood of Russian literature but also from new inventions such as the cinematograph. The centuries-old rural way of life which he had found in the mountains and valleys of the Japan Alps was fast disappearing before new social pressures.

In the face of these pressures, Weston felt that traditional customs were worth preserving. He wrote about the importance of the tea ceremony:

> at least, in an age when an overwhelming tide of materialism, for which Japan of these latter days has chiefly to thank Germany and the rest of the 'Great Powers' of the western world, has swept in upon the nation's life with often devastating effect, it is a good thing that there should still linger on here and there a custom that reminds those who observe it of something beyond human efficiency and the supremacy of human power.[57]

In light of the last statement, it is not surprising that *Japan* is the most Christian of his books. His earlier works are completely free of what might be termed Christian cant and make very little reference to Christianity. In 1926 his concern with the influence of 'Russian ideas' on the labour movement led him to point out that 'there is something significant in the fact that the men who have exercised most influence in forming the sounder elements of the Japan Labour movements had been men of pronounced Christian idealism and of recognised Christian character', and he described Kagawa Toyohiko, a Christian labour leader, as 'the Father Dolling of Japanese slum work'.[58]

Christianity was not only an influence on moderate labour leaders such as Kagawa or Suzuki Bunji, but it also influenced educators such as Tsuda Umeko. One of the themes which he dealt with in Japan was rising status of women in Japanese society. Here, again, he pointed out the important influence of Christianity by stating that:

> the ablest and most earnest leaders in women's philanthropic work for women – as is the case for those of the opposite sex – are mainly persons of high Christian character. To this must be added the further significant fact, that in Japanese society and business in general there is to-day a steadily increasing respect for the honesty and strength of truly Christian men and women.[59]

After more than thirty years of writing about Japan, had the leopard finally revealed his Christian spots? It is true to say that Weston's interest in Japan was first and foremost a Christian one. But more important to Weston in 1926 was the fact that Japanese society had changed. He viewed changing Japan with unease for he saw the traditional way of life of country folk, which he had been privileged to witness, being replaced by the materialistic values of an industrialized society, though he believed that a better society might still be realized through the influence of Christianity.

Weston's efforts in popularizing mountaineering as a recreational sport certainly contributed to the creation of a better society. Indeed, his contribution must be regarded as one of the significant lasting legacies of British influence upon Japan in the late nineteenth and early twentieth centuries. Walter Weston was genuinely fond of the Japanese. He wrote, 'no other race with which we are acquainted have the love of Nature so strongly inborn and so widespread in them. It pervades their whole life, and colours the entire range of their religion, art, and poetry, as well as of their daily pursuits and their holiday recreations.'[60] He shared with them his love of nature in all its forms. His attachment was to a rural Japan and its traditional values, and not to the industrialism and commercialism of modern Japan.[61] The very success of Japan's industrialization could be said to have made Japan less attractive to Weston. Weston practised Anglo-Japanese relations at the personal level and its results cannot be measured in material terms. Nevertheless such an approach can produce profound results.

7

BABA TATSUI (1850–1888)
AND VICTORIAN BRITAIN

Helen Ballhatchet

Baba Tatsui was born in 1850, three years before the American Commodore Matthew Perry with his five 'black ships' helped to stimulate a period of unprecedented political, social and economic upheaval for Japan, which was to continue beyond Baba's lifetime. Fear of domination and exploitation by the west encouraged wide-ranging efforts to emulate its strength, in which intellectuals as well as more practically minded Japanese became involved. Baba Tatsui, 'accomplished, warm-hearted, high-spirited, rather wayward and impetuous, greatly-gifted',[1] above all else 'filled with a desire to do something for his country'[2] was one of these intellectuals. His dedicated attempt to introduce Japan to what he saw as the source of western strength – freedom of speech and representative government – ended in his premature death in poverty in Philadelphia, but it began in Victorian Britain, where he spent the formative period of his short life. It is on his many-sided relationship with that country that this essay will focus.

The son of a family of middle-ranking samurai in Tosa, in south-western Japan, Baba's first real contact with Britain came at the age of 16, when he travelled to Edo and began to learn English, at the school which Fukuzawa Yukichi had established there. A major channel through which knowledge of the west entered Japan, Fukuzawa developed a close relationship with Baba and greatly influenced him. Fukuzawa had a high opinion of Britain, and it is probably to views disseminated by him that Baba is referring when he tells of the favourable view of the country to which he was first introduced:

> I was told . . . that English laws recognize no difference in the rank or social position of man; that men of all ranks are treated with perfect equality; that justice is impartially administered to all, rich and poor, strong and weak, both high and low; that commerce is carried on by most respectable men, whose integrity and honesty no-one can question. They go everywhere, and wherever they go there they carry

civilisation with them. In short, it is a blessing to a country where the British merchant may come!. . . . Happy I was when I thought that these people would set good examples before our people, and give them the means of the truest happiness and comfort which life can yield.[3]

This passage (from a pamphlet of 1875 addressed to a British audience) is, however, written with ironic intent; Baba's appraisal of Britain and its role in the world was not wholly uncritical, as will become clear.

Baba's opportunity to see Britain for himself came in 1870, when he was sent there to study with four other young men from Tosa. Originally he was meant to study naval engineering, but when the Iwakura Mission visited London in 1872 he was told to switch to the study of law; a result, he suggests in his autobiography, of his linguistic expertise. He 'read through' the standard course in English law,[4] although he seems to have been uninterested in gaining formal legal qualifications, and remained in Britain until 1878 with only one short trip back to Japan in between. This period, which comprised most of his twenties, was crucial to his intellectual development, and to the highly individual way in which he carried out his 'desire to do something for his country'.

On his return to Japan, Baba did not show any interest in the lucrative government posts which were open to those with his educational advantages, but retained his independence and concentrated on using the knowledge which he had gained for what he considered to be the benefit of the country as a whole. Largely as a result of his knowledge of the political structure of Britain, and his conviction that this was a major reason for Britain's stability and consequent strength, he believed that Japan needed open, representative government, rather than rule by the small élite which had brought about the Restoration. Thus he devoted himself to speech-making, journalism and political activism, despite the expectations of his parents that he would use his western education to support the family. In all his activities, the influence of his British experiences was evident. In the early 1880s he became a leading figure on the radical wing of the Popular Rights Movement, but he soon despaired of the possibility of reforming Japan from within and left for America in 1886, after a period in prison on suspicion of having tried to buy dynamite. He felt that the only hope for change lay abroad, in the possibility of building up external pressure by informing western public opinion of the real state of affairs in the Japan of the mid-1880s: the oppressive government and lack of any effective opposition which lay behind the veneer of westernization.[5]

The influence on Baba of his experiences in Britain was as complex as it was deep; luckily his autobiography and surviving diaries give us some information as to his activities there. He spent his first year in Wiltshire with his four companions, making brief, anonymous appearances in both *Kilvert's Diary* and local newspapers,[6] but for the rest of the time he had lodgings in various parts of London. He seems to have taken his studies seriously, but to have found time for other pursuits. He adopted a stray dog which he found in danger of starving, and was a fairly frequent theatre-goer, with tastes which ranged from Henry Irving in *Richard III* to *Ali Baba*. He also read the political novels of Bulwer Lytton and Disraeli and frequently visited the House of Commons, where he was, of course, able to watch the same Disraeli clashing with his great rival, Gladstone.

Baba's period in London coincided with Gladstone's first cabinet and Disraeli's second, both of which carried out major social reforms. He seems to have been particularly interested in the controversy provoked by the Eastern Question, both inside and outside Parliament. The whole affair, he later recalled, gave him 'every opportunity to observe the benefit of possessing the representative institution for the mass of the people'[7] and moved him so much that a few days after the outbreak of the Russo-Turkish War in April 1877 he confided to his diary that he was 'thinking whether I shall go to Turkey to try fighting because I have never done it'.[8] Baba was also in London when John Stuart Mill died in 1873; the public response to this made a deep impression on him: 'However short a man's life may be, his actions may live long in the memory of his posterity. Tatui Baba admired very much John S. Mill's straightforward and fearless treatment of social prejudices.'[9]

Baba never became deracinated. As his writings, both during and after his stay in Britain, show, he always remained conscious of his Japanese identity. Even though he was not always able to feel proud of Japan, he was always working in what he perceived to be its best interests. On the other hand, his long experience of life in Britain must have produced tensions. In particular, there is strong evidence to suggest that English became a more natural language to him than Japanese, at least in terms of writing. His autobiography, which was probably written more for his own reference than with publication in view, was in English, as were most of his surviving diaries, even those written while he was living in Japan. His Japanese writings, mostly transcriptions of speeches, all underwent revision by other people before they were published, presumably because Baba did not have sufficient confidence in his written Japanese style. Although Baba was famous for his oratorical skills in Japan, one may therefore speculate about the extent to which his long stay in Britain made it difficult for him to communicate with Japanese who did not share his background. Certainly there are hints in his autobiography of frustration in his dealings with Japanese who were less familiar than he was with western ideas and customs; their 'absurdity and ignorance were beyond description'.[10]

Baba's written English is not that of a native speaker, but it is vivid and perfectly comprehensible. His conversational fluency also seems to have been sufficient to allow him some participation in London social life, although it is not clear how far this was because of his personal qualities, and how far he was being lionized as an exotic presence. His diaries suggest that he moved primarily in two, probably overlapping, circles of middle-class liberals. The first circle centred on a prominent Unitarian minister, Moncure D. Conway, and the second on a political pressure group, the National Association for the Promotion of Social Science.

Conway was an American with strong anti-slavery views. He originally arrived in England in 1863, in order to counter Confederate efforts to discredit the Union, but was invited to become minister of the South Place Religious Society, then in Finsbury Place, and remained there for twenty years, until 1884. It is not clear when or how Conway and Baba met, but Baba's diaries show him to have been a frequent guest at the Conway house, and he even merits a brief reference in Conway's autobiography, published in 1904, where for some reason Conway refers to Baba as 'a learned ex-priest and statesman'.[11] This may be merely a lapse of memory on Conway's part, or it may suggest that Baba showed some interest in Conway's religious activities, possibly as a result of Conway's sympathetic attitude to non-Christian religions. A more obvious influence, however, was in the area of public opinion-forming. Conway was noted for his skill in public speaking. He also privately published pamphlets, which he sent to friends and to public figures, and engaged in journalistic activities, in order to spread his political and religious ideas. Baba also published pamphlets, both in Britain and subsequently in the United States; in Japan he made his real impact on the Popular Rights Movement through public-speaking and journalism.

Baba's links with the Social Science Association probably came through a barrister, George Wager Ryalls. A more cloudy figure than Conway, Ryalls also features frequently in Baba's diaries, and presumably acted as his law tutor. From 1873 to 1877 Ryalls was secretary to the Social Science Association, and was probably the person who introduced Baba to it. The Association aimed to provide a bridge between government and informed public opinion, encouraging debate and pressing for reforming legislation in areas such as the legal rights of women, the treatment of criminals, and public health. Although ostensibly politically neutral, it had close ties with the Liberal Party and was at its most influential around the time that Baba was associated with it in the early 1870s. Baba mentions the Association both in his autobiography and in his diaries. The annual congresses, held at different British cities, were impressive affairs, attracting local support and national publicity and attended by local dignitaries and national figures, including many MPs. Baba mentions attending the congresses of 1873 at Norwich and 1875 at Brighton. At Brighton he even spoke, to oppose the opium trade with China and the injustice of the rights of extraterritorial jurisdiction enjoyed by westerners in Japan. These rights were held as a result of clauses in the treaties which Japan had unwillingly signed with Britain and the other western powers in 1958; Baba was also to write two pamphlets in English protesting about these treaties while in Britain, long before they really became a serious issue in Anglo-Japanese diplomatic relations.

From February 1873 Baba also seems to have been a fairly regular attender, always with Ryalls, at the fortnightly sessional meetings of the Association, which were held in London from November to June each year. Among others recorded as present at such sessions are more people whose names appear in Baba's diaries as friends or acquaintances. Worthy of mention, perhaps, is Miss E.A. Manning, who was closely involved in the National Indian Association. Baba seems to have developed some links with this organization too, and this may help to explain the references to India and the (detrimental) effect of British rule which are found in his speeches and writings.

Baba's links with the Social Science Association helped to shape his experience of life in Britain, and inevitably influenced his ideas of what should be done in Japan. The members of the Association were middle class: lawyers, doctors, politicians, businessmen, and women who were active in education and social reform. Reformist but not revolutionary, their basic desire was to improve the efficiency of the status quo. Conscious of a responsibility to society, particularly to those less fortunate than themselves, they believed that it was possible to achieve improvements through the pressure of informed public opinion on government.

Baba was also active in a third social circle, which he was undoubtedly instrumental in forming, a circle composed of Japanese students in London. In the early 1870s he estimated that they numbered about a hundred and he was apparently appalled at the extent to which feudal rivalries were keeping them apart:

> One would imagine that two Japanese meeting in the street of London would warmly grasp each other's hand and inquire after each other. But ... they passed each other as if they did not know to what country each belonged ... they were still the Samurais of different provinces governed by different Daimios ... they thought that it was necessary to treat each student as their enemy unless he belonged to the same clan.[12]

Baba got them to form a society, its object being to hold meetings once a month with speeches or discussions both in Japanese and English, and during at least the second part of his stay in Britain 'devoted his principal time' to its activities.[13] This society was obviously modelled on the Social Science Association, and seems to have been fairly successful; certainly it survived Baba's departure, at least until 1886. This London society in its turn spawned a similar organization in Tokyo, the Kyōsondōshū (Co-existence Society), in which Baba became heavily involved on his return to Japan in 1878. He clearly wanted to encourage freedom of

111

speech and develop popular pressure for reform of the type generated by the Social Science Association. The young western-educated professionals of the Kyōsondōshū, most of whom were in government employ, were an ideal target for his efforts.

Baba's later speeches and writings also demonstrate that he was very much affected by the intellectual climate in mid-Victorian Britain. His political ideals – his belief in freedom and Japan's need for representative government – were founded upon an evolutionary understanding of human development which clearly owed a lot to the ideas of Herbert Spencer and others, such as Walter Bagehot, who gave the development of liberal democratic institutions an important role in human progress.[14]

Baba was not the only intellectual in Meiji Japan to fall under the influence of Spencer's ideas. In Japan, and other parts of Asia, Spencer's scientific analysis of human development was seen as offering a viable framework to those who were trying to construct programmes of development which would raise their countries up to the level of the west. As in Europe and America, his appeal was to those on both sides of the political spectrum; it is well known that in early 1890 the Meiji government even asked him for advice about the pace of political change, and that he warned against the possibly detrimental effect of allowing westerners to live freely among the Japanese. On his return to Japan, Baba was to use his liberal interpretation of evolution to launch an effective attack on Katō Hiroyuki, president of Tokyo Imperial University, who had invoked Spencer in a controversial attempt to refute the theory of natural rights.[15]

Baba was influenced by Spencer to the extent of expounding his ideas in a similar way. Typically he would begin a speech or a longer piece of writing with a scientific observation, which he would use as a device to illustrate the more general social or political principle which he wished to explain, and would introduce more such analogies as necessary. In arguing for the key role of political freedom in social progress, for example, he drew on Spencer's famous analogy between human societies and animal organisms. The members of a society interacted in the same way as the organs within the human body and, like an organism, a human society would become more differentiated and complex as its development advanced. There was, however, one crucial difference between human societies and animal organisms: while the controlling thoughts and sensations in animal organisms were concentrated in the brain, in a society they were diffuse. Moreover, while the object of the higher animals, such as man, lay in the domain of the senses and the intellect, societies existed to enable man to enjoy his natural freedom.[16]

Baba was particularly concerned with placing the recent political history of Britain, France, and Japan into an evolutionary framework of development. He took a more optimistic view of the results of abrupt revolutionary change

112

than Spencer, who saw revolutions as causing disorder, and contributing to dissolution rather than evolution. Baba, however, saw political upheavals as a natural part of progress. The extraordinary upheavals of both the French Revolution and the Meiji Restoration had been necessary to remove extraordinary obstacles in the way of evolutionary change. It was the revolutionaries, not the conservatives who tried to suppress them, who were really working to improve society.[17] Evolution was the inexorable force of progress in history; governments ignored popular pressure for political change at their peril:

> When man, through the natural process of evolution, burns with desire for equality of rights and plans to expand freedom and rights, governments must give way to this tide of events, and change. This is the law of the strong prevailing over the weak, of the struggle for survival.[18]

Ultimately, however, Baba agreed with Spencer that smooth change was more desirable than periodic violent upheavals. He therefore looked at the ways in which the forces of dissolution and evolution might be harnessed so that abrupt change would no longer be necessary. Inevitably he decided on a British-type system in which evolution and dissolution were kept in equilibrium through a system of representative government, with conservative and progressive parties keeping each other in balance, and with freedom of both speech and information.[19] At one point he even argued that to bring about universal male suffrage was in fact to introduce 'the survival of the fittest by peaceful means'.[20]

In this way, Baba interpreted and developed the ideas which he had encountered primarily in Britain, so that they both agreed with and justified his own political principles, and could also be applied directly to the situation in which Japan found itself. Freedom of thought, speech and action played an essential role in his vision of the smooth evolutionary development of man, as did the existence of a stable, organized society, and the willingness to cast aside any custom which had outgrown its usefulness and was preventing further growth. However, as the Japanese government of the late 1870s onwards responded to the growing political consciousness of the country by imposing progressively stronger restrictions on freedom of speech, and as these policies had a growing impact on the fledgling political parties themselves, it is not surprising that Baba experienced increasing difficulty in reconciling his vision of the future with the trends that seemed, in reality, to be developing, and that he was eventually driven to the conclusion that Japan could not be reformed from within.

As well as this general debt to the intellectual climate of mid-Victorian Britain, Baba also made use of concrete references to Britain in his speeches and writings. He praised the balance of the political system, which meant that conservative and progressive forces held each other in check. This had enabled Britain to avoid the political extremes which had caused so much suffering in France.[21] He also praised the emphasis which British politicians gave to the state of public opinion – in Britain itself, and, when foreign policy was involved, in other countries too.[22] On the other hand, he pointed to the bad state of employer–employee relations – the exploitation of labour by capital despite the existence of trade-union legislation – and the even worse situation of the agricultural tenant, particularly in Ireland.[23] He also had observations to make about India. In 1873, Mori Arinori, a leading Japanese 'westernizer' who was at that time Japan's representative in the United States, suggested that the Japanese language would be unable to cope with the linguistic demands being made upon it by Japan's adoption of the techniques and institutions of modern western civilization. He therefore proposed its abolition and replacement by English. Interestingly enough, Baba strongly disagreed. He replied by producing the first English-language grammar of Japanese, in order to demonstrate that it was just as good a language as any other. In the Preface, he warned that if English was selected as the language of education in Japan this would have the disastrous effect of preventing communication between the educated and the uneducated, as had happened in India.[24] Elsewhere, he refuted the claim that Britain was not oppressing India by emphasizing that Indians had no role in governing their country, and revealing that while in Britain he had heard Indians saying that if Britain and Russia were at war, they would support Russia.[25]

Baba's attitude to Britain was therefore mixed. His idealism was offended by the contradiction between the image of Britain, with its ideals of justice and civilization, and the way in which these ideals tended to be flouted in practice. Nowhere is this clearer than in the two pamphlets which he published while in Britain, in an attempt to awaken British opinion to the uncivilized behaviour of many British merchants in Japan and the injustice of the extraterritorial clauses in treaties between the two countries which allowed such behaviour to go unpunished.[26] The fact that these pamphlets were written in 1875 and 1876, just after Baba's short trip back to Japan, suggests that he was acting in response to the shock of what he had discovered there. Certainly the first pamphlet in particular, 'The English in Japan', contains a powerful attack on British hypocrisy, in which rhetorical techniques are used to withering effect. The emotion is such that one is also tempted to conclude that he had made an additional, even more painful, discovery: that he could not enjoy the sort of social standing with the British in Japan that the treatment he had enjoyed from his liberal acquaintances in London had led him to expect. Thus, after the passage quoted at the beginning of this essay, in which he painted an ironically rosy image of Britain and its civilizing role in the world, he went on to say that this vision had been 'blasted' by what he actually experienced of the behaviour of the British in Japan:

> they are very noble-minded philanthropists according to their professions. But look at what these very noble-minded philanthropists do.
>
> They take every opportunity to grasp gains from the inexperience of our people, and they make no scruple to deceive the ignorant. . . . When they promote their interest at the expense of our nation through some means of deception, they never appear to feel any moral remorse; on the contrary, they boast and laugh at their dupes, saying, 'These Japanese are very green.' I often heard these remarks made by Englishmen who perhaps think it justifiable to cheat any one when they have the opportunity.[27]

Yet, despite the pain and indignation caused by the way in which the British government had taken advantage of the relative weakness of Japan, Baba still felt able to appeal 'to the opinion of the British public in England, who are always ready to judge impartially, and are justly distinguished for their love of "fair play"'.[28] He stressed that Japan was an independent nation which should be treated by Britain as an equal. While there were inevitable differences between English and Japanese law, this did not mean that Japan should be denied the 'indisputable right of an independent nation to have sole jurisdiction over all those who reside within the territory'.[29]

The pamphlets were printed by Trübner, the London publishers, at Baba's own expense, and distributed by him to friends and notable public figures, such as Gladstone and Disraeli. It is not clear how much, or how little, impact they had on anyone apart from Baba's circle of friends in Britain;[30] if anything their tone, particularly that of the first one, probably caused offence. The only review that seems to have appeared even interprets 'The English in Japan' as an attack on Christianity.[31] Before his death, however, Baba felt able to reflect with satisfaction on the significance of his appeal to British public opinion as an independent Japanese citizen rather than as a government official.[32]

In his last year in London, Baba was clearly feeling low. Physically he was unwell, mentally he was unsure of his future course. He knew that he would have to return to Japan sooner or later, but he did not know what would await him there. When a Japanese friend returned to Japan in March 1877 Baba noted in his diary, 'I think Kikuchi [Dairoku] will be disappointed in Japan, especially with the society.'[33] In May, however, he wrote, 'Am I happy? I do not think so. Shall I think the present was happy when I look back in ten years hence. [sic].'[34] Then, in January 1878, there occurred a dramatic incident which took the need to make a decision out of Baba's hands.

Baba seems to have enjoyed intellectual confrontations with his fellow Japanese in London; presumably this was part of his policy of encouraging the development of freedom of speech. He became involved in a quarrel with Manabe Kaisaku, one of the Tosa samurai in whose company he had first come to Britain, and whose abilities he much despised. In the presence of other people, an infuriated Manabe spat into Baba's face. Soon after this, Baba visited Manabe's lodgings in Notting Hill and proposed that they should go to France, so that he could obtain satisfaction for the insult done to him, in the form of a duel. When Manabe refused to take this proposal seriously, Baba picked up a knife which happened to be lying nearby, and cut Manabe about the head to the extent that he seems to have started bleeding fairly copiously. He then sobered up and went with Manabe to give himself up at the local police station. Baba was brought to trial, but given a conditional discharge in recognition of his poor state of health and his stated intention now of returning to Japan. He never saw Britain again, although he constantly conjured up its image in his speeches and writings.

Back in Japan in May 1878, Baba threw himself into activities designed to raise the level of political consciousness of the Japanese people. Using the Kyōsondōshū as his base, he started a series of public lectures on a variety of social, legal and political topics. For a time, he was successful and the Kyōsondōshū flourished, attracting the support of a wide circle of Meiji intellectuals. But his activities depended on an atmosphere which encouraged freedom of speech, and therefore on a stable political situation. Three days after Baba's return to Japan, however, Ōkubo Toshimichi, one of the more progressive of the government leaders, was assassinated; the government ban on public speech-making by government employees in May of the following year was a virtual deathblow to the Kyōsondōshū, and the situation went from bad to worse, with more general restrictions on political speeches and political groups in 1880, and the ousting from the cabinet of Ōkuma Shigenobu, the other leading progressive, in October 1881. Baba was thus driven to take up a more radical position, and to be increasingly outspoken in his criticism of the government. This in turn led to his being banned from speaking on political topics in the Tokyo area for six months in 1883. His relationship with other political activists was also somewhat uneasy. He played an important role in the formation of the Jiyūtō (Liberal Party) but resigned after a public disagreement with Itagaki Taisuke, its leader, and in any case had a low opinion of the organizers of the party outside Tokyo, who seemed to him ignorant and narrow-minded.

Baba is interesting as a case study of the young western-educated Meiji intellectual. Despite the young age at which he went to Britain, and the fact that English became his natural written language, he never lost a strong sense of Japanese identity, and never argued that Japan should adopt western culture wholesale. In his political speeches and writings in Japan, he frequently drew on his knowledge of Britain, but, as we have seen, this was not always to praise. Neither did he adopt a strategy of criticizing Britain only when in Japan. He was willing to criticize Britain to the British, and Japan to his fellow Japanese. The more he knew of Britain, the more he

116

knew of its imperfections; this enabled him to criticize Britain, and must also have encouraged his positive feelings about Japan. On the other hand, his knowledge of the way in which the British political system worked, the important role of the opposition party in the two-party system, and of pressure groups such as the Social Science Association, must also have made him painfully aware of the gap between the general level of political consciousness in mid-Victorian Britain and early Meiji Japan.

While in Britain, and for a time after his return to Japan, Baba felt, at least on the surface, that the gap could be, and was being, closed, and that he had a significant role to play, but the harsh realities of Japan in the mid-1880s put paid to his idealism. Baba had spent so long in Britain that he probably understood the British political system better than any other Japanese then living. But he had also spent so long away from Japan, at a time when both he and Japan were at crucial periods of development, that it was difficult for him to accept, and work within, the Japanese system. It was also difficult for him to communicate his views to, and understand the viewpoint of, those who did not have the benefit of his experiences. Unable to act effectively in Japan, he abandoned all possibility of working for reform from within, and embarked on the lonely path in America which led to his tragic early death.

FURTHER READING

Nobutoshi Hagihara, *Baba Tatsui* (in Japanese), Tokyo: Chūō Kōronsha, 1967.

Nobutoshi Hagihara, 'Baba Tatsui: an early Japanese liberal', *St Anthony's Papers*, 14 (1963), pp. 121–43

——*Baba Tatsui zenshu*, Tokyo: Iwanami, 1987–8. The four volume complete works of Baba's writings in both English and Japanese, as well as other related materials.

8

TWO PIGGOTTS: SIR FRANCIS TAYLOR PIGGOTT (1852–1925) AND MAJOR GENERAL F.S.G. PIGGOTT (1883–1966)

Carmen Blacker

F.T. Piggott, later Sir Francis Piggott, went to Japan in 1888, at the express invitation of Itō Hirobumi, to act as legal adviser to the Japanese government on the matter of the forthcoming Constitution. He stayed in Japan for three years, became a personal friend of Itō, and found time, in the intervals of his legal work, to collect material for a book on Japanese music, another on Japanese gardens, and yet another on Japanese design motifs.

Of his son F.S.G. Piggott it may be said that a deep emotional attachment to Japan was the dominant commitment of his life. His devotion to Japan was the 'thread' which ran from his earliest memories as a child, and which, though temporarily 'broken' during the war, was picked up again immediately afterwards and held unwaveringly until his death in 1966.[1]

Both Piggotts were pillars, not to say *tokobashira*, of the Japan Society. FT indeed was credited with the title of founder and earliest member of the Society. FSG was the guiding energy behind its revival after the war.

In 1887 Mr F.T. Piggott was a barrister of the Middle Temple, the author of *The Law of Torts* and other works on English law. When the Meiji government asked for an English lawyer to be sent to Japan to advise the prime minister on points of English law which might bear on the future Constitution of Japan, it was he who was selected. He set sail with his family forthwith, and arrived in Yokohama in January 1888 to find that already a new house, in foreign style, had been specially built in Azabu Ichibeimachi to accommodate him. Here the Piggott family remained for the three years of their stay in Tokyo. They had a brougham, with a *bettō*, and took an active part in the life of the Rokumeikan, playing tennis and *dakyū*, and becoming skilled kite fliers.[2]

In responding to Itō's invitation, F.T. joined the ranks of the three thousand or so *o-yatoi-gaikokujin*, or foreign employees, more familiarily known as *yatoi*, recruited by the Meiji government during the forty-four years from 1868 to 1912. These were the men, and the scattering of women, whom Basil Hall Chamberlain called the 'creators of New Japan'; the engineers, technicians, language tutors, music teachers, railway and shipbuilding experts, military and naval consultants, financial and legal advisors, whom the government called in from Britain, America, Germany and France to advise and supervise in the creation of the new regime. Thus it came about that the Japanese Navy, the army, the educational system, the banks, the codification of the law, medical instruction, posts, telegraphs, railways, improved mining methods, prison reform, chemical laboratories, the abolition of torture, the Yokosuka dockyard, were all for an initial season in the hands of British, American, German or French 'advisers'.

Nearly half the number were British, and three-quarters were employed during the first fifteen years of the period. The recruitment of so many foreign experts posed a formidable burden on the budget of the Meiji government, which footed the bill directly and entirely. The salaries paid to these people were usually larger than those paid to top Japanese civil servants, generals and admirals, and in two cases larger even than that of the prime minister. The investment was, however, expected to yield quick returns. The *yatoi* were not expected to stay in Japan for the rest of their lives on their ample salaries. They were to see that their skills were passed on to Japanese successors who as quickly as possible were due to replace them. As Chamberlain put it, 'it takes longer to get a Japanese educated abroad than to engage a foreigner ready made'. The government in calling in these experts could be likened to a wise patient who summons the best available physician to administer the marvellous cure which the patient requires. But, the medicine administered, the physician is not afterwards detained. The patient is left to stand on his own feet.[3]

FT before he reached Japan had imagined himself helping to draft the Constitution of the country, preparing alternative forms of articles and engaging in learned discussion as to which form would best suit the Japanese scene. The reality, he recalled, proved very different, and far less inspiring than he had imagined. All he was required to do was to answer a series of abstract questions, rather like an examination paper, sent to the office every morning by the secretaries working on the draft. The questions were often elementary, but none the less difficult to explain. How to convey to a 'logical people' like the Japanese, the mysteries of our unwritten Constitution, where, for example, the Sovereign has the right of veto but may not constitutionally exercise it, and where money bills are passed only with the consent of the Lords, though it would be unconstitutional for them to withhold their consent? There was no doubt that Itō was interested in the British Constitution, and was anxious to discover how much of it could reasonably be embodied in the Japanese draft. He it was who had specifically requested that an English lawyer be sent to explain the points which were still unclear to him.

But he made it clear in the first of his many interviews with FT in short detached sentences uttered in intervals of smoking, that the difficulties of fitting the British Constitution into the concise written articles then being drafted were so great that only the broadest principles would prove helpful and relevant. This was disappointing news; but it was at once clear to FT nevertheless that it would be honourable and congenial to work under him, and that there was 'a glamour about his presence' which accounted for some of the enormous influence he wielded. 'I know you English well, how you all love work', he said. 'I expect you to work and give me all the help in your power.'[4]

In fact it was to be French and German influence, rather than British, which was to prove dominant in the making of the Constitution. Boissonade on the French side and Hermann Roesler on the German, competed for a hearing in the Foreign Ministry and the Cabinet. To F.T., however, it was never made clear until the very end that no foreigner was to be allowed any hand at all in the drafting of the Constitution. It was to be entirely the work of the Japanese themselves. FT, like the other foreign advisers, was there in the capacity of a 'living reference book'.[5]

Final assessments of the Meiji Constitution of 1889 do not attribute much to British influence, and it is difficult to assess what effect may have resulted from FT's answers to the daily questionnaires presented to him in his office. It is sad too that so few papers and diaries survive which might tell us more of his views on the final product.

A unique album compiled by FT has, however, been preserved, and is now in the Diet Library. It contains all the visiting cards, invitations to balls, soirées and banquets at the Rokumeikan, to garden parties, to Imperial cherry viewings and performances of *bugaku*. It contains the menus, always in French, for the banquets, featuring ten or eleven courses. Visiting cards were left by Counts Itō, Okuma and Oyama, by General Yamagata Aritomo and Vice-Admiral Enomoto, with a huge red card from the Chinese minister, Li Shu-chang. All the foreign scholars of Japanese called, for there are cards from W.G. Aston, B.H. Chamberlain, Ernest Fenollosa, Sir Edwin Arnold and Captain F. Brinkley. Scarcely had the family settled in before they were invited to dinner with Count Itō, to a ball at the Rokumeikan and a garden party at Count Okuma's 'Country Residence Waseda'. Sir Edwin Arnold gave a reading, in aid of the Tokyo Relief Fund, on 27 June 1890. Le Ministre d'Autriche Hongrie invited them to dine on 29 May. The Bachelors' Ball gave a 'Fancy Dress cotton-crêpe Ball', Polonaise at 9.15 p.m. Mr Percival Lowell invited them to the Ueno Race Course to see a game of Dakiu or Japanese 'Polo'. The English ladies of Yokohama were at Home with Dancing at the Public Hall. The Minister of the United States gave a Musical At Home, at which Mr Van de Polder sang Verdi's *Un Ballo en Maschera*. Le Ministre de la Marine et la Comptesse Saigo invited them 'de venir passer la soirée au Roku-Mei-Kwan le jeudi 22 November 1888 à 9 heures. On dansera. Un train special partira de Shimbashi à 1 heure du Matin.' Mrs Hugh Fraser gave a Christmas Party in 1890 at which twenty-one courses or dishes were listed on the menu, including turkey with truffles, sirloin of beef, lobster salad, plum pudding, plum cake and orange jelly, *Punch au champagne* and *Pudding Diplomate* featured on many menus. The album testifies to the sparkling social life which FT, on the generous salary paid to him as a senior *yatoi* in the 1880s, enjoyed during the three years of his stay in Tokyo.[6]

What has come down to us is in fact the aesthetic by-product of his three-year stay in Japan. An accomplished painter, musician and an apparently compulsive writer – he wrote two novels in later years under the pseudonym of Hope Dawlish, and during his time as chief justice of Hong Kong he was said to be afflicted with a *furor scribendi* – he found time during his leisure hours to write what is in fact the first comprehensive account in English of Japanese music and musical instruments.

The Music and Musical Instruments of Japan, 1893 and 1909, is a remarkable compendium of Japanese musical history and lore, derived both from written authorities including the eighteenth-century encyclopedia *Wakan Sansai Zue* (the section on musical instruments), and from a certain Mrs Maeo who taught him to play the *shamisen*. There are sections on the 'musical degrees' awarded to blind musicians by the Yoshida family, and on the strange musical monopolies which ordained that the teaching of the Sō-no-koto should be entirely in the hands of the Yotsutsuji family. All the varieties of Jōruri-bushi are enumerated and described, likewise the varieties of *nagauta*, *kouta* and *Bon-odoriuta*. There is a rigorous analysis of the Japanese scale, and of the ten different tunings of the *koto* which produce variations in the scale. All the varieties of *koto*, *biwa* and *fue* are carefully described together with drums, gongs and even the bugle called *charumera* used by itinerant vendors of sweets. The glissades used in *koto* playing, we learn, are called *hikiren* and *uraren*, and a diagram is given showing the seventeen pipes of the *shō*, with their various names, lengths and notes.[7]

All this is leavened with personal reactions to Japanese music of an oddly intemperate kind. For the *hichiriki* in particular FT had a special loathing. It was the 'most villainous of vile-sounding instruments' which emitted 'gruesome and unearthly sounds'. 'How the *shakuhachi* can have given pleasure to people who delighted in the gruesome dronings and wailings of the *hichiriki* is a question of musical pathology not given to us to understand.' As for Japanese singing, it was a 'mere horrid sound, disfigured by excruciating quarter-tones'. It was a paradox that a people with so sensitive a musical ear that they could faultlessly tune a thirteen-stringed *koto* could tolerate such slurs and slides. It is a book full of vigour, as well as of erudition.[8]

The Decorative Art of Japan (1910), an elegant example of book production in late Meiji Japan, is a similarly vigorous study of the patterns executed in the woodwork of the temples of Nikkō and Shiba, where every square foot of available space was 'smothered in ornament'. Where most visitors merely gaped, FT, with Owen Jones's famous *Grammar of Ornament* in mind, observed and analysed. The resulting book is a fascinating exposition of the principles underlying the intricate diaper designs, the lattices, lozenges, zigzags and angles of grace. In lattice work in particular he believed the Japanese to have evolved a unique series of designs, a natural progression from simple to subtly intricate, in which 'cunningly balanced distribution of light and shade' played an important but unobtrusive part. The 'charmed circles' too, in which heraldic *mon*, composed of leaves, clouds, waves and flowers, are confined, are fully treated. In a final chapter he argues that all key-patterns originate, not in ancient Greece as was prevalently supposed, but in the Chinese *Pa kua* pattern of broken and unbroken lines.[9]

On leaving Japan he was appointed procureur and advocate-general in Mauritius in 1893, and afterwards became chief justice in Hong Kong until 1912. He revisited Japan several times before he died in 1925.

His son F.S.G. Piggott, commissioned at the age of 17 into the Royal Engineers and twice military attaché in Tokyo, has been described as the most *shinnichi* (pro-Japanese) English gentleman to be generated by the Anglo-Japanese Alliance. The great aim and object of his life was to promote warm and friendly 'Anglo-Japanese relations', and 'mutual understanding and goodwill between our two countries'. The best thing Britain ever did in his eyes was to form the Anglo-Japanese Alliance in 1902, The worst mistake it ever made was to repudiate the Alliance, under American pressure, at the Washington Conference in 1921. The Japanese understandably felt rebuffed, isolated and humiliated, and no explanations ever atoned in their eyes for this act of betrayal. The disastrous worsening of 'relations' which occurred through the 1920s and 1930s could be traced to this single simple cause.

His devotion to Japan began during his father's three-year stint in Tokyo. He arrived at the age of 4, and for the next three years passed what appeared in retrospect to be an idyllically happy childhood in mid-Meiji Tokyo. The bright side of Japan, so entrancing to many foreigners at the time who saw in it a vision of an innocent, unsullied paradise, threatened by nothing of its own making but only by the dark satanic engines introduced from the west, inspired him for the rest of his life. Only 'understand' the Japanese, he believed, and their traditional virtues of loyalty, trustworthiness, simplicity, courtesy and valour would blossom into warm friendships and enrich the rightful amity between the two countries. The key to this 'understanding' was not difficult to find, though it required patience and hard work. He was sure that he himself had found this key, and that it was his duty to show others how to find and turn it.

He returned to Japan in 1904 at the start of the siege of Port Arthur, as a lieutenant in the Royal Engineers and as one of the first of the new language officers, required to learn the language in order the better to observe and instruct the Japanese army.

In 1904 the approved methods of learning Japanese differed markedly from those of today. There were virtually no textbooks or grammars, and such dictionaries as existed made little provision for colloquial usages. Nor were there any English teachers who might explain matters in more familiar terms than could a native speaker. Nor again was the 'homestay', so important a part of the modern student's training, for a moment considered possible. To expect a European student to live with a Japanese family, to be absorbed into the routine of that family, to sit on the floor without chair or table, and above all to subsist on Japanese food, which was considered almost inedible and in any case to satiate without nourishing, was wildly out of the question.

The most sensible method was rather to assign to every language officer a suitable Japanese teacher, and set them to live together in a comfortably furnished house, equipped with a proper staff of cook and maids. The language officer must as much as possible avoid the society of his compatriots, associate only with Japanese, and speak only Japanese.

FSG was accordingly allotted Mr Sano Yoshitsugu, a 'samurai of Mito', and together they settled down in a house with six rooms in addition to *genkan*, kitchen, bathroom and veranda, for a rent of 24 yen a month. The resident staff included an excellent cook, Yoshikawa-san, whom FSG quickly trained to provide a different English breakfast for every day of the week. Sunday was sausages, Monday poached eggs, Tuesday omelette, Wednesday kedgeree, Thursday fried eggs and bacon, Friday boiled eggs and Saturday kidneys. Six years later, when FSG returned to Japan a married man and re-engaged Yoshikawa-san, the routine was unquestioningly resumed; nothing his bride could do or say would persuade him to alter the Monday menu to sardines.[10]

To the end of his life, indeed, FSG's devotion to Japan never extended to its cuisine, and he remained unpractised in the use of chopsticks. *Sushi, sashimi* and *misoshiru* were to remain caviar to the future general. There were periodic exams for language officers, and these F.S.G., under Mr Sano's tutelage, passed with acclaim. He quickly acquired, during this tour of duty and the next, a remarkable and elegant mastery of all the refinements of Meiji-spoken Japanese. He could speak with appropriate courtesy to almost anyone throughout the complex hierarchy of Japanese society, and in consequence began to form the network of friendships and associations which were to remain *kokoro no takara*, the treasures of his heart, for the rest of his life.

Nor was it only the spoken language in which he excelled. By 1911, his third visit, his mastery of written Japanese was such that in his spare time he was able to compile his *Elements of Sōsho*, the first work on the cursive script to be published in any European language.[11] The book was reviewed by Basil Hall Chamberlain in the *Transactions of the Asiatic Society of Japan* with words of high praise. 'The Japanese cursive script,' he wrote, 'is perhaps the hardest subject which it is given to mortal man to tackle. Those whom circumstances force to grapple with it feel like convicts condemned to hard labour in a Siberian mine. Nothing can turn their misery into joy. . . . But

Captain Piggott's volume, the result of his own laborious days, at any rate now sheds a ray of light upon their gloom. They will stumble a little less henceforth ... even sometimes feel a sort of enthusiasm for their never-ending task.'[12]

Meanwhile his first two tours of duty coincided with some of the most dramatic events in Meiji history. The Japanese victory over Russia seemed to bring not only new pride and confidence to Japan, but also new enthusiasm for Britain, which had supported Japan as a loyal ally in her hour of need. FSG was invited to tour the Manchurian battlefields at the end of hostilities, and wherever he went, through Dairen, Port Arthur, Mukden, the Yalu River, he was overwhelmed by the warm affection shown to him, as a representative of Britain, by Japanese officers and civilians. In 1906, too, when the Garter Mission arrived in Japan, there were 'almost incredible demonstrations of enthusiasm up and down Japan', the Union Flag being seen on an equality with the Rising Sun in remote mountain villages.[13]

He was in Tokyo also when the death of the Emperor Meiji occurred, followed by the suicide of General Nogi, and he witnessed the funeral of the Emperor on 13 September 1912. 'The most impressive ceremony I had ever seen', he recalled forty-three years later, the enormous crowd utterly silent, the only sound to be heard being the the creaking of the ox wagon bearing the catafalque as it passed down the sand-strewn streets.[14]

After 1913 he was not to return to Japan for nine years; but he was heartened by the staunch support given by Japan to Britain during the First World War. In 1921 he had the painful experience of witnessing, as a member of the Military Section at the Washington Conference on disarmament, the abrogation by Britain of the Anglo-Japanese Alliance. Mr Balfour, who had been a member of the cabinet which had negotiated the Alliance, told him that having to end it was like killing his own child. FSG on his part warned Mr Balfour that the Alliance was in Japanese eyes an indissoluble marriage bond; they would be deeply injured at a rejection which seemed like a divorce with no unfaithfulness on their side to justify it. They would not only 'lose face'; they would see Britain's act as an example of the high crime of ingratitude. American pressure, however, left no alternative. The Alliance was ended, and in FSG's eyes the later catastrophic worsening of 'relations' proceeded straight and simply from that one cause.[15]

He returned to Japan for two more spells of duty, 1922–6 and 1936–9, both times as military attaché at the Tokyo Embassy. The year 1922 was enlivened by the visit to Japan of the Prince of Wales and Lord Louis Mountbatten, whom FSG, now a lieutenant-colonel, accompanied on their tour. An attack of jaundice early in their visit proved an unexpected blessing; for it ensured that he was absent on the occasion when, after a banquet given to the party in the Nijōjō, the royal guest kicked a water melon through one of the exquisitely and pricelessly painted *fusuma*. FSG's nicely balanced dual loyalties thus escaped being put to the test.[16]

During his last two tours of duty he had unrivalled opportunities through his network of personal friendships and his contacts, both civil and military, with most of the leaders of Japan, to observe changes in the army and the country. He was apparently unable, however, to perceive any warning signs of a gathering storm. Relations, he realized, had worsened, but this was a natural reaction on the part of the Japanese to their sense of *koritsu*, or isolation, after the dissolution of the Alliance. He was apparently completely unaware of the ominous signs of the rise of ultranationalism, of totalitarian military rule, of the aberrant Shinto cult of the emperor.

His autobiography is accordingly silent on such subjects as the rape of Nanking, the takeover of the army by fascist ideologies, the encroaching myth of Japanese racial superiority, 'government by assassination' and the overthrow of the rule of law by army officers who believed that their proximity to the 'Imperial mind' gave them the right to determine values.

Even after his return to England in 1939, FSG continued to believe that all would ultimately be well, and that mutual goodwill would soon be restored. He applauded Sir Robert Craigie when, in October of that year, he declared that of the current misunderstandings between Britain and Japan, 70 per cent were nonsense, based on uninformed prejudice, 20 per cent were genuine misunderstandings, and only 10 per cent presented any real difficulty.[17]

To the very last, indeed, the 'shadow' side of Japan continued to be invisible to him. During the autumn of 1941 he kindly agreed to give me Japanese lessons twice a week. I would bicycle over to his house at Ewhurst where, in a study of military tidiness but filled with fascinating books and photographs, he set me to read the primary school *tokuhon*, to work through a long forgotten grammar, and to practise calligraphy, in which he had lost none of his old skill and elegance. As the autumn advanced, relations deteriorated, until in the middle of November the Konoe Cabinet fell and General Tōjō became prime minister. No one could be worse, was the general cry. But General Piggott was undeterred in his optimism. It was quite wrong to say that Tōjō was pro-Axis, he declared. He was simply pro-Japanese. Never treat Japanese as you might Germans; give them the special understanding they require, and you will have the staunchest, most trustworthy friends in the world. And he would pause in the reading and writing exercises to recollect 'very Japanese words', such as *yasegaman*, or *giri*, which he described as 'a self-imposed moral obligation with a sentimental impulse', and instances of Japanese nobility and loyalty in personal relations.

The attack on Pearl Harbor in December was accordingly the more terrible a blow to him because it came as an incomprehensible shock. He could not believe, for some time, that he had been wrong. But it was not long before he rallied and, realizing that he numbered among the half dozen or so Englishmen who could read and speak the language of the new enemy, he offered his services as instructor at the School of Oriental and African Studies in London. Here crash courses in Japanese were being hastily devised, with inadequate textbooks and home-made teaching materials, both for service personnel and for certain 'bright boys' wrested from their studies of Latin and Greek and set to learn Japanese instead.

He was appointed senior lecturer, and accordingly took his place alongside the rather motley group of teachers, Japanese ex-journalists, Canadian *nisei* sergeants, the dazzling Mrs Aiko Clark, assembled to turn the young men dressed as army privates and naval ratings into capable translators and interrogators.[18] Of his relations with the famous class known as Translators V, which has continued to meet for an annual dinner ever since, Louis Allen recalled that his ramrod military figure presented an odd contrast with the 'bunch of scruffy private soldiers, still in their teens, all of them loathing the army and every aspect of military existence'. He was a strict disciplinarian, never hesitating to complain to higher authority over instances of lateness or frivolity, but kindly, nevertheless, when any of them proved incapable of learning Japanese and were consequently RTU, returned to unit. 'Even Hobbs couldn't bowl', he would commiserate.

All the existing textbooks proving useless, he resorted to Rose-Innes' *Character Dictionary*, taking the class systematically through the book and awarding star ratings to each character and its cluster of compounds. They found afterwards, as I did myself, that what he taught them of permanent value was to 'accumulate subterranean layers of meanings and compounds which did in the end pay dividends, improbable as that seemed at the time'. Rose-Innes (together with *Kenkyusha*) accordingly went to Burma with its owners, where its covers acquired a patina of fungi from tropical humidity and where the four-starred words played their part in subsequent dealings with captured prisoners of war.[19]

The war at last over, FSG devoted much time in trying to save his old friend General Homma, 'who loved England more than any Japanese officer', from execution, and to lighten the sentence of imprisonment imposed at the insistence of the Russians on his other old friend Mr Shigemitsu Mamoru. He quickly made arrangements for the revival of the Japan Society, and ordered me to edit the first number of the *Bulletin*, for which the ration of paper was four pages or eight sides.

He made one more triumphant visit to Japan, in 1955 at the invitation of Mr Shigemitsu, then foreign minister. He and his daughter Juliet were met at Haneda Airport by Mr Shigemitsu and a hundred old friends, sons of old friends, and grandsons and daughters of old friends. They stayed in the Imperial Hotel, were invited to a tea party with the Emperor and Empress, to whom he found himself able to converse with all his old skill, to a dinner party given by the Crown Prince, and to a lunch party given by Princess Chichibu. He paid his respects at the tomb of the Emperor Meiji, and at the tomb of Itō, his father's friend, at Omori. He had dinner with Mr Yoshida, surrounded by dogs, at Oiso. A hundred members of the Tokyo Tennis Club sang 'For he's a jolly good fellow!' The war vanished. It was true that there were more cars in Tokyo, and that the three bronze statues of Yamagata, Oyama and Terauchi outside the Diet had been replaced by those of 'three unclothed young women' of doubtful origin. But he was convinced, nevertheless, that 'the old virtues of courtesy, cheerfulness and industry' were even more pronounced than before, and that, best of all, there still remained a latent feeling of respect for Britain which only required nourishing to blossom once more into the spirit of the heyday of the Alliance.

He returned from this trip, he told the Japan Society, feeling like the wayfarer in Verse 6 of Psalm 126, who goes forth sorrowing, bearing good seed, but comes back rejoicing, bearing sheaves.[20]

He died in 1966, before the face of Japan changed so much that he might have been forced to notice that some of the old landmarks were gone. 'I was given the task of helping to re-establish mutual trust and confidence,' he wrote; 'this task, to the best of my ability and with all my strength, I have tried to accomplish.'[21]

9

AN AMUSED GUEST IN ALL: BASIL HALL CHAMBERLAIN (1850–1935)

Richard Bowring

> To have lived through the transition stage of modern Japan makes a man feel preternaturally old; for here he is in modern times, with the air full of talk about bicycles and bacilli and 'spheres of influence', and yet he can himself distinctly remember the Middle Ages.

> *Things Japanese* (5th rev.edn, 1905)

For the student of Meiji Japan, this is surely the most memorable of all beginnings. Here, in a carefully crafted sentence that was reworked for every new edition, Chamberlain embarked upon his own 'attempt at an interpretation', expressing a sense of the momentous with that disarming lightness of touch that he used so often to good effect. At first it seems a strange way for a scholar to approach the task, to potter here and there among the bric-a-brac, but it reminds us that Chamberlain was, after all, that kind of gifted amateur who gave the phrase 'English gentleman' its substance. 'The title', he writes, 'cost us much cogitation.' Everywhere the signs of studied insouciance, as if an undoubted sharpness of wit, intellect and tongue could not possibly be allowed to show. It is easy to see how he soon gained a reputation as an archetypal gentleman-scholar, that Confucian role that the English were quick to use to best advantage. He inspired great respect and reverence in his students; and famous students they turned out to be: with such famous scholars as Ueda Kazutoshi (Mannen), Haga Yaichi and Okakura Yoshisaburō among them. It was a role that seems to have come so naturally that one is slightly surprised to find that Chamberlain himself never lived in the England that he left at the age of 6. Brought up by grandparents in Versailles, with equal fluency in French and English and at home with German, Spanish, Latin and Greek by his late teens, Chamberlain was a cosmopolitain, at home everywhere and nowhere.

128

The story that emerges from this period is that of a sickly youth with bad eyesight and chronic bronchitis, both mentioned so often that one tends to suspect a degree of wilfulness about it all. The letters that he was to write from Tokyo to Lafcadio Hearn, who was living on the Japan Sea coast, would constantly harp upon the same subjects – bad health and the dreadful weather – and yet he was to outlive most of his contemporaries. Study at Oxford and work at Barings were eventually rejected in favour of that doctor's panacea, travel, and he arrived in Japan, surely more by accident than by design, in May 1873. He was 23.

As a natural linguist, he plunged straight into learning Japanese, both spoken and written forms. Soon after his arrival he was offered an appointment teaching English at the Naval Academy, a post which he maintained with the occasional break for foreign travel from 1874 to 1882. As a foreign employee (*oyatoi gaikokujin*) he was extremely well paid, with a free house and a servant thrown in, and a teaching load that can hardly be described as onerous. As was the case with those in the diplomatic corps, this allowed him plenty of time for academic and other pursuits. Visits to the Noh theatre appear to have been one of his chief delights, but it was in the area of scholarship that he was to make his mark.

The academic life of the time revolved around meetings of the Asiatic Society of Japan (founded in 1872) and it was at these meetings that Chamberlain began to publicize his work in Japanese language and literature. The years from 1874 to 1886 were spent studying the language, investigating dialects and translating. His first book, *The Classical Poetry of the Japanese* (1880) contained translations of sixty-six poems from the *Man'yōshū*, fifty from the *Kokinshū* and four Noh plays. Much time was also spent with the likes of Ernest Satow exploring the country, partly because of an interest in dialect (Aizu in 1879, for example) but also partly to escape the humid heat of Tokyo during the summer months. He was an avid mountain walker and was probably the first westerner to penetrate the mountains in a number of areas. This interest in travel and his general curiosity was to give both life and depth to his subsequent writings on Japan.

The years from 1880 to 1886 were spent furthering research into three areas: Japanese literature, philology and travel. In 1881 he started learning Korean with Satow. This particular task was part and parcel of his more general interest in clarifying the origins of Japanese. The results can be seen in a number of articles on such topics as sound change in old Japanese, the roots of Japanese verbs, and of course his complete translation of the *Kojiki*, which he started while on leave in England in 1880 and which was published by the Asiatic Society of Japan in 1883. It is perhaps worth stressing the appalling difficulty of this work, which he had the temerity to tackle after only seven years studying the language. It was and still is a monumental achievement. The event also caused considerable stir among Japanese scholars. The introduction touches on a number of highly

129

contentious subjects and deals in an even-handed manner with matters of early society, religious beliefs, language and politics. It faces squarely the problem of the credibility of sources and ridicules the idea that the dates for the early reigns were anything but spurious. Despite volumes of subsequent scholarship on the *Kojiki*, Chamberlain's introduction is still worth reading today. The healthy scepticism that directly contradicted the prevailing dicta of Japanese textbooks on the subject was such that if the work had been written in Japanese it would undoubtedly never have seen the light of day. Certainly, if it had been produced even ten years later it must have run into trouble. Such unencumbered research into tricky fields was to become an object of some envy to later less fortunate Japanese.

There were other areas too on which he saw himself duty-bound as a foreigner to comment: becoming a member of the Rōmajikai on its inception in 1884, he began to argue the case for simplifying and changing the Japanese writing system. Also in 1884 he started to pay frequent visits to the Fujiya Hotel in Miyanoshita, Hakone, where he was eventually to live for a good part of each year.

The year 1886 brought the offer of a post at the Imperial University as the first Professor of Japanese and Philology. Although his tenure lasted a mere four years, in a sense it was here that he had his greatest impact on Japan and the Japanese vision of themselves and their language. His lecturing duties were concentrated on general linguistic theory, which was of course only in its infancy and for which he used textbooks such as *Lectures on the Science of Language*, written by Max Müller with whom he was personally acquainted. He also introduced the principles of comparative grammar and philology. His students testify to the importance of his lectures, which led them to look at their language through foreign eyes, comparing it to Korean and Ainu, and bringing forth connections which they had hitherto been unaware of. The comparison with Korean, the study of historical change in language according to carefully researched principles, and his attempt to study Japanese morphology through romanization unencumbered by the restrictions of the native syllabary, were all major advances. Throughout his writings one can also trace a constant scholarly concern to correct the uncritical adoption of folk-etymology that was so characteristic of traditional Japanese lexicography. Neither can there be any doubt that the very presence of a foreigner teaching Japanese grammar at the Imperial University – surely the ultimate and final indignity, as Yamada Yoshio later put it[1] – was in itself a tremendous spur to Japanese scholars themselves.

The matter of Japanese grammar is in fact another difficult area in which Chamberlain's efforts were of importance. English grammar had developed in relation to the grammars of Greek and Latin, so that a comparative element had always been present. Japanese grammar, however, perhaps precisely because Chinese was so utterly different and alien, had emerged in almost total isolation and did not offer a rich tradition. What home-grown grammar there was died with the coming of the west. It might be said with some justice that the writing of Japanese grammars, and indeed the teaching of them to the Japanese themselves, was a particularly galling example of intellectual imperialism; but in the area of grammar the exercise can, to a certain extent, be justified. We do not know in detail what the Japanese reaction to Chamberlain's grammar was (it was published in outline form in Japanese and he must have lectured on the subject), but the comparative element was invaluable. In fact, Chamberlain's grammar as revealed in *A Handbook of Colloquial Japanese* (1888), is a very useful book even today, when so many more teaching aids and textbooks now exist. Where one might expect the simple imposition of European grammatical categories, one has instead a careful description and a measured analysis of why these categories do not in fact fit. Words like 'adjective', 'conjunction' and 'pronoun' are used as initial pointers rather than Procrustean beds. The book is in fact a major contribution; his treatment of a series of problems from *wa* and *ga* to the passive of intransitive verbs is a model of concise intelligent analysis. Not, of course, the first such grammar of the spoken language but certainly the clearest and the best.

We do not know for what reasons Chamberlain eventually decided to leave his university post, but leave he did in 1890. He was honoured with emeritus status. Perhaps it was because he was becoming too uncomfortable with living in Tokyo and saw a secure financial future coming from his writing? Certainly, for the next twenty or so years he spent much of his time at the Fujiya Hotel, where he kept a library that was to reach 10,000 volumes. He became known by his sobriquet of Ōdō Sensei, Teacher of the Kingly Hall, a name that played on his personal names: Basil Hall. We know from his letters to Lafcadio Hearn at this time that he still suffered from weak eyesight and arranged for a series of young Japanese to come and read to him in English every afternoon. Ueda Bin was among these, as well as a youth called Sugiura Tōshirō, whom Chamberlain was to look after almost as a son and whose studies at Oxford he later funded. He devoted himself to three main projects: *Things Japanese* (1890), which was to be reprinted six times (each time with major revisions), Murray's *Handbook for Travellers in Japan* (1890), which grew out of Satow and Hawes's *A Handbook for Travellers in Central and Northern Japan* (1881) and which he coauthored with W.B. Mason through a further five editions before he left Japan, and further academic work on the language and customs of the Ryukyus. It is presumed that royalties kept him in fair estate.

It would be wrong, however, to get the impression that he remained immobile during these years. As part of his study of Ryukyuan, he travelled to the Ryukyus in 1893 and made sure that he also visited Britain and Europe as often as he could (1892, 1896, 1906, 1908, 1909, 1911). This judicious mix of further scholarship, editing new and revised editions of old works, and travel continued until 1910, when he finally decided to return to Europe for good. It is perhaps symptomatic of a desire for a complete break that he did not take many of his books with him but asked Sasaki Nobutsuna, whom he had known since 1902, to find a way of disposing of his library. Half eventually ended up in the possession of his former student Ueda Mannen; half can now be found in the library of the Faculty of Humanities of Nihon University. So in 1911 Chamberlain returned to Europe and set up residence in Geneva. There he lived studying and working in retirement until his death in 1935, retaining a certain interest in Japan, but becoming increasingly involved with the disasters that befell Europe and seeking consolation in his old love of French literature.

As a coda to this later part of his life, it is interesting to record that Basil was by no means the most famous of the three Chamberlain brothers. It was his second brother, Houston Stewart Chamberlain, who had the most impact. After being educated at Versailles and then Cheltenham, he went to live in Germany, studied in Geneva, and became a passionate Wagnerian. His fame is based on the book *Die Grundlagen des 19. Jahrhunderts* (1899) which expounded the heady theory of Aryan racial supremacy and which eventually became a central text of Pan-German nationalism. It was translated into English in 1910 under the general supervision of A. B. Mitford, who, as it happens, had been attaché in Japan from 1866 to 1870. Mitford added a eulogistic preface that he was later to regret. The connection between Mitford and Basil is unclear, although it is tempting to suggest that Basil may have played some part in helping his brother gain Mitford's co-operation. In 1908 Houston, divorced from his first German wife, married Wagner's daughter Eva. After moving to Geneva in 1911, Basil visited Houston in Bayreuth a number of times sharing, as he did, a passion for Wagner. The relationship continued on a reasonably even keel until 1914 and the outbreak of the First World World. Thereafter Basil broke off contact, appalled and embarrassed by the virulence of his brother's anti-British propaganda. Houston took German nationality in 1916, and received the Iron Cross from the Kaiser for his services to the German nation. But Basil must still have felt something for his brother, for when Houston found himself in dire financial straits at the end of the war, Basil came to his aid. Not that this seemed to change any of Houston's strong convictions. It was largely due to his work that the Wagner myth became linked to the emerging movement that culminated with the rise of Nazism. In 1923 he met the young Hitler and afterwards wrote him a letter expressing ecstatic support and admiration for the future saviour of the German nation. His funeral in Bayreuth was a grand affair at which the whole of Germany paid its respects. Basil was not apparently present, but he did arrange for Eva to receive an annuity after Houston's death.

Basil never apparently pronounced directly on his brother's views in public, but the letters sent from Geneva to Sugiura Tōshirō register his dismay at the growing 'scandal about brother Houston', and later passages in revised versions of *Things Japanese* refer with considerable scorn to the concept of the 'Yellow Peril'. Letters sent to his brother are kept in the 'Chamberlain Nachlass' in the Richard Wagner Gendenkstätte in Bayreuth and remain to be studied.

The existence of such a brother with such views naturally makes one reflect on Basil's own attitudes towards questions of race and culture. In common with many intellectuals of the age, he himself was fascinated by matters of racial origins and the movement of peoples; all his academic work in Ainu, Korean, early Japanese and the labour that went into translating the *Kojiki* would seem to have been generated by a desire to penetrate to the origins of the Japanese via the route that he knew best: comparative philology. But there also seems to be an almost miraculous absence of bigotry. Not that he was afraid to have strong opinions. Indeed, one of the attractions of his writing is that, although reticent in some respects, he is often willing to be open and candid. In common with most Englishmen in Japan, he considered that his role as educator was justified and self-evident. By and large it was obvious that Europeans had reached a far higher level of civilization and that in most things they 'knew better' than the Japanese. For the Ainu he had nothing but contempt. They were savages, 'weak-brained', 'unreliable', 'in comparison to whom the peasantry of Europe are *savants*'. His study of Ainu nomenclature on the Japanese islands ends on the following harsh note:

> Evidently the Japanese Government cannot, with the best of intentions, preserve the race from extinction. The Ainos must without delay be subjected to all the necessary scientific tests. Their language must be analysed, their folk-lore registered; for soon there will be nothing left. . . .
>
> By some European travellers this *japonization* of the present generation, and the probable speedy extinction of the race, are mourned over. The present writer cannot share these regrets. The Ainos had better opportunites than fell to the lot of many other races. . . . But so little have they profited by the opportunites offered to them during the last thousand or two thousand years, that there is no longer room for them in the world. . . . The Aino race is now no more than a 'curio' to the philologist and to the ethnologist. It has no future, because it has no root in the past. The impression left on the mind after a sojourn among the Ainos is that of a profound melancholy. The existence of this race has been as aimless, as fruitless, as is the perpetual dashing of the breakers on the shore of Horobetsu. It leaves behind it nothing save a few names.[2]

For the Japanese, of course, Chamberlain had a good deal more time. He would hardly have spent almost forty years of his life living in Japan if that had not been the case. And yet, in comparison to a man like Lafcadio Hearn, who actually became naturalized as a Japanese citizen, he never lost sight of his own Europeanness. It was precisely the lack of balance in Hearn, the way in which the villain was always either the westerner or Christianity, with which he took issue. The most sober statement of his own convictions comes from a letter written to Hearn in 1891:

I have myself gone through many phases of opinion, but the net result is that they appear to me far inferior to the European race – at once less profound, less tender, and less imaginative. Much of what strikes one as originality at first is only, so to say, a relative originality as compared with Europe; after a time one finds out either that the thing, whatever it may be was borrowed from China, or else perhaps that, though superficially pretty, it is not really worth so much as the corresponding thing in the West. Take poetry, for instance. It is perhaps the best instance. I threw myself with the greatest ardour into Japanese poetry, even to the length of trying to compose it. I read practically all, from the *Manyōshū* downwards, and I now see that all of it together hardly contains so much imaginative power as half-a-dozen of Wordsworth's sonnets. There is a dryness, a jejuneness in all Japanese thought. All this is very sad to write, *and I would not write it publicly*, for the reason that many would ascribe the adverse judgement to other motives than dispassionate comparison. Each man must go through the successive stages in his own person. On the other hand, how absolutely the most charming of all countries Japan is to live in, – how delightful the scenery, how safe the roads, how kind everywhere the welcome, how easy the life! These things must be weighed in the balance against the absence of that greater imagination which has been the root of all our European achievements alike in literature, science, and social life.[3]

Such a statement should be seen in the light of Hearn's own somewhat uncritical enthusiasm for a Japan that, at this early stage, he himself understood only very imperfectly and would have understood even less had it not been for Chamberlain's friendship and advice; but it is a good illustration of the kind of candour that makes one trust the author: he was always scrupulously fair to his own feelings and judgements. A later letter to Hearn, dated May 1894, contains the following: 'I care little for the Europeans here. Barring a few real friends – Mason and half a dozen more – they seem to me to be deteriorated by their surroundings. Brinkley and all that lot disgust me by their sycophancy of the Japanese. Besides them there are the diplomats; but they look down on common folk.'

There is much in *Things Japanese* that reflects a real admiration for Japan, and in any case the time and effort that Chamberlain invested in studying the language and the culture presupposes such admiration. The entry on 'Art', for example, is full of praise and delight in everything from Japanese ceramics to painting, and yet even here he could never quite bring himself to utter the word 'genius'; the entry for 'Literature' makes for somewhat painful reading: 'Sum total: what Japanese literature most lacks is genius. It lacks thought, logical grasp, depth, breadth, and many-sidedness.' Of course, he was not alone in this; perhaps Wagner and *waka* will remain forever irreconcilable. What we cannot accuse him of is making such judgements lightly. A similar statement about Japanese literature had already been made by him at an early stage, well before his 1891 letter to Hearn. In his first book, *The Classical Poetry of the Japanese* (1880), he managed to write with enthusiasm that the technique of 'pivot-words' produced an impression 'delightful in the extreme, passing, as they do, before the reader, like a series of dissolving views, vague, graceful, and suggestive', but his overall impression was still mediocrity, of a 'poverty of the intellectual constitution' and of 'prettiness and a sort of tender grace'.

Perhaps his low opinion of Japanese literature came as a result of the heroic battles that he waged to translate poetry into a 'suitable' idiom. The early translations are instructive, because they show clearly that he had a particular view of what was 'poetic' in English and found the Japanese lacking. The introduction to this particular book contains the following remark:

> The versions claim to be, not paraphrase, but as fairly faithful translations as the widely divergent genius of the English and Japanese tongues and methods of thought will permit, *only such originals as proved themselves sufficiently pliable having been allowed to pass muster.*[4]

The demand that the Japanese should adapt and the implicit use of the vocabulary of the parade ground is revealing here. The original needed constant supplementation to be fitted into the English pattern and so one finds, along with a patina of poetic language that today strikes one as quaint in the extreme, an uncontrollable urge to pad. It is a classic dilemma, of course, but may be one important clue to his constant dissatisfaction with the Japanese. Two examples may be instructive, both from the *Kokinshū*; one by Sosei and the other attributed to Hitomaro:

> Amid the branches of the silv'ry bowers
> The nightingale doth sing: perchance he knows
> That spring hath come, and takes the later snows
> For the white petals of the plum's sweet flowers.

> With roseate hues that pierce th'autumnal haze
> The spreading dawn lights up Akashi's shore;
> But the fair ship, alas! is seen no more:
> An island veils it from my loving gaze.[5]

These renditions probably reveal more about the inflexibilities of English taste at the time than they do about the Japanese originals. As might be expected, the principle is that Japanese should yield to English in all things. By illustrating with disconcerting clarity the degree to which translations are bound to time and contemporary attitudes, they act as a sobering reminder of inescapable limitations in the art of interpretation.

What is Chamberlain's importance for us today? The academic work on the *Kojiki* and Ryukyuan aside, it is surely as the author of *Things Japanese* that he is read and known. It is here that the fascination with bricolage, the delight of the collector rummaging around in 'facts' that brought such obvious satisfaction amid the constant hypochondria, is presented with so light a touch that the book is a constant pleasure. Acerbic at times, but never unfair and always scrupulous, it is a perfect blend of observer with observed; it speaks of the fascinations of interpretation and understanding. Only someone of supreme confidence in his ability to produce balanced judgements could have ventured into such dangerous terrain and emerged so unscathed, even in the light of a history he could not possibly have foretold. Like all the best books, it teaches us a little about ourselves. As he wrote to Hearn in October 1893: 'I confess that patriotism, anywhere, is a thing altogether distasteful to my mind; for I was born cosmopolitain, began to travel and to learn foreign languages at the age of two and a half and now feel at home in no country but an amused guest in all.'[6]

10

BRITISH TRAINING FOR JAPANESE ENGINEERS: THE CASE OF KIKUCHI KYŌZŌ (1859–1942)

Janet Hunter

TECHNOLOGICAL EDUCATION IN EARLY MEIJI JAPAN

One of the major problems facing the Japanese government and private entrepreneurs in their attempts to establish a modern manufacturing sector in the early years of the Meiji period was an absence of skilled manpower. They had at their disposal neither a skilled labour force capable of operating the newly introduced technology as production workers, nor trained engineers capable of installing and repairing machinery and of utilizing it creatively and efficiently in the Japanese context. In order to try and bridge this technological gap, many foreign experts were brought to Japan, and Japanese students were sent to study overseas, but this was a costly operation. In an attempt to reduce the financial burden which this entailed, and to minimize the nation's dependence on other, more industrialized nations, the central authorities sought to establish an environment in which necessary skills were transmitted to Japanese, and foreigners dispensed with, as rapidly as possible. Much of this skill transference took place within an environment of practical, on-the-job training. It was not until the 1890s that the state moved in a systematic manner to provide a comprehensive system of technological training and large enterprises began to implement their own internal training programmes.

One important exception to this was the government's establishment in the early 1870s of a college for advanced technical training, whose aim was to produce graduates with the skills required to work in western-style manufacturing. Conspicuously, the proposal came from the Ministry of Industry (*Kōbushō*), which, unlike the Ministry of Education, had a vested interest in the provision of technological training. The college was the brainchild of Itō Hirobumi, who in 1871 had become vice-minister in the

Industry Ministry, and Yamao Yōzō, another Chōshū man who took Itō's place after the latter's departure with the Iwakura Embassy at the end of that year. In 1872 ministry officials drew up the official regulations for a college of technology. Originally known as the *Kōgakuryō* [yakuryō], the college was in 1877 renamed the *Kōbu Daigakkō*, a designation normally translated as the (Imperial) College of Engineering. The College effectively served as Japan's major source of advanced technological education in the years before 1885, when Japan's industrial growth began to gain momentum.[1]

Hugh Matheson, of the trading form Jardine Matheson and a close contact of Itō's, was approached with a request to seek out an appropriate individual to serve as principal of the college. As a result a young man called Henry Dyer was appointed as principal and director of studies at the princely salary of ¥660 per month, well in excess of that received by his ministerial employer. Dyer sailed from Southampton to take up his post in March 1873. On the same ship was Hayashi Tadasu, Itō's private secretary. Dyer, who was then still only 25, had studied at Glasgow University and appears to have accepted the job with enthusiasm. He had already devoted some effort to studying engineering teaching methods abroad, and laid his detailed plans for the college curriculum during the voyage. His proposals were accepted unconditionally by the Japanese authorities.

Dyer had very clear ideas about the role of engineers in modern industrial society. Engineers, he believed, united nations through providing them with communications, and if only for this reason were a revolutionary force in society. Whether Dyer had a particular interest in Japan before he was offered the job is unclear, but while he was in Japan he undoubtedly gained a sincere interest in the country and its affairs, and affection and respect for the Japanese people. Later on he took great pleasure in refuting the idea, prevalent, then as now that the Japanese were imitative rather than original. This attribute, he believed, was due to little more than lack of experience, and he had little doubt that the Japanese, given time, would produce highly original work. In later life he was deeply concerned that the influence of the west might submerge and undermine Japanese culture and traditions:

> One of the chief faults of the British people, and to a great extent of all Western peoples generally, is that they are so pleased with the advancement and excellence of their own institutions that they cannot understand why any other nation cannot be content with what contents them, and this tactless, unimaginative charity has been the main cause of their troubles in all parts of the world.

Following Dyer's appointment, other British nationals were hired to undertake the teaching of Japanese students at the college. In the years up to its absorption into the new Imperial University of Tokyo in 1885, twenty-one foreigners served on the senior staff of the college, the majority of them British. Almost all were young, usually in their twenties, and many later became famous in the world of scholarship and research. Most well-known were, perhaps, John Milne, regarded as the founding father of seismology, and W.E. Ayrton, Professor of Natural Philosophy, who became world famous for his experimental work in the field of electricity. While the foreign staff of the college had a relatively free rein in devising and teaching courses to students, they remained ultimately responsible to the Japanese authorities. In the Ministry of Industry Dyer was responsible to Vice-minister Yamao Yōzō. Yamao, like Itō one of the group of five Chōshū samurai secretly sent to Britain in 1863, had himself studied at Anderson's College in Glasgow, and knew Dyer. His declaration that engineering was 'the base on which to construct the road to better public welfare' would certainly have struck a sympathetic note in the principal of the college.

The education offered by the college was in many ways revolutionary for its time. In devising the curriculum, Dyer drew upon not only his experience of Scottish engineering education (well in advance of its English counterpart), but also his knowledge of technological education at colleges overseas. Students pursued a six-year course, for the most part studying together for the first two years, and then specializing in one of a variety of subjects, which included mechanical engineering, civil engineering, telegraphy, mining and metallurgy. Courses had a strong practical bent, and students were particularly fortunate in being able to use the college's connection with the Ministry of Industry to secure assignments to works and factories of various kinds during vacation periods. The college was at the time one of the very few comprehensive colleges of further technology, which taught all branches of applied science within a single institution. For engineering educators outside Japan it subsequently served as a centre of excellence, whose best techniques were emulated when establishing new institutions and remodelling existing ones.

From the time the first students graduated in 1879 up until its incorporation into the Imperial University, the College of Engineering produced over 200 graduates in the various branches of engineering. By the turn of the century, many of Japan's leading industrial and strategic enterprises were run by ex-students of the college. Students were most intensively used in practical operations by the public and private sectors. Relatively few (11 per cent) went into education. The majority were thus involved in practising rather than preaching their skills, predominantly in the areas of railways, mining, shipbuilding, shipping and textiles. Many also came to be involved in enterprise management, and were directors and managers of major enterprises. One of these engineers was Kikuchi Kyōzō, a textile engineer and manager. Kikuchi's career demonstrates the degree to which the engineering education he received served as the springboard from which he could make a major technological and managerial contribution to one of the leading sectors in Japanese industry in the half-century prior to the Second World War.

THE CAREER OF KIKUCHI KYŌZŌ

Kikuchi Kyōzō was born in the autumn of 1859,[2] the third son of Kikuchi Yasunari of Ehime Prefecture, Shikoku. The family was a prosperous one, and was well known in the locality, with many generations of family head having served as local headmen. In 1876 Kikuchi left his home, accompanied by his younger brother, Tanaka Kyōtō, to travel to Osaka. The voyage on a small steamer captained by a Briton was, he later confessed, a stunning introduction to the rapidly changing world of early Meiji Japan. In Osaka he took up a place at the Osaka English school (Ōsaka Eigo Gakkō), which was later to become the Third High School. He worked hard, and did consistently well in the three-monthly tests, the only shadow on the horizon being the rumour in 1877 that if Saigō Takamori's men were victorious in their struggle with the government forces the students would have to revert to learning Chinese rather than English. In November, 1878, Kikuchi, against the advice of his father, travelled to Tokyo, where he determined to secure an engineering education. At a time when many ambitious young men were reluctant to enter business, preferring instead politics or work in the bureaucracy, Kikuchi regarded engineering as a means whereby he could make a notable contribution to the strengthening of the country and its industrial growth. He studied for entrance to the Imperial College of Engineering in a rented six-mat room in Kanda, and was accepted despite having studied English for only two years.[3] His studies there began in 1879. After pursuing the general course for the first two years, Kikuchi, who was particularly interested in shipping technology, opted to specialize in mechanical engineering. This was the area for which Henry Dyer himself was responsible, and the relatively small number of students in the school (only three students graduated in mechanical engineering in Kikuchi's year) would have enabled Kikuchi's progress to be closely monitored by his principal.

A relatively wealthy background was an important asset in enabling Kikuchi to study at the college. Early students had been granted state bursaries, but the government's financial exigencies in the wake of the Satsuma Rebellion of 1877 had led to these being abolished. Afterwards, only the privileged few could afford to support their sons in the college. Kikuchi spoke warmly in later life of the continuing support of his father throughout his years of education in Osaka and Tokyo. After his brother, Kyōtō, joined him at the college a year later, the two brothers would receive ¥17 monthly—¥7 each for school fees and expenses, the remaining ¥3 for pocket money. The family's investment was handsomely rewarded. When Kikuchi graduated with the degree of *kōgakushi* (engineer) in April 1885, his score of over two hundred marks secured him the highest classification of degree possible.

Kikuchi's first idea had been to set up in shipbuilding with his brother. Following his graduation he went to work at the state-run Yokosuka

Shipyard, at the miserly salary of ¥30 per month, less than one-twentieth of that paid by the same employer to his former principal. First-hand experience of shipbuilding, however, and a growing awareness of the huge capital sums involved, tempered his initial enthusiasm. Leaving the yard in March 1887, he moved to Osaka, and within a month had been employed at the government Mint, succeeding as engineer there Saitō Tsunezō, who had been three years above him at the College of Engineering. His new salary was double his previous one. He was there only a few months, though, before he was approached by an acquaintance on behalf of the new Hirano Cotton Spinning Company, which was seeking a textile engineer. Kikuchi knew next to nothing of textile technology, and his response was that he would only consider moving to Hirano if the company were willing to send him to Britain to study the business. Somewhat to his surprise, the management agreed to his proposal, and Kikuchi found himself in the awkward position of having to give in his notice to the Mint after less than five months' employment. So embarrassed was he that he asked a friend to do it for him.

The Hirano Spinning Company was formally incorporated in August 1887, one of the wave of new companies founded in the latter 1880s in the wake of the success of Shibusawa Eiichi's Osaka Cotton Spinning Company. Kikuchi was employed the same month as Chief Engineer. His appointment marked the beginning of a lifelong commitment to the development and expansion of Japan's cotton-spinning industry, and the basis from which Kikuchi achieved his position as one of Kansai's leading industrialists.

Two months later, on 12 October, Kikuchi's departure from Yokohama initiated the second, and equally important, stage of his British engineering education. The ship sailed to Marseille, and forty-three days after his departure Kikuchi was in Paris, whence he proceeded to London. He planned to be away from Japan for a year. His employers had undertaken to pay him ¥120 per month through the agency of Mitsui Bussan in London. In return, Hirano would guarantee Mitsui sole agency in the shipping of their new machinery to Japan. Kikuchi's tasks in Britain, therefore, were to negotiate the purchase of the machinery and to further his own knowledge.

Even before Kikuchi's departure the management of Hirano had determined to opt for ring spindles, which reduced the requirement for skilled labour, rather than the mule spindles still widely used in Britain. The source for the machinery was to be the firm Platt Brothers of Oldham, a company which provided almost all of Japan's spinning machinery in the early years of the development of the industry. Kikuchi drove a hard bargain with the London Office of Mitsui Bussan, securing the same terms as those granted to Hirano's competitor, the Osaka Spinning Company. He acquired ten spinning machines from Platts with a total spindleage of nearly 5,000, half the amount operated by the Osaka Company. More than fifty years later the same machines were still in use at the Hirano Mill of the Japan Cotton Spinning Company.

Kikuchi utilized the remainder of his time in Britain to acquaint himself in more detail with the techniques of spinning. In the evenings he attended a course in the principles of spinning at Manchester Technical School, by day he undertook practical observations of the spinning process at a factory in Middleton owned by a certain Mr Wood, introduced to him by Platts. Rumour had it that he was not averse to slipping the girls on the shopfloor a coin or two in order to be shown how various operations were handled. Commentators reported that he went about his business promptly and efficiently. From Britain Kikuchi crossed to America, sailing back to Japan from San Francisco.

Kikuchi's trip to Europe gave him knowledge of advanced spinning techniques. He was to make two further trips to the west. One was in 1896, when, travelling with other textile engineers, he again purchased new machinery, visited woollen mills in France and Germany, and returned via the United States. His final trip was in 1911, when, accompanied this time by his wife, he journeyed via Siberia to Britain and travelled extensively in Europe and America. Both these trips were important in business terms, but it was his first visit, at a time when Manchester was the undisputed leader of the cotton spinning industry, that constituted an essential part of Kikuchi's 'British education' and had a deep-rooted and lasting impact on his career.

By the time Kikuchi returned to Osaka in November 1888, the construction of the factory was virtually completed under the supervision of Imada Kiyonoshin, engineer of the Osaka Arsenal, and the necessary machinery had arrived from Britain. Installation of the new machines was entrusted to the installation engineer, Mr Dransfield. Work went on day and night to get things ready, and by the end of April 1889, the factory was in a position to commence operations. During Kikuchi's absence, in June 1888, the presidency of the Hirano Company had been assumed by Kanazawa Jinpei, vice-president of the Osaka Shipping Company and a major figure in the Kansai business world. Kanazawa, however, tended to visit Hirano only infrequently, around once a month, which meant that most of the day-to-day running of the business was left to Kikuchi.

The whole of Osaka boasted only five or six trained engineers at that time, and the status of a technician in Japanese society was very ill-defined. Kikuchi found that many people in Osaka regarded an engineer as superfluous once the installation of machinery had taken place. Kikuchi found himself held at arm's length, and even within the factory voices were heard to the effect that Kikuchi was not worth the high salary which he was receiving. He took the view that if he were to become truly respected in the Osaka business world he had to be seen not just as a technician but as an effective operator in the field of management and the economy in general. Fortunately, Kanazawa, recognized Kikuchi's ambitions and abilities and appointed him as engineer and manager concurrently.

Kikuchi was also compelled to adapt himself in other ways to gain acceptance among the people of Osaka. Referring in his reminiscences to the proverbial frugality of the Kansai inhabitant, he commented that he had gone out his way to make various petty savings to improve his image. Such economies included dressing in shabby clothing and travelling third class on the train – anything, it appears, to avoid looking like the graduate which he was. This led to his being trusted and respected by the inhabitants of Osaka, but it aroused the contempt of his former classmates, amongst whom he gained the reputation of being intensely miserly.

Although Kanazawa had given Kikuchi a managerial post, he was not immune from a prevailing reluctance to grant engineers a higher status. He adamantly opposed those within the company who suggested that he appoint Kikuchi to the board of directors, on the grounds that he was not a capitalist, and his relations with Kikuchi were not always harmonious. As the cotton industry expanded rapidly in the Osaka area, however, competition for Kikuchi's scarce services threatened to make him reappraise his attitude. The initial pressure came from the newly established Amagasaki Spinning Company. In June 1889 one of the company's founders, Fukumoto Motonosuke, visited Kikuchi at work and asked about the possibility of his either transferring, or making his skills available in some other way to the new company. Kikuchi's response was that because of the substantial sums Hirano had expended on his training in England he remained under an obligation to the company, and must abide by the board's wishes. Direct approaches were then made by Amagasaki to Hirano, and as a result of the ensuing negotiations agreement was reached to share Kikuchi's services. In return Amagasaki would pay to Hirano a lump sum of ¥2,000 as a contribution to the cost of sending Kikuchi to Britain. In the view of the Amagasaki board, such an arrangement was the most rational way of acquiring the expertise the company needed. To hire a foreigner would be even more expensive, and much more difficult. One dissenting voice on the board claimed that Kikuchi had no capital to bring to the company, but was persuaded that at this stage what the company needed was skill rather than capital. Formal agreement between the two companies was reached in September 1889; if Kikuchi wished to resign from either he had to give a year's notice and recommend a successor, and the companies in their turn had to notify Kikuchi a year in advance should they wish to dispense with his services, or pay him a year's salary in lieu.

Amagasaki was not the only company to see the value of an engineer such as Kikuchi. The same year another spinning company, Settsu Spinning, was founded in Osaka. Its president, Hirano Heibei, was a relative of President Kanazawa of Hirano, and through a privately negotiated deal between the two presidents Kikuchi also made his services available to Settsu in the spring of 1890. Settsu, too, was to pay ¥600 to Hirano and ¥700 to Amagasaki for Kikuchi's educational expenses. Hirano, in fact, did rather well out of its financial dealings for Kikuchi's services. The company estimated its total expenditure for Kikuchi's British trip as ¥3,900, and claimed that with ¥2,000 from Amagasaki and ¥600 from Settsu its net outgoings were ¥1,300. However, if Kikuchi's view that the trip cost only ¥3,000 is to be believed, the great bulk of the cost was clearly borne by the other two companies. These financial manipulations, however, did not undermine Kikuchi's position. By the middle of 1890 he was in charge of production at three major spinning companies with a total spindleage of 42,000 – 12,000 at Hirano, 10,000 at Amagasaki and 20,000 at Settsu. This amounted to around 20 per cent of Japan's total spindleage at that time.

Kikuchi tried to balance out his duties to his three employers. Every day he spent the morning at one of the three companies, and the afternoon at another, taking care to allocate his time in a way which none could object to. However, the companies differed in the degree of recognition granted him. His original company, Hirano, resolutely refused to admit him to a directorship. He shifted from engineer/manager to adviser, and in 1898 severed his connection with the company. Amagasaki, by contrast, appointed him to a directorship in January 1893, and at Settsu, too, he became chief executive and then, in 1897, director. He earned the salary of ¥50 per month for his part time work for the company. From 1898, therefore, Kikuchi divided his efforts between Amagasaki and Settsu. He would work daily at the Settsu mill from 7.00 a.m., and then move on to Amagasaki at midday, returning home in the evening.

After Kikuchi's departure and the death of Kanazawa in 1899, Hirano found itself in increasing difficulties. Ironically, through a merger with the Settsu Company its connection with Kikuchi was resumed. The association between the two companies had always been close: their initial contacts had been rooted in family ties between the two presidents, they had installed the same machines, using the same engineers from the Osaka Arsenal and Manchester, and had shared their Japanese engineer. In 1902, the smaller company, Hirano, was taken over by Settsu, of which Kikuchi had already been a director for several years and which was flourishing under his leadership. Settsu continued to prosper. It was renowned for its ability to pay very high dividends of 30–40 per cent to its shareholders, and even in bad years they rarely fell below 20 per cent.

During this time Amagasaki, too, had been going from strength to strength. As early as 1893 it was operating three factories. In the face of internal opposition, Kikuchi had become a director, and in 1901 the outgoing president, resigning over the bankruptcy of a bank with which he was intimately connected, recommended Kikuchi as his successor. The engineer had at last made it to the top. Under Kikuchi's leadership the company expanded apace, taking over several other spinning companies on the way. The value of the company increased rapidly. By the time of the First World War much of the company's income rested not on its spinning operations but on careful investment of its assets.

When Kikuchi added the Settsu presidency to that of Amagasaki in 1915, it was only a matter of time before a merger was implemented. In June 1918 this came in the formation of the Dai Nihon Spinning Company, a giant of the spinning world with a capital stock of ¥30.5m. By 1936, when Kikuchi withdrew from day-to-day management to become chairman of the board, this capital had risen to ¥110m. Under Kikuchi's presidency in the 1920s the company took over two more smaller textile companies and moved into rayon production, then a new product. Kikuchi had been a leading advocate of local production overseas since before the First World War, and Dai Nihon was also at the leading edge of the strategy to establish Japanese mills in China and Manchuria. With Kanebō and Tōyōbō, Dai Nihon thus dominated an industry which played a critical role in the development of the economy up to the 1930s. Kikuchi himself held the top posts in the powerful Japan Cotton Spinners Federation (Dai Nihon Bōseki Rengōkai), and, as the *Ōsaka Asahi* commented in an article on Kikuchi in December 1940, 'the course of his life is, as it stands, the history of spinning'.

In 1940 Kikuchi resigned from his post as chairman of the Dai Nihon board. He died two years later, in December 1942, at the age of 83. His clutch of business directorates in textiles, banking, shipping and insurance, his honorary doctorate of engineering, his membership of the House of Peers, all testified that it was indeed possible for an engineer to become a *genrō* of the business world, and to achieve respect and influence far beyond it.

ENGINEERS AND INDUSTRIALIZATION

The students trained by Henry Dyer and his colleagues at the Imperial College of Engineering played a crucial role in providing scarce skills for industries of strategic importance.[4] It is estimated that in 1890 there were only 131 graduate engineers in private industry, and in 1900 still only 385. The majority worked in heavy industry; far fewer were in textiles, which was less technology intensive. The textile industry as a whole had only eighteen trained engineers in 1890, though by 1900 there were seventy-seven. As we have seen, Kikuchi, simultaneously gave of his knowledge to no fewer than three companies.[5] Without access to these skills, companies would have had to turn to expensive foreign specialists, or perhaps muddle through by a costly process of trial and error. In Kikuchi's case, the cotton spinning industry within which he worked played a critical role in Japan's early industrial development. It was an early example of successful import substitution, and a major earner of crucial foreign exchange. Up to the 1930s the cotton textile industry was, after silk, the second-largest employer of factory labour in the country, and the second most valuable export commodity. The early successes of the industry owed an untold amount to the contribution of just three engineers: Yamabe Takeo of the Osaka Spinning Company, Saitō Tsunezō of Mie and Kikuchi Kyōzō.

The engineering education which men like Kikuchi received both in Japan and in Britain, also served as a basis upon which such men could become involved in management. Hired as independent professionals rather than 'company men', the relative autonomy they enjoyed because of their employers' dependence on them, pushed them into making overall production decisions. Many of Kikuchi's fellow students, like Kikuchi himself, moved into management, and influenced industrial development well beyond its narrow technical sphere. With company structures less formalized than they later became, the scope for the able individual to move from technology into management was considerable. Nevertheless, the Imperial College's emphasis on practical training left a lasting legacy. Engineer-managers rarely lost touch with the shop floor; instead they were the beginning of a proud 'practical' tradition in Japanese engineering.

This fusion of technical and managerial skills, graphically illustrated in the career of Kikuchi, played a crucial role in Japanese company development at a time when skills of all kinds were scarce. Among the British educators at the Imperial College of Engineering, Henry Dyer, looking back at his experience in Japan, was in no doubt as to the major contribution made by his students, and the part which he himself had played in this:

> The best proof of the value of the training they have received is the excellent work which the students have done since they left college, as there are few engineering or industrial works in Japan in which they are not to be found taking an active part in management. . . . Former students of the College are now to be found not only in all the most important engineering and industrial undertakings in Japan, but a considerable number of them are actively engaged in China and Korea, so that the College has been a most important factor in bringing about the changes in Japan and in influencing conditions in the Far East generally.

11

HAYASHI TADASU (1850–1913)

Ian Nish

Hayashi Tadasu was born in 1850 in Edo, the son of a doctor practising Rangaku (Dutch-style) medicine. He was quick to take up the study of the English language in Yokohama. Thanks to his father's prestige at the shogun's court and the patronage of Sir Harry Parkes, the British envoy, he was sent by shogunate officials with a group to England in 1866. He stayed in London from January 1867 and entered University College School in the autumn. Before long he and his companions were recalled to Japan as the Bōshin civil war approached. Hayashi was just in time to join the last stand of Tokugawa supporters and went north to Hokkaidō to serve that cause with Admiral Enomoto (Takeaki). He was captured after the battle of Hakodate and languished in prison for two years, expecting execution. Although he had been on the defeated side and did not have useful clan affiliations, Hayashi was released because he seems to have been regarded as useful by the officials of the Emperor Meiji by reason of his knowledge of English. He was allowed to enter the service of the post-Restoration government in 1871.[1]

In the following year Hayashi accompanied the Iwakura Mission as second secretary, serving in effect as interpreter. He visited the United States and went on to act as advance party to prepare the ground for the Mission in Britain. There, he committed an indiscretion and had to return to his homeland early in the company of Kido Kōin.[2]

In 1873 he entered the Kōbushō (Industrial Affairs Bureau). In 1882 he accompanied Prince Arisugawa during his visit to Europe to represent the Emperor Meiji at the coronation of the Tsar Alexander III, which was postponed. After various postings he came to notice as governor of the newly established Kagawa prefecture in 1888 and of Hyogo prefecture two years later. Hayashi had surmounted the obstacle of his Tokugawa background and secured remarkable promotion as a Meiji official.

In May 1891 Hayashi's patron, Viscount Enomoto Takeaki, became foreign minister and invited Hayashi to join the ministry as vice-minister, an office he was to hold for four years. His qualification was his outstanding knowledge of English, and his ability to deal with foreigners. But he had had no experience as a diplomat overseas, apart (that is) from his membership of the Iwakura Mission and the Arisugawa Mission. At all events he served the second Itō cabinet and was attached as aide to the ailing foreign minister, Mutsu Munemitsu, who was appointed in 1892 and wanted Hayashi, for whom he had great respect, to stay on.[3]

In his vice-ministerial position he played a substantial part in the negotiations for the Anglo-Japanese commercial treaty which was eventually signed in July 1894. It was part of Mutsu's strategy that the site of the negotiations should be in London away from the frenzied anti-foreign atmosphere of Tokyo at the time. But Hayashi and Mutsu had to lobby strongly with Hugh Fraser, the British minister, before the talks in London got under way.[4]

Hayashi also played a major role during the Sino-Japanese war, especially in the peace-making process. The peace negotiations began early in 1895, first in Hiroshima and later at Shimonoseki and Mutsu went to western Japan to accompany Prime Minister Itō as plenipotentiary. From April he was forced to withdraw to Kyoto because of illness. The role of the vice-minister in Tokyo became critical because he was the channel of communication with Mutsu and with the other negotiators. Since the European powers – Russia, France, Germany – interfered in the peace process through their ministers in Tokyo, Hayashi's role became one of substance rather than acting merely as an administrator and postbox. For his shrewd handling of this international crisis, probably the first major one which the young Japan had faced, he was duly honoured. Strangely enough, he was more highly esteemed by Mutsu during this crisis than he had been by his earlier patron, Enomoto.[5]

Shortly after the conclusion of the negotiations, recriminations were made against the minister in Berlin, Aoki Shūzō, who belonged to the Yamagata faction and was not respected by Mutsu and Hayashi, for having mishandled the Germans and misinformed Tokyo. This disagreement was to play a significant part in Hayashi's later career. In October he was made a baron for his pains during the war.

As soon as the Triple Intervention was resolved, Hayashi was posted on 21 June 1895 as minister to China, his first diplomatic posting. In March 1897 he moved to St Petersburg as minister to Russia, Sweden and Norway. It is notable that, while he took on the Russian assignment, he was never posted to Berlin, where he may have felt that the main roots of the Intervention were to be found. During his Russian posting he went as Japan's representative to the First Hague Peace Conference, which had been convened at the initiative of the young tsar, Nicholas II.

But it was Hayashi's promotion to the Court of St James that was the high point of his diplomatic career. He was posted to London in February 1900, taking over from Katō Takaaki who had cultivated cordial relations with Britain over the years of Russian expansion from 1895 to 1899.

Hayashi's conversion to the need for an alliance with Britain came comparatively late. In 1897 he had been an advocate of an agreement with Russia over Korea. But in 1900, when he was waiting in Tokyo prior to leaving for his new post in London, he told G.E. Morrison, *The Times* correspondent in Peking, who was in Tokyo on a short visit, of his ambition to achieve an alliance with Britain during his period as minister there.[6] The ideas, which he was to put forward in London, had their origins before he left Tokyo. This is confirmed by the evidence in his *Secret Memoirs*, where he states that he discussed the issue with the two Elder Statesemen Itō and Inoue, and 'formed the impression that they were in favour of an alliance with Great Britain'. But he received no positive mandate to present such views to the British government.[7]

Hayashi entered the lists at the foreign secretary's diplomatic reception on 17 April 1901. He asked whether it was possible to have some lasting arrangements between Japan and Britain to safeguard their respective interests. He avoided speaking of an Anglo-German-Japanese alliance and confined his remarks to some permanent understanding between Britain and Japan alone, in order to combat the power of Russia becoming strongly entrenched in Manchuria. There had been discussions from the spring onwards for some sort of Anglo-German-Japanese understanding, but when the Germans withdrew from the 'project', it was Hayashi with the foreign secretary, Lord Lansdowne, who kept the idea in play. It is hard to say with which country the origin of the Alliance lay, because diplomats are always reluctant to be seen to be taking the initiative. Be that as it may, Hayashi had a central role in keeping the Alliance project alive.[8]

Hayashi's *Secret Memoirs* are a valuable source on this subject; but they convey a picture of Hayashi's own initiative which goes beyond anything which would have been allowed to a minister in his country's foreign service. They lay stress on the undoubted progress made in these informal discussions but fail to show that Tokyo took a more cautious line. Important as was Hayashi's persuasiveness with Lansdowne, he could make little headway in Japan on account of the change of cabinet and the government crises there during May and June. What rankled with Hayashi was the meeting between Prime Minister Katsura and Yamagata, Inoue Kaoru and Itō himself, representing the Elder Statesmen in August before Itō, the most senior Japanese statesman, set off from Japan on his round-the-world trip. The cabinet could perhaps not prevent Itō from going abroad or indeed prevent his including St Petersburg in his itinerary. But Hayashi felt it should not simultaneously have agreed to proceed with the British overtures.

Britain's first draft of the Alliance was passed over on 6 November. Itō was by this time staying in Paris, before going on to Russia. The Tokyo cabinet decided that Hayashi should go over to Paris to obtain Itō's consent for Britain's proposals. Hayashi could not have been happier to confront Itō over what seemed an untimely idea of visiting Russia at such a sensitive time. He could not talk Itō out of going to the Russian capital, but Itō followed his advice and went straight to Russia, only changing trains in Berlin. Meanwhile Tokyo made it clear to the Japanese Legation in Russia that Itō had no official mission but could discuss with the Russian leaders 'freely and without reservation'. Hayashi was sarcastic about this fudging by the Tokyo cabinet.[9]

By the end of November, the Japanese cabinet definitely committed itself to accepting a treaty with Britain. News of this was allowed to leak out judiciously. The foreign minister passed the Japanese counterdraft to Hayashi so that he too was made aware of the position. In order to consult Itō, Hayashi was told to send the draft agreement by the hand of some responsible person to Itō wherever he was. On 1 December, Matsui Keishirō, the first secretary at the London Legation, was delegated to take the draft to St Petersburg, where Itō was still staying. Eventually Japan replied to Britain's draft on 16 December and the negotiations went smoothly to the end, the draft being given Itō's blessing during his brief stay in London in January 1902.

After the treaty was signed on 31 January and duly published, Hayashi drew up his report on 'the truth behind the alliance' (*Nichi-Ei dōmei no shinsō*).[10] It amounted to a detailed and damaging account of Japan's two-headed diplomacy – of seeking to conduct private parleys with Russia while being partially committed to talks with Britain. The report was in two parts. Hayashi appears to have penned the first memorandum on the day following the signing of the Alliance on 31 January 1902. It contained serious allegations regarding Japan's true motives. On 30 March he prepared – or more likely had prepared in his office – a more detailed memorandum which amounted to a historical survey of the negotiations. It was a substantial document occupying thirty pages of print. This too contained a damning section entitled 'The progress of the negotiations and Marquis Itō's trip to Europe'.[11] It was eventually forwarded to the Foreign Ministry by safe hand. It was to be carried by Konishi Kotarō, a junior diplomat, who was returning to Japan on board the *Bingo Maru* in the middle of May. It was not therefore available in Tokyo before Itō had returned to Japan in triumph and presented to the emperor the telegrams he had exchanged while he had been overseas.

The Foreign Ministry commissioned a young official, Ishii Kikujirō, to draw up an account of the alliance negotiations as seen from Tokyo.[12] It is not known what the motive was or whether it was a matter of political significance. At all events, it was not compiled as a matter of great urgency. According to Ishii's own account in his *Diplomatic Commentaries*, which was translated into English and published in 1936, the memorandum was written for the first anniversary of the signing of the agreement in 1903. There are serious gaps in this account of events in that it makes no mention of the councils of the Elder Statesmen and is, perhaps understandably, weak regarding events in Europe.[13]

Hayashi was duly honoured for his services to the Alliance, both by

Britain, which conferred the Grand Cross of the Victorian Order on him, and by Japan, which made him a viscount. He is described by one British diplomat as 'the prime mover, if not the creator, of the Alliance'.[14] But for his efforts and his persistence, the Alliance might not have come into being. He had to press the matter on Tokyo; and he had to intercede with Itō both in Paris and in London. But his personal success has to be set against the fact that he had a brush with Itō at this time, and while they may have made it up during Itō's visit to London in January 1902, it was damaging for Hayashi's career to lose the goodwill of an Elder Statesman.

In its early stages the Anglo-Japanese Alliance was an alliance of mutual ignorance. Perhaps this was to be expected at a time when diplomacy was secret. But whereas the Japanese government took steps to correct the British public's ignorance of Things Japanese, Britain did not particularly address the problem. It was the object of Hayashi's embassy in London to educate the great British public and to create a good atmosphere. The press, book publishers and journal publishers appear to have been the targets for the enlightenment. On the whole, there was a considerable coverage of Japanese events and Japanese culture in the 1900s.

During the Russo-Japanese War of 1904–5 Hayashi's legation became a focal point in the war effort. On the military side, the attaché, Colonel Utsunomiya, was abetting the efforts of Colonel Akashi to stimulate forces hostile to Russia in Europe and thus damage the tsarist war effort on the home front. The Finance Minister Takahashi Korekiyo was present raising loans for Japan, while Baron Suematsu Kenchō, Itō's son-in-law, was actively trying to win over British and European opinion by his propaganda activities.[15] Hayashi meantime was negotiating the revised Anglo-Japanese Alliance, which was signed in August 1905 (though its existence was not immediately made known). Again the negotiation had been conducted by Hayashi in London rather than in Tokyo.

In view of these efforts – and what Hayashi described as 'the anxiety and strain' felt at the time – it was fitting that the London Legation should be given embassy status in December 1905 and that Hayashi should become the first Japanese ambassador to Britain, indeed the first Japanese ambassador anywhere in the world. However, he was recalled to Tokyo on 20 March 1906 after six strenuous years without enjoying his new status to the full. This was because Katō had resigned as foreign minister early in March and Hayashi was invited to take over at short notice.

In May he became foreign minister (for the first time) in the first Saionji cabinet. He was immediately immersed in a conference on the Manchurian problem which had surfaced because of the continued occupation by Japanese armies of large parts of Manchuria following the Portsmouth Treaty. He was worried about the deteriorating international reputation of Japan after the war because of the Manchurian problem. In September he opposed the establishment of advisers to the Kwantung leased territory and took leave from the Foreign Ministry temporarily because of illness. He argued, plausibly, that he had come back from Europe to be immediately plunged into a high cabinet post and was exhausted. But in 1907 he was back, negotiating important treaties with Korea, France and Russia and thus stabilizing the East Asian situation. For his efforts he was made a count.

Alongside these successes, Hayashi had difficulties over Aoki Shūzō who was Japan's ambassador in Washington. After he had been in the United States for eighteen months, Aoki reported that he had in his personal capacity suggested an American–Japanese treaty, along certain lines, to President Theodore Roosevelt and that this had been favourably received. Hayashi noted that the project made no mention of the immigration issue, which was, in his view, the sole problem requiring attention. The matter was presented to the cabinet, who rejected Aoki's initiative. It was also considered and rejected by Itō and by Katsura who was visiting him in Seoul.[16] Hayashi, therefore, replied to Aoki, recalling him to Tokyo for taking the law into his own hands without receiving instructions. This misunderstanding over policy towards the United States was to have wider implications for Hayashi's last years.

The majority of the Elder Statesmen became critical of Hayashi. Yamagata and Katsura, who might be described as the leader of the Opposition, denounced Hayashi's Manchurian policy.[17] Eventually the Saionji ministry itself was forced into resignation and on 14 July 1908 Katsura returned to form a new cabinet. According to Hayashi's memoirs, he immediately concluded a treaty with Washington (the so-called 'Root–Takahira Pact') which 'closely resembles the draft prepared by Aoki. . . . What was the reason which made Katsura regard its conclusion as a necessity when last year he opposed it, is unknown.'[18] It seems to have been one result of the bitter personal dispute between Hayashi and Aoki, in which the latter (some six years his senior and probably the most senior member of Japan's diplomatic service) was able to mobilize the support of influential clan friends whose disagreements with Hayashi were wider than the American issue. At all events, Hayashi felt thereafter a sense of grievance that he had not received due thanks and recognition from the state for his labours. After the end of his rather ineffective period as foreign minister, Count Hayashi was now able to enjoy true retirement for the first time. He had already begun working on his memoirs while he was at the London Legation. During his leisure in 1909 Hayashi began to dictate his memoirs to a reporter of *Jiji Shimpō*, to which he had contributed articles anonymously for some years past. The final version, *Nochi wa mukashi no ki*, was published in December 1910. It was generally understood that some portions had been omitted from the book as published.[19]

In August 1911 Hayashi joined Saionji's second ministry as minister for communications and for a while also acted as foreign minister. But the cabinet was short-lived and resigned in the following year when it failed to secure a consensus over increasing the army by two divisions.

On 10 July 1913 Hayashi died in Tokyo at the age of 63. But, like his friend and superior, Mutsu Munemitsu, he left an unexploded bomb behind. He opened the portion of his memoirs which had not been included in the published book, supplemented by other original material, for publication in the newspapers. Immediately after his death, his memorandum on 'The Truth Behind the Anglo-Japanese Alliance' began to be published in serial form by *Jiji Shimpō*. But the government stepped in and banned the publication because it was based on secret official documents, it still being an age of secret diplomacy. Naturally journalists were infuriated by the suppression of the series and versions became available. In particular, *Jiji Shimpō*, whose proprietor Fukuzawa was Hayashi's son-in-law, brought out a four-page supplement on 21 August.[20]

Britain's attitude to the Japanese version of the documents when they appeared in 1913 is given in the Tokyo Annual Report for that year:

The 'Reminiscences of Count Hayashi of the Anglo-Japanese Alliance' ... which were distinguished by their indiscretion, were banned by the Ministry for Foreign Affairs, but nevertheless were published in a local newspaper. They professed to give the history of the negotiations leading up to the Alliance, as vouched for by Count Hayashi, who was himself the prime mover, if not the creator, of this compact. The reminiscences, which were, I take it, the work of a disappointed man, went to prove that the Imperial Government had been inconsistent, if not insincere, in its dealing both with Great Britain and with Russia. They did not, however, do much mischief, and were soon relegated to the category of 'back numbers'. I understand that the publication in question is only a portion of much more extensive reminiscences written by Count Hayashi, but that the Minister for Foreign Affairs has taken steps to prevent the issue of the remaining portions.[21]

Andrew M. Pooley, the Japan correspondent of Reuters, claims that he was able to come into possession of further articles and that the remaining portions were offered to him by a Japanese in October. He duly bought them, translated them and was planning to incorporate them with the other parts of his material in a publication, despite the protestations of the Hayashi family and the Japanese government.[22] In spite of interference by the Japanese police, Pooley was able to smuggle a translation to London. But he himself was under investigation on blackmail charges in connection with the Siemens bribery scandal during much of 1914; he was later prosecuted in the courts and detained for part of the time. Thus he was not able to proceed with the publication immediately. But the assorted Hayashi materials were published under the slightly misleading title *The Secret Memoirs of Count Tadasu Hayashi, GCVO* by Eveleigh Nash late in 1915 in a remarkably elaborate wartime edition. Pooley boasts that revelations in the English language may have created no small surprise to the literary public abroad.[23] It has, however, to be said that the British government knew most of the story already.

The revelations, therefore, did not come as a shock to British officials or journalists who were also aware of the background to the Itō mission in general terms.

Questions have been asked about the authenticity of Pooley's manuscript, notably by Professor Hilary Conroy.[24] It has to be said that the original manuscript on which it is based can be verified from Japanese Foreign Ministry records, and on the whole it is not inaccurate. The raw material taken from Hayashi's writing is authentic (allowing for translation difficulties), but the title 'Secret Memoirs' is misleading. Cheque-book journalism was rife in Tokyo at the time. Pooley was an exponent of it in his private capacity, though Reuter's denied all connection with it. But, while his methods may have been underhand and his book not without its inaccuracies, the general message which he conveys is accurate.

As the British chargé wrote, Hayashi was a disappointed man at the end of his official life. He felt bitterness tinged with a desire for self-justification. One of the factors in his desire to publish the truth may have been Hayashi's yearning to be a journalist – shared incidentally with his contemporary, Katō Takaaki – and an inclination to 'publish and be damned', which was uncommon among Japanese bureaucrats. But, if this was one motive behind Hayashi's desire to clear his name by publications late in his life, there was also an undertone of bitterness, of bearing a grudge against Japanese society and the ruling elite. What was the nature of his complaint? On the surface, he had been eminently successful. After a brief but brilliant diplomatic career from 1895 to 1906, he had been plunged into Japanese politics at the highest level, becoming foreign minister twice and communications minister once. Indeed, he had been a minister until a year before his death.

He had entered into the party structure, joining the Seiyūkai ministries of Saionji. But, in doing so, he had alienated the formidable coalition of forces around Prince Katsura, the Chōshū-dominated political clique associated with the name of the Elder Statesman, Field Marshal Yamagata. It followed policies which Hayashi instinctively abhorred: a continued military presence in Manchuria; a tough line towards the United States over emigration; an increase in the army in Korea; and an increase of the overall strength of the army. Into the bargain, he had alienated one of the lesser luminaries in the Chōshū coalition, Aoki Shūzō, who felt disgraced by his recall from the Washington embassy.

Hayashi claimed to be a victim of political intrigue, and to have been denied his just rewards. By manipulation his opponents apparently withheld what Hayashi sought most, membership of the Privy Council (and possibly certain retirement moneys).[25] This does not entirely explain the mystery since the publication of 'the real facts behind the British Alliance' was not only aimed against Katsura but also against Itō who had died in 1909. Hayashi had the misfortune to have alienated not only the Katsura group but also the most influential statesman of the late Meiji period, Itō Hirobumi. He was short-tempered and had a strict code of honour, which did not readily allow him to make the compromises which were sometimes needed in Meiji times.[26]

Hitherto we have dealt with Hayashi as the political man. It is now necessary to write of him as a scholar, a man of culture and, in particular, as a writer. Not unnaturally he used his talent in English to translate what seemed to be some of the nineteenth-century English classics. In 1875 he translated John Stuart Mill's *Principles of Political Economy* (*Keizairon*) and in the years that followed published in nine parts Jeremy Bentham's *Principles of the Penal Code* (*Keiho Ronko*). Much later in life he published a short novel in English *For His People* (1903). As we have seen, his reminiscences appeared in 1910 as *Nochi wa mukashi no ki*. He also wrote *Itarii-shi*, a history of Italy. Hayashi was also one of the patrons of the movement in the 1900s to replace Chinese ideographs by Roman letters – this at a time when nationalism was growing and Japanese-ness was at a premium. But Hayashi in his day was a force for international trends in Japan. He was a Meiji gentleman of a special kind. He had a code of honour and propriety which he felt had been transmitted from generations past, but he was always attentive to opinion abroad. He was always ready to stand up for his beliefs.

In this composite picture of Hayashi, his contacts with Britain obviously played a large part. From his year in London as a youth to the time when he left as ambassador in 1906, he was regarded as an anglophil. Like many in Japan his idea of the Meiji gentleman had been moulded by his conception of the Victorian English gentleman. In appearance he was bearded and high-collared in the Victorian fashion. He was a consistent advocate of the Anglo-Japanese Alliance. When the third alliance came into existence in 1911, it was widely attacked because it was linked to arbitration agreements. Although he was out of government, Hayashi in *Jiji Shimpō* pointed out that this was a narrow view which did not take into account the ever-increasing tendency among civilized nations to substitute arbitration for war.[27] In the Coronation number of the *Japan Times*, 22 June 1911, Hayashi wrote that there could be no doubt about the Alliance's continuance: 'the only point against which Japan must guard is a wantonly aggressive policy'. Not that Hayashi's sights were solely fixed on Europe; he also had a vision for Japan as the following quotation from 1909 will show: 'The Pacific Ocean will, at a not very distant date, become one of the principal theatres of commercial and political activity.'[28]

If Hayashi had respect for Britain, Britain also had respect for Hayashi. He was much honoured. He received the Honorary LD of the University of Cambridge in 1905 and the DCL of Oxford. He was president of the Japan Society of London from 1900 until 1906 – his only rival in length of service being Ambassador Matsudaira Tsuneo in the 1930s. Lord Lansdowne, the British foreign secretary for most of his years in London, found him loyal and straightforward. After his return to Japan, Sir Claude MacDonald, the

British ambassador in Tokyo, thought him, like Katō Takaaki, to be friendly to Britain, 'frank and honest, very English in his proclivities' and a source of insider information on happenings in Japan and the Japanese court.[29] When Sidney and Beatrice Webb met Hayashi in October 1911 during their leisurely travels in Japan, they recorded their impressions of him in their travel diary thus: 'A sort of Japanese Arthur Balfour with a detached philosophic mind and delightful manners.'[30]

In Japanese circles, Hayashi has been less conspicuous. There is no major biography of him. He does not merit a mention in the *Biographical Dictionary of Japanese History*. So the lack of recognition which Hayashi sensed in the last years of his life may be said to have outlived him. And perhaps unjustly. In our eyes, Hayashi was a remarkable son of the Meiji period, combining a desire for national progress with a sensitivity to internationalism which not all of his contemporaries exhibited.

12

MARIE STOPES (1907–1958) AND JAPAN

Carmen Blacker

Marie Stopes's connection with Japan has been overshadowed by the drama of her later life. The fame and notoriety she acquired as the pioneer of birth control in England, as the crusader for married bliss and wise sex education for women, as the writer of *Married Love, Enduring Passion* and *Radiant Motherhood*, which dealt in floridly romantic yet acceptable language with subjects hitherto 'unmentionable', as the fierce opponent of the Roman Catholic Church and Gandhi, as the author of a play banned by the Lord Chamberlain – have obscured almost entirely the 'Japan' period of her earlier life. Few people now read her *Journal from Japan* (1910). Fewer still have even heard of her *Plays of Old Japan: the Nō* (1913). And fewest of all are aware of the determining drive which first directed her to Japan, her extraordinary love affair with a professor of botany in Tokyo University.[1]

It is arguable, however, that without these earlier 'Japanese' events, her attention might never have turned to the field of birth control. A palaeobotanist she might have remained all her life, and the debt of gratitude which every woman in this country ultimately owes to her, might be directed instead to some other less interesting, less courageous, less intransigent and less exasperating pioneer.

Marie Stopes went to Japan in 1907 with a grant from the Royal Society to study the cretaceous fossil plants to be found in the rocks and coal-seams there. Her family was evangelical and intellectual; her father was an authority on prehistoric flint implements and her mother an enthusiast for women's suffrage and rational dress. Her upbringing was strict. But she showed early promise of a superior intellect and an almost incredible capacity for prolonged hard work. She took her BSc. at University College London in geology and botany, in only two years, and in 1903 left for Munich to study for a doctor's degree in palaeobotany under the renowned Professor K. Goebel. She was the first woman to work at his Institute, the regulations being changed at her insistence to admit her, and after a year of ferociously hard work presented a thesis on fossilized cycads which won her the degree of Doktor, *magna cum laude*.

In Professor Goebel's laboratory she met Professor Fujii Kenjirō, then aged 37, on leave from Tokyo University to study botany in Europe, and already an authority on the gingko tree. He proved a far more congenial companion, with his leanings to poetry and philosophy, than the beer-drinking and duelling German students. She went to the opera with him, and on walks in the mountains to collect specimens, and soon after her return to England in 1904 to take up a lectureship in Manchester University, Fujii also came to London.

An exchange of letters began between them which records their gathering tenderness for each other. In April 1905 they went on an excursion, possibly to Hampstead Heath, when they became secretly engaged. Fujii was at the time married, with one child in Japan. But his wife, he assured Marie, was already unfaithful and suing for a divorce. Marie therefore saw no moral objection to exchanging vows, and on that occasion 'he won from her lips the first kiss she had ever given to a man, a kiss she considered as binding as a marriage vow'.[2]

From the moment of this secret betrothal their correspondence becomes rapturous. Fujii's letters over the next eighteen months are remarkable for the unbridled and imaginative expression of the torrent of feelings which overwhelmed him. Endearments with no equivalent in Japanese poured from his pen. 'Oh my love,' he cries at the end of June,

> My heart begins to beat with supernatural melody. . . . If I am to die now, I wish either to be killed by you . . . or I wish to die with my body in your arms and my lips on yours. . . . Dearest, beloved heart of mine, there were no flowers and no letters which were ever been kissed so many times as I did with yours.

He sailed for Japan in July, and as the distance widened between them their correspondence became more and more impassioned. 'Dear, terribly sweet one', he calls her, 'star of my heart' and 'dearest, sweetest mine and ours'. By October he tells her, 'sweetest of all, oh dear half, you created love in me, your hand-touch began to propagate in my body like an electric current. . . . Without you I shall be a dead mass of blood and bones.' His heart sobs with impatience, he calls her name in bed before sleeping, he dreams of holding her tightly round, with cheek on cheek.

She in her turn wrote him rapturous letters of love and longing, called him 'dear living dream', begged him to learn to waltz, and wanted most to sit on his knee, resting her head against him. She had been starved of kisses for so long that she feared his first kiss might kill her when they met. Each took it for granted that they would be married as soon as possible, he addressing her as 'oh my dearest sweet wife' and she signing herself 'deine Braut, your wife'.

At last a prospect arose that they might be reunited. Marie applied to the Royal Society for a grant to travel to Japan to study the fossil angiosperms to be found in the rocks and coal there. She rightly guessed that these would prove to be of a much later date than the carboniferous fossils found in European coal, and would hence afford entirely new evidence for plant life during the late mesozoic period. Her work promised to be so exciting that the Society agreed to award her the first grant that they had ever given to a woman. She sailed for Japan in June 1907.

From the moment that the news of her imminent arrival reached Fujii, his letters dwindle abruptly to short, infrequent postcards. He is very busy, he is ill, the time is not convenient for him, she had better come a year later. . . . Poor Marie arrived in Japan on 8 August to find awaiting her a letter, addressed to dear Miss Stopes, which told her that he had decided that her view of love was after all wrong.

> That I should have loved any lady, in such strong way as I loved you is quite out of my natural thought, and the thought of any Japanese. I told you in earlier times that love is immoral with us. And now I know that it is really so, if it had such a strong power over me against my natural habit. . . . I hope you will marry some nice Englishman. Yours sincerely, K. Fujii.

In 1911, two years after returning to England from Japan, Marie took the incomprehensible step of publishing the entire correspondence, changing only the proper names. She is Mertyl Meredith, he is Kenrio Watanabe. The letters, purportedly edited by one G.N. Mortlake, are stated to be 'real. There is added to them no fiction, no studied literary effect.' For those to whom truth is dearer than fiction, they will carry the zest of a true revelation of the psychology of the Japanese mind. The lovers, who were both poets, are now dead, but their love, though it had no physical consummation, was so deep and vivid as to carry eternal life. For the rest, the letters speak for themselves. The book appeared under the title *Love Letters of a Japanese*, charmingly published in white and gold buckram by Stanley Paul & Co.

A discerning Japanese friend has queried the authenticity of these letters. So utterly out of character would it seem for a professor of Tokyo University, in the late Meiji period, to have written to a woman in the manner described, that it is easier to believe that Marie Stopes invented the entire correspondence herself. Against this view lies the fact that there are seven letters from Fujii among the Marie Stopes Papers in the British Library which are identical, word for word save for the proper names, with what is transcribed in *Love Letters of a Japanese*. There is also a later series of letters from Fujii to Marie Stopes, written during a visit to England in 1925, which contain indubitable hints of nostalgia for a vanished romance. It is known furthermore that shortly before her death in 1958 Marie destroyed a great many old letters. Nor could she possibly have invented the English, completely authentic of its kind, in which Fujii's letters are written. We conclude that the correspondence as printed is, as claimed, 'real'.[3]

A possible alternative explanation is that for eighteen months Fujii had been indulging in a fantasy: the fantasy of being in love with a foreign woman, a remote, 'outside' being who oddly enough enabled him to give free expression to feelings and emotions which he could never have expressed to a Japanese girl, and which was foreign to the pattern of Japanese culture. Japanese literature contains no love letters which express in such unrestrained terms the writer's natural flow of emotion. Not even Yosano Akiko, as torrid a romanticist as has come down to us from that period, could hold a candle to Professor Fujii's effusions. He indulges in the same kind of fantasy as might a poet pretending to be in love with a goddess or a statue, and thereby acting out a role which releases unknown and unexperienced emotions. But when the ship approaches Yokohama, and the dream threatens to become reality, then, oh horror, escape and advise her to marry a nice Englishman instead.[4]

It speaks much for Marie Stopes's strength of character and determination that, despite this humiliating rebuff and the collapse of her hopes of marriage, she should have steeled herself to make the ensuing eighteen months in Japan so full, stimulating and productive. Her *Journal from Japan* records a good many of her activities, though it is irritatingly reticent about proper names and the technicalities of her fossil work.[5] She arrived to find Tokyo a city of grey wooden houses, lit at night by lanterns, where the only traffic was rickshaws and carts, and where the streets were often ankle deep in mud. But it was a very green town, and Mount Fuji was often visible. She chose to live in a small Japanese house in Koishikawa, which she 'fitted up', with *futon* and no western furniture, for £3, her kitchen items costing no more than a farthing each. A little maid cooked her Japanese meals. Her base was the Botanical Institute of Tokyo Imperial University, an ugly western building with a tin roof, but which boasted one of the new fossil-cutting machines. Here, throughout her stay, she worked long and hard on the cretaceous fossils brought back from her trips to mines, beaches and riverbeds.

Barely ten days after her arrival in Japan, indeed, she was on her way to the Yubari coalfields of Hokkaido, where a rich haul of fossil angiosperms promised to lie embedded in rocks and coal-seams. Here she was allocated a policeman, several coolies and two interpreters, with which retinue she proceeded to climb down mines and to wade up riverbeds in search of the nodules in which were hidden the fossil plants of the cretaceous era. Despite torrential rain and swollen rivers, she returned with a very creditable collection of nodules, though no coal-balls.

Other trips to discover Triassic fossils she made to Okayama, to the Miike coalfield in Kyushu, and to the mines on the island of Amakusa. Thanks to her energetic collecting and expert cutting of the fossils, her laboratory soon acquired celebrity enough to be visited by Dr Koch, the bacteriologist, by Sven Hedin and by Sir Claude MacDonald himself.

It is clear that no one at all in Japan had an inkling of her romance with Fujii, and clear too that she continued to encounter him from time to time in the Botanical Institute. But heartbreak and humiliation in no wise inhibited her from a social life which was 'most gay and delightful'. The British community invited her to balls and banquets; she went to an Imperial garden party. She in her turn started a ladies' debating society, and gave regular At Homes in her little house. She chose to bicycle everywhere in Tokyo, even to a dance at the Belgian Embassy in a 'traily pink frock'.

How was Marie Stopes, a single woman, insistently professional, touchy and insensitive, very much 'the first woman scientist from the west to work in the University with Japanese men of science' – how was such a woman regarded by the Japanese men of science?

Her position was certainly an anomalous one. But it appears that the professors of Tokyo University on the whole had the courtesy to treat her as a kind of honorary man. Her *Journal* records frequent faculty meetings, New Year visitors, dinners where she is the only foreigner present.

But she was particularly and almost miraculously fortunate in winning, early in her stay, the friendship and warm affection of one of the most distinguished scholars and scientists to emerge from Meiji Japan. Dr Sakurai Jōji, later Baron Sakurai, had been one of the first students sent by the Meiji government to study science in England. He entered University College London in 1876 to study physics and chemistry, winning a gold medal for chemistry after his first year. He returned to Japan in 1881, and the following year was appointed, at the age of 24, professor at Tokyo University. A succession of honours, responsibilities and tokens of international acclaim were to follow over the rest of his life. He was to become president of Tokyo University, a privy councillor, a member of the House of Peers, founder-president of the Japan Society for the Promotion of Science and an Honorary Fellow of University College London. At his death in 1939, *Nature* carried an obituary which described him as

> 'the great promotor of scientific research in Japan, ardent lover of peace and friendship amongst men, and one of the finest spirits and greatest gentlemen of this or any age. Proud indeed must be his homeland to have produced one who was honoured, respected and beloved by men of science of many nations, and proud are we in England to have had him in our care during his formative years of study at University College London.' This great and good man was indeed 'the friend of all men of goodwill throughout the world'.[6]

This was the man who befriended Marie Stopes in the autumn of 1907 and who allowed none of his responsibilities to interfere with the loyal affection in which he continued to hold her for the rest of his life. None of her letters

161

to him survive. But his letters to her, written with an impeccable elegance and courtesy seldom seen today, are in the British Library. They span a period of thirty-two years, during which she ceased to be the enterprising, eccentric woman botanist he had first encountered in Tokyo, and became by degrees one of the most notorious figures in the British Isles, celebrated for her crusade for emancipation in a subject just as 'unmentionable' in Japan as it was in England. Throughout the vicissitudes of her marriage, its annulment on the grounds of non-consummation, her dramatically successful *Married Love*, *Enduring Passion* and *Radiant Motherhood*, her *New Gospel to all Peoples*, a message sent straight from God through her to the bishops at Lambeth in 1920, her second marriage, her birth-control clinic, her violent controversies and litigations with the Roman Catholic Church, her play banned by the Lord Chamberlain[7] – never once did he waver in his steady loyalty and affection, wise understanding and encouragement.

His first letter invites her to tea in his house in Akebonochō, to meet three professors. She accepted, was entranced by his roses and promptly invited him to a dance at the Hotel Metropole, Tsukiji. Most politely he replied that he had had no practice in dancing for a quarter of a century, but would much like to accept if he could merely be a 'looker-on'. He must have overcome his scruples, however, for the next day he wrote to say that 'the waltz I had the pleasure of dancing with you was a perfect enjoyment'.

Thereafter, for the rest of her stay in Japan, he watched over her welfare, lunched with her every Friday, introduced her to influential friends, took her to the Nō and demonstrated to her his skill in the chanting of *utai*. From this last event arose the scheme that they should collaborate over a book which might introduce to the English reader the medieval beauties of the Nō.

After her departure for Canada in January 1909, he wrote to her regularly, addressing her as Rose, 'because of all the flowers it is the rose I love best, for its noble sweetness and its prickly stem'. She in her turn addressed him as Noble. Thereafter he was to rejoice with her on her marriage, commiserate with her on its failure and congratulate her somewhat amazedly on the runaway success of *Married Love*:

I *have* read your wonderful book, and am so amazed that I don't exactly know what to say about it. This much however I can say that I admire your boldness more than ever, your fearlessness in speaking out what nine hundred and ninety-nine people out of a thousand would never have dared to say. At the same time, I feel I *must* say that there are certain things which, as it appears to me, would have made your work holier and more poetic, if left unsaid, such for example, as the description of the actual process of – you know.

He was to visit England, to attend international congresses and to promote schemes of scientific cooperation, five times more. He invariably made time to see her and to stay with her family. 'I do pray that God may watch over you and guard you wherever you go', he wrote. When her letters, owing to illness or absorbtion in birth-control lecture tours, became infrequent, he was thrown into an agony of anxiety. 'I was getting *quite desperate*,' he wrote in June 1923, 'and was beginning to fear that I must, in some way unknown to me, have offended you. I feel *such a relief* in knowing that after all I did not offend you.' He complimented her on her only son Harry – 'he is the loveliest and most beautiful child I have ever seen'. He joined her party to watch the Coronation procession in 1937, having come to England with Prince Chichibu who represented the emperor. His last letter thanks her for her Coronation poem, and deplores the war in China.

But the permanent monument to their friendship was their book on the Nō. They went together to a performance of Nō in November 1908. She was apparently instantly captivated by its beauty and mystery, and the suggestion that they should collaborate on a book seems to have come from her. He was to do a first translation, which she was then to 'work into a finished product'.

To date no single volume had appeared in English devoted to the Nō. Translations of single plays or brief passages by Chamberlain, Aston, Dickins and Sansom had found their place in general studies of Japanese literature and poetry. But Yeats and Ezra Pound did not begin their discussions of the Nō until 1913, Yeats's *Hawk's Well* did not appear until 1917, and the classic study by Arthur Waley, *The Nō Plays of Japan*, was not to follow until 1921. In a very real sense therefore, Marie Stopes and Dr Sakurai were pioneers in offering to the English-reading public translations of four Nō plays, with an introduction by Marie remarkably perspicacious for its time.

Their collaboration was carried out entirely by correspondence, their letters travelling by the Trans-Siberian Railway, larger packets going all the way by sea. After some discussion as to what plays to include in their book, they decided on *Motomezuka*, or 'The Maiden's Tomb', *Kagekiyo* and *Sumidagawa*, which Dr Sakurai considered 'very pathetic and beautiful', together with a full resumé of *Tamura*. None of these plays had been translated before.

On her return from Japan she must have worked hard and quickly, for on 15 October 1909 he can congratulate her on 'having got the Nō pulled into shape', and to express amazement that she had accomplished so much in the time. On 15 November she was able to read a version of *Sumidagawa* to the Royal Society of Literature, with a very competent introduction describing the 'wonderful old plays, full of poetry, pathos and indescribable charm', the music and its unfamiliar scale, and the peculiar difficulties of translation. She had the satisfaction of observing that at the end of her reading, many of her audience were in tears.[8]

The version she gave was, however, full of rather serious mistakes of translation, which Dr Sakurai speedily corrected. By September 1912, in the same letter that he reports being in the funeral procession of the Emperor Meiji, passing a million people along the route in utter silence, he writes that the resumé of *Tamura*, though 'wonderfully correct on the whole', still needs a good deal of correction. Two months later, however, he had received the completed manuscipt of *Plays of Old Japan: The Nō*.[9] 'What you have done is really a wonder', he wrote, modestly disclaiming the decidedly scant acknowledgements she makes of his own part in the venture.

She sent him only three copies of the book, which reached him in June 1913, and for which he expressed warm gratitude. He ordered a dozen copies from Maruya for distribution to friends such as Professor Fujii . . .

Her introduction to the book, to date one of the best general accounts of the Nō in English, gives vivid expression to her own most unusual delight in the plays and her hope of conveying to English readers something of the beauty of this unexplored literature. In a section entitled 'The Effect of the Nō on the Audience and on me', she comments on the absorbed, learned audience, who follow the chanting on their own scores so as not to lose a word, and who are versed enough in classical poetry to enjoy the rich texture of allusions and hidden quotations which fill the plays. Indeed, considering that her own grasp of Japanese was probably limited to a few useful colloquial phrases, she writes remarkably percipiently about pillow-words, pivot-words and the complex allusions which characterize the language of the Nō *utai*. She confessed herself entirely captivated by these elemental tragedies, so potent in their combination of music, dance and symbol.

She decided to render the whole of the texts, irrespective of the difference between *utai* and prose, into some kind of poetic rhythm, for English prose was too jagged and coarse to convey the melodious effect of the medieval Japanese. The *utai* passages, in fact, are rendered remarkably successfully in blank verse, while the *kotoba* passages are in a longer metre reminiscent of *Hiawatha*. It is sad that this book has been so entirely forgotten. I know of only one person who possesses a copy.

Marie Stopes was to make two appearances before the Japan Society, both of them as a first woman. She was the first woman to read a paper to the Society, with her 'Value and Interest of Japanese Fossils' on 9 March 1910. And on 25 April 1920, when she took the chair for Arthur Waley, it was the first occasion in the history of the Society that a meeting was presided over by a lady.

Her fossil lecture is lucid, and far more informative than her *Journal* about what exactly she was doing with fossils in Japan, and why they were important. Her greatest find, the 'first petrified flower to be found in any country', is actually illustrated in the *Transactions*.[10]

Arthur Waley's paper ten years later, for which she took the chair, was entitled, 'The Nō: A Few Translations'. Here, with no further introduction than brilliantly to transpose *The Duchess of Malfi* into Nō form, he read the felicitous translations of *Hagoromo*, *Ikenie* and *Hachinoki*, which were to appear in his book the following year. He was known to date only for his *170 Chinese Poems*, *More Translations from the Chinese* and *Japanese Poetry: The Uta*. *The Tale of Genji* was not to follow until 1925. She on the other hand was the author not only of *Plays of Old Japan* but also of *Married Love*, which by 1920 had sold nearly a million copies, and of *A Letter to Working Mothers: On How to Avoid Weakening Pregnancies*. It is likely that she had read his works, but very unlikely that he had read hers. It is even less likely that any single member of the Society attending the meeting had even heard of the notorious writings.

No chairman's remarks, alas, are recorded for this meeting, nor any discussion which might have followed the paper. The encounter between two such powerful yet disparate characters must be left to the imagination. For many of us, the scene may well exceed the boggle-threshold.[11]

Marie Stopes never returned to Japan. Nor did she ever attempt to bring her gospel of birth-control to Japanese women. There is no record of any advice or encouragement sent by her to Ishimoto Shizue, on whose shoulders the task largely fell. Warned by Dr Sakurai in 1929 that Japanese law dealt stringently with any propaganda for family planning, and that her books, if translated, would be banned from sale, she doubtless felt her energies better spent in England. After 1945 she increasingly turned her attention to literature and poetry.

She has been described as one of the most remarkable women of the twentieth century, remarkable not least for the fundamental irony of her life: she who devoted so much of her energies to teaching women how to avoid the misery and exhaustion which too often had been their lot hitherto, and to guide them instead to the ways of mental and physical happiness, was unable to find this happiness for herself. She died in 1958 at the age of 77 still in pursuit. Her own discontent at the last, however, in no wise diminishes the magnitude of her accomplishment; her fearlessness, her obstinacy, her lucid writing, her tireless initiative have left all women in this country in her debt. On the one occasion when I met her, in January 1956, she was living alone in a large eighteenth-century house near Dorking, the walls covered with beautiful frescoes, the rooms stuffed with papers, files and books. No family, no devoted disciples surrounded her. But she still remembered the Nō as among the great things in world literature, and she may have realized herself to be perhaps the only western woman to have been the recipient of two such remarkable series of letters from Japanese men.

13

SIDNEY WEBB (1859–1947) AND BEATRICE WEBB (1858–1943) AND JAPAN

Colin Holmes

Sidney and Beatrice Webb stand as important figures in the history of the labour movement in Britain. In particular, alongside other prominent intellectuals such as H.G. Wells and George Bernard Shaw, they are viewed as the personification of the Fabian Society. Indeed, in the course of their long lives (Sidney Webb lived between 1859 and 1947 and Beatrice Webb between 1858 and 1943), the Webbs devoted most of their time and energies to the development and advance of Socialism. Their contribution came in a variety of forms. They were intimately associated with works of scholarship which presented the case for socialism at a time when the prevailing intellectual climate did not guarantee its easy acceptance. In the case of Sidney Webb, his commitment also took him into the Labour cabinet in 1924 as president of the Board of Trade and again between 1929 and 1931 when he served as colonial secretary. Related to such endeavours, the Webbs were responsible for the foundation of the London School of Economics. They remained deeply involved in the early development of this institution, which they hoped would provide through its activities a more scientific understanding of society.[1] To a great extent, therefore, they devoted their lives to the public good, and in order to acquire the knowledge with which to argue their case, they showed, like Marx, a restless interest in social enquiry. Between June 1911 and May 1912 this intellectual prurience took them on a world tour which incorporated a visit to Japan.

The Webbs have left a written testimony of their journey. It lies particularly in 530 pages of typescript in Beatrice Webb's diary, 'which she never had the time or much inclination to work up into a planned book on the Far East', and also in a considerable number of letters.[2] Although a published account of the journey never appeared, there is no doubt that the tour assumed an importance in the Webbs' development: 'It certainly preceded a change of political direction as decisive as the shift in attitude which followed the

Australian visit of 1898 and the expedition to the Soviet Union in 1932.' When they returned to Britain they were more critical of imperialism and also particularly 'aware of the rising tide of nationalism in Asia'. Even so, it has been claimed that 'In retrospect the journey seems to look like a long ante-room to the next phase of the partnership.'[3] In fact, leaving the personal development of the Webbs on one side, their observations on Japan are of continuing interest; so are their additional scattered comments on that country. But this is to anticipate. There is a need to set the scene for the Webbs' observations.

Before the late nineteenth century Europeans curious about Japan faced considerable difficulty in their attempts to gain knowledge of that country. The contrast in this regard between China and Japan is staggering. Since the expulsion of Christian missionaries in 1639 Japan remained largely isolated from the western world. It was not until the mid-nineteenth century that Japan's period of isolation began to fade. As it did so, 'One result was a flow of Japanese woodblock prints, decorative art and fabrics to Europe and sumptuous Japanese displays at International Exhibitions in London, Paris, Vienna and the United States.'[4] A boom or craze for *japanoiserie* appeared. This interest in the exotic, similar to the earlier passion for Chinese art and flowers, is also reflected in the first production in 1885 of Gilbert and Sullivan's *The Mikado*.

This drawing of Japan into the community of nations encouraged Europeans to travel to the Far East, particularly in the 1870s after the opening of the Suez Canal. 'In Victorian and Edwardian Britain the superior classes were travelling classes. They were always going abroad. Their lives were a constant bustle of arrival and departure, their portmanteaux and hatboxes were plastered with foreign labels, and many of the myriad letters that they wrote and received carried the postmarks of exotic places.'[5] Japan could not escape this curiosity about 'abroad', even if the Mediterranean exercised a more powerful attraction and fascination. Furthermore, some Europeans began to work in Japan: two outstanding examples are Basil Hall Chamberlain, brother of the noted Teutonist, H.S. Chamberlain, and W.G. Aston, a superb linguist and pioneer student of Japanese literature.

These developments led to an increase in writings on Japan. Publishers in Britain and other European countries, were keen to have books on Japan on their lists. 'English books on Japan abound',[6] a writer observed in 1904. There is also little doubt that publishing houses, certainly in the Victorian period, were anxious to slant, or massage, the image of Japan. Their interest lay in portraying it as a 'strange and singular country' in spite of its growing westernization.[7] Such writing helped to enhance the appeal of Japan.

However, this image did not exist in isolation in the years leading up to the First World War. It has been claimed that 'The essentially frivolous image of Japan formed by Europeans in the second half of the nineteenth century was abruptly challenged by the Japanese victory over China in 1895.[8]

However, this claim is not completely justified. The defeat of China in the Sino-Japanese War was not regarded as significant by military strategists in Britain. A recognition of Japan's military potential did not occur until the Russo-Japanese War of 1904–5. Colonel Charles A'Court Repington, who covered the war for *The Times* played a key role in influencing British public opinion in this direction. Japanese military successes in the war against Tsarist Russia also encouraged a wider recognition of Japan as a significant political force in Asia and led the British to congratulate themselves on having secured the 1902 Anglo-Japanese Alliance – in such circumstances the British became partial to portrayals of their ally as the new Britain of Asia.[9]

In the early twentieth century a quickening of British interest in Japan can be detected. Social commentators who agonized over the 'condition of England' question and the relative decline of Britain in the world regarded Japan and Germany as the two exemplars pointing the way towards the society of the future. In these circumstances some Englishmen, such as Alfred Stead, acted as unofficial publicists for Japan. Stead helped particularly to publicize the writings of Nitobe Inazō whose *Bushido: The Soul of Japan*, which first appeared in 1899, went through a number of English editions. Indeed, the section on *bushidō* in Stead's edited book, *Japan by the Japanese*, which appeared in 1904 and carried a fulsome dedication to the emperor of Japan, was written by Nitobe. Stead, the son of W.T. Stead, the well-known newspaper editor, was also responsible in 1906 for *Great Japan: A Study of National Efficiency*, which made its own distinctive contribution to the condition-of-England debate.

These images of Japan and the growing British interest in that country during the so-called 'Age of Imperialism' provide the background to the visit by the Webbs. In the case of those British who trekked to the Mediterranean, it has been claimed that, 'the only local people with whom the majority . . . had contact were shopkeepers and servants, and even with these contact was kept to a minimum'.[10] As regards the Webbs and Japan, their contacts remained equally but differently limited. 'Arriving with excellent introductions from the Japanese Ambassador in London, they started by meeting the outgoing prime minister, the vice-minister of foreign affairs, a financial magnate and a scattering of University professors.' In such company the Webbs showed themselves to be 'assured and indefatigable travellers'.[11] But how did they view Japan? What impressions of that country did they receive?

Before the Webbs set foot in continental Asia they had encountered the Japanese in Hawaii in 1898. At this time they had been presented with a number of positive stereotypes of the Chinese on the island but with a relatively unfavourable image of the Japanese. 'The Japanese are not regarded so favourably [as the Chinese] by the capitalists. They are usually allowed to be more intelligent and more versatile but they have objectionable notions as to leisure and a quite intolerable personal independence. They have even been suspected of mediating a strike against their labour contracts. . . . then they have shown signs of wishing to take part in politics and bitterly resent being excluded from citizenship as Asiatics.'[12] The Webbs recorded such opinions. It is not known if, at this stage of their development, they endorsed these sentiments.

When they entered Asia on their Far Eastern tour they found that among westerners a similar set of split images prevailed, with the Chinese being more highly regarded than the Japanese. In other words, the generally positive image of the Japanese which circulated in Britain was less in evidence among westerners in Japan. This difference in perception relating to the Chinese and Japanese intrigued the Webbs and they could not resist the opportunity to speculate on the reasons for it. Were the Europeans affronted by the Japanese insistence on 'equality of consideration and treatment'?[13] Did they

> resent the extraordinary energy and persistency, the concentration of purpose, and the undeniable efficiency with which the Japanese have made good their position as equals of the white race, and as its rivals in war and trade; even its successful rivals, before whose steadily growing power the foreigner is losing ground in Japan itself, in finance as well as in commerce?[14]

In fact, the Webbs had no doubt on the sources of the antipathy:

> The success of the Japanese comes as an unpleasant shock to the dignity, or the self-conceit of the Englishman; and he has an uncomfortable feeling that the Japanese may actually beat him in some respects: as he actually does in intellectual curiosity and open-mindedness, and in intellectual humility; even perhaps in family and national altruism, and in patriotism.[15]

Such sentiments suggest that, for their part, the Webbs developed a favourable impression of Japan and the Japanese during their visit. By contrast they had little positive to say about China and the Chinese. They did not remain content with making this observation. They tried to explain why the two countries had followed their respective paths. In the case of the Japanese they observed:

> What has made these wonderful achievements possible is the character of the Japanese people: its extraordinary idealism or mysticism which manifests itself in its all-pervading reverence – reverence for the parent, reverence for the teacher, reverence for the local landed-proprietor, reverence for the official, above all reverence for the Emperor: which is seen in the amazing patriotism and self-sacrifice for Japan; and which is accompanied by a remarkable capacity for deliberate plan, persistent effort and the subordination of the present to the future.[16]

This emphasis on subordination and discipline appeared more than once in the Webbs' analysis. After rejecting various possible reasons for the

169

formation of the Japanese national character, the Webbs focused eventually upon the fact that the Japanese, unlike the Chinese, had been drilled and disciplined by centuries of strict 'feudalism' with its dominant emphases on universal obligation and self-subordination. 'This, on the whole, seems the most plausible explanation – just as Carlyle ascribes the national development of England to the stern discipline of the Norman Conquest.'[17]

In a diary entry headed 'On the "Homeward" Sea 16th to 25th April 1912' which was written 'on a crowded ship, disturbed by three crying babies and two dogs, in unpleasant moist heat which only the cool draughts of the incessantly-going fans made endurable' Beatrice Webb allowed one critical comment on the Japanese to intrude. 'One sees in front of them, the danger of becoming vulgarised by their success as practical men – of losing the substance of their ideal, in the shadow of accomplishment.'[18]

Nevertheless, criticism is sparse in relation to celebratory comment and it can be readily understood why George Bernard Shaw could write to the Webbs in 1916: 'You are utopian and pro-Jap.'[19] The Webbs' favourable image of Japan appeared notably in the diary of Beatrice Webb, in private communication with friends and also in their published observations relating to the tour of the Far East. In the last it is possible to find additional strands of critical comment which deserve attention. The Webbs did not approve of the social treatment of women in Japan. This concern arose not only from the degree of subordination practised within the family but also from the power over women wielded by factory owners and geisha masters. The Webbs also expressed their concern that the Japanese had failed to introduce a medical system at all comparable to those in the west. Furthermore, they pondered how quickly the Japanese bureaucracy would be 'clever enough to jump to a systematic application of the policy of the national minimum in sanitation, education, leisure and subsistence, BY WHICH, AS ENGLISH EXPERIENCE TEACHES US, THE COUNTRY CAN ALONE BE SAVED'.[20] Even so, as in their private papers, the Webbs remained anxious to emphasize that Japan was 'so civilized a country' and they stood firm and square in their belief that 'it is still the land of the Rising Sun'.[21]

These positive images springing from the visit to Japan did not totally prevail for all time. The end of the First World War induced in the Webbs fears for the future. 'There is always the question of questions: is Europe going to recover or are we now on the eve of the first stage in the decline of the white race?'[22] A fear of Asia, known as 'the Yellow Peril', had emerged in the course of the late nineteenth and early twentieth centuries in countries as far apart as Australia, Germany, Russia and the United States and echoes of it sounded in Britain. In the case of the Webbs the fear of Japan, an integral component of the Yellow Peril syndrome, came late. But, having settled, it did not depart. The apprehension stood revealed in a comment of 20 July 1920 when, after expressing fears from the future, the diary entry continued:

And very naturally we do not see our successors in the coloured races we have always deemed inferior to our own. Over them we are accustomed to rule – with one exception – cold blooded scientific Japan. Is she going to lead the coloured races, not only to revolt but to supremacy? This may seem a childish fear. But whichever race proves to be united in its purpose – a purpose coinciding with the nature of things – and shows itself capable of pursuing that purpose scientifically must become the leader, if not the ruler of the human race – or at any rate, of all other races having no fixed purpose, or not possessing the scientific capacity to achieve such purpose as they have.[23]

This observation hints at a possible Yellow Peril in the future. By this stage, however, the Webbs had not become totally consumed by a fear of Japan. The young Hugh Dalton noted in 1922 that the Webbs' veneration of things Japanese, even though perhaps more evident in the past than the present, still continued to excite a degree of mild ridicule.

By the 1930s, however, the Webbs' fears had heightened. The military aggression of Japan during these years delivered the decisive blow. To the Webbs the imperialist adventures of Japan in Manchuria and China threw down a challenge to the United States, the Soviet Union and Britain. In their reading of the future the Webbs envisaged a world dominated by the United States, the USSR and Japan. By contrast Europe would 'sink into insignificance – as Greece did before the advent of Christianity'. In this unfolding of the world political scene the Webbs postulated in 1935 that the best hope for the future lay in the development of communism in Europe.

Will any section of the Europe of today, before it is too late, become Communist and get a new start? It is significant that the only one of the three great powers – the USSR, USA and Japan, who is today a member of the League of Nations, is the communist – the creation of Lenin! The situation is an ironical paradox – a monstrous outcome of the war to end war . . . what a comedy![24]

In 1937 the role of Japan continued to obsess the Webbs: 'The world events which every day animates our evening listening to the news is the Sino-Japanese War.'

By now the Webbs could reverse their earlier assessment and write of the Chinese in glowing terms. 'China . . . has been finding herself, a new self, patriotic and with an understanding of science and a growing appreciation of the new civilization of the USSR.'

Such developments, influenced by the sinews of war, meant it was 'conceivable that the communism of this race with its ancient and accomplished civilisation, may be different, and in some respects better, than that developed out of the hotch potch of barbarism of Czarist Russia'.[25] In contrast, the Webbs' attachment to Japan had turned to ashes. Hence Beatrice Webb could write with all that passion born out of disappointment:

> we have always been admirers of Japan: alike before and after our visit in 1911. But since the Great War she has been an evil influence in the world, intensely imperialist, militarist, insincere in her religious faith, reactionary in her political and economic doctrine. Japan has, in fact 'lost her head' and I think her soul.[26]

How can these observations be viewed and understood? A study of the western image of Japan between 1850 and 1905 remarked that

> one sees and believes largely what one wants to. . . . Those who believed that a non-western, non-white, non-Christian country such as Japan could not possibly, by sheer force of things, develop into an industrial society or towards more progressive politics refused to accept evidence to the contrary.[27]

In contrast, 'The excessively pro-Japanese . . . tended to exaggerate changes out of all proportion.' Such selective inattention is not peculiar to those people interested in Japan. On the contrary, an assessment of Victorian and Edwardian travellers came to the conclusion that 'Travel did not broaden their minds. Too often their mental horizons contracted as their physical horizons widened and they returned home settled rather than disturbed in their views about life and art, God and man, good and evil.'[28] Indeed, the tendency to selectivity is not confined to the Victorians and Edwardians alone.

In the case of the Webbs and Japan their perceptions during the Far East tour were influenced by the images they had accepted before ever they set foot in the country, images which they derived partly from the publications relating to Japan which proliferated in the course of the nineteenth and early twentieth centuries. It is particularly interesting, even if it has gone largely unnoticed, that Sir Charles Eliot, scholar, diplomat and, for a period, vice-chancellor of Sheffield University, as well as a friend of the Webbs, had written on the Japanese in the course of a visit to the Far East in terms which presaged the Webbs' assessment. Eliot had observed: 'the Japanese are Asiatics who can imitate Europeans, and that is the root of the matter. That is what really differentiates them from other Asiatics.'[29] Influences such as these (Eliot's text was known to the Webbs), and the ideological baggage derived from years of reflection on the most efficient form of social organization, which the Webbs took with them on their journey to Asia, help to explain the 'earnestness and tunnel vision' which they revealed on their trek to the east.[30]

It is clear that when the Webbs reported on Japan in a favourable light in the years before the Great War, during the Far East visit, and on other occasions, they did so partly as a result of what were widely perceived in the west to be the qualities of *bushidō*. In its origins *bushidō* was the moral code of the *bushi*, the samurai, the military class of pre-modern Japan. Its first systematic exposition appeared in the seventeenth century, at a time when the function of the warrior class was changing from a purely military role to that of providing general social leadership. The individual samurai was expected to show devotion to duty and loyalty to his lord; he was also charged with subordinating personal considerations to moral principle. In practice, significant lapses occurred from this high standard and by the early twentieth century the traditional concept of *bushidō* had declined in social significance.

Nevertheless, some western commentators seized upon what they understood to be its essence, particularly its emphasis on self-subordination, and suggested that it could play a role in the future evolution of European society. A number of British observers, deeply fearful of the relative decline in Britain's world position, proved particularly assiduous in purveying its relevance to the European experience. In this exercise they were assisted by a number of Japanese writers who gave a stamp of authority to such activity. Apart from Nitobe Inazo, it is interesting to come across a series of lectures given by Y. Okakura at the London School of Economics, the Webbs' creation, their intellectual child, in 1905. In his discourse Okakura claimed that without the code of the *bushi* Japan would not have made the progress she had during the previous forty years. Did the Webbs join the audience to hear this message?[31]

Among British writers who dwelt on the code of the *bushi*, a prominent place is filled by Colonel Charles A'Court Repington whose writings, such as his article in *The Times* on 4 October 1904, emphasized both the military and social importance of *bushidō*. Others, including Sir Ian Hamilton, in *A Staff Officer's Scrapbook during the Russo-Japanese War* (1905), followed suit in stressing that self-sacrifice for the state had brought about the greatness of Japan. This kind of emphasis stretched beyond military writers such as Repington and Hamilton. Alfred Stead, deeply influenced by the work of Nitobe Inazo, gave the concept a recognizable prominence. Indeed, he equated it with 'the totality of the moral instincts of the Japanese race', in other words, 'the soul of Japan'.[32] It is hardly surprising, therefore, to read Stead's ringing proclamation: 'The transformation of modern Japan [was] itself the fruit of the teaching of Bushido.'

The cult of *bushidō* did not exercise universal influence in writings on Japan which appeared in Britain. An article in *The Athenaeum* in 1904 adopted a particularly jaundiced perspective and, among experts, Basil Hall Chamberlain reflected a critical posture in his book *The Invention of a New Religion*, which appeared in 1912. However, such voices did not totally drown the choir which loudly sung its praises.

But did the Webbs make any contribution to the circulation of this particular theme? A visit in 1908 to Hadleigh Farm Colony to view the work of the Salvation Army resulted in the following complimentary comment on the Army's officers: 'in respect to personal character all the men and women constitute a *Samurai* caste, that is they are the men and women elected for their power of subordinating themselves to their cause, most assuredly a remarkable type of ecclesiastic'.[33] This notion of self-sacrifice, subordination, the repression of the self for the good of society, all growing out of the concept of *bushidō* as it came to be understood, is also a key component in the Webbs' perceptions of Japan on their Far Eastern tour. In expressing such interest the Webbs did not stand alone among their Fabian contemporaries. In his novel *A Modern Utopia* which appeared in 1905 H.G. Wells called his ruling élite 'the Samurai'. In 1907 in a Fabian pamphlet Oliver Lodge referred explicitly to the role of *bushidō* in creating 'the magnificent spectacle of Japan'.[34]

The influence and presence of *bushidō* in the Webbs' observations of Japan in the early twentieth century has lain virtually unnoticed. By contrast, two critical observations have been directed at the image of Japan which they projected on the basis of their tour in the Far East.

First, they have been accused of suppressing unfavourable aspects of Japanese society, of failing to portray it warts and all. Attention has been drawn specifically to their failure to emphasize the arrest and subsequent execution in January 1911 of twelve Japanese socialists allegedly involved in an assassination plot, an incident which had been raised at the Labour Party Annual Conference in 1911. There are echoes here of the later charge that they glossed over crucial aspects of life in the Soviet Union when they visited that country in 1932. The purges, the labour camps did not feature in their survey of life in the Soviet Union. In the case of Japan the generally celebratory tone of the Webbs' observations has already been conceded.[35]

Second, the Webbs have come under attack for their so-called 'racialism'.[36] It has been claimed that clear signs of this trait appeared in comments made during the tour of the Far East as well as elsewhere in their writings.

A reading of Beatrice Webb's diaries and papers leaves no doubt that she displayed a particular and persistent interest in race and racial characteristics. She can be found observing that a person was Jewish, even in situations where ethnic origin had no significance. This interest in Jewishness cannot be treated as exceptional: she could also find time to comment on the perceived racial characteristics of the Irish, that 'ramshackle race'.[37] In making such comments no line divides Beatrice Webb from her husband. Sidney Webb might have prided himself on a more scientific approach to ethnic and racial issues. However, this passion for scientific exactitude did not inhibit his capacity for commenting on the historical significance of racial and ethnic origins.

The opinions of the Webbs on the Chinese have been regarded as a particularly striking example of their capacity for race-thinking. To Beatrice Webb the Chinese were 'essentially an unclean race'.[38] To Sidney Webb the Chinese could be described as 'a race of ants, or bees of gregarious habits, but incapable of the organization of the ant-hill or the hive'.[39] Such assessments have been deployed to mount a bigger case against the Webbs. It runs as follows. 'The Webbs were not alone in voicing the racialism of the left. . . . It may not have been a complete accident, then, that Oswald Mosley emerged not from the Conservative but rather from the Labour Party.' The racial attitudes of early socialists were in turn related to 'the paternalism with which they approached the British working class as well as the "lower races" and of their failure to make the concept of equality an integral part of their Socialist position'.[40]

This assessment, by placing an emphasis on race-thinking among socialists, directs attention from the wider currency of such thought in the late nineteenth and early twentieth centuries to which the Webbs' comments on racial groups are related. It is often assumed that those who engage in racial categorizations and classifications form part of the periphery of society or inhabit a form of 'underworld'. In fact, in the years before the First World War this form of categorization was widespread in respectable circles.[41] Some confirmation of this claim comes in a standard history of anthropological theory: 'No major figure in the social sciences between 1860 and 1890 escaped the influence of evolutionary racism'.[42] There is also evidence to suggest that race-thinking, albeit in a less sophisticated shape, circulated as popular currency.

But what of this race-thinking and Japan? It has been claimed that the Webbs' account of the Far East while displaying a racial hostility towards the Chinese and being characterized generally by an 'élitist' and 'illiberal' perspective, showed no signs of treating Japan and the Japanese in racial terms. In the case of Japan, 'the rule of white political, intellectual and moral superiority did not apply'; in other words, 'the Webbs exempted the Japanese from their racialist judgements'.[43] In view of the widespread diffusion of interest in race and racial categorization at this time any such claim is surprising. Not only is it surprising, it is also inaccurate.

It is certainly the case that if a search is undertaken in the Webbs' travelogue for any assertion of white superiority over the Japanese it is impossible to uncover it. However, race-thinking does not always move along such a narrow, confined axis. One of the distinctive features of social thought emerging in the Victorian era is that of 'bright racialism' or, as it has been glossed, 'the admiration for cultures other than one's own'.[44] The Webbs' observations on Japan, their laudation of Japan and the Japanese fall into that particular conceptual box.

In displaying this trait the work of the Webbs resides in good company. Philip Lyttleton Gell wrote to Lord Milner in 1904:

I shall turn Japanese for they at least can think, and be reticent!. . . . I fail to see any Western people in a position to set the Japs an example, in their diplomacy. . . . their organization, their strategy, their virile qualities, their devotion and self-control. Above all, their national capacity for self-reliance, self-sacrifice and their silence.[45]

This further testimony to 'bright racialism', in private correspondence, also hints at the significance, yet again, of *bushidō*. Public testimony could be equally revealing. In an age when members of the educated élite were brought up in the classical tradition, the influence of Greece and Rome on the evolution of western civilization did not encounter any challenge. Hence there is considerable significance in the view of Valentine Chirol, appearing in 1896, in which he referred to the Japanese in the same breath as the ancient Greeks and the Italians of the Renaissance.[46] A stubbornness or inability to recognize 'bright racialism' in the Victorian era and in the years leading up to the First World War, restricts an understanding of the racial discourse taking place in these years to which the Webbs contributed and by which they were influenced.

How different it all appeared soon after the First World War! Japan's expansion into Asia marked the end of the Webbs' portrayal of Japan as an exemplar, even if it did not reduce their interest in Japan and things Japanese. In itself the changing image of Japan which can be traced in the Webbs' work is of more than passing significance. It is frequently claimed, and the case is indeed overwhelming, that once their formation has taken place stereotypes possess massive durability. In short they persist long after the conditions which created them have died away. However, the prospect of change cannot be completely overthrown. The shift in the Webbs' perception of the Japanese, from the essentially good to the undoubtedly evil and dangerous, reveals a transition of considerable magnitude.

But, to repeat, whatever changes occurred in their perceptions, Japan remained to the Webbs historically significant long after the Far East tour became a memory to a couple growing old together. To the end they never ceased to reflect on the ideal form of social organization, and their late attachment to communism, the new civilization, can be viewed partly as a reaction not only against the prospect of a world dominated by American capitalism but also against its possible control by Asia, particularly the Japanese. Applauded and then feared, Japan and the Japanese never ceased to intrigue, indeed obsess, the Webbs. Contemporaries of Beatrice and her 'darling boy', as she often called Sidney, could at least agree on this aspect of the Webbs' life and work.

14

MALCOLM KENNEDY (1895–1935) AND JAPAN

Jon Pardoe

Malcolm Duncan Kennedy was born in Edinburgh on 5 January 1895. His father, James Young Kennedy, an oil merchant, was president of the Municipal Commissioners of George Town (Penang) and commandant of the Penang Volunteers. His mother, a McLeod by birth, came from a military family. Malcolm was the youngest of four brothers and three sisters (one sister died in childhood).

Malcolm's mother took him to Penang soon after he was born. However, by early 1899 his father was bankrupt following a severe slump in the local economy, and the family returned to Britain. In 1904 the Kennedys moved to Ealing and Malcolm attended Durston House, a local preparatory school. In 1907 he joined his brother Angus, six years his senior, at Trinity College, Glenalmond in Perthshire. Glenalmond, founded in 1854, particularly emphasized the preparation of potential officers for the British and Indian armies. Malcolm passed into Sandhurst in 1913 and in January 1914 obtained a commission in the 2nd Battalion (the Scottish Rifles) of the Cameronians.

Kennedy served in the trenches in Flanders through the winter of 1914/15 and was seriously wounded on 10 March 1915 at the Battle of Neuve Chapelle. A leg injury left him permanently unfit for active service. Early in November 1916 he was passed fit for light duties and was posted to Eastern Command Headquarters in London. For Captain Kennedy (as he now was) this new appointment was not at all to his liking: he enjoyed leading troops in the field as much as he loathed desk work. Time dragged on and uninteresting day followed uninteresting day.

To add insult to injury, it was Kennedy's lot to be duty officer on Christmas Day 1916. An item that day in Command Orders stated that the General Staff had decided to revive the pre-war practice of sending officers to Japan to study Japanese, and spend periods attached to Japanese army units. Initially, two officers were to be selected, and applicants wishing to be considered were to submit their names through the proper channels.

Although Kennedy fulfilled all the stated requirements he did not at first seriously consider putting his name forward. However, on Boxing Day, when he was again on duty, he found the same notification repeated in Command Orders. The prospect of going to Japan for two years now appeared far more attractive than a desk job in London. A few days later, having obtained the necessary approval from his Colonel, Kennedy submitted his application. After an interview at the War Office he was seconded, with six other officers, for a three months' preliminary course in Japanese at the School of Oriental Studies (London). This began on 12 March 1917. At the end of the course the officers took an examination and Kennedy was one of the two selected to go to Japan.

On 4 September 1917 Captain Kennedy boarded the Japanese passenger liner *Katori Maru* at Birkenhead. At the end of a two-month voyage, during which the ship called in at Cape Town, Ceylon, Penang, Singapore, Hong Kong, Shanghai and Nagasaki, the ship reached Kobe on 5 November 1917. From there Captain Kennedy travelled by train to Tokyo to report to the British Embassy.

The practice of sending British officers to Japan to study the Japanese language and the Japanese military system had been initiated in 1903 as a consequence of the Anglo-Japanese Alliance, which had been signed in the previous year. Each year two or three officers were sent out from the British army and one or two from the Indian army. The scheme was intended to build up a reserve from which future military attachés could be selected, and, in the event of Britain and Japan fighting a common enemy, it would provide officers for liaison work. In the event there was little requirement for liaison officers. The scheme did, however, train all British military attachés who served Japan in the 1920s and 1930s.

The first year of the language officers' stay was mainly spent in studying Japanese, but after this (usually a further two years) they also completed one or more periods of attachment to Japanese units or military training establishments. In addition, they attended manoeuvres and, in many cases, travelled extensively in Japan and Japanese-held territories. These officers worked under the orders of the military attaché in Tokyo, for whom they prepared intelligence reports on the Japanese army.

From his arrival in Japan in November 1917 until the summer of 1918 Kennedy lived in Tokyo and continued his language studies, a programme which was only broken by embassy functions and short trips to nearby places such as Hakone, Shimoda and Yokohama. Most of his acquaintances were either British or American – embassy officials, missionaries and businessmen. In the next two years he was to travel widely in Japan and the Far East and visited western Honshū, Shikoku and northern Kyūshū in the course of a tour of the Inland Sea area in September 1919. He also visited Hokkaidō some twelve months later.

Captain Kennedy's first attachment to the Japanese army came at the end of 1918 when he arrived at Shizuoka, the base of the 34th Infantry Regiment. Kennedy was struck by the contrast between Japanese and British officers' messes:

Wednesday 27th November 1918

At noon was introduced to, and had tiffin with, the officers of the Regiment. Terribly formal sort of show! Had to stand at the entrance of the Mess Room, bow, and then state who I was, why I was, how glad I was to meet them, and so on! While doing this, all stood to attention (about 100 of them) facing me, and when I had finished, all solemnly bowed and hissed through their teeth! A Japanese Mess is very different from a British one – a great barn-like room with bare white-washed walls and bare wooden tables with wooden benches. No table linen or decoration of any kind. For food, each officer has a large bowl of rice and a plate of awful-looking garbage. A piece of raw 'daikon' [radish], a cup out of which he drinks green tea, and a small box containing his chop-sticks, completes his luncheon paraphernalia! They simply bolt their food, and when they have finished, wash their chop-sticks in their tea, which they then drink, and then clean out their rice bowls with the same liquid and drink that down also! By the noise they make in eating and drinking, it sounds more as though they were inhaling their food! This, however, is a sign of politeness, to show they appreciate it! Finally they have a regular 'field-day' picking their teeth with tooth-picks provided for that purpose![1]

From February to July 1920 Kennedy attended a course for captains at the Chiba Infantry School. Kennedy's attachment to the School proved a useful source of intelligence since he was able to see Japanese army training in all fields of infantry tactics and weaponry. Compared to the lessons learned by the British army from the First World War the Japanese appeared backward, particularly in their use of massed infantry formations and inexperience with tanks and bombing.

A farewell outing on Thursday 22 July 1920 given for Kennedy by Major General Kawamura, the head of the Infantry School, showed an unexpected side of the Japanese officer class:

About a dozen of the more senior instructors . . . came also, as well as two of the Chinese officers [who had attended the course]. . . . As soon as we got to Yawatajuku, about 20 minutes by train on the Hojo line, we all trooped off to the Azumaya, a local 'ryokan' [inn], and changed into 'yukata' [informal cotton kimono for summer wear] provided by the pub. From there we padded down to the sea, and about midday set off in a large sampan. The sea all along this coast is very shallow, and you can wade out 2 or 3 miles with the water barely up to your waist. On the outward journey the boat was propelled by means of punt-poles, but 2 or 3 times struck sand-banks, on which occasions we all, including the old 'kakka' [lit. Your Excellency – i.e. the General] himself, got out and pushed her into deeper water! Some 2 or 3 miles out are sort of 'mazes' made of light bamboo sticks. The fish enter these mazes and then forget the way out, and the fishermen come down with sort of shrimping nets and scoop them out. On this occasion we acted as the fishermen and it was really a splendid sight to see the old general and pot-bellied old colonels, clad in 'yukata' tucked up round their middles and wearing 'tenegui' [face-cloth] on their heads, all paddling about in the water and scooping up fish with as much zest and enjoyment as a party of children at the seaside! . . . After fishing and paddling about for an hour or two, we set off back in the 'sampan', our means of propulsion this time being by two 'sendo' [boatmen] pulling and one pushing from behind! On the way back we consumed some of the fish we had netted, some raw and some fried. It was low tide when we got back, a stretch of sand a mile or more in width being exposed. . . . Got back to the inn about 5 p.m. and after a tub we sat down to a 'go chiso' [a feast], which carried on till about 8 p.m. when we had to get into our proper clothes and set off to catch the 8.25 p.m. train back to Chiba, everyone, the usually very stern-looking old general himself included, being very full of vim and vigour! As I was the 'guest of honour', I had to sit beside the latter by the 'toko-no-ma' [alcove forming the focal point of the main room of a Japanese house; the place of honour is that nearest the alcove]; but far from being dull as I half-expected it to be, General Kawamura was in great form, and altogether it was a most cheery evening.[2]

The Japanese police, both civil and military, kept a close watch on the activities of foreign military officers:

Wednesday 23rd June 1920

A policeman fetched up about 5.30 p.m. to see me with the rather bright excuse that he wanted to know what decorations I was entitled to wear! . . . After he had left I asked my cook if the police ever came while I was out, and was told that they had been twice. Was surprised to hear that at Shizuoka the Kempei [military police] came time after time, always wearing [plain clothes] to find out where I had gone to![3]

Nevertheless, in the period up to the Washington Conference in 1921, which brought the end to the Anglo-Japanese Alliance, the British military attaché and language officers were given access to information on the Japanese army which was denied to other countries. They were often the only foreigners who were permitted to attend Japanese military exercises. This meant that British officers often had to parry awkward questions from their foreign counterparts, who noticed that their periodic absences from Tokyo often coincided with certain manoeuvres in remote country districts.

Before the end of his tour of duty as language officer in November 1920, Captain Kennedy spent the period from September to October visiting Vladivostok, which was occupied by Japanese forces, and Manchuria. After spending three days in the vicinity of Vladivostok, Kennedy travelled by train via the Trans-Siberian and Chinese Eastern Railways to Harbin in northern Manchuria. In the next two weeks he visited Mukden, Liaoyang, Dairen and Port Arthur. He returned to Japan travelling via Antung, Seoul and Pusan on the south coast of Korea.

Kennedy was most impressed by the kindness and efficiency of the Japanese officers who were his hosts during this visit. Instructions were telegraphed from one place to another to ensure that he would be met from his train and guided to wherever he wished to go. Horses and guides were provided when required and accommodation arranged. He also received free travel passes covering his journey by ferry to Vladivostok and by rail all the way from Vladivostok to Changchung in southern Manchuria where the zone under Japanese military control ended. Kennedy realized that this kindness also served another function. The guides who accompanied him were almost invariably *kempei* (Japanese military police) who were able to keep a close watch on his movements. Whenever he left one area and was met by another *kempei* the latter always knew every detail of Kennedy's background and travel plans. Such surveillance was nothing unusual – it was something that foreigners became accustomed to both in Japan, and especially in Japanese territory overseas.

Although this was an unofficial visit which Kennedy had arranged personally with the main aim of visiting the battlefields of the Russo-Japanese war, he wrote an intelligence report on what he had seen during his journey. In his report on Japanese forces in Manchuria he included the locations and sizes of various units and information on their commanders. He discussed the 'bandit problem,' the quality of Chinese troops in Manchuria and the hostile attitude of many European residents to the Japanese. He also devoted a long section of his report to what he had learned from the journey regarding the deteriorating relations between Japan and America.

By November 1920 Captain Kennedy's three-year tour of duty in Japan had come to an end. He returned to Britain and was transferred to Far Eastern Intelligence at the War Office. It was a common occurrence for a language officer to be appointed to the relevant section in Military Intelligence at the War Office on returning from a tour of duty abroad. Kennedy was thus moving up the chain of information: formerly he had written intelligence reports which would be forwarded to Military Intelligence at the War Office; now (as the Far Eastern Section's Japan expert) he was reading the reports sent by language officers in Japan.

Kennedy shared an office (Room 322) with Major R.B. Denny of the

Somerset Light Infantry, the Far Eastern Section's China expert. The Far Eastern Section was grouped with the Russian Section under the overall command of Colonel Napper Tandy.

Kennedy, as the War Office's Japanese expert, was responsible for relations with the Japanese military attaché and his staff, Japanese language-officers and other visiting Japanese military personnel. With his superior officer in Far Eastern Intelligence (Major 'Roy' Piggott and subsequently Major King) he had frequent meetings with their Japanese opposite numbers, either at meals in their respective clubs or when Japanese officers visited the War Office. Kennedy also gave occasional talks on Japan and its army at the School of Oriental Studies to groups of prospective language officers. He wrote several reports for the War Office: one was on the education of Japanese officers, another was on the future of the Anglo-Japanese Alliance. He also liaised with the Far Eastern Department of the Foreign Office.

Both Piggott and Kennedy were closely involved in the arrangements for the visit of the Japanese Crown Prince to Britain in May 1921. Piggott was attached to the prince's suite and Kennedy was involved in the security arrangements for the visit in liaison with the Metropolitan Police Special Branch. Kennedy was invalided out of the army in March 1922 due to his leg injury. This was the result of a compromise reached in 1921 when Major Piggott had supported Kennedy against a medical board which sought to retire him immediately.

During Kennedy's last year in Japan (1920) the military attaché, Brigadier-General Woodroffe, had persuaded the Japan subsidiary of Shell Oil, Rising Sun Petroleum (RSP) to create a position for Kennedy as an adviser. In 1921 Major Piggott successfully requested the company to hold this post open until Kennedy's retirement from the army.

Kennedy began work at the RSP Company's Yokohama head office on 24 April 1922. Apart from Kennedy the company had two, Japanese, advisers. Kennedy's work was varied. It included, in the course of his two years with the company, several business tours to sell the company's products to local kerosene buyers and to investigate local market conditions. These tours included visits to buyers in Fukushima Prefecture (Koriyama and Aizu Wakamatsu) a hundred miles to the north-east of Tokyo, to buyers in Nagoya (150 miles to the west of Tokyo) and to Sendai and Mito (to the north-east). The most important part of his work, however, was establishing (or re-establishing) contacts with government departments, particularly the Ministry of War. In fact it was the Japanese government which allocated the largest and most lucrative contracts.

With the departure from Japan of A.P. Scott, the managing director who had accepted the idea of employing a socio-political adviser, Kennedy's position became insecure. The acting manager, Hugh Malcolm, regarded Kennedy's socio-political job as unnecessary and his employment as a waste of money. From April 1923 onwards Kennedy found himself with more and more time on his hands as Malcolm brought Kennedy's work to a near halt.

On 7 July 1923 Kennedy took his family to the hill resort of Hakone where his wife and child were to spend the summer away from the oppressive, humid heat of Tokyo. Kennedy joined his family there at weekends. They were together at Hakone on 1 September 1923 when the Great Kanto (Tokyo area) Earthquake struck. The house which they were renting collapsed on them. Kennedy managed to dig himself out, and, with the help of others, was able to rescue his wife and son. Fortunately they were unhurt. Nearby several people were killed when a hotel collapsed.

By the end of 1923, the Rising Sun Petroleum had successfully re-established its operations in Tokyo and Yokohama in the wake of the earthquake. Kennedy once more had time on his hands. In November 1923 the family moved to Seoul in Korea where Kennedy was to help with the company's sales campaign.

On 14 February 1924 Kennedy was informed that the RSP Company's head office in London had recently sent a telegram to Japan stating that A.P. Scott, the former manager, was to return to Japan as an adviser to the company and would be employed mainly on social and political work. As a result Kennedy's job was to be ended and he would be given the choice of resigning or being absorbed into the business organization of the company. If he chose the latter, he was told, he would be sent to Moji and be employed almost entirely as a travelling sales representative. Kennedy decided to resign, chiefly because if he became a touring sales representative his wife would be left, even more isolated, than she had been in Tokyo.

The Kennedys arrived back in Britain in mid-August 1924. By this time 'Roy' Piggott, now military attaché in Tokyo, had arranged for Kennedy to have an interview with Sir Roderick Jones, the chairman of Reuters, for the post of Tokyo correspondent. On 26 August 1924 Kennedy had an initial interview with Sir Roderick. Then, after a second interview, on 23 October, he was offered the position of part-time correspondent in Tokyo. Captain Kennedy sailed for Japan on 31 January 1925 on board the NYK Line's *Hakone Maru* to take up his new appointment. A letter from Reuters' chief editor, Herbert Jeans, was his main source of guidance for his new career. This letter warned him to tread warily, especially when cabling news on US – Japanese relations.

Kennedy's major source of information for his journalistic work, apart from reports from Reuters' Japanese ally, the Kokusai News Agency, was the daily news briefing provided by the heads of the Information (*jōhō*) Section of the Japanese Foreign Ministry. Like other foreign journalists, Kennedy relied heavily on these official briefings. He could also draw on his contacts with officers in the Japanese War Ministry and General Staff and on information provided by his friends in the British Embassy. He was on especially good terms with successive British military attachés ('Roy'

Piggott, Leslie Hill, Arthur James and Hugh Simson), whom he provided with any information which he was able to glean on the Japanese army.

The task of reporting news from Japan accurately and honestly was not helped by the fact that many papers were unable to afford full-time correspondents, and many journalists, both British and American, were employed as 'stringers' who were paid only for cables which were accepted for publication. Since American and British newspapers had discovered that sensational stories were popular with the public, the journalists realized that sensational stories were popular with editors and owners. Speed and sensation were at a premium – not accuracy or honesty. Reuters' head office sent out frequent editorial orders impressing on its correspondents the need to beat the 'Opposition' in the race to be the first with the news. As a result Kennedy became increasingly disgusted by what he saw as the decline in journalistic standards:

Monday 17 August 1932

I must say it rather disgusts me the way I am thanked and congratulated for anything of a sensational or 'human interest' nature, while serious matter is at a discount. I suppose it is simply a question of what 'the great British public' want, but it is a pretty damning indictment of their standard of intelligence and serves well to explain their extraordinary ignorance on matters about which they presume to pass judgement. It is very riling, too, to find [Reuters' head office in] London dating my mail items in such a way as to make them appear cabled. Rank dishonesty, I consider it, and often very misleading.[4]

Kennedy, however, was determined to report what he considered to be important, serious news: the Japanese political scene and Japanese foreign policy, particularly as it affected British interests in the Far East. Although Kennedy's contract with Reuters was not due for renewal until mid-1934, by the end of 1933 relations between the two sides reached such a pass that neither party wished to extend it.

Soon after Kennedy's return to Britain on 19 July 1934 his old friend 'Roy' Piggott mentioned a possible job – working for the Government Code and Cipher School. Following an interview at the War Office on 24 November 1934 with the head of GC & CS, Commander Denniston, Kennedy received a definite offer of a post. He began work in the Japanese Section on 1 October 1935. In the meantime he supported himself and his family by freelance journalism and lecturing on the Far East – an ideal opportunity to further the cause of Anglo-Japanese friendship and to counter the rising tide of anti-Japanese feeling in Britain.

In May 1935 the publishers Nisbets had requested Kennedy to write a book on Japan and her problems. But by November he was having recurring problems with Nisbets, who were unhappy about the effect that Kennedy's pro-Japanese views would have on the book's sales. Although Nisbets backed down in their confrontation with Kennedy, their apprehensions were justified. Kennedy's book which sought to explain and to some extent justify Japanese action in Manchuria also floated the idea of Anglo-Japanese co-operation in China. Kennedy's book was strongly criticized in a review in *Punch*:

> The Japanese nation, it seems, is grossly misjudged. It really consists of innocent children, forced to stand on the defensive against the threatening tyranny of those sinister bullies, China, Russia, America and Great Britain. We must therefore be sympathetic and helpful whilst the Yamato race proceeds with its benevolent expansion. Such, at any rate, is the view maintained by Captain M.D. Kennedy in *The Problem of Japan* (NISBET, 15/-). It is an astonishing piece of propaganda, for in order to make his contentions even plausible the author is compelled to impute the basest motives to all the nations and their League and to explain away some extremely stubborn facts. In this he is not uniformly successful.[5]

As this review suggests, Kennedy and the other members of the pro-Japanese lobby in Britain failed to stem the rising tide of anti-Japanese sentiment in the 1930s. There were three principal reasons for this. First, its most active adherents were those who had lived in Japan: it was thus numerically weak. Lacking resources for large-scale publicity, it concentrated on lobbying leading political figures such as MPs. The battle for British public opinion was lost largely by default. Second, its efforts were constantly being undermined by the erratic and largely inept propaganda effort emanating from the Japanese Embassy. Third, the actions of the Japanese military in China together with the deterioration in Anglo-Japanese relations left the pro-Japanese lobby in an invidious position and completely sabotaged its publicity work. It was not that Kennedy and the pro-Japanese lobby had been defeated in detailed debate. It was merely that they had been outnumbered by their opponents and overwhelmed by the march of events in the Far East.

Kennedy stands alongside Sir George Sansom and G.C. Allen as one of the three British writers on Japan in the inter-war years of major significance. Of these, only Kennedy and Sansom had a mastery of the Japanese language. Sansom, although a Foreign Office official who wrote many official reports on Japanese trade and industry, was principally interested in Japanese history, art and culture, whereas Kennedy preferred to investigate the contemporary scene and covered in his writings wide areas in what are now known as the social sciences.

Kennedy's views were given consideration in official circles but never had any significant impact on British Far Eastern policy. The Foreign Office, with its embassies and consulates, had its own sources of information on the Far East and its own experts. Its emphasis on good relations with the United States ran at cross-purposes with Kennedy's advocacy of an

Anglo-Japanese rapprochement. That Kennedy's writings made hardly any impact outside his circle of acquaintances in the British War Office and Foreign Office should cause little surprise given the hostile turn of world events and Britain's growing emphasis upon amity with Washington.

FURTHER READING

M.D. Kennedy, *The Military Side of Japanese Life*, London: Constable, 1924.

M.D. Kennedy, *The Changing Fabric of Japan*, London: Constable, 1930.

M.D. Kennedy, *The Problem of Japan*, London: Nisbet, 1935.

15

SIR CHARLES ELIOT (1862–1931) AND JAPAN

Dennis Smith

Sir Charles Eliot's name has hitherto figured as little more than a footnote in the history of Anglo-Japanese relations, in part because he was directly involved with Japan as a diplomat and scholar for no more than the last decade of his life. However, he was one of a distinguished line of British diplomats in East Asia who made significant pioneering contributions to oriental scholarship; furthermore, his time as ambassador in Tokyo included the ending of the Anglo-Japanese Alliance. Eliot moved into a significant position in Britain's relations with Japan when he was appointed ambassador to Tokyo in August 1919. His first two years as ambassador coincided with the decline and final ending of the Alliance, which had been the keystone of Anglo-Japanese relations. There followed four years of readjustment to a new, less formal pattern of relationship. Eliot was a convinced advocate of close Anglo-Japanese friendship, and the abrogation of the Alliance was deeply painful to him. He had a deep and genuine regard for Japan and its culture and he despised the racial prejudice against the Japanese which was characteristic of his time and generation. Eliot's affection for Japan was vividly demonstrated by his decision to remain there after he retired from the diplomatic service, and he spent his final years researching and writing on Japanese Buddhism. Unfortunately, he was unable to translate his vision of Anglo-Japanese amity and co-operation into reality, but his genuine regard for Japan moved Major-General F.S.G. Piggott, himself no mean admirer of Japan, to write of Eliot that 'few, if any, men understood and loved their country's ally as much.'[1]

The tall, 58-year-old bachelor who stepped from a Royal Navy cruiser at Yokohama on 6 April 1920 to take up the position of ambassador brought with him an awesome reputation for intellectual brilliance. Indeed, even experienced Japan hands in the embassy experienced a frisson of apprehension. Eliot's appointment to Tokyo was the pinnacle of his career, and was the culmination of a varied, and indeed chequered, career which had

187

shown spectacular promise in its early stages but had become extraordinarily becalmed during its middle phase.

Charles Edgcumbe Eliot was born on 8 January 1862, the son of an Anglican clergyman. He had a conventional upper-middle-class Victorian education, first at preparatory school, then at Cheltenham College and finally at Balliol, which he entered in 1880. By the time he arrived at Oxford, two of his principal personal characteristics had surfaced: sparkling intellectual brilliance combined with emotional and psychological fragility which had led to a nervous breakdown which had forced him to postpone going to university. At school, and then at Oxford, Eliot displayed striking linguistic aptitude. As an undergraduate he carried off a raft of prizes for both western and oriental classical languages, and during his life he acquired competence in close to twenty languages, including Arabic, Turkish and Chinese. Further, he became a substantial linguistic scholar, writing the first English-language grammar of Finnish and subsequently a Swahili instruction manual.

When Eliot left Oxford in 1886, he was undecided about his future, but a chance encounter with Lord Dufferin pointed him in the direction of the diplomatic service. Predictably, he passed the civil service examinations with ease and was posted to St Petersburg, where he could capitalize on his knowledge of Russian which he had incidentally acquired at Oxford. In 1892 Eliot was transferred to Tangier, and a year later he moved to Constantinople. Inevitably qualifying in Turkish, he stayed there for five years during which he developed himself into one of the leading authorities on the Ottoman Empire and what was then called the 'Eastern Question'. His expertise was revealed in 1900, when he published the highly regarded *Turkey in Europe*, writing under the pseudonym 'Odysseus'. By the time this work appeared, Eliot had served in Washington for a brief period, been knighted for service on the international commission set up to bring some order to the byzantine affairs of Samoa and been appointed consul-general at Zanzibar and commissioner of the British East African Protectorate.

Eliot would later tell one of his officials in Tokyo that his four years in East Africa were 'the happiest and most interesting' of his life'.[2] His appointment at the age of 38 put Eliot effectively in control of all British possessions in East Africa, and he seemed destined for the peak of the Foreign Office hierarchy. Instead, East Africa came close to prematurely but permanently ending his diplomatic career. Eliot became a passionate advocate of white settlement in what would become the White Highlands of Kenya, but the extension of white settlement could only take place at the expense of the Masai tribes who currently occupied the land. Eliot had taken a deep dislike to the Masai and was not averse to disturbing them. However, the Foreign Office was anxious to avoid confrontation with the Masai and Eliot was warned to take no action which might provoke it. Throughout his diplomatic career, Eliot showed a tendency to bend or even disregard his instructions from London if they contradicted his own deeply-held views. In 1904 this cavalier attitude to his political masters brought professional disaster when he continued to sponsor white settlement on Masai lands. Finally, London formally instructed him to reverse his policies, and Eliot responded by resigning from the diplomatic service.

Eliot had hoped that when he returned to Britain he could secure an official inquiry which would exonerate him and lead to his reinstatement, but no inquiry was held and his career as a diplomat appeared to be over. Eliot spent the next thirteen years as a senior university academic, first as vice-chancellor of the newly established University of Sheffield and then, from 1911 to 1918, as vice-chancellor of the University of Hong Kong. Eliot did not find life as a vice-chancellor particularly congenial, and he made sporadic but unsuccessful efforts to mobilize highly placed contacts to secure a return to official life. However, his university service did give him the opportunity to indulge his passion for marine biology and, more significantly, to collect material for and write a substantial part of his *magnum opus, Hinduism and Buddhism*, which appeared in three volumes in 1921. Eliot might well have remained an academic for the rest of his working life had it not been for the unusual circumstances which the First World War and the collapse of the Russian Empire created in East Asia in the summer of 1918.

On 2 August 1918 Eliot returned to the diplomatic community when he was appointed British high commissioner for Siberia. Eliot owed his appointment to the quite fortuitous fact that, being in Hong Kong, he could be at his post in Siberia shortly after the first substantial Allied forces landed at Vladivostok. The post of high commissioner was only temporary, but Eliot was so anxious to re-enter public life that he accepted it with alacrity, and was later to claim that it 'rejuvenated' him. Eliot was to have been the British representative on an Allied body responsible for co-ordinating the policies of the interventionist powers. However, Eliot would be the only commissioner appointed by a major interventionist state since both the United States and Japan did not make similar appointments and the co-ordinating body never functioned. In Siberia Eliot gained new renown as a linguist, and gained new fame as a provider of hospitality.[3] In general, he navigated the chaos of post-revolutionary Siberia skilfully. In early 1919 the Foreign Office found some difficulty in finding a successor to Sir Conyngham Greene as ambassador to Japan. On the strength of the accomplished manner in which he had acquitted himself in a very difficult situation, Eliot was offered the embassy in Tokyo.

Unquestionably, Eliot brought formidable qualities to his post. He was an acknowledged expert on 'the orient', having devoted much of his diplomatic and subsequent academic career to service in and study of the non-European world. When he arrived in Tokyo he had spent almost all the previous nine years in East Asia, first in Hong Kong and latterly in Siberia, and he had stayed for long periods in and immersed himself in the study of the most significant regions of the Far East, particularly China. He was reasonably competent in Chinese and he was putting the finishing touches to a major work on two of the great spiritual traditions of Asia. His previous diplomatic service had not involved dealing with Japan, and when he took up his post he did not speak Japanese, but he had visited the country several times, and his year in Siberia had naturally involved intense and sustained exposure to current Japanese policies in north-east Asia. On the debit side, Eliot had held no regular diplomatic appointment for sixteen years and the prolonged interruption of his career meant that he did not have the normal network of diplomatic and personal contacts within the Foreign Office, and this was a defect which three months' briefing in London in 1919–20 could only partially rectify.

Eliot took up his post at a decisive period in Anglo-Japanese relations, for the Alliance was beginning to come under serious scrutiny. Events during and after the First World War had brought attacks on the Alliance from numerous different directions. The Alliance was unpopular with the United States, where it was seen as an essential prop to Japanese expansionism on the Asian continent. Similarly, in China Japan's formal connection with Britain was viewed as a support for previous and current Japanese pressures on China. From a British perspective, the Alliance had been an essential plate in the armour defending Britain's interests in East Asia, first from Russian and then from German threats. The defeat of Germany and the disintegration of Russian power removed these dangers and consequently the Alliance appeared increasingly redundant. Also, Japan's activities in China and Siberia during and after the First World War often conflicted with perceived British interests, while the argument that the Alliance gave the British a restraining hand over Japanese policy seemed to be contradicted by events. Finally, the international environment which emerged out of the First World War was uncongenial to formal alliances. More specifically, the Anglo-Japanese Alliance and membership of the League of Nations might well prove incompatible. However, these threats to the Alliance took time to develop and converge. Eliot left for Japan on St Valentine's Day, 1920. The government's policy at that time, which was to retain the Alliance, albeit in a modified form, to take account of Britain's responsibilities as a member of the League of Nations, was almost identical with Eliot's own view. The ambassador-designate was convinced that the Alliance should be kept, and until its abrogation Eliot remained an unwavering supporter of it. After its demise he would be a regular mourner at its grave.

In the event, having Eliot, a staunch advocate of the Alliance, in Tokyo had no decisive impact upon the debate about its renewal since the final decision was taken entirely in London. Eliot's first substantial expression of opinion on the Alliance following his move to Tokyo was 'a masterly statement of the case for renewal', which impressed Curzon. Again in December 1920, Curzon found Eliot's stout defence of the Alliance more persuasive than the generally lukewarm report of the Foreign Office committee which had been specially constituted to consider the matter.[4] However, from February 1921 Canada began a concerted attack on renewal because of its adverse effect on Anglo-American relations, and by June 1921 the Alliance had become a main topic at the Imperial Conference. At that conference, Curzon still basically favoured renewing the Alliance, but its future was increasingly bound up with imperial and Anglo-American relations. By the summer it was clear that the Alliance's fate would be decided as part of the proposed international conference on Pacific and East Asian affairs, which was to be held in Washington. By this time Eliot had virtually no influence on decisions regarding the Alliance, and in fact he did not try to exert very much. As early as July 1921 Curzon was complaining that both information and views coming from Tokyo 'strike us as somewhat meagre'.[5] In Tokyo, Eliot was active in calming Japanese suspicions of Britain's policies, but he sensed that the Anglo-Japanese relationship based upon the Alliance was drawing to a close. After the abrogation of the Alliance had been arranged at the Washington Conference and it had been replaced by the Four Power Pact, Eliot wrote to Curzon that 'I confess that I regret the termination of the Anglo-Japanese Alliance, but it was really dead before its termination.'[6] Eliot may have been tempted to repeat the moral gesture he had made in East Africa nearly two decades before and resign over the issue, but he did not.[7] Instead, he remained in Tokyo with a brief to soothe Japanese feelings and work out a new framework for Anglo-Japanese relations.

After the Washington Conference Eliot was in a unique position as the only ambassador to serve in a country with which Britain had had a prolonged Alliance and which had been terminated by mutual agreement. It was a difficult, indeed potentially embarrassing, predicament. However, by June 1922 Eliot was able to put a brave face on the end of the Alliance: 'those who believe that real friendship between our two nations is possible cannot but feel some regret, be they British or Japanese, at seeing a close tie replaced by an advantageous understanding. But still a cause of chronic misunderstanding has been removed.'[8] In this second phase of his ambassadorship, Eliot fulfilled the normal tasks of assessing and keeping London informed of the nature and direction of Japanese foreign policy, of dealing with concrete issues between Britain and Japan and of sustaining and improving Britain's image in Tokyo. All of these roles, were of course, complicated by the end of the Alliance, and because of the disappointments and sensitivities of the Japanese after the Washington Conference, it was vital that they be handled carefully. The Foreign Office was conscious of the delicacy of Japanese feelings, and soon after the Washington Conference Eliot had been specifically instructed to ensure that 'now that the Alliance has gone . . . [we] must do what we can not to make Japan feel we have abandoned her'.[9] These were instructions which Eliot obeyed to the full in both letter and spirit.

The least conspicuous, but none the less important, aspect of Eliot's work after the end of the Alliance was public relations. The state visit of the Prince of Wales to Japan in the spring of 1922 provided an early opportunity to improve Japanese attitudes towards Britain. The success of the visit was threatened by a series of thinly veiled anti-Japanese articles in *The Times* and the *Daily Mail* and by the Prince appearing to be uninterested in Japan during the early part of his visit. However, the Prince perked up as the visit progressed and Eliot believed that this brought a material improvement in Anglo-Japanese relations.[10] Eliot wasted no opportunity to bolster Britain's image in Japan. After the Kanto earthquake on 1 September 1923, Eliot pressed for urgent and substantial British assistance. He was only partially successful and was frankly disappointed by the British reaction, but he was instrumental in prodding the British government into donating £25,000 to Tokyo Imperial University to help restore its library. Eliot accompanied his subordinates on visits to numerous civil and military establishments throughout Japan, frequently impressing his hosts with the passable Japanese which he had acquired since his arrival in Tokyo. It is, of course, hard to assess Eliot's role in maintaining Britain's image after the end of the Alliance, but his contemporaries spoke highly of his efforts and it was, perhaps, in the words of *The Times* obituary for Eliot, 'a solid if not outwardly brilliant achievement'.[11]

When analysing Japanese foreign policy, Eliot, like most pre-war western observers, imagined the decision-making process to be a contest between 'the military party and the more peaceful elements in the State'.[12] Eliot believed that the latter group had established their dominance after the Washington Conference. Thus, in June 1922 he 'felt inclined to expatiate on the change in Japan's foreign policy, the apparent decrease in chauvinistic spirit of the nation and the abandonment of aggressive designs on China and Siberia'. He grudgingly gave the Washington Conference some credit for this, but he felt that the main cause was the failure of previous expansionist adventures to bear substantial fruit: 'all classes, and especially business people, cannot help feeling that half of the annual budget was devoted to naval and military expenditure with no adequate return, while many urgent needs were neglected'.[13] On a broader canvass, Eliot frequently referred to the weakening effect which Japan's post-war economic problems had upon its foreign policy. The range and depth of these difficulties discouraged foreign adventures and, in Eliot's final analysis, made Japan 'a weak rather than a strong power'.[14] One of the frequent refrains in Eliot's despatches was that Japan attached the highest priority to being recognized as one of the great powers and on being seen to co-operate with the others. He wrote that 'it is no exaggeration to say that they often put the manner before the matter, their national dignity before material advantage',[15] and he put great emphasis on the way in which Japan was treated and referred to by the British.

Eliot could point to specific examples of Japan's retreat from expansionism. The Japanese had retired gracefully from Tsingtao after the Washington

Conference, and they had evacuated their forces from eastern Siberia exactly on time, despite attempts by the British, initiated by Eliot, to have them stay long enough to destroy large stockpiles of arms in Vladivostok.[16] In broader terms, Eliot opined that 'I do not think that any sane Japanese dreams of using force against Australia or Singapore, or of annexing the Philippines or Dutch Indies.'[17] Eliot was not completely starry-eyed about Japan's future policies, however. Writing in 1922, he warned that 'I do not, of course, mean to imply that an era of unbroken peace and guilelessness has commenced. The majority still believe in the mission of Japan, a vague phrase but not excluding ideas of conquest.'[18] Writing two years later, when the Japanese had been ruffled by the American immigration bill, Eliot cautioned London that 'in international relations the Japanese should [sic] take care to be correct and courteous but that if foreigners do not like Japanese methods they can go elsewhere'.[19]

Japan was most clearly interested in China, and there was very considerable interest in London in what would be the thrust of Japan's China policy under the new Nine Power Treaty, which had been one of the major achievements of the Washington Conference. Consequently, analysing Japan's ambitions and activities in China became a major part of Eliot's responsibilities between 1922 and 1926. When he tried to probe the roots of these policies, Eliot thought that he detected a certain ambivalence and even contradiction. On the one hand, he reported, Japan wished to be seen and clearly recognized as one of the great powers, and 'no international action must take place without the co-operation of Japan'. On the other hand, the Japanese obviously felt that they had a special position in China; during and after the First World War Japan had tried to expand its hold on China by political and military means, but after the Washington Conference they hoped to pursue their ends by economic means. However, the chaotic state of China was a grave disincentive to investment which might have been the spearhead of Japanese penetration of China. Consequently, Eliot wrote, Japan did not have 'a firm and consecutive policy' in China, but, generally, the Japanese were weak and indecisive in their dealings with Chinese affairs.[20] Eliot pressed on London his view that British and Japanese interests in China did not conflict and that Britain should pursue policies in tandem with Japan rather than with the United States, but such ideas found no favour and brought Eliot into conflict with the Foreign Office.

Eliot encountered almost no serious concrete difficulties in Anglo-Japanese relations after the Alliance ended. The one exception to this was the Singapore base project. Until the end of the First World War British interests in Asia had ultimately been protected by the Anglo-Japanese Alliance. However, a comprehensive review of imperial defence in 1919 had highlighted Britain's strategic weakness in Asia caused by the lack of any base capable of accommodating modern capital ships at precisely the time when the Royal Navy was coming to regard Japan as the hypothetical enemy. In June 1921 doubts about the future of the Alliance with Japan and steady pressure from the navy and the Australasian dominions persuaded the cabinet to approve the development of Singapore as a major base for the British battlefleet. The British were careful to ensure that the Singapore base was excluded from the restrictions placed on new naval fortifications by the Washington naval treaty, and the project became the most important single element in British naval strategy in the 1920s. No amount of official evasion could conceal the fact that the Singapore scheme was aimed at Japan. It reflected the strident anti-Japanese tone adopted by the Royal Navy, which was in part a ploy to extract the maximum possible resources for the service from the Treasury, but it was also symptomatic of increasing forebodings of a threat from Japan which afflicted the Royal Navy.[21]

As ambassador in Tokyo, Eliot could not of course directly influence imperial defence policy, but he was troubled by the potential damage which building the Singapore base posed for Anglo-Japanese relations. Eliot never clearly opposed building the base, but he did warn of its impact upon Anglo-Japanese relations: 'Well-informed Japanese did not regard the proposal as a menace, but they were hurt that their old ally and professed friend should take an early opportunity after the Washington Conference of erecting fortifications as near to Japan as was convenient under the new regulations.'[22] Eliot wrote this appraisal shortly after the first Labour government had decided to suspend work on Singapore as part of its policy of stimulating further disarmament. Eliot had no influence on this decision on the Singapore base, but when the general election at the end of October 1924 produced a Conservative victory and a government likely to resume work on the project, Eliot wrote directly to Austen Chamberlain, the new foreign secretary, warning him that the Japanese–American immigration controversy had spawned an increase in anti-foreign feeling in Japan, and that the Japanese were unusually sensitive to foreign actions. At the very least, he pleaded for a conciliatory message to be sent to Japan, assuring them that Singapore was not aimed at curbing them, although 'I am bound to add that I don't think they will believe it'.[23] Eliot's hope that construction of the base would remain suspended was not fulfilled, although the project had to withstand a violent assault from Winston Churchill, then chancellor of the exchequer, before work on it was resumed. Eliot was left to try and mollify the Japanese and carry on his quiet public-relations exercises.

By the time the new Conservative government decided to resuscitate the Singapore scheme Eliot's influence on London had declined appreciably. Throughout his ambassadorial career, Eliot had irritated some of the most important Foreign Office officials with his opinions, his often convoluted method of argument and his occasional failure to follow instructions. The main London official whose patience Eliot tried was Victor Wellesley, who had been head of the Far Eastern department until his elevation to the post of assistant under-secretary of state in February 1924. Wellesley was a formidable influence upon Britain's policies in East Asia, and his increasingly exasperated comments upon Eliot's despatches reflect a belief that Eliot was too pro-Japanese and generally out of sympathy with the course which British policy was increasingly taking, especially in China. There was always an undertow of anti-Americanism in Eliot's opinions, and he disliked the gravitation of Britain's East Asian policy towards that of the United States at the expense of British relations with Japan. Shortly before he retired, Eliot made his views clear: 'So far as the East is concerned I personally feel that it is to our advantage to work with Japan rather than with the United States but I can imagine that considerations of world policy may dictate a contrary course.'[24] Victor Wellesley's view cut directly across that of Eliot:

The fact is Japanese interests and British interests in the Far East do not harmonise while the American and ours are identical. It is this which makes cooperation with the Japanese so difficult and forces us more and more to cooperate with the Americans. Close contacts with America has become the only right policy for this country to pursue.[25]

In reality, the weight of the argument and of real influence lay with Wellesley, and although Eliot tried to initiate closer Anglo-Japanese consultation on Chinese affairs, Britain continued to incline towards the United States.

The estrangement between Eliot and senior officials in London contributed to the decision taken by Austen Chamberlain to retire him from the diplomatic service. While on leave in Britain in 1923 Eliot had received the impression that Curzon had assured him that, when his term in Japan expired, in early 1925, his appointment in Tokyo would be renewed or he would be offered another ambassadorship. Eliot passionately believed that he still had much to offer the foreign service, and correctly surmised that Chamberlain had decided to dispense with him because the foreign secretary's 'opinion of me has been mostly formed by information given by the Foreign Office. I may have enemies there.' Eliot lobbied for an embassy either in Cairo or Turkey; alternatively, he was prepared to accept the governorship of Singapore or Hong Kong. Chamberlain's claim that Eliot was being required to retire because of logjams in promotion within the diplomatic service provoked a riposte which reveals much of Eliot's self-confident character:

I have a very exceptional knowledge of Asia, its inhabitants and their languages. How many people have you in the public service who know China, Japan and Russia as I do, or the near East . . . as I do? To throw away such knowledge and experience is simple waste and not . . . in the interests of the service as a whole.

Chamberlain would not relent and when, in October 1925, Eliot plaintively stated that 'I am helpless and you can treat me as unjustly and illogically as you like', Chamberlain coldly brought the correspondence to an end.[26]

After his forced retirement, Eliot did not return to Britain. He decided to stay in Japan and collect material for and complete his work on Buddhism in Japan. During his period as ambassador he had travelled widely in Japan searching for sources, and when he finally left the embassy in February 1926 he moved into the Nara Hotel and, with the assistance of a network of contacts in Buddhist institutions in Nara and Kyoto, he immersed himself in religious texts. In the years that remained to him, Eliot continued his lonely, solitary life in and around Nara. However, he did maintain contact with some of his closer associates from the embassy. Most notably, he became uncharacteristically close to George Sansom, then commercial counsellor; Sansom was in the final stages of completing his *Cultural History of Japan* and perhaps as an author Eliot felt close fellow-feeling with his erstwhile subordinate. By early 1929 Eliot had drafted much of his book on Japanese Buddhism, but his health was deteriorating rapidly and there is some suggestion that his vaunted intellectual powers were beginning to wane and progress on his book slowed drastically.[27] In December 1930 Eliot became seriously ill, and by February 1931 his condition was clearly terminal. He became determined to return to England, and he did set out for home but on 16 March 1931 he died as his ship passed through the Straits of Malacca. *Japanese Buddhism* was still unfinished and George Sansom undertook to complete it and prepare it for publication. The text was in some confusion and Eliot had been too ill to write anything on Nichiren. Sansom contributed a chapter on Nichiren and it took three years to shape the complete text into its final form. The complex and frankly imperfect work was only published four years after its author died.

It is not easy to assess Sir Charles Eliot's contribution to Anglo-Japanese understanding. Eliot himself was disappointed with the way in which the two nations drifted apart during his tenure of the Tokyo embassy. He was particularly distressed by the abrogation of the Alliance, but the important decisions concerning its renewal were taken in London, and it is difficult to see how the ambassador, geographically isolated in Tokyo, could have exerted more influence. Once the Alliance disappeared and it became necessary to build new frameworks for Anglo-Japanese relations, Eliot's instinctive empathy for Japanese sensibilities helped to project an image of a Britain which had not entirely abandoned its old ally. Eliot tried to reassure the Foreign Office that post-Washington Japan was not a threat to Britain's interests. As ambassador, he maintained a personal correspondence with four foreign secretaries, and the influence of his opinions emerges clearly in Austen Chamberlain's address to the Imperial Conference in October 1926 which, when discussing Japan's retreat into placidity, not only used the same arguments as Eliot, but also expressed them in virtually the same words as Eliot's personal letters.[28]

196

When Eliot tried to convince decision-makers in London that his conception of a close Anglo-Japanese relationship was desirable, he failed. The causes of that estrangement were fundamental, and the Foreign Office mandarins were too suspicious of Japan, and of Eliot's well-known pro-Japanese sentiments, for them to be able to accept his arguments. As one of Eliot's successors pointed out in 1931, Britain was now less important to Japan, which was concentrating its attention on relations with the United States, on the emergence of Soviet power in north-east Asia and on the the tide of change in China.[29] To the Japanese, relations with Britain were becoming little more than peripheral, while the British were increasingly inclining their East Asian policies towards those of the United States. The misfortune for a man of Eliot's convictions was that he was quite unable to reverse, or even slow, the estrangement of the former Allies.

16

THE PEACEFUL OVERTURE: ADMIRAL YAMANASHI KATSUNOSHIN (1877–1967)

Haruko Fukuda

Relations between Britain and Japan changed fundamentally in 1921, the year in which the Anglo-Japanese Alliance of 1902 was abandoned by the British in the course of negotiations for the Naval Limitations Treaty signed between the major powers in Washington the following year. The consequences of that treaty and another that followed in 1930 were to affect popular opinion in Japan profoundly and to lead to dramatic and often violent divisions in Japanese politics. The outcome of that divide in the years which followed is only too well known.

Admiral Yamanashi Katsunoshin was one of the principal architects of those two treaties and by his own admission sacrificed his own naval career for what he believed to be the national interest. This chapter must necessarily begin with this preface, for it is in the history of the two treaties that his name is remembered by posterity. The part he played in these events and the vision he held at that time will be recounted later in this chapter. But in the period between 1894 and 1920 the naval dimension was the core of Anglo-Japanese relations and indeed of the Alliance. *The Times* obituary of December 1967 recorded, 'Admiral Yamanashi, who died on Sunday in his 91st year, had, from the beginning of his career in the former Imperial Japanese Navy, been closely associated with the Royal Navy.'

Though he kept silent on these and other events of which he was a principal witness, when he had outlived his colleagues he did leave his account to later students of history. He lectured to the Japanese Naval Defence Staff between 1959 and 1966 when he was between 82 and 90 years old. It was characteristic that he did so specifically without passing judgement on those events or the personalities involved. Those lectures in their entirety tell much of the history of the Imperial Japanese Navy. Remembering the handsome old Admiral with his kindly eye standing erect to deliver his talks on Nelson, Farragut and other naval leaders whom he admired, his pupils published these lectures posthumously.[1] Much of this chapter is based upon them.

Admiral Yamanashi Katsunoshin, Hon. KBE, Hon. CMG, was born in Sendai on 26 July 1877. He was the eldest son of a samurai, Yamanashi Bunnoshin of the Date clan. The family lived in a large house and estate, now the site of a girls' high school. He went to school there and studied the oriental classics, but at the age of 13 was sent to a Congregationalist school in Sendai and was taught by American missionaries. He often said that though he never became a Christian he was a Christian sympathizer and supporter. In later years he was much influenced by Zen Buddhism and was a close friend of the great Zen philosopher Suzuki Daisetsu. It was his friendship with Suzuki which led him to a close association with R.H. Blyth, a Briton who was to play a critical role with Yamanashi in the realization of the Declaration of Humanity of the Emperor Shōwa of 1946. He declared in one of his very last lectures, when he was 90, that his spiritual leader throughout his life was Kōkan (Kobayashi Shuho), the chief priest of Myōshinji of Kyoto. Indeed, his style of life was ascetic in the Zen tradition. The small house in which he and his wife spent their later years was spartan: with few ornaments except for a framed piece of calligraphy by his most noble pupil, the Crown Prince, and his photograph.

On 29 January 1895, aged 18, Yamanashi entered the Naval Academy at Etajima and from that day was to come under the influence of Britain and the Royal Navy.

The Sino-Japanese War had broken out the previous year and the new cadets were more than aware of their destiny as the chosen élite of the nation, devoted to the Emperor Meiji. Stephen Howarth in his history of the Imperial Japanese Navy writes: 'A new cadet approaching the wide parade ground and classical Western-style buildings knew that he was someone special – not only a Japanese, but one picked from rigorous and highly-competitive nation-wide examinations to become part of the Emperor's foremost fighting arm.'[2] One of those proud cadets, Yamanashi recollected that there were three or four barbettes on the shore of Etajima with 15-inch Krupp guns on which they conducted their firing practice. They used tackle to move them from side to side; they practised Nelson's broadside, and ramming. He explained to his students more than a hundred years later that Japan's best battleships of the early twentieth century, *Fuji* and *Yashima*, were built to ram: the tactics of the Sino-Japanese War were for the Japanese battleships to ram and board the *Ting* and *Chen* with their much superior armament. Much of the training at Etajima was therefore occupied with cutlass drills, which Yamanashi thought inelegant compared with the Japanese art of the sword; but as he said, the navy still lived in the tradition and custom of the days of sail.

So much did the habits of the Royal Navy permeate the Imperial Japanese Navy that the staple diet on board Japanese vessels was biscuits and lime juice. In the early days of the Imperial Japanese Navy the Japanese had no national anthem. The instructors from the Royal Navy taught the Japanese cadets *God Save the King*, while the French who had come earlier taught them the *Marseillaise*. As Yamanashi recalled, there were curious occasions in which the Japanese solemnly sang the British or the French anthem in deference to whichever of their instructors were present, as if to pretend that those were the anthems of the Japanese navy.

The part played by the Royal Navy, and Admiral A.L. Douglas in particular, in training the embryonic Japanese navy is well known. A letter written by Yamanashi for an English friend the best part of a century later gives a generous and poetic insight into these pioneering, brotherly days:

> It is quite evident that the Admiralty sent the very persons best fitted for this memorable mission. They all represented fine British national character in a true sense. The respect and esteem of all who came across the party were universal and immense and a tender affection long survived following their noble work. . . .
>
> The class of junior cadets . . . had been chosen, after passing examinations, from various clans of feudal lords and, though not of rich families, all retained hereditary brave and chivalrous martial spirit. In view of the small number of cadets, the sudden appearance of the gallant British Mission, complete with their families, turned the place into a quaint English settlement. The language, customs and social manners quickly permeated the young impressionable minds, making the whole atmosphere like a foreign quarter of refined, decent people, entirely different from the time old remnants of the feudal age. . . .
>
> It is said that Commander Douglas did his best to impress on the cadets the importance of military discipline, and sedulously devised various means of doing this: he nominated a gentleman of high character to give a special lecture on Robert Southey's biography of Lord Nelson, with the result that all the cadets came to worship Nelson as their ideal hero. Commander Douglas modelled his moral training of the cadets on the following subjects – discipline, duty, justice, faithfulness, salute, benevolence, patience, obedience, orderliness, economy. . . .
>
> It may not be an overstatement if we say that the ruling spirit, discipline and manifold faculties of the Japanese Navy, which had such brilliant success in the two great wars of 1894 and 1904, were chiefly the product and fruits of the above-mentioned inestimable work of Commander Douglas and his staff. Besides strictly naval attainments, we received far-reaching and broad teaching of British social customs, free institutions, liberal thinking and a sense of duty, with the result that England was esteemed as the guiding example of island monarchy.[3]

Before the British, the Japanese navy had relied on help from the Dutch, the soliciting of whose assistance in Nagasaki in 1853 marked the end of

Japan's two centuries-long isolation from maritime commerce, and also from the French. In that letter and in his lectures Yamanashi praises L.E. Bertin, the French engineer who established the Yokosuka Dockyard and designed the battleships which won the Sino-Japanese War, thus gaining the funds to build the ships which were to be decisive in the Russo-Japanese War. Yamanashi was adamant that Bertin's name should never be forgotten in the annals of the Japanese navy.

The Royal Navy's involvement in Japan had in fact begun a decade before Douglas's arrival. According to Yamanashi, when in 1861 the Russian gunboat *Posadonnik* suddenly anchored at Tsushima and built barracks, the Japanese immediately determined on enlisting the support of Sir Harry Parkes. Without delay the governor of Hong Kong and the commander of the China squadron arrived with three or four ships. It took the Royal Navy six months to drive out the Russians. The British had previously obtained a Russian naval journal published in St Petersburg which told of the Russian intention to capture Hokkaidō and 'as an hors d'oeuvre, Tsushima': so when the *Posadonnik* appeared, the British consul at Hakodate reported back to London, 'they have come as expected'.

Yamanashi's first overseas tour was in *Kongo*, a sail-steamer of 2,300 tons, to Australia. When he returned in September 1898, he was to serve in the then most modern battleships *Fuji* and *Yashima*. These, the first ironclads Japan ever possessed, were both built at Barrow-in-Furness and were delivered two years after the Sino-Japanese War.

Yamanashi talked of *Fuji* and *Yashima* with very great affection: looking back *Fuji* was 'a dream'. One can see with what excitement the young naval officers in the twilight years of the last century welcomed the arrival of the first modern warships from Britain. They had just won their first international sea battles, established the navy's credibility with the country, and were walking tall. As a young officer on *Yashima*, Yamanashi found the routine rigorous and often arduous. Amongst his colleagues was Nomura Kichisaburō (later admiral and ambassador in Washington at the outbreak of the Second World War). But it was these experiences on *Yashima* that first taught Yamanashi the qualities of leadership he valued. To inspire loyalty, skills in organizing men alone were inadequate; leaders must *love* their men, not be sticklers for inessentials, and always be prepared to sacrifice themselves first. Eighteen months later, on 15 May 1900, he was instructed to travel to England to oversee the construction of the battleship *Mikasa*. He was to remain in England until 13 March 1902 when *Mikasa* left Portsmouth for Yokosuka.

The victory of the Imperial Japanese Navy in the Sino-Japanese conflict had finally persuaded the Diet to vote a ten years' warship budget of ¥200 million. The Emperor Meiji personally offered to contribute ¥300,000 per annum from the Imperial Household's budget, while the military and civil personnel of the government were to offer a tenth of their salaries. On this budget the four battleships *Shikishima*, *Hatsuse*, *Mikasa* and *Asahi* were commissioned. The last of these to be completed was *Mikasa*. The Imperial Navy was then moving into the modern world of the standard Royal Navy models of 12,000 tons, with four twelve-inch and twelve six-inch guns. *Fuji* and *Yashima* were the first battleships to have underwater torpedo tubes, two forward and two aft.

The year 1900 is remembered as being of particular importance. It was the year of the Boxer Rebellion, the incident in which the Japanese military displayed to the rest of the world its strength, spirit and skills. The Japanese naval force was led by Rear Admiral Fukushima and the army was also strongly represented. Yamanashi considered the Japanese participation in the Boxer Rebellion a prelude to the Anglo-Japanese Alliance of 1902. Though the Japanese had won the Sino-Japanese War they had subsequently been forced by France, Russia and Germany to give up territories they had acquired. Thus the Germans obtained a long lease in Shantung Bay and the Russians regained Port Arthur and the Liaotung Peninsula. Yamanashi regretted the latter very much as the possession of the Liaotung Peninsula could have solved Japan's future emigration problem. No one, even including Yamanashi, thought it possible for Japan to win a war against Russia, yet an eventual conflict was thought inevitable. The atmosphere was electric: one of fear, yet determination amongst the men of the navy, the army, politics and diplomacy. Despite the tension Yamanashi recalled that the atmosphere in Japan could be likened to the time when cherry blossom begins to open in unison, with a hint of brilliance, quite contrary to the prevailing air of constraint and reserve which pervaded the Japan of the post-war period.

It was in that atmosphere of tension that Yamanashi sailed for England, arriving in London in August. He was to oversee *Mikasa*'s construction at Vickers-Armstrong's shipyard in Barrow-in-Furness. As he passed through the Suez Canal he saw a German battleship of 10,000 tons bound for the East.

Mikasa became the flagship of the Imperial Japanese Navy, and he held a life-long affection for her. Stephen Howarth writes:

> *Mikasa* represented an abiding Japanese predilection: for her time she was the biggest, strongest battleship in the world. Four hundred feet long between perpendiculars, her beam was 76 feet, her draught just over 27 feet. Her motive power came from vertical triple expansion boilers of the Belleville type, not one of the latest, but one of the most reliable kinds available. With them she could steam at up to 18 knots and with a maximum fuel capacity of 2,000 tons of coal, her theoretical maximum radius without refuelling was 9,000 sea miles at 10 knots. Her armaments were impressive: four 12 inch guns, two for'ard and two aft; fourteen 6 inch and twenty 3 inch quick firers; a dozen 47 millimetre guns, the small 2½–3 pounders; and four underwater torpedo-tubes. Her flying bridge, however, was open and unprotected.[4]

She was the pride and emblem of maritime Japan. Yamanashi watched her being built at Barrow, sailed her back, and when in 1962 the ship was repaired and preserved in Yokosuka as the permanent and unique memorial to the spirit of the Imperial Navy Yamanashi was the sole survivor of that generation to attend the opening ceremony. As he wrote to his friend in Britain, it moved him very much.

The years he spent as a young sub-lieutenant in Britain included the nine months of negotiations between Landsdowne and Hayashi which culminated in the Anglo-Japanese Alliance. The treaty was signed on 30 January 1902 and announced simultaneously in London and Tokyo on 12 February. The jubilation that followed was expressed in the cries of 'Banzai' by Keio University students outside the British Embassy in Tokyo. Yamanashi pays tribute to Joseph Chamberlain and his determination to conclude a treaty with a people of totally different religion and culture and which ended that splendid isolation which had been the hallmark of the British Empire. For Japan it was a major triumph; for the first time she was accepted diplomatically on equal terms with other powerful nations. The day after the announcement of the treaty Yamanashi was travelling on the train to Portsmouth. An Englishman approached him and said to the young Japanese naval officer, 'That was a good piece of business'. Yamanashi thought this characteristic of the British, quite unemotional unlike the French.

That 'business' of mutuality of benefit was of course the containment of Russian power. Japan was able effectively to defuse the Franco-Russian Dual Alliance, while Britain gained a lever in maintaining its position in the China trade which the Russians had been threatening since the Boxer Rebellion. As far as Japan was concerned the Alliance laid the diplomatic foundation with which she could fight a war against Russia any time thereafter. For the twenty years from 1902 to 1921, when the Alliance was abandoned, the treaty was to protect the interest of those two imperial island nations.

To Yamanashi the Anglo-Japanese Alliance of 1902 was the cornerstone of world diplomacy and he regretted very much its end in 1921 during the Washington Conference. He thought that Britain was the loser in that decision and often quoted Churchill from the talks the great British statesman held with the Japanese prime ministers Yoshida and Kishi in the post-war years. Yamanashi was of the view that the end of that alliance had far-reaching implications for the dissolution of the British Empire and in particular the independence movement in India.

In his lectures Yamanashi not surprisingly devotes a considerable amount of time to the Russo-Japanese War. It must have been a disappointment to him that he was not on board the *Mikasa* which he had nursed at Barrow, though he would never reveal such personal feelings. He played a very active part in the blockade of Port Arthur as the navigation officer of the battleship *Saien*. At the start of the war he was the torpedo officer, then leader of a landing party on the battleship *Fuso*, to which he returned as navigation officer later. He vividly recounts his first-hand experience of the war. There is obvious pride in the successful co-ordination of tactics and manoeuvre.

It is not necessary to recount his record of events as he saw them; the war has been much discussed elsewhere. Yamanashi concludes that the Japanese victory had a profound impact on the rest of the world. First, in terms of purely military tactics, artillery assumed much greater importance, so that battles could not now be won without trenches. Submarines and aircraft entered the scene for the first time. Second, in terms of political implications, it was catalytic in starting the Russian Revolutionary movement, and Germany could now concentrate its strength on the west and the Balkans. Third, in diplomatic terms Britain began to promote relations with France instead of Germany. But the greatest legacy of the victory over Russia was the psychological impact it had on the rest of the world, in that it signified the end of the absolute supremacy of the white race and awakened hope amongst the peoples of Asia and Africa. Nehru was said to have gained absolute confidence that the independence of India was not so far away.

As a participant in this major war Yamanashi emphasized to his students that he fundamentally believed that military science had no place without a deep understanding of religious and moral philosophy. War was a social phenomenon, a part of human life whose techniques could not be studied in isolation. All his lectures are laced with his immense knowledge of western and oriental philosophies, the Christian religion, the literatures of the east and west, and of world history from the earlier times. The breadth of knowledge which he obtained from his very wide reading is remarkable, and the influence of the education he received at Etajima is much in evidence.

Yamanashi returned to Britain again in 1909 on the cruiser *Ikoma* and spent some time with the Royal Navy. There is little record of this visit. Between the Russo-Japanese War and the First World War Yamanashi spent much of his time in the Navy Ministry, as private secretary to the minister of the Navy and as ADC to Admiral Count Yamamoto.

During the First World War relations between the Royal Navy and the Imperial Navy were at their best in the Indian Ocean. After collaborating in the capture of Tsingtao in 1914 from the Germans,[5] the British were keen to obtain Japanese naval support in the Pacific and the Indian Ocean, where the German armoured cruisers *Gneisenau* and *Scharnhorst*, and other light cruisers including *Emden*, had dispersed from west of India to the Falkland Islands. In early August 1914 Yamanashi (then Captain) was ordered to take passage on *Ibuki* to Hong Kong and Singapore.

Ibuki and *Chikuma* joined the British fleet and it was *Ibuki* which joined the Anzac squadron in the hunt for the *Emden*. Yamanashi however spent the four months until December 1914 with the British Command in Singapore and served as staff and liaison officer under Vice-Admiral Jerram. Among his colleagues was Vice-Admiral Egerton, whom he was to encounter again at the time of the Geneva Conference in 1927. Yamanashi remarked to his pupils that he was impressed by the perseverance of the Royal Navy and the superiority of the naval craft in use. However, he was not so impressed by their planning and tactics. The British were, he felt, far-sighted and effective in organization but the Germans were superior in analysis and planning. Spending four months with the British command he sensed the underlying mistrust of the British towards the Japanese.

Though Churchill, as First Lord of the Admiralty, expressed the official attitude of the British in 1915 to the Japanese naval attaché in London, the relations between the two governments, if not the two navies, were less than perfectly cordial. Churchill wrote:

> The signal success which has been achieved between the navies of Japan and Great Britain has been reflected in the relations established between the two Admiralties. When the history of this great war comes to be written, the ungrudging and wholehearted assistance of Japan will form a striking chapter, and the cordiality that has united the naval staffs of both countries will endure as one of our pleasant memories. For the moment our attention is turned to the naval operations in the North Sea and the Mediterranean, but we know that should the need ever arise we can rely with confidence upon the powerful aid of the Navy of Japan.[6]

In reality Britain felt that Japan could assist the Alliance more in the Mediterranean and the Baltic, while the Japanese (particularly the army, whose tutors the Germans had been) felt that Japanese interests were not sufficiently at stake to do so.

The Japanese side thus demanded terms for their assistance in these theatres which the British felt were hardly worth meeting. However in early 1917 Britain asked for two cruisers to patrol off the Cape of Good Hope. When the Japanese requests for British support in Shantung and the ex-German Pacific islands were met, the Japanese in fact sent two cruisers to the Cape as requested, and twice the number of ships requested to the Mediterranean. A few months later when Britain asked Japan for twelve more destroyers for the Mediterranean the Japanese eventually agreed to send what they could afford. Four of the best ships, brand new and the most advanced of their type were sent in May. In the autumn of the same year, however, Britain, needing more ships in Europe, offered to buy some battle-cruisers from Japan. This offer was refused; and Britain's feelings of mistrust increased.

The Japanese Mediterranean squadron continued to operate in conjunction with the Allied forces until the end of the war. The arrangement was one of automatic collaboration and this worked well, so that after the war the mood in Britain became more generous. The Japanese Mediterranean fleet was invited to visit Britain and did so.

Meanwhile, Yamanashi was to return to Britain again in 1916, accompanying the admiral he most admired, Admiral Akiyama Sanuyuki, through Russia. That was the last year of Imperial Russia and he tells of the splendid champagne parties he attended in Moscow and St Petersburg. It was also the year of the Battle of Jutland.

The Imperial Navy was a more willing supporter of the Royal Navy during the First World War than the Japanese government, which put obstacles in the way of providing assistance. At the end of the war Japan received a German passenger/cargo ship, which was named *Taiyo Maru* by the new owners. It is among the small ironies of history that Yamanashi's own brother-in-law, Fukuda Koichi, repaired this almost sinking ship as chief naval architect of the Mitsubishi shipyard; that Yamanashi's unceasing efforts to avoid war through negotiations for naval limitations treaties resulted in his brother-in-law losing his job; and finally that *Taiyo Maru*'s last sea-going mission was to be used as a reconnaissance ship on the eve of the attack on Pearl Harbor.[7]

The next decade of Yamanashi's life saw the climax of his naval career amid possibly the most important turning point in the history of twentieth-century Japan. Before these serious events there were happier interludes, again involving close liaison with the Royal Navy. Yamanashi was flag captain of the squadron which brought the then Crown Prince (Emperor Shōwa) to Britain in 1921. Again in 1923 as vice-admiral he was the principal escort to the Prince of Wales on his visit to Japan, leading a fleet to Hong Kong to meet the Prince's squadron, and escorting him to the Indian Ocean on his return voyage home. For this service he was awarded an honorary KBE.

The history of the naval limitation treaties is too complex to recount here. The political struggle in Japan over the two treaties, and the background to the 'Declaration of Humanity' of the Emperor Shōwa, were the two subjects on which Yamanashi kept silent throughout his life. In his eighty-fifth year, however, he lectured on the treaties, stressing in his preface both that his own responsibility for the treaties had been great, and that all others concerned were now dead.

In his account Yamanashi characterizes the Washington Treaty of 1921, which determined the capital ships tonnage ratio at 5 : 5 : 3 for Britain, America and Japan respectively, as the 'peaceful overture' to the eventual war against America. For him the negotiations were themselves a form of war without recourse to weapons. On this stage he put into practice his most profoundly held belief, that for a warrior the use of weapons must be founded in absolute human morality, never used in search of personal honour. The realism with which he approached the Conference reveals that Yamanashi was no mere pacifist.

Rear-Admiral Yamanashi went to Washington as deputy chief of the Special Committee on Arms Limitation: the Special Committee's chief was the navy minister Katō Kanji, while the delegation was led by Admiral Katō Tomosaburo in the capacity of envoy plenipotentiary.

The Washington Treaty had its origins in the American desire to build the strongest navy in the world, rivalling the British, and in her ambitions in China and the western Pacific. In 1900 the relative naval strength of Britain, Japan and the United States had been in the approximate ratio of 100 : 25 : 20. However Theodore Rooseveldt's administration had begun the build-up of American seapower, so that by 1921 the ratio had changed to Britain 100, the United States 75 and Japan 49. America's motivation for the naval build-up and expansion westward into the Pacific had its origin in the Spanish–American War of 1898 and the annexation of Hawaii – an event unwelcome to Japan. In China, then dominated by the European powers, US Secretary of State Hay had propounded his 'open door policy' and the doctrine of 'equal opportunity'.

The prelude to US naval expansion in the west Pacific was the arrival of Sperry's mission to Japan in 1908 with sixteen ships, flaunting America's new naval strength. (Yamanashi was one of the officers who entertained the visitors on that occasion.) In 1915, while the other world powers were engaged in the First World War, the US Navy Board was announcing that the US navy 'should be equal to the most powerful navy maintained by any other nation in the world'.

Meanwhile, the issue of Japanese immigration into California had begun to be troublesome. Altogether, over thirty years, US–Japanese relations had become ever more difficult and mutually antagonistic. In this climate of opinion the Japanese Navy was becoming increasingly nervous. The budget discussions of the decade 1910–20 were dominated by the so-called 'eight–eight plan' calling for the building of eight battleships and eight cruisers. This was finally to be approved in 1920, though the burden on the exchequer was two-thirds of all government expenditure of the time. Katō Tomosaburo, Yamanashi and others felt that a naval limitation treaty was inevitable as the limit of taxation, and thus of the naval budget, had now been reached.

Yamanashi states that Britain's position was never very clear to the Japanese. On arrival in Washington, he wondered what understanding had already been reached between Britain and America. Admiral Beatty visited his room and said abruptly: 'We have no money.' Dispensing with conventional salutations he launched forth on how it was essential to maintain naval superiority for the defence of widely scattered colonies but that the lack of financial resources meant inevitable concession to American demands. He urged Yamanashi and his colleagues to follow suit. It was imperative that Britain agreed to equality with the United States, but she could not accept a superior Japanese navy; the Japanese had to accept the ratio of 5 : 5 : 3.

Much of the negotiation concentrated on the definition of capital ships, but there followed discussions on bases. On this latter point, Yamanashi and Chatfield had preliminary talks to agree a position between them which amounted to maintaining the status quo. Yamanashi then talked to Pratt, who remained favourably disposed to Japan throughout, and the treaty was satisfactorily concluded.

The treaty, however, did not extend to cruisers and other supporting vessels. America proposed applying the same ratio to those ships also. However, the French chief of staff, Admiral Le Bon, telephoned Yamanashi and asked to see him: he could not return to his country with the same miserable ratio for cruisers as for capital ships. Yamanashi, knowing that Katō Kanji would be in favour of killing the American proposal, went to see their leader, Katō Tomosaburo, who understood this French reluctance. The Italians also joined in and no agreement was reached on cruisers.

Talks continued on this issue throughout the 1920s and in 1927 there was another meeting of the principal powers in Geneva. Among the British delegation was Yamanashi's old colleague Vice-Admiral Egerton. The Americans, however, came in large numbers, including many shipbuilders. At the time of the Washington Conference public opinion in the United States had largely supported the limitation; but by this time the atmosphere had changed dramatically. The British felt that they needed many cruisers for the defence of their colonies, and that the Americans should not need such a large navy. The Japanese delegate Saitō Minoru (Commander-in-chief in Korea, later Prime Minister), who was much respected by both Britain and the United States, tried to mediate but the impasse could not be resolved.

At Ramsay Macdonald's suggestion another meeting of the powers was arranged for 1930 in London. Japan decided to send the former prime minister Wakatsuki Reijiro as envoy plenipotentiary to the conference, supported by navy minister Takarabe Akira. The prime minister, Hamaguchi Osachi, was from the start totally committed to coming to terms with the other powers in a new treaty. To Yamanashi he said: 'I am prepared to stake my life over this issue for the Country, the Emperor, and the people. Vice-Minister, please help me'. Hamaguchi was indeed to stake his life as he eventually died directly as the result of an assassination attempt. Since the navy minister, Takarabe, was away in London, Yamanashi as the navy vice-minister was the effective head of the Navy Ministry and was to play the principal part in obtaining Japan's signature of the London Treaty of 1930. In his memoirs of his father, his son records the size of that task.[8] Not only did he weave together the various strands of opinion within the navy itself but he devoted tireless efforts to the handling of public opinion through the press, lest the opportunity to preserve peace be lost.

Yamanashi's task was principally to reconcile the interests of the navy and the country at large, but also to gain the acquiescence of those who were opposed to the naval limitation treaties. He proposed including in the delegation someone from this opposing camp, since he feared that the London Conference would spark off a political confrontation within Japan itself; but this suggestion was rejected.

The Japanese wish was to achieve 70 per cent of American (and British) tonnage for cruisers and support vessels and 78,000 tons for submarines. Though the torpedo specialists led by Suzuki Kantaro objected to submarine tonnage being fixed while surface ship tonnage was to be variable, the Naval Command and the Navy Ministry agreed that this was their ultimate negotiating position. Yamanashi insisted that these relative proportions must form the basis of agreement. In any event Wakatsuki's delegation managed to negotiate up the ratio from 10 : 10 : 6 to 10 : 10 : 6.975. The minuscule difference between this and the desired 10 : 10 : 7, and the fixed submarine tonnage of 78,000 tons, were to lead to disastrous political division in Japan. Britain insisted on no further building of submarines, thus by the end of 1936 the existing Japanese submarine tonnage of 78,000 tons, without replacements, would fall to 52,000 tons.

On the ratio of surface ships the Japanese yielded to the other two powers in achieving just less than 70 per cent while Britain and the United States yielded to Japan in maintaining parity. Though Japan had achieved slightly less than her declared target of 70 per cent, Wakatsuki was persuaded that to get the treaty through Congress it was imperative not to involve the American negotiators in loss of face. The Japanese prime minister, anxious to have the treaty accepted under budgetary pressure, persuaded the navy to accept what amounted to a loss of face on its part. In order to carry shipbuilding interests, he made the signing of the treaty conditional on once more attempting to negotiate for the continuation of shipbuilding capacity in Japan. But this was a feeble protest; should the delegation fail to reach agreement on this point the treaty was to be signed regardless.

Yamanashi arranged for the Imperial Family's agreement through Prince Fushimi, then the most senior member of the Imperial Family in the navy, and also personally obtained the agreement of Chief of Staff Katō Kanji and his deputy on condition that he should obtain the prime minister's agreement for the savings from the treaty to be spent on qualitative improvements in the navy and quantitative upgrading of its air strength. Thus foundations for the signing of the treaty were carefully laid.

On 1 April 1930, when the navy's official decision was to be communicated to the prime minister, at a meeting between the prime minister, Admiral Katō Kanji and Yamanashi, Katō (who was supposed to remain silent) suddenly stated that from the standpoint of military manoeuvres the US proposal was unacceptable. Thus the navy's wholehearted acceptance of the treaty was brought into question.

The Japanese government was in crisis. Yamanashi, however, resolved to push the treaty through and sent the decisive telegram to Wakatsuki to go ahead with the treaty. For him too the honour of his navy was at stake, but to abandon the treaty at this point was to place the navy in even greater difficulties. His telegram is legendary in recent Japanese history, as is his admission that its sending was like spitting blood. Yamanashi's task, however, was not yet complete; he engineered the apparently triumphant return of the delegation by sending his deputy to Harbin to forewarn them of the difficult atmosphere at home.

Prince Fushimi, and Admiral Tōgō too, initially supported the treaty; but under the influence of less enthusiastic protagonists such as Kāto Kanji, they soon became disenchanted. Yamanashi regrets in his lecture that nothing could be done to prevent the build-up of a political crisis.

The crisis came over the issue of *Supreme Command*. It was a constitutional requirement that the ministers of the navy and the army should be serving officers of the two armed forces. These were of course members of the government, while the chiefs of staff were not. The issue of Supreme Command arose over the interpretation of the law, which was ambiguous as to whether the authority of the minister of the navy to commit the navy was equal to that of the chief of staff (Articles 11 and 12 of the Meiji Constitution). This question arises from the traditional tenet of the navy that it owed its allegiance to the Emperor and no one else. The interpretation of the constitutional relationship between the government and the armed forces was to become an explosive issue for Japan for the next decade.

Yamanashi offered his resignation as vice-minister of the navy on 13 June 1930. It was his way of demonstrating the navy's commitment and its acceptance of the treaty in the face of mounting debate over whether the navy was indeed in agreement. He explained in his letter of resignation to the prime minister that it was the navy which was placed in a sacrificial position, and in order to avoid further damage to its morale and to stem the conflict of opinion he felt it necessary to leave his post. He asked the prime minister to remember the understanding they had reached on the naval budget with the reduced naval capacity. His final request, to bear in mind the achievements of Admiral Kātō Kanji, says everything about his perception of the crisis. When Yamanashi left active service two years later (he had been Commander-in-Chief at Sasebo in 1931 and at Kure in 1932), Wakatsuki regretted his retirement saying: 'a great man like you should be the Minister of the Navy now: that you are retired makes me fear for the country'. Yamanashi replied: 'A matter as important and solemn as arms limitation cannot be achieved without sacrifices. I did what I did fully prepared to become that sacrifice.'

At this final point in Yamanashi's naval career it is appropriate to mention the high regard in which he was held by Japan's greatest Second World War admiral, Yamamoto Isoroku. Yamamoto, planner of Pearl Harbor, had from the first been convinced of the necessity for naval limitation and of the impossibility of conducting an arms race against America. Often quoting Yamanashi, he passionately though unsuccessfully argued for the continuation of the treaty after 1936, when the treaty was scheduled to expire.

After leaving the navy Yamanashi retired to his small house in a suburb of Tokyo. His son remembers that Yamanashi had bought the land during the London Conference; he must have been making contingency plans for the possibility that his naval career might come to an end. When he left active service he was 54 years old. He spent the next six and a half years devoting himself to reading and gardening. His rose garden was his pride and joy. He enjoyed English literature, and Shakespeare and Longfellow were his particular favourites. 'There is a tide in the affairs of men' from Julius Caesar was one of his favourite lines, and well expressed his outlook on life: he often said to his son, 'However right and great the objective there is always the need to choose your timing and tactics to achieve it.' To a naval man the word 'tide' must have had its particular appeal.

In 1939 Yamanashi was to begin his second career, as an educator. He was appointed by the Emperor to take charge of Crown Prince Akihito's education, and became president of the Peers' School. His son recalls that these were probably the happiest years of his life, despite the responsibility for the safety of the Crown Prince and the sadness of war. When at the war's end the Occupation forces ordered the school's closure no one could have been better suited to negotiating with them: Yamanashi changed the school's constitution, opening it to competitive examination, and thus persuaded the Americans to allow the continued existence of this famous institution.

In the immediate aftermath of the war Yamanashi was once again to play a crucial role in the history of twentieth-century Japan. In the autumn of 1945 the future of the Emperor and the Imperial system was highly uncertain: this was to be secured chiefly through the Emperor's Declaration of Humanity on 1 January 1946. Yamanashi never spoke of his role in this episode, but the evidence that it was he who first conceived the idea (of the Emperor renouncing his 'divinity') is now indisputable.[9]

Through his friendship with the Zen philosopher Suzuki Daisetsu whom he employed at the Peers' School, Yamanashi had encountered R.H. Blyth, an Englishman from Ilford in Essex and an authority on Haiku poetry who had spent the war years in Japan. Recognizing Blyth's personal qualities, Yamanashi had asked him to join the Peers' School staff to teach English. Blyth, directed by Yamanashi, played the critical part – first in seeking out the Americans' reactions via his friends at GHQ, then in working with Yamanashi in drafting a suitable text for the emperor. Finally he acted as go-between in agreeing the text with the Americans.

Once again, Yamanashi's political skills had been employed in obtaining assent to his idea for the preservation of the Emperor's and the Imperial Family's existence and position in Japanese life. The Imperial Household Ministry was at first opposed, but through another channel at court Yamanashi heard that the Emperor was more than willing to publish a Rescript in the New Year. Yamanashi proceeded to organize the whole scheme with the collaboration of Prime Minister Shidehara, Imperial Household Minister Ishiwata, Blyth, and General Dyke and Dr Henderson of GHQ. Preparations were made very quickly in the final weeks of 1945.

Yamanashi never revealed the true process of history over the Declaration of Humanity. That he kept his silence to his death is a testimony of his absolute loyalty to the Imperial Family. It seems that this was something almost sacred to him. When the American historian Woodard visited him when he was in his eighties, he raised his hands above his head and clapped his hands loudly.[10] He asked his visitor which of his two hands had produced the sound. He said it would not have been appropriate if the Emperor had pronounced words given by the Americans, yet equally it would not have been acceptable if his words had not been agreeable to the Americans. Thus he explained that it was the culmination of the momentum of history that resulted in the Declaration of Humanity of 1946. But when Woodard mentioned the yellow piece of paper (on which Henderson had written the words, 'His Majesty disavows entirely any deification or mythologizing of his own Person'), the old admiral asked: 'Do you have that paper?' Woodard replied: 'No, you asked that the paper be burnt.' Yamanashi was satisfied. He did not wish to leave any evidence of the process by which the emperor's new status had come into being. It was of course Blyth who took the yellow piece of paper back to Henderson asking him to burn it in front of him.

Yamanashi was a perfectionist; he was not a brash warrior; he always tried to attend to detail so that his purpose would be accomplished without leaving room for further manoeuvre. He had the foresight of a military man that was often lacking in politicians, and he attached much importance to foresight as his actions were always based on moral conviction from which he knew he could never escape.

At the end of the war Yamanashi was entrusted with the task of choosing an American tutor for the Crown Prince – Yamanashi himself would have preferred a Briton to take on the task of teaching the young prince English, but it was the emperor's wish (almost certainly for political reasons) that this post should be given to an American. He preferred not to have a religious fanatic, but a person with some experience of life – not a young man but someone of middle age. With the aid of Blyth he chose Mrs Elizabeth Gray Vining, a widow of Quaker convictions. She herself has written of her association with the Imperial Family and her time in Japan in the immediate aftermath of the war. Of Yamanashi, who helped her settle in Japan, she wrote:

> He was one of the finest and most lovable men I have ever known. . . .
> He had all the qualities of the ideal samurai: courage, a stern sense of
> duty, loyalty, truthfulness, love of beauty, an ascetic grace of living in
> the face of poverty, kindness, dignity. In addition he had a Navy man's
> experience of great spaces and broadening knowledge of other lands,
> other navies, other ways of life and thought, which the land-bound
> warrior seldom has and without which he is blind and fatally prone
> to hubris. Mr Yamanashi was a man of peace, and his opposition to
> the militarists terminated a distinguished Naval career in 1933.[11]

She went on to say, 'there can be few left today who had themselves lived out the philosophy of the samurai as Mr Yamanashi has done . . . the samurai virtues of loyalty, contempt for money, frugality, simplicity, stoicism'. Those words, for those who knew him in person, strike a chord in their hearts. His dignity was awesome and one dared not speak without necessity; yet he was overwhelmingly kind.

He was a patriot, not a simple pacifist; he possessed the realism of a statesman though always he called himself a *gunjin* – a military man. He disliked war hawks; he deeply believed that morality must be at the basis of warriors' conduct in their use of weapons and that, as he repeatedly taught his students, the most dangerous thing in life is the pursuit of personal glory. You only needed to meet him to know that these were his fundamental beliefs. Blyth respected him very much and often said that if Yamanashi were Japan's prime minister and Suzuki Daisetsu Japan's archbishop, Japan would be a much better country.

Many of his students wrote about their teacher, Yamanashi, but Yamanashi always said he would never write or talk about himself, as he believed, with characteristic humility, that one should never broadcast one's own thoughts or achievements: that was for others to do. At home, his son remembers, he never uttered a cross word to his children. He introduced them to western culture: on his way home from the Washington Conference he brought back a gramophone and records of classical music by Schubert, Wagner and Beethoven; he had in his library the literature of the west as well as China, which provided much inspiration to his descendants. He was a regular visitor to concerts and opera whenever the opportunity arose. Not only to his own children but to many who were his pupils, in the Navy, Sendai-ryo, and the Naval Defence College and others who came across him, he was a teacher who taught a scale of human values of which he was a living example.[12]

His loyalty and devotion to the Imperial Family was absolute. This was in the true tradition of the Imperial Navy, whose officers believed that their first allegiance was to the Emperor, not the government. It is in this context that his resignation in 1930 seems so poignant. He could not hide his immense pleasure when the Crown Prince and his brother Prince Hitachi visited the *Mikasa* in 1962.

Shortly after the Second World War the Emperor was asked by the court journalist and writer Nagayo Yoshiro, in whom had His Majesty placed his greatest confidence and trust in the turbulent years of the Shōwa era? The Emperor replied without hesitation: 'Yamanashi Katsunoshin'. This must have been the greatest accolade and honour that Yamanashi ever received.

17

ARTHUR WALEY (1899–1966): POET AND TRANSLATOR

Phillip Harries

Of all the British scholars, writers and translators who have helped to shape our knowledge and our image of Japan over the last century, Arthur Waley is among the first to come to mind. His name is familiar to all students of Japanese culture and also to large numbers of educated readers with no special interest in the orient, who owe to him their knowledge of Japan's greatest works of literature. From 1919, when he published his first translations from the Japanese, down to the present day, his work has provided a window on Japanese sensibility and a genuine experience of the richness and the intrinsic value of Japanese culture.

Arthur Waley was born in 1889 and was educated at Rugby and at King's College Cambridge, where he gained First-Class Honours in Part One of the Classical Tripos in 1910. At that point he was forced to abandon thoughts of staying on at Cambridge, owing to the loss of sight in one eye. It is ironic that he should subsequently have taken up the study of Chinese and Japanese, which place far greater demands on the eyesight, and that he remained an avid reader right up to his death. After leaving Cambridge, he spent a year in Spain learning Spanish, followed, as far as can be determined, by a year in Germany. Then in 1913 he obtained a post in the Print Room of the British Museum, moving that same year to its newly formed Oriental Sub-department, where his chief was the poet Laurence Binyon. In this post he soon found himself wanting some knowledge of Chinese and Japanese, and set about learning both simultaneously. It thus appears to have been pure chance that brought him to the two languages that would occupy so much of his life. He had from his early days been a keen and brilliant linguist, with a strong interest in literature; and when he began the study of Chinese and Japanese, he already knew Dutch, French, German, Italian, Portuguese, Spanish and a little Hebrew and Sanskrit, not to mention the Greek and Latin he had read at Cambridge.

The first translations from Chinese poetry were privately published in 1916, and his first book of these translations came out in 1918, with another following in 1919. His translations of Japanese poetry appeared in that same year, and from then on the stream of translations, books and pamphlets continued. He gave up his post at the British Museum in 1930, but he never moved far from that area of London, living in a succession of houses around Bloomsbury, until his move to Highgate in 1963. During the Second World War he worked as a censor at the Ministry of Information and in 1948 he was appointed honorary lecturer in Chinese Poetry at the School of Oriental and African Studies in the University of London. His honours included a CBE in 1952, the Queen's Medal for Poetry in 1953 and a decoration from the Japanese government in 1959. In May 1966 he married Alison Grant Robinson and one month later he died at his house in Highgate.

Such is the bare outline of Arthur Waley's life. Like his own shy, reserved and austere exterior, it hides much that will possibly never be known. For all his wide range of friends and connections among leading writers, artists and thinkers of his day, such as the Bloomsbury Group and the Sitwell Circle, he seems never to have belonged wholly to any one group and remained an enigmatic figure often aloof and unpredictable. Memoirs, sketches and appreciations of him abound, but surprisingly enough there is as yet no full biography and much obscurity remains. The fate of many of Waley's personal papers is uncertain: according to his wife, Alison Waley, unknown numbers of them seem to have vanished in strange circumstances not long before his death, and other papers have become dispersed. Fascinating glimpses of his private life can be gleaned from Alison Waley's memoirs, *A Half of Two Lives*, which take us from their first meeting in 1929 right up to his death. From the work of the American scholar Marian Ury, we have an increasingly clear and sympathetic picture of Beryl de Zoete, with whom Waley had a perhaps unusual but deeply significant relationship, extending from 1918 until her death in 1962.[1] The influence of these two women, particularly the latter, on Waley's artistic achievements must have been profound, but, as with so many aspects of his life, it has yet to be properly assessed. In the end, however, Waley's achievement stands by itself, independent of the details of his life: it lies in his published works, above all in his translations.

While there can be no doubt of Waley's great achievements and stature in the field of Japanese literature and culture, it remains a fact that, notwithstanding the immense status and the sheer bulk of *The Tale of Genji*, the greater part of his output came from the Chinese. *The Bridge of Dreams*, the final volume of *Genji*, appeared in 1933, and thereafter Waley produced very little concerning Japan, whereas his output from the Chinese continued in profusion. It is therefore hardly surprising that China weighs more heavily in critical comment on his work and in what he himself had to say on the specifics of translation. This physical preponderance of matter from the Chinese has of course affected the way in which his reputation is framed, but what is equally important in our perception of his achievement is an essential difference in the type of work he chose to translate from the two languages.

Waley has been acknowledged a poet in his own right. But this is on the basis of his Chinese poems alone, and no recognition seems to have been given in this context to his translations from Japanese. For instance, Cyril Connolly writes of 'Waley's *Translations from the Chinese* which can surely be judged as an original contribution to our poetry'.[2] When Waley is included in such a general anthology of English poetry as *The Penguin Book of Contemporary Verse*, he is represented by two Chinese poems, and the compiler, Kenneth Allott, comments: 'He has perhaps a better claim than Ezra Pound – see Mr Eliot's introduction to Pound's *Selected Poems* – to be regarded as "the inventor of Chinese poetry for our time".'[3] It is clear that not only were Waley's translations from Chinese accepted as actual poems in English, they were perceived to have influenced English literature itself. In the Introduction to the 1962 edition of *A Hundred and Seventy Chinese Poems*, Waley tells how the poet and critic Edward Shanks turned away from him saying, 'That man [i.e. Waley] has done more harm to English poetry than anyone else.'[4] While we may not quite agree with this sentiment, it does show how deeply Waley's translations from Chinese entered the consciousness of the reading public and of practising poets.

Why then did this not happen with his translations from the Japanese? In the first place, the number of Japanese poems is very much smaller: Waley produced only the one rather slim volume, *Japanese Poetry: The Uta*, in 1919, and thereafter only a handful of isolated poems, confined mostly to primitive or folk poetry. Yet this is not an answer to the question; it is only a symptom of a deeper difference between the two halves of Waley's oeuvre. Essentially, Waley's achievement with Japanese literature lay in genres other than poetry; this is not to deny the highly poetic nature of the works he did translate, merely to point out that after his first venture into the field Waley did on the whole eschew translating Japanese poems. He appears, indeed, to have had a completely different attitude to them, a sense, virtually, that they could not succeed as English poems. The whole tone and presentation of *Japanese Poetry: The Uta* is that of a primer or book of instruction, for Waley is quite explicit in his introduction that 'The translations in this book are chiefly intended to facilitate the study of the Japanese text; for Japanese poetry can only be rightly enjoyed in the original.'[5] This was something that he surely never felt towards Chinese poetry, with which he had a genuine sense of creating new English poems: 'I was trying to turn a Chinese poem into an English one', he says in his 'Notes on the "Lute Girl's Song".'[6]

Readers too were much less sure of the merits of the Japanese poems. One reviewer remarked, 'The poems do not give the same thrill as those little decorative masterpieces – the Chinese translations.' More specific shortcomings are then mentioned:

One labels them sentimental and derivative, suspecting them to be the products of an over-conscious literary cult, and at the same time one admires their delicacy and simplicity. But one is not very much interested in delicacy and simplicity as such. Simplicity and delicacy are not praiseworthy in themselves, but as the means to an end. The end is, in this case, to reproduce a mood in the reader's mind; and few of them are likely to do it adequately.[7]

This is not the place to debate the validity of this view or the translatability of Japanese poetry in contrast to Chinese, but it must be admitted that the translations from Japanese are less successful than those from Chinese. It is obvious that Waley was making little attempt to create fresh literature, only to provide a literal version for the interested layman. Waley's turns of phrase are frequently felicitous and full of poetry, as one might expect of such a gifted translator, but the poems as a whole do indeed fall short of the ones he translated from Chinese, lacking somehow their power, conviction and integrity.

Underlying this difference of approach, there is no doubt some essential difficulty in casting Japanese poetry into English: the short form and short line, less amenable to Waley's lovely English rhythms; the smaller range of topics; the lower incidence of concrete images and the greater reliance on modal shading. But there is also the matter of personal affinity. Waley in his translations from Chinese certainly showed strong preferences and sympathies for certain poets, notably Po Chu-i, following a principle long known to translators:

> Examine how your Humour inclin'd,
> And which the Ruling Passion of your Mind;
> Then seek a Poet who *your* way do's bend,
> And Chuse an Author as you chuse a friend.[8]

Alison Waley, in a letter to the late Ivan Morris, recalled that Waley would not translate anything that 'did not excite, grip and haunt his imagination'.[9] One feels that this was certainly true of the Nō plays and *The Tale of Genji*, but not of the Japanese poems, which, perhaps, he felt as a scholar bound to make accessible in English but which he did not feel compelled to transform into English poetry. This is not to suggest that he failed to appreciate the poems. On the contrary, his comments show deep understanding and feeling, while his translation of the poems in *Genji*, for all that he casts them in prose, are highly successful. In fact, his choice of prose rather than verse for these poems embedded in the narrative demonstrates his sensitivity to what would work in English and his feeling for the longer structures of which the poems form only a part.

Given Waley's success with his other translations from Japanese his neglect of poetry may seem unimportant. It does, however, have an effect on attitudes

217

towards him. Since his early success and outstanding reputation were based on his Chinese poems, it is as a translator of poetry that he has primarily been perceived. Furthermore, his first translations appeared at a crucial time for English poetry. The Imagist Movement had just reached its height; T. S. Eliot's Prufrock poems had just been published, and his *Gerontion* and *The Wasteland* were soon to follow. Waley himself used to join Ezra Pound, Eliot and other poets at their weekly meetings in Soho, and he can well be considered part, even though not in the ordinary sense a member, of the Imagist and Vorticist groups, which exercised a major, progressive influence on the development of poetry. This was at the same time that the 'Georgian' poets were pursuing their conservative path, which may well explain the reaction of Edward Shanks quoted above. Pound had long maintained a strong interest in Chinese and Japanese verse and the Japanese Nō plays, while the Imagist poetic is inconceivable without the influence of haiku. Waley's work is, therefore, inextricably caught up in the history and formation of twentieth-century English poetry, and his achievement is looked upon in this light. An intriguing question is why he remained aloof from haiku, which had meant so much to the Imagists and which had not been adequately translated at that time. Here too we must fall back on personal affinities: there is no doubt that Waley's essential style, the rolling phrase, the full and singing line, do not suit the terseness of haiku, which is much more the style of Pound, keen as he was to encourage excision and the breaking up of the poetic line.

So the Chinese poems remain the touchstone of Waley's talent and the basis of his reputation. An additional reason for this is the intrinsic accessibility of poetry. Owing to its brevity, its concreteness, its more obvious rhythms, textures and devices, poetry is on the whole more susceptible to analysis, criticism and discussion, particularly with regard to the minutiae of translation. It is therefore easier to dissect Waley's technique in his poetry, while the structures and methods of prose or drama are more opaque. The Nō plays and *The Tale of Genji* are more diffuse, less tractable, less capable of exerting influence, as well as less obviously integrated into the English tradition. While their quality is acknowledged they are less frequently analysed and discussed.

With the Nō plays, Waley found an area of Japanese literature that obviously excited his imagination and brought out the best of his talent. His book of translations appeared in 1921, but he had already published some extracts in journals in 1920. The plays earned immediate acclaim, both as drama and for the poetry of their expression. These are densely textured verse plays in the original Japanese, and their length, together with their deeply spiritual and emotionally charged nature, gave Waley scope for his own sensitive and beautifully affecting English. In later years he admitted to finding some of his translation 'overladen and wordy', but this is too hard a judgement.[10] Although terseness has its virtues, the cadences of Waley's translations seem to match to an astonishing degree the pace and the dignified yet intense, often agitated, emotion of the Japanese.

It cannot have been a simple desire to introduce Nō drama to an English-speaking audience that prompted Waley's translations, for there were translations already in existence, of which Waley was well aware. Nor were these earlier ones necessarily inferior: Pound's adaptations of Ernest Fenollosa's translations had been published in 1916, and they were accounted then, as they are still today, good poetry, although, admittedly, there were mistakes to be corrected. What seems to have inspired Waley was a genuine need to put into English the beauty he had discovered. Despite some reservations, he reveals in the Preface to his plays a more positive attitude than with his Japanese poetry: 'Though English versions of Nō can at best be little more than makeshifts, I think I have managed . . . to retain in one or two passages in each play something of the original beauty.'[11] This is too modest. What Waley brings to his translation and how he transmutes his material into moving English poetry can be shown by comparing Waley's and Pound's versions of a short passage from the play *Kagekiyo*, which has been counted one of Pound's best.[12]

Literal version:

> Shut in by the pine that is my gate,
> I spend the years and months.
> Since I do not see the pure light,
> I cannot tell the passing of the time
> And in the dark hut
> Sleep in vain.[13]

Pound:

> Sitting at the gate of the pine wood I wear out the
> end of my years. I cannot see the clear light, I do
> not know how the time passes. I sit here in this
> dark hovel.[14]

Waley:

> Behind this gate,
> This pine-wood barricade shut in alone
> I waste the hours and days;
> By me not numbered, since my eyes no longer
> See the clear light of heaven, but in darkness,
> Unending darkness, profitlessly sleep
> In this low room.[15]

The poetry shines through Waley's version. He has added some words and repetitions, but they are wholly effective. The structure and movement

219

follow the original. His diction and phrasing have a plangency and sense
of desolation that are utterly convincing.

Four years after the Nō plays, in 1925, Waley produced the first volume
of *The Tale of Genji*, that huge and profound eleventh-century narrative
that was arguably his greatest masterpiece. Subsequent volumes appeared
in 1926, 1927, 1928, 1932 and 1933. The four-year gap between the fourth
and fifth volumes is unexplained: no other major work appeared during
this time. But he did give up his post at the British Museum in 1929, and
it may be that his personal circumstances were so unsettled and his other
professional commitments so time-consuming as to interfere with work of
this magnitude. At the same time as he was working on *Genji*, as part of his
general background studies he also translated substantial portions of several
court diaries, including that of *Genji*'s author, Murasaki Shikibu. In addition
he produced his version of *The Pillow Book of Sei Shōnagon*, which forms
a charming portrait of late tenth- and early eleventh-century Japanese court
life, consisting of a mixture of his own narrative and Sei Shōnagon's own
words, a pattern he later used in the highly successful *Life and Times of Po
Chu-i* (1949). In *The Pillow Book of Sei Shōnagon*, he shows that talent for
bringing other ages and cultures and their human actors vividly before our
eyes in all their universal humanity that informs his translations and was an
essential element in his success.

As with the Nō plays, in *The Tale of Genji* Waley did not approach
a text entirely unknown to the English-speaking world. An abridged and,
it must be said, unsatisfactory translation of the work had appeared in
1882.[16] Although Waley never mentions this version, it is unlikely that he
was ignorant of it, for his reading was wide-ranging and comprehensive.
There are indeed small similarities between the two versions which suggest
that, at the beginning at least, Waley was influenced by his precursor.[17] But
what Waley brought to his work was a superb ear for the English language,
a keen sensitivity to the human heart and mind, and an astonishing insight
into the nature of Murasaki's art. He also brought an integrity and unity
of style and conception that raise the work from a mere translation into a
classic of the English language. It is as much a tribute to Waley as to Murasaki
herself that one commentator should say, 'There is nothing rash in adding
her [Murasaki's] name to the names of the great novelists. Certainly there
are passages enough in this final volume which produce that strange effect
of revelation by which one recognizes great art.'[18]

Among the novelists to which Murasaki was compared were Jane Austen,
Proust and, significantly, Virginia Woolf: 'Curiously enough, for the modern
reader Murasaki's style carries with it a suggestion – to which it seems
Mr Waley himself is sensitive – of that of Mrs Virginia Woolf. . . . To what
extent this resemblance has been furthered by the translator it is difficult
to tell.'[19] Virginia Woolf herself was not without reservations about *Genji*:
'No; the Lady Murasaki is not going to prove herself the peer of Tolstoi

and Cervantes or those other great storytellers of the western world. . . . All comparisons between Murasaki and the great Western writers serve but to bring out her perfection and their force.'[20] But 'force' is surely not what one expects of Virginia Woolf's own novels; and there is little doubt that she and Waley shared the same views on the function of art and literature: both shared the ideals of the Bloomsbury Group, which saw the higher life as a mixture of human relations and aesthetic experience, exactly the qualities which Waley perceived in Prince Genji and his world. It was not only because he knew *Genji* to be the acknowledged masterpiece of the Japanese literary tradition that Waley was drawn to the work, but also because he saw in it something of his own vision and that of the artistic milieu of his time.

The mode of Heian Japanese narrative is essentially lyrical, not merely because of the abundance of poems in the text, but by its very structure, use of dominant images and unifying motifs and its manner of presenting thought and feeling. Virginia Woolf's novels too have been called lyrical.[21] Both writers share a skill in their use of interior monologue and their ability to give the appearance of entering their character's minds. With Murasaki it is a feature of the language and a literary tradition which discovered aspects of psychology and character portrayal centuries before they were discovered in the west. With Virginia Woolf it is a conscious artistry, one which, interestingly enough, owes its origins to the influence of China and Japan on the formation of the Symbolist and Impressionist aesthetic, which fostered the new modes of the twentieth-century novel. For Waley, then, who was by no means a peripheral figure in the literary circles of his time, but a genuine formative influence and expression of his age, *Genji* was the ideal work. His success in translating it is a measure of how far he found his own aspirations embodied in the work and the extent to which he knew as a creative artist he was answering the interests of the English literary world.

The last twenty years have seen an increase of interest in Japan and in scholarly research on its culture and literature that Waley could scarcely have imagined. Translations appear in an endless stream. It is therefore only to be expected that Waley's work should be re-evaluated in the light of present-day standards of scholarship. Mistakes and distortions in Waley's version of *Genji* are certainly there to be pointed out, and a new translation of the work appeared in 1976, which is indeed more accurate in strict linguistic terms.[22] But there is no question of Waley's *Genji* being supplanted. Waley understood to an uncanny extent the essence of Murasaki's art, and close comparison of his translation with her original text serves only to show how extraordinarily well he captured it, even while he made those adjustments that render her world more intelligible to an English reader. Part of the success of Waley's version is that he made the work his own. In so doing he inevitably imposed something of himself and his age on it, but only from that could come the integrity, the conviction, the sheer beauty and appropriateness of style that made it an English classic.

221

What was the nature of Waley's achievement? His contribution to under-standing between Britain and Japan is so obvious that it scarcely needs comment. In the first place, he made some of Japan's greatest literature available in English as classics in their own right, introducing Japanese literature to a wider English-speaking audience than it had ever had before, and making works such as *The Tale of Genji* an indelible part of the British consciousness. He was also an expert source of knowledge on Japanese culture and a humane and sympathetic influence on our understanding, as we may see from the piece he published in 1929 as a briefing for a group of officials and still worth reading today for correcting some popular misconceptions about Japanese civilization.[23]

Equally important has been his influence on two generations of scholars and experts on Japan. For many who today pursue the study of Japan in many walks of life, he was the first inspiration and a model of humane, sensitive scholarship to which to aspire. He was above all a man of letters, a devotee of literature and, not least, a creative artist. For him, Japanese literature was but one part of that spectrum of writings that constitute the world's literature and show both the variety and the universality of human experience. His wide knowledge of other languages and literatures informed and deepened his understanding of the Japanese. Without such breadth his insight and understanding would have been diminished. From his wide reading, as well as from his innate sympathy of mind, he surely derived his ability to form those apt analogies that made an alien custom seem at once familiar. He succeeded in translating a whole culture and society along with the words of its literature, and brought Japanese civilization and aesthetics as a truly felt experience into English intellectual and artistic life. His translations, as Virginia Woolf said of *Genji*, are 'always filled with the rush and bubble and chuckle of life'.[24]

18

TSUBOUCHI SHŌYŌ (1859–1935): SHERBORNE AND JAPAN – AN EPISODE IN CROSS-CULTURAL RELATIONS

Brian Powell

A historical connection between the small Dorset town of Sherborne and the cultural modernization of Japan might seem unlikely. The people of Sherborne themselves might be surprised to learn that around 1921 the name of their town was frequently on the lips of a group of young Japanese intellectuals working under one of the most influential scholars of the time.

The scholar was Tsubouchi Shōyō (1859–1935), known primarily in the west as the first Japanese to translate Shakespeare in full. After an early experiment with *Julius Caesar* in 1884, Tsubouchi started regular work on a complete Shakespeare translation in 1909. He began with the four tragedies (*Hamlet* in 1909) and completed the project in 1930 with *Henry V*.

We would probably think of a complete translation of Shakespeare's works as a worthy enough achievement for any scholar in one lifetime, but Tsubouchi Shōyō was active in many other fields as well. The theatre historian Kawatake Shigetoshi, author of the longest and most fully documented biography of Tsubouchi, claims for his subject the achievements of two or three people in the world of literature and two in the world of education. As an aside he also mentions that Tsubouchi was sometimes teaching as much as forty hours per week.[1] He was also a not infrequent visitor to the pleasure quarters.

In terms of publications Tsubouchi Shōyō's output was extraordinary. The *Selected Works* published in 1926–7 already comprised fifteen volumes, and in this only two of the Shakespeare translations appear, although by this time thirty were already available in print. What is more astonishing is the range and volume of his reading in western books evident from the bibliographies and notes in his articles. At each stage of his career Tsubouchi Shōyō seems to have had access to great numbers of contemporary western works on the subjects in which he was interested. He was clearly a voracious reader. He also made sure that he had all the latest publications. Many of his articles refer to western books published in New York or London in the same year that the articles were written.

A good example of Tsubouchi's exhaustive reading and enviable access to secondary sources was his work on the pageant. Tsubouchi Shōyō turned his attention to the pageant in the middle of 1920 and within a year had published numerous articles utilizing all the important secondary material available. He even seems to have had a view of the commemorative pamphlets of the Sherborne, Oxford and Yorkshire pageants of the time. By 1923 Tsubouchi's interest in pageants had played itself out and he turned his attention to children's theatre. In the meantime he had provided comprehensive accounts of British and American pageants and several blueprints for Japan's own version; there had also been a few productions of pageants in Tokyo and Kyoto, two of them written by Tsubouchi himself.

At the time the most substantial study of pageantry in the west, of course known to Tsubouchi, was Robert Withington's *English Pageantry*, published in two volumes by Harvard University Press in 1920. The last few sentences of the Preface to this work read as follows:

> The subject is interesting because it is close to the people. One root is in folk custom; and from the beginning, the populace has claimed pageantry for itself. As a form of artistic expression it is not, perhaps, so high as the masque; but of late years, from the soil cultivated by pageantry for centuries, a new form has arisen, calling itself by the same name. And this bids fair to play a considerable part in the community life of our country, as well as of England, for some time to come.

Such words matched the mood of the times in Japan and Tsubouchi's own mood at that stage of his career. By 1920 many young intellectuals were preoccupied by the ideological dimension of Taishō democracy, Japan's slow and hesitant move away from absolutism. Among the Left there had been vigorous debate on the subject of *minshū geijutsu*, art created by and for the people at large, and the theories of Romain Rolland and the work of the Swedish educationalist Ellen Key were eagerly discussed. The anarchist Ōsugi Sakai had developed a theory of popular arts in three influential articles published between 1914 and 1917, in which he had concluded that the people must create their own art or surrender their destiny as a newly arisen class.[2]

Although Tsubouchi was mysteriously ill on several occasions when he might have come into contact with the Imperial Family, he was not left wing and would not have agreed with the aggressive tone of Ōsugi's writings. He was, however, deeply involved in education and believed that for the necessary regeneration and reform of all aspects of Japanese culture every possible type of educational facility must be mobilized.[3] Drama was to be an essential part of this process, and by 1919 Tsubouchi was beginning to perceive a direct application for drama in the fostering of a new culture for the whole Japanese people. Up to this time his interest in education and his interest in the theatre had developed in parallel. The time was right for a new venture that would bring the two together.

Tsubouchi Shōyō's previous work in theatre had been varied and important. He had been active in supporting the move towards greater realism in the kabuki theatre during the 1880s. There was virtually no theatre other than kabuki at the time, and kabuki was presentational rather than representational. The famous actor Ichikawa Danjūrō IX had initiated a form of kabuki *jidai mono* (period piece) referred to as *katsureki geki* (plays of living history), in which some regard was paid to historical accuracy and psychological realism. Tsubouchi himself wrote such plays and two of them became classics of twentieth-century kabuki.

Tsubouchi had also contributed significantly to the recognition of plays as literature, a status they had never had in Japan before. Apart from *Shōsetsu Shinzui (The Essence of the Novel*, 1885) and the subsequent debate with Futabatei Shimei, which did not attract much attention at the time, in the early 1890s Tsubouchi engaged in a highly public debate with Mori Ōgai that centred on *Macbeth*.[4] In 1894 and 1895 Tsubouchi published a series of theoretical articles entitled 'Wagakuni no shigeki' ('Japan's historical drama'), in which he argued for certain principles to be observed in playwriting. Tsubouchi, already a teacher at a prestigious new private college, was publicly regarding drama as a legitimate subject for academic debate.

In the early 1900s Tsubouchi became interested in creating a new Japanese dance drama, believing that this was the way forward for a theatre whose best actors were still trained in kabuki acting technique. He wrote a few dance dramas himself and one is still occasionally performed.

Finally, from the late 1900s Tsubouchi Shōyō was involved in his most radical venture yet. Propelled, it must be said, by his less cautious protégé Shimamura Hōgetsu, Tsubouchi presided over a largely student arts club with the name of Bungei Kyōkai (Literary Arts Association). Dedicated to the proposition that new actors – *and* actresses – should come from outside kabuki, that is, should be amateurs trained to be professionals of a new type, Bungei Kyōkai mounted a number of notable productions, perhaps the most famous being *Hamlet* in 1911, the Association's first public performance and the first complete production of a Shakespeare play in Japan (the translation was Tsubouchi's). Bungei Kyōkai was a mixed society affiliated to what was by then Waseda University, and to Tsubouchi's chagrin, although he himself had caused a scandal some years previously by marrying a *geisha*, Shimamura Hōgetsu fell in love with Matsui Sumako, the Association's leading actress. Mainly because of the public outcry that their highly publicized love affair occasioned (Shimamura was married and had children), Bungei Kyōkai split up before it had a chance to be successful.

225

Although Bungei Kyōkai has just been described as a 'radical' venture for Tsubouchi Shōyō, many of its student members did not see him in this light at all. In the context of Japanese established theatre, which can only be described as essentially conservative, it was radical to plan and realize public productions of western plays using mixed casts of actors who had had no previous connection with the professional theatre. Tsubouchi himself, however, had no wish to move too far away from the norms of the kabuki theatre, which he much admired. In training his actors and actresses, he taught a method of delivery that owed much to that of kabuki. The stage movement that he encouraged in his productions was similarly redolent of kabuki and resulted sometimes in what were referred to as Bungei Kyōkai mannerisms.

Hence it is not surprising to find that the language of Tsubouchi's Shakespeare translations, which were by now regularly appearing in print, had a rhythm and sonority that would not have been out of place on the kabuki stage. The principles he followed in translating Shakespeare differed as he became more involved in his task and early on he was many times close to despair, but he finally settled on a form of modern Japanese (*gendaigo*) that employed to the full his unusual resources of vocabulary.[5] The contemporary playwright Kinoshita Junji (*b*. 1914), himself a translator of Shakespeare, has discussed at length the five stages through which Tsubouchi himself wrote that he passed during his search for the perfect linguistic medium. On behalf of all modern Japanese playwrights Tsubouchi Shōyō fought a long battle with a classical stage and literary language that seemed intractable when it needed to change to meet the demands of the modern age. Paradoxically Tsubouchi Shōyō succeeded more with his translations than with his own original plays.[6] There is a prevailing dignity of tone about Tsubouchi's Shakespeare, together with 'a free selection of words, antiquated and newly coined, simple and ornate, elegant and vulgar, native and foreign, which would remain within the grammatical structure of colloquial Japanese (*kōgo*) and would be intelligible to average people by hearing alone'.[7]

The other strand of Tsubouchi Shōyō's life had been as an educationalist. While a teacher at the forerunner of Waseda University (Tōkyō Senmon Gakkō), which he joined in 1883, he had regarded his main duty as providing information and interpretation to his students on a wide variety of subjects, but concentrating on western history, politics and law. As his interest in literature deepened during the 1880s he devoted more of his energy to establishing literature as a valid academic subject at Tōkyō Senmon Gakkō. He succeeded in persuading the university to create a literature department in 1890 and in 1891 he founded *Waseda Bungaku*, a journal soon to be highly influential in literary circles. In 1896, however, he took part in a different kind of educational venture. In that year Waseda founded its own middle school, and Tsubouchi Shōyō became its first head. He was now involved in the practical education of impressionable young people and this stimulated a strong interest in ethics. In 1903 he published what is known as a seminal work in the history of ethical scholarship in Japan.[8] Tsubouchi in his writing on ethics was critical of the romantic individualism of Takayama Chogyū then in vogue, warning that it threatened the continuation of society as it was constituted at the time. During this period Tsubouchi also edited two Japanese readers for use in elementary schools. For a few years, therefore, Tsubouchi's position required him to consider ways in which the consciousness of young Japanese could be shaped in a way that he thought was appropriate.

For the next ten years he had little opportunity to develop his ideas further on this subject, as his energies were taken up with the theatrical activities which have been briefly described above. In 1920, however, he was plunged into despair by the failure of a new historical play, even, in May, walking out of a performance because he was not able to endure the barracking which it was provoking in the audience. He abandoned his long-standing attempt to reform the established theatre and threw himself into pageants.

For five years since his resignation from Waseda University (as Tōkyō Senmon Gakkō had become in 1902) representatives of the university and of the students had been trying to persuade Tsubouchi to give some lectures. He had always refused, but finally in June 1920 he relented. He proposed lectures on 'drama as a practical matter; drama as an organ of popular self-education; drama as an organ of social management'.[9] The subjects proposed speak eloquently of Tsubouchi's new preoccupation at the time: how to develop drama as an educational and social force. Tsubouchi Shōyō's ambitions for drama were high and urgent, and he had given his course of lectures before June was out.

Tsubouchi followed up these lectures with a proposal that an organization be created to foster the study of 'cultural projects' (bunka jigyō). After discussions with Waseda representatives it was decided that although the office of this organization would be located in the Literature Department, it would have no formal association with the university. It was given the title Bunka Jigyō Kenkyūkai (Society for the Study of Cultural Projects) and it was to admit as members men and women both from the university and outside. One might note in passing that Tsubouchi Shōyō is again associated with an organization promoting some measure of sexual equality, in spite of the very bad publicity that Bungei Kyōkai had received as a result of the love affair between his student Shimamura Hōgetsu and Matsui Sumako. Tsubouchi would, as it were, barter his obligation to lecture in the university for active support of the new society. The Bunka Jigyō Kenkyūkai held its inaugural meeting on 11 October 1920 and there were immediately 300 applications for membership.[10]

The Society's syllabus was divided into two sections, one for education in literature and the arts and one for national literature and the arts. The latter was to study and foster new national performing arts (covering music, songs, dances and drama) and new popular festivals. Lectures were given by a number of Waseda lecturers covering a broad range of topics in drama and popular education. It was clear, however, that Tsubouchi Shōyō was the main moving force and he used the Bunka Jigyō Kenkyūkai as a platform from which to publicize and give practical realization to his developing ideas on pageants.

Pageants seem largely to have died out in Britain now, but they were still flourishing in the late 1940s and through the 1950s. Historians of the pageant would specify 1905 as the year from which pageants as we know them date. In 1905 the Sherborne pageant was put on and this is defined as the first 'modern pageant'.[11] The Sherborne pageant was devised to commemorate the founding of the school, bishopric and town of Sherborne 1,200 years before. Beginning with, for a pageant, a fairly modest cast of around 100, it ended up with 900. It started a fashion for pageants which swept the country and continued unabated on both sides of the Atlantic for the next decade. The originator of the Sherborne pageant was a former Sherborne school teacher named Louis Parker, and the Parkerian pageant became the norm for all subsequent pageants.

Robert Withington draws a clear distinction between the pageant that Parker created and the 'pageantic revels' that had existed before.[12] Processional pageants of various kinds had existed since the Middle Ages, the most splendid of all being the Lord Mayor's Show in London. These, however, according to Withington, had consisted of a series of unconnected floats; there had been no unifying purpose to the procession, apart from entertaining the spectators. 'It is for this reason that the pageantry of the past may be called "aesthetic", while that of the present [1920] is "educational". The first existed primarily to entertain; the second seeks rather to instruct.'[13]

The overall aim of the Parkerian pageant was the education of a community in its own past. Parker hoped that when the whole process of planning, rehearsing and performing the pageant was over, the people of the locality would have a clearer sense of the history of the area and would have renewed feelings of continuity with that history. To these ends Parker insisted that the pageant must have certain key characteristics. First, it had to be based in a particular locality. The pageant was a community project and the subject of the pageant was the history of the locality itself. A pageant had also essentially to be drama. Drama in his time would have meant a clear structure, realism in characterization and dialogue, and a strong sense of direction. Pageants were also to be historically accurate, as far as possible. Before a pageant was written, exhaustive research was to be done in local records; although any major historical events connected with the locality would be known about, such research might well uncover forgotten but significant episodes from its past, and these might well contribute to the educational function of the pageant.

Another concern of Parker's was to counter what he referred to as the 'modernising spirit'. His pageants were to correct and give structure to the nonsenses of the past, but they were sensitive to tradition and intended to be modern only in a limited sense. Parker says, 'This modernising spirit, which destroys all loveliness and has no loveliness of its own to put in its place, is the negation of poetry, the negation of romance. . . . This is just precisely the kind of spirit which a properly organised and properly conducted pageant is designed to kill.'[14]

Parker was also opposed to the participation of professional actors and was particularly critical of the 'hired performers' that had appeared in recent Lord Mayor's Shows. He wanted to involve the whole community. The various episodes of the pageant should be written by local playwrights and poets; the music should be composed by local musicians; the costumes should also be the work of local people. The only concession he was prepared to make was in the matter of the musicians in the orchestra. These, he allowed, could be professional. By keeping the project firmly based within the community it was also hoped that the various social classes would co-operate more than they usually did. They would understand the others' point of view and perhaps more sympathy and understanding would be aroused between the classes. There is no hint here of redressing any social injustices that may have existed, but in the context of the times Withington is able to term the Parkerian pageant 'essentially democratic'.[15]

The central feature of the modern pageant was to be the procession, but Parker did not want this to be a procession or processions through the streets. The site of the pageant was to be one large open area and processions would proceed across it. Dances were also important. The pageant was to be built up from a series of what were termed 'episodes', which should each tell a complete story.

Tsubouchi Shōyō was deeply impressed by what he read of western pageants. He saw in Japanese history a wealth of local incidents which would provide excellent subjects for pageants. He thought the potentiality of pageants to fulfil his cherished ambitions for Japanese drama was considerable, and he was anxious that knowledge about the western pageant should be disseminated with all speed. In the second half of 1920 and through most of 1921 he used every opportunity presented to him to speak or write on the subject of pageants. Many of his ideas were very similar to those of Parker and other English pageant masters, but some were significantly different.

Tsubouchi also drew a distinction between the public revels of the past and the pageant that he wished to create in Japan. The costumed procession (*kasō gyōretsu*) was an established feature of Tokugawa life and most *han* held one annually. These, however, had two features with which Tsubouchi could not agree. First, they were solely for entertainment and Tsubouchi had even stronger educational ambitions for his pageants than Louis Parker. Second, they were fixed, each procession being the same as those that had gone before. Western pageants, though there were hundreds if not thousands of them in the first two decades of the twentieth century, were one-off events requiring planning over a long period and achieving their educational and social objectives through the memory of the huge investment of time and community effort that had been needed to mount them. Tsubouchi by contrast felt that Japan's first local pageants would probably be of a low quality and that therefore new ones should be written by each locality every year. Eventually a masterpiece would emerge. Until this happened Tsubouchi recommended regular efforts in the community in order that an instinct for artistic creation could be widely fostered.[16]

Tsubouchi wanted to give dignity to the frivolity of the o-matsuri mood that infected whole communities whenever there was a local festival. Louis Parker had a similar object in mind, but the impression given by comments on actual examples of Parkerian pageants is that there was plenty of scope for the participants to enjoy themselves. Tsubouchi by contrast repeatedly uses the word genshuku – dignified, serious, grave – to characterize his pageants, as if the frivolity of Japanese festival crowds somehow needed more correction than that of their counterparts in the west.

Tsubouchi Shōyō's aims in promoting pageants were different from Parker's. He was more concerned with 'elevating' the taste of the Japanese people at large. He referred to medieval western pageants as 'folk plays' (minshūgeki) and to the Parkerian pageants as 'folk plays for the new age' (shinjidai no minshūgeki), and although Withington uses 'folk play' to describe the Sherborne pageant, in Tsubouchi the idea of community consciousness is much less strong. Tsubouchi hoped pageants would be an instrument by which to create a cultural movement that would raise the standards of drama nationally and improve general appreciation of theatre. New 'national arts' (kokumin geijutsu) would result, leading to a new culture for Japan.[17] His vision of the future for Japanese pageants was something comparable to the drama festivals of ancient Greece or Oberammergau.[18]

Tsubouchi's aims for his pageants meant that they did not have to be confined within the boundaries of one locality. To be sure, appropriate localities existed in abundance in Japan; Tsubouchi provides a long list of them, in which Kyoto and Kamakura figure prominently. But he also believed that national festivals, such as Bon and Shōgatsu, could be profitably organized along the lines of pageants. National memorial days commemorating famous historical personalities of Japan's past could also be celebrated in pageant form. The organizing body need not be a local community at all. Universities, large companies, shrines and temples could all create their own pageants.[19] The Japanese pageant was to be the primary force for cultural change on a national scale.

If Tsubouchi's ambitions were rather more grand than Parker's, he was at one with him on the question of performers. Pageants were not to be drama schools. Performers were not to see them as a convenient stepping stone for a rapid entry into the professional theatre. Tsubouchi's reasons for preferring amateurs, however, were rather different. While Parker wanted to encourage the local population of the area sponsoring the pageant, Tsubouchi was anxious to discourage those who might use the pageant to further their own hopes of a glamorous stage career. Tsubouchi Shōyō had had bitter experience of the attraction of what one might call the ascribed attributes of the acting life for those whose ambitions had initially seemed seriously theatrical.

Tsubouchi accepted much of what Parker recommended for the technical structure of pageants. He used the loan word *episōdo* to denote the basic units in the programme. He was aware of the problems of outdoor performance and had his classes at the Bunka Jigyō Kenkyūkai to practise voice projection. He wrote short plays suitable for outdoor performance and used them as training texts for his students. He also composed three specimen pageants, of which the most important was *Atami-machi no tame no pe-jento* (*Pageant for the Town of Atami*), published in February 1921. The *Atami Pageant*, as it is usually called, was intended for the opening of the Tokyo–Atami railway, but for some reason was not performed on that occasion. Meanwhile Tsubouchi's students at the Bunka Jigyō Kenkyūkai were so enthusiastic that they wanted training to continue through the Tokyo summer heat, and from among them soon came calls for an actual performance.

Tsubouchi, always keen to follow theory with practice, and at this time being publicly scathing of those who did not move beyond theory, acceded to this request.[20] As a text he selected four sections from the nine of the *Atami Pageant*. He found an open site in central Tokyo,[21] and he, his pupils and his whole household (a somewhat different pattern from Sherborne) spent the summer preparing for the event. As often happens with pageants, rain forced the postponement of this one several times. It was finally held on 2 October 1921, but even then heavy rain fell until the last few minutes. Seating had been arranged for 1,500 spectators, but only between 600 and 700 attended. The response from the society whose level of artistic appreciation Tsubouchi Shōyō hoped to improve was rather poor, but this was Japan's first pageant and deserves mention for being that.

If the *Atami Pageant* had been performed as Tsubouchi had intended in writing it, Louis Parker would have approved of it, as it would have involved the whole community. It was to start with a choral prologue, in which local elementary school teachers and their former pupils, wearing western clothes and accompanied by music played on western instruments, sang a song celebrating Atami as a park for the whole world. Part 2 was an 'episode' showing how the god Kotoshiro nushi no kami came to live in Atami, peacefully engaging in fishing and farming. The performers of this part wore masks. Part 3 was also an episode and related the miraculous transfer to land of the great hot spring that had spouted out at sea. The next two episodes (Parts 4 and 5) concerned Yoritomo's connection with Atami. Then Part 6, entitled 'The Flow of History', was to be a procession

231

of children in historical costume representing famous figures from the Hōjō period up to the beginning of the Tokugawa period. Part 7 was a country dance (*inaka odori*) performed by Atami *geisha*, and it ended with the arrival of foreigners with long noses. Part 8 was an episode depicting the casting and test-firing of a cannon by Edogawa Tarōzaemon and Sakuma Shōzan. Part 9 was to be the finale, with joyous singing and dancing by great crowds of people, and including the inevitable formal addresses by local dignitaries, who were allowed five minutes each.

Planned and executed as intended, the *Atami Pageant* would probably have achieved all that the western pageant was aiming at. A large number of performers of all ages and a multitude of costumes would have been needed. Those essential integrating agents in Japanese society, the elementary school teachers and the local dignitaries, were neatly placed at the beginning and the end. Music and dance were used in abundance. The rich mythological and historical past of the area was utilized to produce a feeling of continuity with what had gone before, and the hopes of Atami for the present and future were amply represented. Parker's insistence on historical accuracy was also observed. Parts 4 and 5 were specifically designated by Tsubouchi in the texts as episodes to be performed in the *katsureki* style. *Katsureki geki*, as has been touched on above, were the 'plays of living history', historically accurate and relatively realistic, that had begun the reform of kabuki in the 1880s and so bored traditional kabuki audiences in that and the following decade.

The *Atami Pageant* was never performed in full. Part 2 on the mythological origins of Atami was performed in the garden of the Waseda Ōkuma Kaikan in October 1924 and apparently well received. Another Tsubouchi Shōyō pageant on Shōtoku Taishi had been planned for the autumn of 1921 but had not taken place. In 1922 there were a few performances in Japan that could be called pageants, including a notable one in the Chion'in in Kyoto performed by Ichikawa Sadanji II; but pageants never became the contemporary fashion as in Britain and the United States. Soon the Bunka Jigyō Kenkyūkai became inactive; Tsubouchi himself transferred his interest elsewhere and the pageant itself became not much more than an interesting episode in the story of Japan's cultural debt to the west.

Tsubouchi clearly expected too much of the Japanese pageant. While in the west there had been, for whatever reason, a spontaneous outburst of interest in the idea of local pageants, Tsubouchi could only hope to induce such an interest from above in Japan. Throughout his writing on pageants the tone is similar to that adopted earlier when prescribing how the development of modern theatre should proceed in Japan. We should not be surprised at this. First, teachers were expected to be unhibitedly prescriptive, and second, in addition to the respect traditionally accorded to teachers, Tsubouchi Shōyō had the authority which accompanied a knowledge of his subject that was unrivalled in his generation. If Tsubouchi could hold up the Bungei Kyōkai production of *Hamlet* in 1911 each night by lecturing for an hour to an audience of intellectuals on how to appreciate the play, he could well instruct local communities in how their pageants should be organized. It was difficult, however, for him to instruct them in the enthusiasm which had resulted in pageants the length and breadth of Britain.

Perhaps a more important reason for the failure of the pageant was that Tsubouchi tended to regard it as able to provide the foundation for a new Japanese theatre. Louis Parker had no connections with the professional theatre, and in Britain the pageant was quite separate from the drama that was watched in theatres. Tsubouchi had been preoccupied since the 1880s with the task of reforming the Japanese theatre. His attempts, theoretical and practical, to introduce a limited amount of rationality into the kabuki period play had been rebuffed by the audiences on whom the theatre depended. The new dance dramas that he created in the early 1900s are of only limited significance in the history of modern kabuki. His courageous attempt to address the crucial problem of an acting method for modern Japanese theatre turned sour on him as notoriety rather than fame followed the fortunes of Bungei Kyōkai. Each had been a stage in his search for an appropriate theatre for modern Japan and each had seemed to him a failure. Pageants, which to Tsubouchi appeared to be transforming local theatre in Britain, combined several of his previous interests and were seen by him as having the potential to achieve what he had been unable to achieve before. Very soon, however, he had passed on to something else – this time, *kateigeki* (family drama), plays for children to perform within the family, which would in turn raise the cultural level of families throughout Japan. More enterprises followed.

The single constant thread running through Tsubouchi Shōyō's activities since the later 1900s was his translation of Shakespeare and it is difficult not to agree with the theatre historian and critic Ozaki Kōji that his greatest achievement lay in giving Shakespeare to Japan.[22] Between 1909 and 1922, with the exception of 1917, he produced at least one translation per year. Many of his translations were later reworked and in 1935 Tsubouchi was preparing a revised version of *Othello* until the collapse that led to his death a week later. Tsubouchi may have seen his other ventures as leading cumulatively to a new theatre art for Japan, but by 1910 or the second decade of the twentieth century Japanese theatre was already fragmented and Tsubouchi's achievements in one area were unlikely to affect others. On a theoretical level the theatre of Tsubouchi Shōyō was developing steadily towards a dramatic art that would revitalize Japanese culture. In reality, after providing the initial impetus towards modern theatre, Tsubouchi left his mark on Japanese theatre in a number of separate ways. The pageant was one of these and we have to conclude that its impact on modern Japanese theatre was minimal.

Shakespeare's plays have transcended many cultural boundaries, and it is hard to imagine Japan in the Meiji period failing to encounter them at some stage. In this sense Tsubouchi stands alongside many others who have laboured to make their own cultures aware of the universality of this great world playwright. What is even more impressive, to return to a point made at the beginning of this chapter, is that Tsubouchi Shōyō did not permit Shakespeare to dominate him. After starting his translation project, Tsubouchi continued searching for other elements of western, specifically British, theatre and literature that might enrich Japan's own developing modern culture. In the area of the pageant his sense of urgency may have led him to assume wrongly that a set of prescriptive principles could produce a nation-wide movement; but that he was receptive to the potentiality of the pageant and willing to do exhaustive research on it, is remarkable. Tsubouchi's interest in British culture was catholic, and if he did not achieve all that he wanted for Japan through his knowledge of that culture, he introduced it more widely to his countrymen than any other Japanese of his time.

19

WILLIAM PLOMER (1905–1974) AND JAPAN

Louis Allen

'I won't have niggers in this place! Get out!' spat-out by the proprietress of a coffee-shop in Pretoria, Transvaal, to two Japanese journalists from the *Osaka Asahi* and the *Osaka Mainichi*. The captain of a visiting hockey team from Natal remonstrated with her, and stopped her throwing the Japanese out of the shop. They were grateful to him, and wired home to their steamship company in Osaka to keep in touch with this young man. His name was Laurens van der Post.

Four months later, in August 1926, a Japanese ship, the *Canada Maru* of the Osaka Shosen Kaisha, called at Durban. Her captain asked van der Post to dinner on board, and gave him an invitation to spend a fortnight in Japan at the company's expense. Not wishing to leave his two friends, the young poet Roy Campbell and the newly hatched young novelist William Plomer, van der Post declined, and was amazed to be rebuked later by both of them for his refusal. Relenting, he agreed to go if they would go with him, but Campbell was unwilling to leave behind his wife and two daughters, so van der Post and Plomer set off without him. It was the breaking up of an interesting literary friendship, for the three of them had been involved in running the avant-garde periodical, *Voorslag*, with which they hoped to start an African literary renaissance. *Voorslag* aimed to rid South Africa of what Campbell called 'this fetish that rules the country – Colour prejudice'. This was the theme, too, of the young Plomer's novel *Turbott Wolfe* (1924), a vehicle for his own intense sexual frustration – a homosexual unable, at the time, to avow it openly – and his protest at South Africa's racial bigotry.[1]

The themes made Plomer an apt guest for Mori Katsue, the captain of the *Canada Maru*, who allowed himself to be persuaded by van der Post to take Plomer along as well.

Mori Katsue was not only a formidable young sea captain (he was 36 when he met Plomer for the first time) but also national kendo champion. Moustached and bearded, he had an exuberant sense of fun, and a strong awareness of his responsibility to what he conceived to be the new duties of his nation. Plomer had become rapidly known as the author of a novel written against racial prejudice, and Mori's sea voyage to South Africa was also a weapon in that struggle. 'I wanted to make a success of the new line', he told Plomer's biographer sixty years later. 'I wanted to break up South African colour prejudice, and I knew that Plomer had written strongly against it.'[2] His ship had luxury accommodation for a dozen passengers, and for six weeks en route to Japan van der Post and Plomer were treated like kings. They were also treated to the spectacle of Mori getting his own way in the face of racial prejudice in a British colony when the ship called at Kilindini, the port of Mombasa. Frustrated in an attempt to see the Governor of Kenya, Sir Edward Grigg (later Lord Altrincham), Mori returned from Nairobi with his two young South Africans to learn that the ship's carpenter had died. Mori was determined that his man should not be buried in a cemetery alongside the coloured population, or at sea. He must be interred where Europeans were buried. The tacit opposition was considerable on the part of the local community, but pressure from the local press and the police, lobbied by Mori, was effective. Rebuffed, as he saw it, by the governor, whom he had entertained on board ship and who had apparently refused him the courtesy of a return invitation, he had returned in the train from Nairobi 'silent, broody and bitter',[3] and the achievement of ensuring his carpenter 'should lie among the decomposed remains of some of his ex-allies as equal' was something he savoured. Plomer wrote:

> So it happened, one sultry evening that the Anglican burial service was read over the corpse of a Japanese peasant by a hot and irate-looking Anglican clergyman in a surplice, probably a cricketer, while Mori and van der Post and I stood by with the crew of the *Canada Maru* – well-behaved and in spotless white ducks, and looking slightly spellbound, like good children at a classy wedding – to witness this unexpected end of some poor mother's son, this triumphant vindication of Japan as a Great Power. As for Mori, he had such a mingled expression of solemnity and satisfaction on his face that he might have been burying a rich and childless uncle. He looked like a cat that has just finished a large piece of its favourite fish.[4]

As the voyage continued, the ship became for Plomer and van der Post a kind of encapsulated version of Japanese life. The crew spoke little English; Plomer began to learn Japanese by helping Mori translate *Turbott Wolfe*, they ate Japanese food and in the evenings listened to one of the officers playing the *shakuhachi*, the long-drawn notes seeming 'a classical lamentation, exquisite and resigned, for some irrecoverable age of primordial peace, an evocation of what the Japanese call *aware* – which had been translated "the ah-ness of things"'.[5] But there were occasionally more disturbing sounds: not the lachrymose love-songs volunteered by another passenger, or Plomer's contribution of *Vat jou goed en trek, Ferreira!*, but a curious dance by Mori – Plomer was sure it was a war dance – which made not merely Plomer but the other Japanese uneasy: 'For a few minutes the atmosphere was uncomfortable; equivocal looks and remarks were exchanged by the Japanese, and we knew without a doubt that he was dancing in honour of *der Tag*. A momentary but ineffaceable impression.'[6]

After arriving at Moji, Mori took his guests ashore to a geisha party and tried to make Plomer succumb to the charms of a pretty, gentle and quick-witted girl:

I think the idea was that I should fall heavily at the outset for Japanese womanhood and accordingly for Japan, but matchmaking is such a gamble, and just as people often give as presents what they themselves like rather than what the recipients want, Mori had chosen the bait he himself would have taken. All the same she was a very nice and obliging girl and may be said to have literally laid herself out to please – nor was she unsuccessful.

Later, Plomer's homosexuality was to declare itself in uncompromising terms, but at this time he seems to have been in a state of hovering bisexuality, and the *sake* and the occasion seem to have lulled him into acquiescence. There was little in the rest of Mori's introductory tour that could not have been foreseen: Kobe, Osaka, a model hostel for workers in a textile factory ('But all that we saw and heard of their lives filled us not with admiration but with horror and pity'), the melancholy tranquillity of Nara and Kyoto in autumn, speechifying in Tokyo, Nikko, the Ise shrine, and early morning in a boat on Lake Chuzenji: 'It was a late autumn morning, and a few red and yellow leaves fell like dead butterflies through the mist and floated on the clear water, through which we could see the lake-bed of coloured pebbles.'[7] *Double Lives: An Autobiography* was published in 1943, and wartime London no doubt sharpened in retrospect those little perceptions of Plomer that behind the screen of beauty and elegance in Japan there lay a thirst for power which would soon have to be reckoned with; but at the time he also recognized the upshot of Mori's package tour, that it had given him, at the price of much physical and nervous energy, a deep view of Japanese life that he might have spent months, perhaps years, in acquiring on his own as a conventional tourist.

When van der Post returned with Mori on the return voyage to Durban, Plomer opted to stay in Japan. Through an introduction from Edmund Blunden, he taught at the Tokyo School of Foreign Languages, then at the Tokyo Kōtō Gakkō, where one of the pupils, Sumida, attached himself to Plomer as a kind of general factotum. Other pupils included the nephew of Baron Shidehara (the foreign minister and future prime minister), a future president of the Sumitomo Bank and several future university professors of English. His 'textbooks' were Boswell's *Life of Johnson* and *Hamlet*, but what impressed his pupils most was his determination to live in Japanese fashion, without any western possessions in his house.

Plomer's reaction to their approval is interesting and ambiguous. One of them wrote him a letter of thanks, which he quotes in *Double Lives*:

> To tell the truth, I expected that we should meet with more starchy, formal treatment which is usual between the people who belong to other nationalities, so I was rather afraid of seeing you. It was interesting for me to find you accustomed to the Japanese manner of living, and seeing you live in a simple way like a man who was thoroughly acquainted with the world, I couldn't help smiling. But I believe the life you are leading now will not be unpleasant for you, because I perceived that you have something of the genuine Japanese character in your spirit – that is, the indifference about the world's affairs, the despise for social talents and a calm and self-possessed attitude.

Plomer sees in this not merely the intended compliment, but also a note of condescension, the same thing

> that may be heard in an Englishman's praise of a foreigner for not behaving like a foreigner; it hints at a conscious superiority. Much has been said about the 'inferiority complex' of the Japanese and much of what has been said is justified. Keen observers, on the other hand, have sometimes stressed that the Japanese do really feel, even if they have taught themselves to feel, on a loftier plane than other races, and that this feeling has been a strong motive power in their great imperialistic gamble . . . Modesty and arrogance, diffidence and assurance, can exist or alternate in one breast, so why not in a whole race?

Some observers of Japanese life have distilled in writing their experiences of three or four decades. For others who have spent merely a brief period there, the impression has been so profound and disturbing that it has lasted the rest of their lives. William Plomer is one of these. Of English extraction but South African birth (1905), he went to school at Rugby and returned to the Transvaal as a young man. Later in life he explored the theme of cultural conflict in fiction and poetry, worked in publishing, and with Naval Intelligence during the Second World War, and became a respected figure on the London literary scene during the 1950s and 1960s, editing Kilvert's *Diary*, composing librettos for Benjamin Britten and so on. But his three years in Japan, from 1926 to 1929, were a period of great change, both for him and for Japan itself, and they marked him for good.

It was the beginning of the reign of the Shōwa emperor, which was to last longer than any other in Japanese history, and which saw the country transformed, first from a liberal democracy to a totalitarian militarist state, then to a nation at war with half the world, and lastly, via the catastrophic defeat of 1945, to the casting aside of weapons and the fulfilment of peaceful economic progress. Plomer saw the early part of this process, chiefly in the domestic side of Japanese life. He was welcomed by Japanese friends and in Japanese homes; but he was aware, too, of the strains and stresses in the Japanese society of the 1920s, and of the nationalist stirrings which, in less than a decade after his departure, were to lead Japan into war.

Three years may seem a short time. But for a curious, sensitive and intelligent mind such as Plomer's, the intensity of impressions counts for more than duration. It was not an uncritical gaze he brought to bear, either. Affection for Japan, in his autobiographical writings (*Double Lives: An Autobiography*), his fiction (*Sado* and *Paper Houses*), and his poetry is mingled with an astringent, ironical scepticism which is not merely personal but a reflection of the debunking mood of the 1920s in general. The mood which produced Aldous Huxley's dismissive peripatetic portrait of Japan in *Jesting Pilate* is merely an exaggerated form of the scepticism about certain aspects of Japanese life which informs the brilliant and quirky account of Plomer's friend, the poet and university teacher Sherard Vines, in his book *Yofuku* (Western Dress). It is no coincidence that Vines took the typescript of Plomer's first volume of Japanese stories, *Paper Houses*, to Europe with him on his return in June 1928, and that Plomer dedicated it to him.

The last story in that book, the mildly Voltairean 'Mother Kamchatka', is described as 'A Fantasy', and depicts a land geographically not remote from Japan and spiritually and socially extremely close. The reader would not be mistaken if he heard echoes of *Candide*: Count Hibachi, the narrator's friend, 'lives in foreign style, and his home I must say is a mansion, for I do not exaggerate when I assert that it possesses a chimney'. The narrator, Mainchance, visiting Kamchatka, sees the national flag flying everywhere: 'an emblem whose design shows commendable simplicity – a poached egg, gules, displayed on a white plate ... a triumph of heraldic economy, for whose sake anyone might be proud to bleed to death, or to be kicked repeatedly in the face by a policeman'. He is decorated by 'His Imperial Effulgence, the Cham' of Kamchatka with 'the *tenth* class of the Unimpeachable Order of the Sacred Gooseberry Bush'; he makes fun of ceremonial suicide – 'the Kamchatkans use a hairpin and coal-shovel; or, since the introduction of western civilisation, simply the more homely spoon and fork'; he finds the natives speak a language 'specially made to prevent clear thinking' because they are afraid of 'plain speaking, home truths and common frankness'; he sees the capital Kooty 'as having no slums because the whole thing is one large slum'; he has a dig at Lafcadio Hearn in the person of Cadwallo Tern, a celebrated writer on Kamchatka, 'a wretched, soft-headed, dreary fellow' who wrote, a considerable quantity of sentimental though pretty stuff which savours too much altogether of wish-fulfilment. Why, he made Kamchatka out to be a sort of paradise. He was very far-sighted, but he could only focus on the remote past. For him, present and future seemed hardly to exist. One result of his long-sightedness was that all the Kamchatka cabmen looked in the distance like Adonises, all the housemaids like a rosebud garden of nymphs and all the gooseberry blossoms like swansdown.

And, of course, militarist propensities are guyed:

Their alleged militarism, I concluded, was partly, nay mostly, congenital, for the warlike habits of two thousand years don't disappear in a night; but partly self-defensive. Besides, before the present Cham entered upon the parental guardianship of his subjects, and of the Almighty, he had made a tour of Europe. There they showed him nothing but guns, tanks, aeroplanes, submarines, poison gas, liquid fire, and death-rays; and simply as a matter of politeness he had to make large purchases of these novelties, so it would be absurd to call the Kamchatkans peculiarly militaristic. By nature they are the most peace-loving people, and in old times were never known to shed blood except when they did: except, for instance, when committing suicide out of sheer loyalty to the Cham; and except for occasional tribal wars and petty feuds, which seldom lasted more than a century, and in which it was only very rarely that more than two hundred lives were lost.[8]

A meeting of the new Kamchatkan social-democrats is broken up by the police (who outnumber the audience), the party is dissolved, and it is then announced that 'a frightful Red plot against the Cham' had been suppressed: 'A law was then enacted that anybody caught thinking dangerous thoughts would have to slit his belly or it would be done for him.' The conclusion, by Mainchance, who has decided to stay in Kamchatka, tempted by honours and a fat salary, lies in the valour of discretion:

I have long since understood the true Kamchatka, but would never dream of saying so. I always say that I am quite certain now that discipline is better than liberty, and that only the young and foolish could have any doubts on the matter. But is that what I really think? Ah, thoughts, thoughts! All thoughts are dangerous. Long live Kamchatka, the true and everlasting Kamchatka!

Plomer's biographer suggests that his return to Europe in 1929, forecast in a letter to Leonard Woolf on 11 June 1928, may have been caused not merely by his increasing awareness of the xenophobia of Japanese society but also because *Paper Houses* was about to be published, and 'if this had been read and understood by some chauvinist fanatic,' wrote Plomer, 'he might have put a violent end to me'.[9] Alexander adds that the danger was real enough, since the volume was translated into Japanese; but it is perhaps worth pointing out that Japan was liberal enough at the time to permit such a translation to be made and printed; just as British society in the middle of the Second World War was liberal enough to permit precious paper to be used for a reprint by Penguin Books of *Paper Houses*, much of which is as sympathetic to Japan as 'Mother Kamchatka' is critical.

Plomer wrote two prefatory notes to *Paper Houses*. The first, dated June 1928, is a statement of grateful affection:

> I admit that I am an admirer of the Japanese for I can respect and love individuals. But I disbelieve in their tendency to nationalistic paranoia and their particular politico-religious superstitions, which I believe to be more insidious and locally almighty than those of nearly all other countries, Russia and Italy included, and which, if persisted in, will have terrible results.[10]

These words were written eight years before the revolt of the young officers in Tokyo, and thirteen before Pearl Harbor. By the time Plomer's forebodings had been only too completely fulfilled, it might have seemed that the portraits contained in *Paper Houses* were too patient and sympathetic to be suitable for a wartime readership. So it is a testimony to the tolerance of London in 1943 that Penguin Books reissued it. Plomer was asked for a fresh introduction, and he did so in terms singularly at variance with anti-Japanese feelings of the time. He evokes the fascination of the life available to a young foreigner in Japan in the 1920s, and makes it seem singularly enviable:

> In the towns there were wonderful theatres, interesting shops, an unfamiliar kind of domestic life, and the varied life of the streets. Travel was easy, unrestricted, and comfortable. There were all the accumulations of a long civilisation to study and enjoy – the arts and applied arts, manners and customs. And above all there were the people, lively and companionable and often good to look at, clean and polite, generous if they liked you, faithful as friends, and capable of deep and violent emotion.[11]

The disfigurement of Japan by uncritical nationalism and militarism, and her grotesque sense of 'divine mission', makes Plomer ascribe to a split personality (the theme of 'A Brutal Sentimentalist') and to the madness which is its accompaniment: 'In the quietest and kindest person there lurked a potential fanatic, full of racial vanity.' 'The Portrait of an Emperor', as Plomer points out, illustrates the excesses of patriotism when it becomes a repressive cult, and 'A Brutal Sentimentalist', shows the tug of war between the humanity of an individual and what is conceived to be patriotic duty. There is no drum beating in the new introduction, and he admits with regret that, to crush the bitter enemy Japan had become, 'the innocent must suffer with the guilty'.[12] What interests him is neither the adulation of sentiment nor the crudities of propaganda, but the reality of his own experience: 'I was not out to prettify Japan or to throw mud at it, but to convey something of what I had seen or learnt there.'[13]

'A Brutal Sentimentalist' illustrates the tug of war perfectly. A Japanese diplomat, Tonoki, falls ill and is visited in hospital by his friend Wilmington. He opens his heart to Wilmington and tells him how hard and stern his life as a child had been after his mother's death. His father, an ascetic, conventional and conservative man, brought him up in terms of prohibitions. At 18 he fell ill for the first time in his life and nearly died. His father came to see him, and stood at the doorway, simply saying his son's name, 'Taro!'. Tonoki had never seen him show any feeling before, but there was no mistaking the mixture of terror, love and anxiety on his father's face:

> I can never forget his eyes at that moment, although he has been dead for many years. . . . 'Why didn't you tell me?' he said in a voice of strange yearning and tenderness that seemed to come straight out of his belly. Neither of us could keep back the tears. From that time I had no doubts. I knew then that the severity of all those years came out of a deep, deep love.[14]

In a later visit, not put off by Wilmington's chaffing at him for being 'so disgustingly sentimental', Tonoki recalls the murder of a Japanese socialist by a Gendarmerie Captain, Amakasu, and the behaviour of a certain Colonel K. after the 1923 Tokyo earthquake. The Colonel had encouraged scapegoat reprisals against the Korean minority and had personally hacked to death with his sword a Korean couple who had taken refuge in his house. Wilmington answers this by quoting examples of European brutality and massacre. But he has misunderstood Tonoki:

> No. Understand that I cannot blame Colonel K., Amakasu and those others. When even civilised men are excited they will do anything, act like savages. They were doing, I suppose, what they believed to be their duty. Their duty to their Emperor and their country. But look at me, Tonoki Taro, forty-four years of age. I am a rather successful and not unimportant official. 'You're absolutely indispensable; I don't know what we should do without you,' the deputy vice-minister for foreign affairs said to me six months ago. I have a wife and three children, a top-hat, and five decorations from foreign governments in recognition of my services. Why? Because I've always done my duty. My duty to whom? To my Emperor and my country. Wilmington, don't you see it is the same Emperor and same country as *theirs*? How can we both be right? If they're right, then I'm wrong. They acted with open violence, but I coldly went away and went on with my work. If they are brutal, I am equally brutal. They may have done what they believed to be right,

but I'm doing what I believe to be wrong. Tell me, how can I go on? Isn't it better to give up, to resign or to die? I'm not afraid to die. You know that. The other day you told me I am sentimental and you're right. To-day you told me that I am not brutal, and you're wrong. For I am brutal and sentimental. I despise myself.[15]

This is the same Japan in which the headmaster of a school from which the emperor's portrait has been stolen commits suicide. It never seems to his widow that he has done anything other than the right and honourable thing. She goes to live with her brother-in-law, who takes in students. One night she hears two of them discuss a third, the young radical Wada:

Do you know what he actually had the effrontery to say to me the other day? I told him he was disloyal to the Emperor. 'I have got nothing against the Emperor,' he said, 'but after all he's only a man.' 'If you ever say or think such a thing again,' I said, 'I'll disown you.' He didn't answer.

The headmaster's widow is flooded with a revulsion of feeling:

To think that that boy, that student, that lazy long-haired good-for-nothing, that *radical*, should mock at the Most Sacred Majesty for which her husband had died! To think that he should dare to *doubt*! She saw again the face of Yoshida [her dead husband] on the floor of his room, the projecting teeth horribly exposed and slavered with yellowish foam, the familiar features fixed in the last grim purpose, the children watching. . . . All her pride, all her love, all her life, summoned up in her at this moment a magnificent renewal of the faith she had never lost.

Naturally, when she encounters Wada that evening, she greets him with a frozen politeness. He merely thinks her a stiff little *petite bourgeoise*. 'As the years went by, she became formal and even prim, devoted to her children and to household affairs. But the words "only a man" haunted her till her dying day.'[16]

Plomer did not reissue *Paper Houses* after the wartime reprint – on villainous paper – but three of its seven stories were published again in *Four Countries* in 1949, intended as characteristic cross-sections of his writing on England, Africa, Japan and Greece. Each has four stories, and the fourth in the Japanese category is a new one, written many years after *Paper Houses*. 'My Neighbour's Creed' is a fictionalization of a strange visionary experience. On a visit to Hiroshima with one of his pupils, he watched a firework display from a boat one evening. It left a domed cloud of smoke hovering over the city, something he recalled in 1945 when he read newspaper reports of the mushroom cloud over Hiroshima after the dropping of the atomic bomb. 'My Neighbour's Creed' has at times too much dramatic irony – 'one can be scorched in the summer at Hiroshima', he remarks of the heat – but the eerie premonition of his pupil's great-uncle who sees passers-by in the street as the dead they will one day be in this very spot, and without their shadows, is far subtler. He has previously said to the narrator (the date is 1927), 'in Hiroshima many people have been born who will never be buried'.

> It was so hot that I felt disinclined to question him, and thought to myself that there had been previous instances of prophets dwelling on the future doom of the cities to which they belonged.
>
> As we headed for him, two searchlights met above the distant bonfire and showed that in the windless air the smoke had risen like a tall column and had flattened out at the top: it appeared motionless.
>
> 'What a peculiar shape that smoke is,' I said, inspecting it through the field-glasses. 'It looks just like a poisonous toad-stool.'
>
> As soon as I said this I thought it sounded rather precious. Why hadn't I said simply 'like a mushroom'? But the smoke was livid and discoloured; it *did* look rather like a poisonous toadstool. . . . When I looked again in the same direction the searchlights had vanished, the smoke was no longer visible, and the bonfire had died down. I wondered if I had imagined the thing, especially when I asked Hajime if he had seen it and he said he had not.[17]

One one occasion Plomer found in Higashi Nakano the perfect illustration of the dichotomy of Japanese life which he was to describe in 'A Brutal Sentimentalist'. He had wanted to move closer in to the centre of Tokyo than his country home in Kami Nerima. He was not put off by its sprawling industries. Far from it. 'It was a city electrical with life,' he wrote 'and, at least to me, of inexhaustible variety'.[18] And although the Kōtō Gakkō seemed to him like one of the factories on London's Great West Road, and the curriculum stiff and over-demanding for the students, he found his fellow masters in the common-room 'as agreeable a set of men as could be wished'.[19] His own work was well paid, not uncongenial, and alternated with long holidays in which he could explore and savour the country and cultivate his private life. His pupil Fukuzawa Morito was an important part of that life, and their hedonistic and sceptical turn of mind was not at risk in what Plomer calls the palmy days of Japan, when 'dangerous thoughts' could still be expressed with relative impunity. There were certainly some absurd attempts at censorship, covering such incongruous items as nude sculpture at an exhibition and the *Private Papers of Henry Ryecroft*, for its supposed power to inculcate dangerous thoughts, a decision Plomer naturally found quite incomprehensible. The government had set aside 3 million yen a year to 'improve national thought', a euphemism for the establishment of a spy system in schools and universities, to keep tabs on socialist and communist secret societies.

There was endless discussion in the house at Higashi Nakano, a good deal of reading and writing, and a great deal of occasionally noisy entertainment. A rarer visitor than the students, but more important to Plomer, was Mori on his return trips from Africa, where he had got to know Plomer's parents, who looked upon him as a model of courtesy, charm and intelligence; qualities he found in them. On one such visit, when all three of them, Mori, Plomer and Fukuzawa, were sharing the sleeping accommodation, Plomer lying awake between the other two, he pondered on the difference between them. He sensed a slight jealousy between them, too, each of them having a special claim to his affection; this, the difference of ages, resulted in a formality of manner.

> As I lay listening to their tranquil breathing, and warmed by the proximity of their bodies, I thought of them as the two poles or antitheses of the Japanese character. Mori was the man of action and duty, perfectly disciplined, all self-control and efficiency; a nationalist and, I suppose a militarist; a quiet but fanatical believer, I had never doubted, in the 'divine' mission of his race; Mori stood for power, war, violence and injustice in the interests of a visionary and doubtful good. Fukuzawa was the intellectual, a temperament, melancholy, and gaily sardonic; aesthete, perhaps an artist, his life made up not of public duties but personal relationships; he stood for peace and quietness, for living and letting live, for internationalism, for the immediate and tangible good, for everything (as William Allingham put it) 'we prize for mirthful, gentle, delicate and warm.' The dualism of the Japanese nature which, for me, was typified by these two friends became ever clearer. They were the two aspects of the Japanese double life. It would have been convenient to be able to divide the Japanese into Thugs and Gentles, but too simple, and erroneous besides, for the thugs were often largely gentle, and the gentles often tainted by the traits or tenets of the thugs. I have even heard it said that every Japanese is a split personality.[20]

Plomer's homosexual nature is the theme that lies behind his novel *Sado*, and it seems clear enough that his relations with some of his Japanese pupils were stronger and more intimate than those that subsist merely between teacher and taught. He waited until he was living in Greece with his friend Anthony Butts before giving final form to the novel, and the place and circumstances of its writing affirm his homosexuality much more strongly than the text. He and Butts had gone to Greece because it was a place where homosexual partners could easily be found, like the Berlin of the 1930s or, as Plomer discovered later, in the neighbourhood of large London barracks, or a regimental centre at Dover, where he could give free rein to an impulse that demanded a partner of a lower social rank who might be paid and would otherwise not be demanding.

The novel proved easy to write when he was in the midst of a passionate affair with a young Greek called Nicky. When that affair came to a disastrous end, with Nicky abandoning him, diseased from the contact, for another rich foreign 'patron', the novel ploughed into difficulties. Its theme under the original title of 'Memoirs of an Emigrant', has been described as 'the dissolution of youthful priggishness and ignorance under the powerful influence of homosexual experience.[21] Plomer's publisher, Hogarth Press, asked him to reduce it, and he agreed to cut it to half the original length. But size and a lack of unity were not the only problems. He told van der Post that he was trying to conduct his life and work in accordance with his 'real nature' (though he did not define that for van der Post, who did not suspect Plomer's homosexuality for many years). It was really the problem of coming to grips with his sexuality in a novel, according to Alexander, that constituted his first obstacle as a writer.

Sado is a thinly disguised debate, not merely about the problems of a young European in his first contact with Japan, but also about sexual identity. A young English painter, Vincent Lucas, is offered lodging in a garden hut owned by a Japanese, Komatsu, and his English wife Iris, whose feelings towards Lucas, at first inchoate, quicken into love, which for most of the book she despairingly conceals. Lucas's young Japanese friend, Sado, also develops a strong passion for him, but feels rebuffed when Lucas forgets to introduce him to a visitor from Europe, Elsa Nicolai.

Lucas, Iris, Komatsu and Sado, form a quartet of people very turned in upon themselves and their mutual relationships, and Elsa, the visitor, acts like a brisk solvent upon the situation. Her presence has another effect on Lucas. She tells him that he has been in Japan long enough, that much awaits him in Europe, and that it is time to be gone. He has in fact been considering this for some time, but it needed Elsa to articulate it fully. Her definite assurance makes his mind up for him. Before he goes, he asks Sado why they have become estranged from one another, and is amazed when Sado tells him it is because he failed to introduce him to Elsa, when he had promised to do so. To Lucas, who had simply forgotten, it seemed a trivial and insignificant thing; to Sado, who had brooded upon the omission, it appeared as a rejection.

Iris, too, in their final meeting, asks him, in fury, how he could be so self-centred not to recognize how deeply she had fallen in love with him. He knows that he can feel affection for some women, but has no need of them at all. And what he feels for Sado is not strong enough to deflect him from his resolve to return to Europe.

Plomer had little difficulty in analysing, in some detail and with some self-indulgence, the inner-directed speculations of Lucas, clearly modelled on his younger self. The greater challenge – and greatest assumption – is the exploration of the reticences and hidden explosive passion in Lucas's young Japanese friend Sado, no doubt modelled, at any rate in part, on Fukuzawa.

He had taken Lucas into his confidence about the most appalling shock of his life, when he had discovered his young sister's suicide:

> On a March morning, when the bamboos, but lately relieved of their burden of snow, were beginning to wave with a refreshing rustle in the glittering windiness of spring, Sado Masaji, going into his sister's small north room on the first floor to tell her a joke, found her lying dead on the floor with her head all bloody. She had cut her throat with a razor, which was lying nearby, and open beside her was a love-story by Turgeniev, the place marked by a letter addressed to Masaji, which he took, read, and destroyed. The chief motives of her action had been unrequited love (of which the unwitting object was in Tokyo) and the despair, under a double ban, of being married.[22]

Lucas's reaction had, naturally, been compassion. But since he knew Sado's suffering was at a depth he could not reach, the compassion expressed itself as pity, as gifts and as occasional flattery to bolster up Sado's highly susceptible self-esteem. Plomer describes the upshot as being like that of a speculator who has had a few successes and then gambles on one big throw:

> Lucas had become the main force in Sado's sad but placid life. At the moment when he first saw him, Sado had happened to be posting a letter to Miss Plover, and had paused half-contemptuously, half joyfully to re-read the address he had written, being in that tranquil mood which is apt to precede sudden and sensational events.
>
>   Lucas . . . had, one might say, invested too heavily in Sado[23]

Conversely, Lucas's role in Sado's 'sad but placid life' became a major one,[24] and the tranquillity Sado had managed to achieve was disturbed by it. Their relationship follows a pattern which is Plomer's own interpretation of his mildly determinist philosophy. We may be passive in the face of fate, but we can be uprooted by a storm from outside for which nothing has prepared us: 'We may reduce ourselves to the most negative state of passive acquiescence in what seems to be a completely barren situation, but all at once circumstances burst in from nowhere at all and blast us off in an unforeseen typhoon.'[25] So self-doubt begins to gnaw at Sado, not just as an individual, but as a Japanese *vis-à-vis* a European. Perhaps this lonely and currently womanless foreigner was simply bored, and was merely pretending to treat him as an equal? Sado did not think of himself as inferior, but simply as 'too different', and reflects that if Lucas had met him in England, in his own set, his behaviour might have been patronizing. Sado could not afford these doubts. Because of what he perceived as Lucas's nature and impact: 'It was simply a question of trust . . . it was not as if Lucas were a woman or casual friend, he involved one in his lively and complex destiny, he seemed vitally concerned in everything he came in touch with, he lived intensely.'[26]

So Sado desires, but mistrusts, the friendship Lucas extends, fearing that it may have been born of circumstance and could not be deep or enduring. 'To think that friendship could be as tortuous and torturing as love!'[27] And over-reserved and hesitant, Sado dare not reach out and seize the happiness Lucas holds out to him.

Lucas, who conceives himself to be emancipated, is none the less aware of an instability in the age in which he lives, which seems to dictate the way he feels about Sado. He has a Gidean – *familles, je vous hais!* – attitude to the constraining effect of the family system on the individual, and he sees himself as a victim of it, just like the Japanese among whom he lives, just like Sado: 'He knew by now that the apparently close texture of the traditional Eastern family often veils, like many another, not only indifference, but hatred and despair.'[28]

Like many young intellectuals of the 1920s, Lucas could imagine communism to be an acceptable alternative, involving, as he saw it, the switch of allegiance from the family unit, in a disciplined and cheerful way, to the community as a whole, asserting that the mass and not the family was the basis of society. But he was *not* completely emancipated from his past and family, and instinctively dreaded the domination of the mass. So he saw himself as a transitional figure, liberated from 'family, bourgeois, Philistine standards'[29] and at the same time retaining a residual fastidiousness which was repelled by the raw ugliness of the mass society that was coming into being:

> And even as he thought of its ugliness he thought also of its beauty, its youth, energy, and promise. But he feared for the individual, trembled for the weak, shrank from the vulgar, at once shunned and hankered for the healthily commonplace, was anxious about culture and freedom, hated levelling, clung to survivals – until now, pitched head foremost into the paradoxical Japanese world which had leapt from feudalism to machinery, he sometimes felt at sea.[30]

He refused to accept the cliché that there was more wisdom in the east than in the west. Both were equally anchorless and uncertain, equally lost, as Sado was, as he was and – again a characteristic reaction, paradoxically individualistic for the determinist Plomer proclaimed himself to be – what he held on to was an affirmation of personal relationships:

> how infinitely precious the occasional individual trying to hold himself aloof from the crowds, like Sado sitting there before him, quiet and affectionate, protestant but resigned, gentle but a little dangerous to interfere with, at once melancholy and amused, disillusioned and hopeful, clothed in the old radiance of human dignity.[31]

Sado's confusion is analysed as characteristic of what Plomer sees as the immense class of unemployed intellectuals, products of innumerable Japanese 'universities' (Lucas/Plomer insists on the inverted commas), coming immediately from a background of small property and individual respectability, and less directly from a peasant background behind that, and ready to plunge into a sentimental Tolstoyan world,

> ideas of going 'back to the land', art colonies living by barter, noble poverty, free-love love-nests, and so on. . . . Conditions of life that were neither ancient nor modern, neither Western nor Eastern, in which only the incongruous was normal, Marxism going along with primitive religion, enlightenment with taboo, reaction with revolution.[32]

So however Lucas may view his own position, Sado does not see him as a transitional, unstable being, but as someone who has 'an assurance, a hold on life, a "Christian" confidence in existence, a vivacity that seemed in its strangeness greatly superior to his own wretched state'.[33]

Lucas is aware that something inhibits Sado's full confidence, and traces it to self-esteem. But the source of Sado's anxiety is not an objective awareness of inferiority, rather an assumption about Lucas's attitudes: 'Yet, kind and tactful as he meant to be, he could not at all realise that Sado's trouble was not that he felt himself inferior to Lucas, but that his every nerve cried out within him that Lucas, while fond of him, *in his inmost heart despised him*.'[34]

Lucas/Plomer's analysis does contain a sentiment which is perhaps not contempt but mildly derisive; not of Sado, but of young Japanese intellectuals in his position:

> At least Sado had not that sort of mind which is so common in Japan, the mind which grows too quickly, without striking deep enough root, and which, depending only on a shallow soil and the favourable caprices of the weather, exhausts its strength before it has produced shade, perfume, or fruit; such minds, common enough when a hitherto isolated race is suddenly overwhelmed by the influx of a powerful alien civilisation, become engaged in a furious attempt to be up-to-date, thirst for the novelty-after-next, and instead of drawing a steady sustenance from their own traditions are blown along on the barren wind of an illusory progressiveness.[35]

Because Sado is not like this, but umbilically linked to the social matrix from which he was trying to emerge, Lucas sees that the cord could be severed or weakened, provided Sado's self-esteem were not wounded in the process. So he determines 'to maintain his attitude of perfect naturalness and tactful sincerity in the hope that Sado might some day learn to stand squarely on his own feet'.[36] Self-esteem, in the end, is the rock on which the attempt founders.

The book has a leisurely, introspective style, much concerned with refinements of feeling, and moments of self-conscious analysis. Like some modern Japanese novels, it has one or two set-pieces – a picnic in the country, a provincial *matsuri*, or festival – which give scope to Plomer's observant eye and retentive memory. But it was no doubt the awareness that he had dealt unsatisfactorily with the homosexual presence in his novel that made him react so sharply to Harold Nicolson's review of the book in, of all things, Oswald Mosley's paper *Action*:

> If my book is (he replied to Nicolson), as you say, 'pretty feeble' as a novel, I can only hope to do better in future; but is it altogether fair to accuse me of a want of courage, and of having failed to 'grasp the nettles'? What nettles? You admit that I have made the homosexual theme 'abundantly plain', and at the same time reprove me for reticence. But am I to blame because it is not possible to be so frank in this country [i.e. England] as in France or Germany or China?[37]

Plomer had of course found Japan much more tolerant of homosexuality than England was then – or was later to be, until the post-war period. There was, after all, a samurai tradition in which love between warriors was perfectly acceptable. And Plomer's awareness of the increasing power of the Japanese army in politics, its racial mysticism and dangerous fanaticism, did not prevent him seeing in some of its publicly visible personal relationships something with which he could sympathize:

> It was common to see two buck privates in uniform strolling about hand in hand with a far-away look in their eyes, and I was credibly informed that this was not an expression of ordinary matiness but of an emotion to some extent encouraged in the armed forces, no doubt in the belief that greater love hath no man than this, that he lay down his life for his emperor, but that there will be an extra incentive if by doing so he is also laying down his life for his friend. Such intense relationships have of course a place in the samurai tradition, sometimes as a substitute for conjugal love, sometimes as an adjunct to it.[38]

This love was, of course, a way of knowing Japan itself. Plomer wrote that he had a happy sense of community with the Japanese: 'I lived with them and in their fashion and was part of their society; I worked for them and played with them; love and habit had made them part of me. Nevertheless, I had not "gone native" and could not.'[39] In a parenthesis which indicates the still ambivalent nature of his sexuality, he adds, 'When at one time I contemplated marriage with a Japanese girl, I saw clearly the complications that might arise'. So although he could see physical love as an ideal mode of apprehending a new civilization, he realized that to stay in Japan would be an exile for which he was not prepared. 'How many lifetimes would one need,' he asks, 'how much luck, health, money and knowledge even to smell the richness of old civilizations and to embrace living bodies to which they had given birth (for it is only through love that one can taste)?'

But the voice of caution was not stilled inside him: 'I was aware of the anomalous existance of exiles everywhere and of their seemingly inevitable

unbalance and distorted perspectives; and I felt, like a familiar pain, inter-
mittent but recurrent, a keen sense of isolation from my own kind and their
culture.' So both these themes, the reluctance to be exiled from Europe for
ever, and the exploration of his 'real nature', are the basic themes of *Memoirs
of an Emigrant* and their final form, the novel *Sado*. If we take the youth
Sado as a fictive representation of Plomer's lover Fukuzawa, which seems
likely enough, the author appears to conclude that, even though both of
them acknowledge that their destinies are to be separated, 'it was clear
that they would part not merely with mutual respect but with a bond
between them so subtle that nothing could shake it'.[40] But this looks like
an aesthetic tidying-up of reality; and of the true grief Plomer seems to have
left behind when he parted from the strikingly good-looking Fukuzawa, who
shared with Plomer a debunking and pleasure-loving temperament, and who
introduced him to Japanese literature and the theatre. The break came in the
early spring of 1929, when Plomer sailed from Shimonoseki, for Pusan in
Korea, in order to return to England via the Trans-Siberian Railway. He
stood on the deck, feeling the vibration of the engines beneath his feet:

> Like a bare stage brilliantly lighted, the receding quay was as clean
> as the deck, unencumbered with gear or goods, and now deserted
> except for one human figure. It was Morito Fukuzawa, a Japanese
> who had shared my life for a long time and had come all the way
> from Tokyo to see me off. From that lonely and lessening form under
> the arc-lamps there presently came, in a voice made strong by emotion
> and enlarged in the empty night by the high roof above him which
> acted as a sounding-board, the Japanese valediction, that forlorn word
> 'Sayonara!' He uttered it four times, at what seemed long intervals, and
> four times over the calm sea I called back those four sad syllables. The
> last time I was surprised by the volume of my own voice, but I knew
> that by the time the word reached him it would be faint, ghostly, final.
> Long after Shimonoseki was out of sight I seemed to hear him still.[41]

Plomer was not only a novelist and short-story writer. He was a poet. In
his *Collected Poems*,[42] the section 'Poems written in Japan' contains eleven
pieces, of varying length, some of them lyrics which are mere exercises in
observation, and not very different from the sort of lyric, half-affectionate,
half-critical, which is the staple of English poets who have lived in Japan.
The genre is skilfully used by D. J. Enright, Anthony Thwaite, James Kirkup
and many others, and at times it imitates a haiku-like brevity of allusion and
notation of nature, like 'White Azaleas':

> Mats of woven grass
> In the lighted room
> Where he lay in bed;
>
> All at once he heard

The audible-by-night
Bamboo waterfall;

Shadows of the trees
Were moving on the ground
Underneath the moon.

Midori came back
With a hiss of silk,
And knelt upon the floor,

In her golden hand
A branch of white azaleas
Crystal-dropped with dew.

In some of the longer poems, a quirkier prosody is the vehicle for the evocation, part history, part observation, of an old inn in central Japan, the Aburaya, where *daimyō* retinues would stop on the way to Edo. From its windows was visible Mt Asama, a dormant volcano:

Placidly a window-screen is opened by the landlord's daughter,
A buxom rustic poetess of seventeen –
Very sentimental, smelling clean
As a white chrysanthemum in a glass of water.

The subjects of her verses are in the usual taste,
Conventional without dullness, and without coldness chaste:
The taste of the sound of silence in the snow,
The vanishing of the twilight shadows of a pine-tree on a lonely beach,
The scented oblivion of the voices of those who were lovers long ago,
And the sense of the irreparable in an opening flower of peach.

In contrast, the second panel of this hotel diptych, the 'Hotel Magnificent' in Yokohama, uses a less broken rhythm but a jazzier vocabulary as a vehicle for Plomer's social vision. It is the same vision he evokes so incisively in such later poems as 'Sounds of Pleasure: Cannes, 1938', a contemptuous view of rich voluptuaries mingled with the forebodings of war:

Japan, they say that Kipling said, is 'not a sahib's land',
But *si sahib requiris, circumspice* in the well-planned grand
Brand-new Hotel Magnificent whose highly-polished floors
Reflect both millionaires and brassy pseudo-Jacobean cuspidors . . .

Here East meets West to the strains of the *Mikado*
Born kicking from the strings of a Filipino band
Whose members have an air of languor and bravado,
And one a Russian emerald lucent on his hand,
A trophy of the ups and downs, the switchback way we go,

252

Pressed upon a supple finger by an exile starving in the snow.

The band strikes up again and from bedroom and bridge-table
In this modern Tower of Babel people glide towards the door;
The band burst out anew, and wistful nasal whining
With hypnotic syncopation fills the ballroom's glossy floor
With two-backed beasts side-stepping, robots intertwining,
Trying to work a throwback, to be irresponsible once more.

Perhaps for Plomer as a tourist, hotel dance-floors were a natural locus of astringent observation, but just occasionally a note of compassion creeps in, as he watches a Greek merchant from Bombay desperately trying to enjoy a holiday 'At Lake Chuzenji':

> 'We ought to go and see that beastly waterfall'.
> 'Who is this young man that follows her round?'
> 'Three hearts'. 'And you?' 'I pass.' 'What's yours?'
>
> A sudden yearning for an evening with geisha
> Cruises along his hardening arteries,
> But sadly he turns his broad back on the lake,
>
> Resigned to missing intimacy with Japanese joys,
> To no longer being young, and to not being free
> From his wife, his daughter, his hotel, or propriety.

But these brief vignettes are not expected to contain the sustained argument that is the armature for a poem like 'Captain Maru: A Nationalist', written in 1935 and early 1936, and published first in the *London Mercury*. It is a blend of reminiscences of Captain Mori, news passed on in letters from Japanese friends about the growing xenophobic nationalism in Japan, and a letter from van der Post recounting a dream in which he had seen Mori with no back to his head. The multi-faceted Mori, urbane and feline, a cultured autocratic samurai 'used to being obeyed', demonstrating to the young British travellers on his ship – 'Abbot of its drilled, monastic life' – his mastery of himself, of judo, of fencing, yet able to relax. Or is he? He 'takes relaxation seriously too' and his sword-dance has a hidden echo for the poet Plomer, now nearly a decade older than the young novelist bound for Japan:

> Maru in his cups does a sword-dance on the deck,
> Bare-legged, with feet as vigorous as hands,
> With a whole ocean for a private room,
> Stamps and shouts according to old rules,
> His face all flushed and big veins in his neck,
> And muscles, eyes, and anger all belong
> To a follower of Saigo, a Kumamoto tough.

The conflict over the Kilindini funeral, and Mori's moral victory, are recalled:

> Two days of Maru, then a surplice and a bell,
> A slow bell and a surly gown, the crew in white
> Under the saw-toothed palms, a shallow grave,
> Pink sunset, distant gramophone, white flowers,
> Heads turned, and honour satisfied, and Maru wore
> The sure smile of a victory of the will.
> 'And thou shalt have
> None other race but mine.'

The poem evokes what the younger Plomer had sensed, the immense power held in restraint inside Mori, the tenacious resolve behind the affable social front, containing rebuffs but remembering them:

> Maru as a traveller always cool and clean,
> Debonair in his many ports of call
> With white silk suit, topee, and gold-topped cane,
> Chose his words carefully, got what he required,
> Exacted deference by being firm and calm
> . . . The pride and hatred duty breeds
> Condensed inside his strong heart's caves,
> Pride grew another shell, gall gained a drop,
> Determination hardened a formidable man.

There is also the Mori who survives a geisha party while his companions succumb to *sake*:

> The drunkard wallows: Maru sits upright.
> The girls are giggling: Maru only smiles,
> And crossing to the window sees the moon
> And quotes a verse about an octopus
> Caught, in the thirteenth century, in a trap.

And the official Mori, eager to show the streets and trams of Tokyo to his friends, and his friends to important Japanese officials:

> . . . using the press,
> The radio, banquets, interviews, the great
> To serve his various ends.
> The Foreign Minister rises from his desk,
> Cordial but cautious, one eye on the clock.

Mori at home is tender with his family, but patriarchal as well as patriotic, and in the excesses of that sentiment Plomer uncannily anticipates the wrath to come which it will ineluctably invite:

For Maru is of course a family man
And skipper of an ever-growing crew
Of little Marus full of national pride.
There only at evening, by the Inland Sea,
Is Maru tender, like a girl with dolls
Handling his young, whose little gowns
Are wreathed already with the blossoming sword.
As virile husband to a docile wife, he thinks
He serves the glory of the State,
Ignorant that he is helping to provoke
Death chemical from fleets with wings.

The poem's conclusion is surrealist in its inconsequence, incomprehensible until Plomer's biographer, and van der Post in *Yet Being Something Other*, recount van der Post's dream vision of Mori:

And now he has appeared to someone in a dream
Or rather a nightmare, menacing, a giant,
With no back to his head, uttering a taunt –
It is the challenge of his race, the short man scorned,
Not satisfied with power, but mad for more.

In a sense, we might perhaps think the poem a poor return for Mori's solicitous friendship, unless we realize that Plomer's awareness of Mori is accurate, that Mori was both genuinely helpful and at the same time used his guests to further not an individual ambition but a national purpose. Plomer understands the rationale behind the purpose: a people feeling itself deprived of the place in the sun it feels it deserves, and resolved to have it. In return Mori/Maru serves Plomer's aesthetic purpose as a symbol of a Japan that is both loved and feared.

The intervention of van der Post in this imaginative recreation of Mori was to be duplicated a decade or more later when Mori, having read van der Post's *Bar of Shadow*, a fictionalized account of his sufferings at Japanese hands when a prisoner of war in Java, wrote to Plomer to protest at the protrayal of the sadistic camp guard, refusing to believe him to be typical of Japanese behaviour. Mori's reaction, when we look at certain passages of *Bar of Shadow*, is understandable. Take, for instance, the physical description of the anthropoidal Sergeant Hara, whose violent brutality in the end brought him to face a war crimes trial and, ultimately, execution:

He was so short that he just missed being a dwarf, so broad that he was almost square. He hardly had any neck and his head, which had no back to it,[43] sat almost straight on his broad shoulders. The hair on his head was thick and of a midnight-blue. It was extremely coarse and harsh in texture and, cut short, stood stark and stiff like the bristles on a boar's back straight up in the air. His arms were exceptionally long and seemed to hang to his knees but his legs by contrast were short, extremely thick and so bowed that the sailors with us called him 'Old Cutlass-legs'. His mouth was filled with big faded yellow teeth, elaborately framed in gold, while his face tended to be square and his forehead rather low and simian.

Even the possession of 'a pair of extraordinarily fine eyes' does little to redeem this portrait of an incomprehensible and uncomprehending primordial bully, prepared to beat his prisoners to death if necessary.

Mori read this portrait with anguish. He wrote to Plomer to reject what he saw as van der Post's distortion of the Japanese character:

> It is very well written, I admit, but I cannot agree with his opinion that Sergeant Hara is the symbol of real Japanese. He is only crazy and lunatic, simpleton and brutal beast. Although I really sympathize with him and his comrades deeply for being tortured by such a bloody fellow and I am ashamed from my heart for such terrible soldiers . . ., I dare refuse to admit his generalized opinion for Japanese nature.[44]

'Japan almost took away my appetite for the English theatre', Plomer wrote in *Double Lives*; 'there the art of acting, which is hereditary, has attained perfection.' The enthusiasm was to recur much later in his life, when his association with Benjamin Britten revealed a talent for writing librettos. Hearing that Britten was to visit Japan in 1956, Plomer advised him to visit a Japanese theatre: 'I strongly recommended the Japanese theatre in its various forms, Kabuki, Bunraku and No – particularly the No. I remember describing a No play, enlarging upon the emotive effect of its strict stylization, and imitating some of the formal gestures used by the actors.'[45]

The composer, his companion Peter Pears and their friend the Prince of Hesse, were in Tokyo in February 1956, and on the 11th they saw a performance of the Noh play *Sumidagawa*. Eight days later, Britten went to see it again and was profoundly impressed. The Sumida River is the locus of a tragedy. A traveller comes up to a ferryman and tells him a woman is approaching. She is searching for her lost child, and her loss has driven her mad. The ferryman is unwilling to take her on his boat, but in the end relents. He recounts the story of a little boy who came to the spot a year before, after an escape from robbers. The ferryman took him across, but the boy died on the opposite shore. It was the woman's son and she weeps. The ferryman shows her where her son is buried. They recite prayers over the grave, and the spirit of her son appears to her. She reaches out to touch him, but he vanishes, as dawn breaks.

The play falls into the group of 'mad woman' Noh plays, and is the work of Motomasa Juro (*d.* 1432). When Britten told Plomer about the impact the play had had upon him, 'It is a very great pleasure to me,' Plomer replied, 'and somehow not altogether a surprise, that your response to Japan was instant and strong. You see now how fortunate I was to be able to live there for a couple of years in my twenties. It struck me as a gong or bell is struck, and the vibrations set up in me will last till I drop.'

Britten asked Plomer to write a libretto on the basis of *Sumidagawa*, intending a fairly straightforward translation, which should retain Japanese setting, words and names. He was apparently unaware that a version already existed, from the pen of Marie Stopes, who provided a libretto for a one-act opera on the theme for the 1913 Glastonbury Festival; and the final version of Plomer's libretto acknowledges the version made by the Japan Society for the Promotion of Science (Nippon Gakujutsu Shinkōkai). Plomer's Japanese was certainly not adequate for the task of translating a Nō play from the original medieval text, and he was not at all keen on the project as Britten envisaged it.

> Though honoured to be asked [he later wrote], I thought the whole project hardly possible. Neither he nor I nor anybody else would want to pastiche of a No play, a piece of *japonaiserie*, and as the original depended entirely upon its *mise en scene*, archaic music, all-male cast, and rigidly formal production down to the last detail of costume and movement, it was hardly transferable to the western operatic stage. What was more, the language and action of the play belonged to an antique Buddhist culture and could only be properly appreciated by highly cultivated Japanese traditionalists. But like the poets Yeats and Waley (neither of whom ever visited Japan), Britten had been enchanted by the No, as I had been enchanted before him, so what was the good of protesting?[46]

Plomer's resistance weakened in face of Britten's resolve, but he felt it necessary to make Britten aware of some problems of pronunciation:

> As my mind begins to run on Sumida River, I feel less inclined to shy at Japanese names and place-names. It may be that some of them will be just as useful to you musically as 'Namu Amida' etc.
>
> As you know, in Japanese all goes by syllables, and each syllable is, in theory, of equal weight, so, if Japanese words are to be sung or spoken, it is better that they should be formally enunciated than slurred or falsely accented. E.g. we ought to have, as nearly as possible,
>
> Mi-ya-ko, not Miyàko
> Su-mi-da, not Sumìda
> Mu-sa-shi, not Musàshi
>
> Naturally when the words are said or sung in a quick tempo, the syllables do not always *seem* to be equally accented: so *shite*, as Ezra Pound so delicately tells us, can seem to sound like *shtay*. . . .
>
> Don't let this worry you, and unless you have strong feelings

in the matter *against* my doing so, I shall proceed to make what seems judicious use of Japanese names. We can cut or alter later, as necessary.[47]

Plomer drew up a draft in October and November 1958. They discussed it over Christmas, and a second draft was produced in March 1959. Then Britten changed his mind. He had been anxious over Japanese costumes – the masks would be 'a colossal problem' for the singers, and he was worried about producing 'Japanesey' music, in fact not a Nō in English but a pastiche. He proposed instead a transposition into a medieval English setting – pre-Conquest East Anglia; or perhaps Israel or Italy. Plomer, aware that Pound and Yeats had made creditable ventures into Nō, both as translation and imitation (though neither of them knew Japanese), was at first not enthusiastic about his work being cast aside:

> I can't say [he wrote to the composer] that I'm astonished at your – I won't say throwing up the sponge, but setting fire to your – and indeed my – kimono. I really don't know *how* the piece could have turned into anything but a pasticcio grosso. But it is a little electrifying to have to think of transposing the story into Christian terms. Think I will, my first thought being that the missing child has come to be regarded locally as a saint (perhaps he could have been martyred) and that his grave has already become a place of pilgrimage. But I rather think that however formalized such a version might be, it might seem odd for the mother to be a man.[48]

(Britten had envisaged the part of the madwoman being performed by Peter Pears).

In the end, he accepted the change, but later suggested that Britten's simple title *The River* should be *Curlew River*, and recast the libretto removing the Buddhist references and replacing them by Christian ones. Between other works, and in the intervals of travel, Britten corresponded with him, and the work was completed in 1964. The recast Nō was now set in 'a church by a Fenland river in early medieval times'. It begins with a monastic procession singing the hymn *Te lucis ante terminum*, with which it also ends. The Ferryman and Traveller remain, as does the Madwoman seeking her son, begging the birds of the Fenland, the curlews, to speak of him. Like the Japanese chorus, the Abbot and monks echo her plea. The Ferryman narrates the boy's adventure in a page of uninterrupted prose, and says that his last words were 'Kyrie eleison'. The river people believe he was a saint and that his spirit sometimes appears. The Madwoman realizes it is her son they speak of, and is in despair:

> O Curlew River, cruel Curlew,
> Where all my hope is swept away!
> Torn from the nest, my bird,

Crying in empty air.
Now the nest of the curlew is silent with snow,
And the lamb is devoured by the carrion crow . . .
The innocent lamb . . .
The heathen crow!
Good people, where shall I turn?
Tell me now!
Take me back . . .
Chain on my soul, let me go!
O River Curlew, O Curlew, cruel bird . . .[49]

Against the background of another Latin hymn, *Custodes hominum psallimus Angelos*, she hears her son's spirit, speaking from the tomb. He emerges from it. She tries to embrace him, and he returns to the tomb, promising they will meet in heaven.

A vision was seen, [*proclaims the Abbot*]
A miracle and a mystery,
At our Curlew River here.
A woman was healed by prayer and grace,
A woman with grief distraught.

The procession leaves the stage, singing the final hymn.

The transposition does seem to work. The linguistic difficulties which even educated modern Japanese have with the language of the Nō texts is matched by the occasional use of medieval Latin. The four central characters are retained, one of them at any rate using a half-mask; the instrumental accompaniment is almost as sparse as it would be in Japan; and whereas in Tokyo, as the composer indicates in a programme note, 'the music was the ancient Japanese music jealously preserved by successive generations, here I have started the work with that wonderful plainsong hymn "Te lucis ante terminum", and from it the whole piece may be said to have grown'. There is, as he admits, nothing specifically Japanese left in what he chose to call 'A Parable for Church Performance', but if stage and audience alike can achieve 'half the intensity and concentration of that original drama I shall be well satisfied'. 'Both brilliant and innovatory', one critic called the result and Plomer's libretto was described as 'the finest, most skilfully designed for music that Britten has yet had'.[50]

It was Plomer's last literary contact with things Japanese. Perhaps by this time Japan had no more to say to him anyway, and his lack of resistance to Britten's Europeanizing of the Japanese theme indicates this. He never returned to Japan, as his friend John Morris did; though he drew a Japanese cup for the dust wrapper of Morris's *The Phoenix Cup*, and signed it with his name in *Katakana*: 'Puruma'. But by this time he was totally absorbed into the literary life of London, and Japan had become an idea rather than an experience. But Japan's mark remained in him. She had made him aware of how different he was from the Japanese; what distinctive things he could contribute to the life of his students; and also what Japan had to give him.

The distinctiveness first: Japan confirmed in him his dislike for the Anglican Christianity in which he had been brought up, its attempt to reconcile suffering with virtue, and puritanism which he found loathsome and its progeny of cant which he termed insufferable. Japan confirmed him in his determinism, his belief that heredity supposes little independence or self-command in the individual; and in his disbelief in progress, based on the ludicrous idea of perfectibility, in his detached and sceptical attitude to religion and politics, and – by reaction against what he had seen in Japan – his admiration for leisure and idleness:

> I had no facile optimism or rosy hopes but, on the other hand, no want of energy or *joie de vivre*. An absence of hopefulness in itself perhaps derived from physical causes, may tend to inhibit effort, particularly in public or political matters, but the lessening of effort is not necessarily a bad thing, if we may judge by the two greatest public efforts of our time, the two world wars. We live in a period when work has become a mania and idleness almost a crime, but it is just as well to remember that the best things the human race has done hitherto would have been impossible without leisure and what would now be called idleness.[51]

So what he taught his Japanese pupils, as much by example as formally, was in almost direct contrast to what everything in their national ethos was urging upon them. He influenced them, he thought, as they did him, in the direction of hedonism and scepticism, in a heightened perceptiveness, an appreciation of creativity, a hostility to social or official repression. And he quite explicitly argued against the waste of promising or potentially useful lives which the Japanese cult of suicide implies. Though later, when he came to write *Double Lives*, he was less confident that his anti-suicide stance was one his maturer self would approve of: 'I might hesitate to dissuade an intending suicide, and there are circumstances in which, whatever the Christian religion or English law may prescribe, I should regard it as only human to help a person to bring about his or her end.'[52]

The lessons he taught his Japanese pupils are probably even more useful to today's hyper-industrious Japanese, though no doubt they will not be in the mood to listen. And what Japan gave to William Plomer may not be the most obvious gifts – but he took them to heart:

> Civilisation has many dialects but speaks one language, and its Japanese voice will always be present to my ear, like the pure and liquid notes of the bamboo flute in those tropical evenings on the Indian Ocean when I heard it the first time, speaking of things far more important than war, trade and empires – of unworldliness, lucidity and love.[53]

20

JAPANESE BIRTHDAY: TAISHŌ II, G.C. ALLEN (1900–1982) AND JAPAN

Sarah Metzger-Court

It seems singularly appropriate that the death of George Allen in 1982 marked the close of an auspicious sixty-year cycle, or *kanreki*, in terms of his long and fruitful connections with Japan. It was a relationship that from its very beginnings – when the young graduate from the English Midlands first stepped ashore in Kōbe – was to endow him with a unique status as both an acute foreign observer and participant in a vital period of modern Japanese development.

Indeed, George Cyril Allen (1900–82) was born in the momentous dawn of Japan's new age – just over three decades after the Meiji Restoration, halfway between the triumphs of the Sino-Japanese and Russo-Japanese Wars, a year after the final abrogation of the detested 'unequal treaties' and two years before the diplomatic peak of the Anglo-Japanese Alliance. Perhaps this accident of birth helps to account for the breadth of historical view (which Audrey Donnithome was posthumously to characterize as his 'rootedness in history') that remained such a constant feature of all his later analysis of Japanese affairs. Even his early upbringing and education, in Coventry and Birmingham, seems in retrospect to have been designed to give him a peculiarly relevant approach to the problems of Japan's rapid industrialization and to have added an extra dimension to his interpretation of the various stages of Japan's modern economic growth.

Since family finances would not stretch to a place at Oxford, Allen proceeded in 1918 – on a history scholarship – into the Faculty of Commerce at the University of Birmingham. This was to prove an event of the most wide-ranging significance, in both personal and professional terms. It was not simply that his fellow undergraduates at the university included his later wife of forty-three years, Eleanora (Nell) Shanks. The Faculty of Commerce itself – brought into existence by the Royal Charter which transformed Josiah Mason's Scientific College into the University of Birmingham in 1900 –

represented something quite unique in the British university system of the early twentieth century. In the words of Margaret Gowing, 'it was designed to produce successful businessmen and embodied a carefully thought-out course of principles and practical knowledge with a Marshallian-type economics combining theory and application and a humanistic spirit applied to utilitarian studies'.[1] Furthermore, it enjoyed the great good fortune of being under the direction of Birmingham's first Professor of Commerce (1901–25), Sir William Ashley, who had previously taught economic history at Harvard and whose great academic achievement was to turn economists from their preoccupation with ideal models to a study of the real world of industry and commerce.

All this contrasted with the curricula of the ancient universities that had firmly turned their backs on what Arnold Toynbee, at Oxford in the 1880s, had once scornfully described as 'the intellectual superstitions known as Political Economy'. It was also very much in keeping with the perceived needs and emerging educational models of Meiji Japan. As a result, it was the Japanese who from the beginning provided the single largest group of foreign students in the Faculty of Commerce at Birmingham, and an early photograph of 1907 reveals no less than three serious-looking representatives of the new Japan in a total student body of twenty-one.[2] The fact that one of the very first Japanese students was an enterprising member of the Mitsui family, who later went on to take control of the great Mitsui *zaibatsu*, bore fruit for the university in 1923 in the form of an endowment for the Mitsui Chair of Finance.

By 1923, however, George Allen himself was already in Japan. He had had a distinguished undergraduate career at Birmingham, emerging with a first-class B. Comm. degree, and went on to foreshadow later economic interests by writing an M. Comm. thesis on 'Restrictive Practices in the Copper Mining Industry' in his postgraduate year. His 'remarkable qualities and particularly a certain fineness of thought and expression' had already attracted the attention of his thesis supervisor, Sir William Ashley. When, in his capacity as Dean of the Faculty of Commerce, Ashley was asked during the spring of 1922 to recommend a young English lecturer of ability to a two-year appointment at the recently opened commercial high school (*Kōtō shōgyō gakkō*) in Nagoya, he had no hesitation in putting forward the name of George Allen.

There is a fascinating and detailed account of Allen's subsequent journey to Japan and initial experiences in a country of which he knew little, least of all the language, in his posthumously published memoirs, *Appointment in Japan*.[3] However, it is important to place this early and unlooked-for career development into a wider, less personal context. The *Kōtō shōgyō gakkō*, modelled directly on the Handelshochschulen of Bismarck's Germany, were an intrinsic part of the Meiji government's drive to give the Japanese education system – especially in its higher reaches – a severely practical, scientific and technological bent wherever possible. By the eleventh year of the Taishō period, when George Allen first stepped on to Japanese soil, such colleges were already well established as an essential cog in the mechanism of a successfully modernizing state and one of the principal routes whereby students could be selected and distributed into occupational areas by ability and specialized training. The new *sensei* from England, with his own rigorous training in economics – both theoretical and applied – and with a natural, unending curiosity about the practical workings of business and industry, was ideally suited to contribute to the forwarding of this particular type of higher education in Nagoya.

For two and a half years, between the autumn of 1922 and the spring of 1925, Allen taught to such good and stimulating effect that his Japanese students – many of whom went on to become the leading businessmen, bankers or commercial experts of their generation – never forgot the experience. Tributes penned more than half a century later by members of the Nagoya Kitankai (alumni association) bear eloquent witness to the deep respect and affection with which George Allen and his teaching were remembered. As translated for the guest of honour at a Tokyo reunion in 1979, they read in part as follows: 'Your lectures . . . still remain vivid in my memory, though more than fifty years have passed since then.' 'Your pronunciation of English was wonderful. I have never heard such wonderful English as yours.' 'Your young face comes to my mind and your lectures on English Industry.' 'I have kept Ashley's *The Economic Organization of England* – the textbook you selected for us.' 'Your white hemp suit was very impressive and enchanting, as well as your hard straw hat and walking stick. Long live our noble Professor!'[4]

Quite apart from the superb image of an uncompromisingly correct and sartorially elegant young English gentleman summoned up by this last tribute, such comments as these are important in another context. They would seem to indicate rather clearly that Allen's earliest lectures bore many of the hallmarks of his prolific later writings, especially on Japan. For it was not merely impressionable young Japanese students who greatly admired his English prose style in all its aspects. At an early stage in her memoir of him, Margaret Gowing comments upon the fact that George Allen's particular upbringing and education made him 'a passionate advocate for life of accuracy, precision, graceful lucidity and style in writing and speech, even on abstruse subjects'.[5] Audrey Donnithorne, his collaborator on an important post-war work, *Western Enterprise in Far Eastern Economic Development: China and Japan*, observed in retrospect that 'he wrote in good clear English, being an enemy of jargon and waffle'. It was this clarity of view and elegance in expression, together with the intellectual stimulus provided by his particular type of comparative historical approach, that undoubtedly helped to form the 'dear memories' which so many of his Japanese students carried away from the lectures halls of Nagoya's commercial high school.

In other ways, too, this prolonged initial sojourn in Japan set the tone for practically all his subsequent work in the field. For George Allen found Taishō Japan an ideal environment in which to apply the new emphasis in economic studies that had been instilled into him by his training in Birmingham and by the natural urgings of temperament. Throughout his professional life, his approach was to be distinguished both by its practicality and by an ability to reach for fruitful points of comparison within the economic systems of Britain and Japan in almost equal measure. In the tradition of William Ashley and George Unwin, he cultivated a broad view of all things economic and retained his own sense of the fundamental relation between the economic and the social. He relished the opportunity to see man at work, as witnessed by detailed descriptions of the traditional workshops he saw all around him in Nagoya, and this later translated itself into a passion for visiting industrial plants and businesses on both sides of the world.

As he tramped the highways and byways of Japan in the early 1920s (narrowly avoiding being cast into Lake Ashi, hotel and all, by the great earthquake of 1 September 1923), his acute powers of observation and enduring interest in the functioning of a real world so different from his own enabled George Allen to build up a unique image of the Japanese people and their institutions. Indeed, it is perhaps a measure of his particular achievement that, on the occasion of the presentation to him of the Japan Foundation Award in Tokyo in the autumn of 1980, he was able to sweep his Japanese audience through nearly sixty years of their own modern history in a single sentence: 'Since I first set foot in your country and remarked on the daikon drying on the pine-trees in the neighbourhood of Nagoya, Japan has been transformed from an agricultural society with a fringe of modern industry to one of the most progressive and admired countries in the world.' For the historian, there is an interesting echo here of the famous remark by Basil Hall Chamberlain on the rapid rate of change in early Meiji Japan: 'to have lived through the transition stage of modern Japan makes a man feel preternaturally old; for here he is in modern times . . . and yet he can himself distinctly remember the Middle Ages'.[6]

For the young George Allen, however, the challenge of interpreting, in an innovative fashion, to his fellow countrymen all that he had seen and imbibed in Japan proved irresistible. Three years after his return to England, as research fellow and lecturer in industrial history at his alma mater, the University of Birmingham, he published the first of a long series of distinguished works on the Japanese economy, *Modern Japan and Its Problems*. Perhaps symbolically, the book was published shortly before his parallel study of *The Industrial Development of Birmingham and the Black Country*.[7] Both volumes were regarded as important and well received – at the time of publication and for many years thereafter – but it is the 'holistic' analytical approach adopted in *Modern Japan and Its Problems* that provides the principal recognizable hallmark of all Allen's work on Japan and marks him out as a pioneer in Japanese studies in the truest possible sense.

For the book is much more than simply a series of 'impressions' from an observant traveller, despite a characteristic and frequent use of living evidence to back up statistical and second-hand materials. Nor – as might have been expected from one who described himself as an economist, and who had already published effectively in Keynes's *Economic Journal, Economica* and the business section of the *Japan Chronicle* – is it exclusively or even largely concerned with the dry detail of banking, finance and population trends. It is, rather, a sustained and novel attempt to interpret the branch of Japanese national life with which the author was particularly concerned (i.e. the economic structure, in all its vital aspects) in the light of his comprehension of the underlying principles of the country's civilization. As stated in a preface that is more enlightening than most, the book set out 'to link up an interpretation of the national character or social organization with an analysis of Japan's political, educational, financial and industrial systems'. Those words might well have been used to describe countless other works, from younger contemporaries and successors on both sides of the Atlantic, that have emerged in the sixty years since G. C. Allens' first book was published. If imitation is the sincerest form of flattery, then the author of *Modern Japan and Its Problems* has been greatly flattered in the general field of Japanese studies. Moreover, the continuing relevance of many of the questions that he posed and the answers that he attempted to provide is highlighted by the recent decision to reissue the book,[8] with an appropriate introduction by one of his most distinguished successors, R.P. Dore.

Although George Allen was to ponder creatively on Japanese affairs for the rest of his life, it was another ten years before his next book on Japan appeared. Furthermore none of the three university chairs that he held between 1929 and his retirement in 1967 had any close or specific connection with Japanese studies. At the astoundingly early age of 28, he was appointed to the Chair of Economics and Commerce at the recently established University College, Hull. From there, in 1933, he went on to hold the Brunner Chair of Economic Science at Liverpool. Although called away, like many academics, for a stint at the Board of Trade and (briefly) the Foreign Office during the war years, he returned to Merseyside in mid-1946 and only allowed himself to be inveigled south the following year by the offer of the Jevons Chair of Political Economy at University College London. There, despite efforts to tempt him elsewhere, he remained for the last two decades of his academic career.

None the less, while still in Liverpool, Allen managed to produce a further trio of notable books on Japan. The first of these – brought out in 1938 – proved that, for a professor of economic science, he had an unusual journalist's feel for an eye-catching title. *Japan: The Hungry Guest* was both a skilled analysis of recent developments in Japan's industrial sector and an effort to dispel some of the complacency and insularity, regarding Japan's particular economic problems and their grave foreign policy implications, that was still so prevalent in his own country. George Allen continued to believe that Japan's social, political and industrial problems 'seldom admitted of western solutions' and that only a better understanding of the peculiar characteristics of the Japanese system would help towards constructive criticism or advice in what was already a critical situation in the Far East.

Much the same theme was to be pursued in a study – arising directly out of the ongoing Sino-Japanese conflict – published for the Institute of Pacific Relations in New York in 1940. It must surely have appealed to Allen's deep-rooted sense of humour that this time his work appeared under the distinctly staid title of *Japanese Industry: Its Recent Development and Present Condition*. Both this and the previous book were characterized by their emphasis on the importance of small firms and plants to the Japanese economic structure, and by their author's reliance on 'private information' and 'personal inspection' in rounding out accounts of advances in the textile trades or providing statistical evidence of rises in industrial productivity. This empirical approach was only made possible by the phenomenal amount of 'leg-work' undertaken by George Allen during a second visit to Japan in 1936. His wife, who accompanied him, makes frequent references, in her letters home, to George just dashing off – full of energy and enthusiasm – to visit yet another mill, factory or small workshop!

By August 1945, however, when the third and certainly best known of this triumvirate of books was completed,[9] the days of such pleasant field trips in the home islands of Japan were long since gone. At least one of the questions raised in the IPR study at the end of the 1930s – regarding 'Japan's staying power in a long war' – had been swept away in terrible fashion. Hostility towards Japan marked British society at all levels and, in many quarters, the ordeals endured by Allied soldiers and civilians in Japanese occupied territories and prisoner-of-war camps had not simply 'placed Japanese studies at a discount' but led to complete revulsion and bitter thoughts of revenge.[10] It therefore says much for the well-balanced, broadly tolerant nature of George Allen's scholarly approach and the depth of his continuing attachment to Japanese culture and Japanese people – in spite of the worst that fanatical military men could do – that he none the less chose this difficult moment in Anglo-Japanese relations to publish the results of a long-running research project dear to his heart.

A Short Economic History of Modern Japan 1867–1937 set out to describe – in Allen's usual lucid, comparative fashion – the process of economic development in Japan between the beginnings of her westernization and modernization and the outbreak of the war with China in 1937. Although written with an obvious scholar's enjoyment of knowledge for the sake of knowledge, the book – in its latter phases – had the important additional objective of wishing to assist in the formulation of a wise economic policy for a defeated and devastated post-war Japan. The *Short Economic History* had an immediate and well-deserved impact and was seen on both sides of the Atlantic as a work that, even in its compact and partially restricted form, successfully filled a very substantial gap in western perceptions of Japan. It received the ultimate academic accolade of entering all the standard bibliographes and became, in the words of Sydney Checkland, 'the staple of most young lecturer's treatment of Japan's extraordinarily conservative modernization'.

None the less, even at this high point of his career, the persistent impression remains that the work of G. C. Allen never received quite the unreserved acclamation and long-term recognition which might have been expected. In the interests of a balanced assessment, it would seem appropriate here to ask why not. On the Japanese side of the equation, there can be little doubt that George Allen ultimately suffered from a dual disability. In the first place, the sheer length of his career and rapid developments within the specialist field of Japanese studies (especially on the far side of the Atlantic) meant that the pioneering author of *Modern Japan and its Problems* suffered the usual fate of pioneers. Even in the immediate post-war period, he was already being overtaken by a new generation of Japan scholars and experts raised in the American academic world. Many of these – W.W. Lockwood, T.C. Smith, J.W. Hall, C.D. Sheldon, Johannes Hirschmeier and, rather later, James Nakamura, Henry Rosovsky, Hugh Patrick, Kozo Yamamura, William Hauser, Susan Hanley and Ann Waswo – turned their own considerable abilities and those of their increasingly numerous graduate students towards the fruitful fields of Japanese economics and economic history. Through four productive decades, they assumed the mantle of a radically new approach to the entire subject. The best of them did not lose sight of the importance of the type of integrated economic, social and even political treatment that George Allen had so splendidly pioneered. Yet they introduced into their work a degree of analytical and statistical rigour – stemming both from the quantitative disciplines of the so-called 'new economic history' school and from the painstaking use of a vast array of primary and secondary Japanese materials – that was largely beyond the reach of those trained long before the war.

For it was perhaps Allen's linguistic limitations that did most to reduce his stature in the field of Japanese studies. In a post-war world of scholarship where, for good or ill, knowledge of the written language became increasingly the yardstick by which merit was to be measured, the former lecturer at Nagoya's commercial high school made no secret of the fact that Japanese *kanji* remained by and large a mystery to him. Indeed, at an early stage in his memoirs he remarks of the language problem that 'I found it easy enough to acquire a sufficiency of colloquial Japanese for the ordinary business of living, but my acquaintance with the characters remained rudimentary'.[11]

This may have enabled him to retain a commendable degree of detachment in his analysis of Japanese affairs and even, on occasion, endowed him with a clear-sightedness that was probably denied to some colleagues who where linguistically better equipped For example, in talking of the dominance of Japanese economists in the field of mathematical economic theory, he wryly observed that 'perhaps their acknowledged success can be explained by the fact that it is easier to communicate with foreigners in mathematical symbols than in ordinary language'.[12]

Such perception notwithstanding, George Allen's own inability to make sense of even a single page of written Japanese must be rated a major handicap in the scholarly climate of post-war Japanese studies. In practical terms, it meant that almost all his information on Japan, especially after his departure in 1925, was filtered to him second-hand and sometimes through highly selective channels. During the crucial war years and for some time thereafter (he was not to visit Japan again until 1954), such sources dried up almost completely. Although he was fortunate in many of the life-long contacts that he made – notably with A. Morikawa, who worked for the NYK shipping line in Liverpool down to 1940 and with whom he continued to correspond on economic matters into old age – there were no real substitutes for direct documentary access to Japanese materials. This also meant that his historical interpretations, which were such a notable feature of his early works, tended to become rather dated and were unable to take account of radically altered priorities and opinions within the field of secondary Japanese literature. An obvious example of this is to be found in the historical introduction to the Japan section of his joint work with A.G. Donnithome, *Western Enterprise in Far Eastern Economic Development: China and Japan* (1954). As an accurate reflection of current interpretative trends within the world of Japanese scholarship, this fares badly in comparison to the language-based research of somewhat younger contemporaries such as W.G. Beasley.

None the less, the doyen of western historians on Japan, Sir George Sansom, who himself enjoyed a formidable command of the Japanese language, retained enormous respect for George Allen's own work. It was a respect based not simply on Allen's academic reputation and publications but also upon his impressive performance as a temporary civil servant at the Board of Trade (1940–4) and in the Foreign Office (1945–6). Although the majority of his work at the Board of Trade had no direct connection with Japanese economic studies,[13] his expertise in the field *was* immediately called upon when he was involved from early 1943 onwards with post-war reconstruction. The labours of this period, which Allen later characterized as 'in many ways . . . the most interesting time', came to fruition in June of 1944 on a major secret paper to which he had contributed the entire section on Japan. While dealing with all aspects of the Japanese economy, the study is particularly concerned with Japan's industrial potential – of which he had received such a favourable impression during his pre-war visit in 1936

– and the steps that might be taken after the war to control some of the less desirable manifestations of Japan's economic structure. These undesirable features include the domination of agriculture by absentee landlords and of enterprise by the great monopolist cartels, the *zaibatsu*.

It was as a result of this work in the corridors of power and at the direct request of George Sansom the British representative on the newly established Far Eastern Commission in Washington, that Allen was called back to Whitehall in August 1945. Here he served for a hectic six months as head of the Japanese section of the Economic and Industrial Planning Staff created within the Foreign Office. With his usual clear view of things, George Allen was under no illusions as to the motivation behind this particular summons from on high. As he wrote in an explanatory letter to the vice-chancellor of Liverpool University, 'The end of the Japanese War has caught the Government unprepared with plans for Japan's future, especially on the economic side, and . . . the need for my services is urgent. . . . It happens that I am about the only English economist who has studied Japanese industry and finance in any detail and at first hand.' Indeed, he was to find to his chagrin that, within the conventional walls of the Foreign Office itself, his type of economic expertise was not always highly valued. He later reported that, on one occasion, the economic clauses of the treaty with Japan were dismissed in Cabinet committee with the contemptuous phrase, 'what sordid things we have to talk about!' His own feeling that 'there wasn't a soul in the FO at that time who knew anything about economics' was to be confirmed the following March (1946) when he received a warm letter of gratitude from his immediate superior, Hall-Patch: 'The Far Eastern Department (in common with all political departments in the Foreign Office) were quite happy to pass this vulgar economic business to somebody else, and I was quite happy to leave it in what I knew to be very capable hands.'

No doubt, George Allen's irrepressible sense of humour kept all this in proportion. In any event, he himself remained convinced that the future stability of the Far East would depend upon the economic policy decisions taken during those turbulent months after the end of the war. He worked enormously hard and, despite an early realization that much of his economic advice went unheeded 'because General MacArthur was doing it all in Tokyo', he and his civil service colleagues continued to bombard Sansom and the Far Eastern Commission with all manner of well-researched and cogently argued papers.[14] The prevailing characteristic of most of these was their adherence to a liberal approach towards Japan – in the midst of a clamour of voices demanding extreme forms of punishment and retribution. They also gave frequent expression to George Allen's own far-sighted optimism with regard to the Japanese potential for economic recovery. Hence, he helped to play down the more unreasonable demands for reparations or civil restrictions, and concentrated upon the encouragement and revival of Japan's devastated industrial infrastructure.

George Allen may have felt himself to be something of a voice crying in the wilderness during those difficult days at the end of the war. Yet he must surely have derived considerable satisfaction from the manner in which the Japanese economy subsequently not only rose phoenix-like from the ashes (with some feathers put in place by his own mediation) but its architects then proceeded to teach the west a number of useful lessons in the not-so-gentle arts of industrial revival, financial solvency, increased productivity, technological know-how, successful competition and the acquisition of trade surpluses and investment potential, the like of which the world has rarely seen. Furthermore, Japan appears to have repeated – in her ability to undergo immense material changes without substantial loss of social cohesion – an achievement that George Allen had earlier remarked upon. Of the Meiji period, he observed with deep perception that 'if it is true . . . that the most vital problems are not problems of economy but of maintaining social unity in the face of economic interests, then it may be claimed that Japan largely succeeded in solving these problems in a period of far-reaching change'.[15]

In the more general field of Anglo-Japanese relations, G.C. Allen deservedly acquired during the later years of his long life the status of elder statesman, or *genrō*. Many honours came his way from a grateful Japanese government, including in 1961 the Order of the Rising Sun and in 1980 the much-coveted Japan Foundation Award. Japanese newspapers continued to pen respectful and affectionate tributes to him, including – in the *Asahi Shimbun* of 4 October 1980 – a wonderful portrait of his retirement years in Oxford. From this it is obvious that he managed to achieve a state of grace denied to his old friend and colleague George Sansom. Sansom had left for a university post in New York in September 1948 complaining that 'years ago, I thought I should be able to imitate an Eastern example and sit contemplating nature in my declining years. I didn't expect to contemplate Manhatten and its denizens'. George Allen, on the contrary and as the *Asahi Shimbun*'s correspondent admiringly observed, sat serenely in north Oxford, surrounded by all the accoutrements of a great scholar, sipping cups of tea that he had made himself and contemplating upon his favourite subject: the human condition, east and west, and 'How many different ways there are of being alive.' This quotation, from E.M. Forster, was a much loved one and appears on the very last page of *Appointment in Japan*.

270

21

IN PROPER PERSPECTIVE: SIR ESLER DENING (1897–1977) AND ANGLO-JAPANESE RELATIONS 1951–1957

Roger Buckley

Esler Dening was the central figure in British dealings with Japan in the years from the ending of the Pacific War until the mid-1950s. Robust, knowledgeable and with an acerbic streak, Dening had the good fortune to be at the hub of Asian affairs during the war and occupation years; he next had the harder task of running the Tokyo Embassy at a time when British opinion in many quarters was decidedly anti-Japanese. Some material has already been published on aspects of his service, but a synoptic reassessment in the light of newly available official records, covering his entire service in Tokyo, is still lacking. This sketch can only begin to repair this neglect and identify some of his successes and failures in the post-war decade. It will look briefly at Dening's work, and comment on the man who remains the most senior and longest serving of all British ambassadors to Japan in the post San Francisco Conference era.[1]

Dening achieved professional success the hard way. He began, after enlisting in the Australian forces during the First World War, as a student interpreter in the Japan Consular Service in January 1920. Since he had grown up in Japan, where his father had been a missionary who later lost his faith and turned to writing, this was not a particularly surprising decision. Yet it was hardly a guarantee of preferment when the diplomatic service reserved preference for its own members and may have viewed consular officers as lesser mortals, fated until the Eden reforms of 1943, to remain part of the 'Cinderella Service'.[2] For twenty years Dening criss-crossed north-east Asia working in Seoul, Dairen, Osaka, Kobe and Harbin, until in 1941 he found himself appointed first secretary at the British Embassy in Washington. The outbreak of the Pacific War clearly accelerated his progress and his capabilities were noted firmly in September 1943 when he was made political advisor to Louis Mountbatten at SEAC headquarters. This was Dening's big break and he made the most of it. He may not have always hit it off with Mountbatten or found his own advice welcome to the supreme commander, but the Foreign Office's 'senior officials had a high regard for the abilities and reporting of Dening'.[3]

Dening ended his years in South-East Asia assisting in the making of some rough policy for handling the chaotic situation in the Dutch East Indies. He was sent from Singapore to report and advise on political developments in Batavia following the surrender of Imperial Japan and the arrival of British and Indian troops. Characteristically Dening spoke his mind and was quick to condemn both the returning, vengeful Dutch and the terrorism of the newly proclaimed independent state of Indonesia. As in his activities in Colombo and Singapore, Dening's telegrams had considerable influence in London. But his frank approach could have its disadvantage and many on the Dutch, Indonesian and Allied sides were not unhappy to see Dening posted home in February 1946. His analyses of the confused situation may have been better than his handling of the participants. He found it hard to suffer fools gladly.[4]

Still, he was clearly due for further promotion and became assistant under secretary for Far Eastern affairs. It was in this post that Dening did his best work and had the ear of the foreign secretary, Ernest Bevin. The next few years were to prove to be the most rewarding of his entire career. Bevin undoubtedly came to rely on Dening for advice on Asian business at a time when British influence was still sufficiently great for the job to give satisfaction. Dening was trusted by Bevin and given considerable discretion to handle an area of the globe that was already passing rapidly out of the British orbit. The secretary of state had more than enough to cope with in tackling the problems of Europe, the beginnings of what soon became the Cold War, the dilemmas of the Middle East and, above all else, maintaining amicable relations with the United States. If, as Alan Bullock has argued, Bevin's dealings with 'Southern Asia were peripheral', because of divided cabinet responsibilities, the marginal nature of his involvement with East Asia was even greater.[5] All this could only work to Dening's advantage provided he retained the support of his master and colleagues. Dening's record in watching the region and shoring up the British position in occupied Japan led directly to his return to Tokyo in 1951.[6] Herbert Morrison commented to the prime minister, Yoshida Shigeru, at their meeting during the San Francisco peace conference in September 1951: 'We are now sending out as Head of UK Liaison Mission, Sir Esler Dening, a great authority on Japan, who would I was sure promote the interests both of His Majesty's Government and of Japan'.[7] Unfortunately for both countries the secretary of state's sugary expectations proved unfounded. For all Dening's skills and knowledge of things Japanese the 1950s were to be a disappointing decade for Anglo-Japanese ties. We must next see how Dening handled business and ask whether his services in Tokyo were doomed to failure.

Dening was a tough diplomat who knew Japan from pre-war days. He had few illusions about the extent of enforced change that the American occupation might have produced on the newly independent nation. In many cases he was dealing with figures who had been career politicians and bureaucrats in the years before Pearl Harbor. He was sceptical of some of the American claims that Japan had been transformed through defeat and occupation into an example to the rest of Asia. Dening's reporting from Tokyo pulled no punches. On the rare occasion when a British minister did visit Japan it was immediately obvious that 'our ambassador is undoubtedly the commanding figure in the Diplomatic Corps and I have no doubt he is both respected and to some extent feared by the Japanese'.[8] This approach by Dening may not have fitted too easily with the shrunken realities of the British position in East Asia.

Yet most of the strains in Anglo-Japanese relations during Dening's years at the sharp end were beyond his control. All that the ambassador could attempt to do was soften some of the acrimony and press his own government to be slightly less severe in its approach to gaining Japanese understanding. There was little or no prospect of genuine reconciliation in the mid-1950s. The British public's memories of the wartime treatment of its prisoners of war and concern over Japanese economic resurgence were far too strong for any ambassador, however gifted, to counter in dealing with his hosts. It left Dening caught between obviously wishing to improve relations with Japan and having to carry out instructions that were far from forgiving, or in the long-term interests of his own government. At times one senses considerable frustration at what was an unenviable mission to halt deteriorating relations.

Dening, although Japanese officials might deny the fact, was generally sympathetic to the Japanese case; when he felt there was misrepresentation and misunderstanding with British public opinion he said so. Yet evidence of Dening's private views on post-peace treaty Japan is not easy to come by since he does not appear to have kept a diary and little personal correspondence is available. To grasp Dening's vision of Japan and his aspirations for improved Anglo-Japanese relations it is necessary to rely on his voluminous official reportage.[9] Here there is remarkable consistency in his opinions and equally little progress in resolving Anglo-Japanese problems.

In March 1953 in an ambitious survey of Anglo-Japanese ties from the turn of the century onwards Dening argued that 'short of pulling out of the Far East altogether, we must seek to cultivate friendly relations with Japan whether we like it or not'. He criticized the United States for thinking that 'Japan's destinies are to be determined by America alone' and suggested that, since Tokyo wanted to go its own way, there ought to be sufficient room for a British role in Japanese affairs. To achieve this objective, however, Dening was not about to mince his words. The ambassador stated that if 'we are to play this part, we must rid ourselves of some of our antipathies and determine how economic competition is to be met'.[10] On British prejudices he warned that 'just disliking the Japanese may prove an expensive luxury'.[11] He noted that 'If their outlook is materialistic and their policy governed by self-interest, I do not know that this differs very much from other nations with whom we have close relations.'

For Dening the heart of the matter was the economic question. For Anglo-Japanese relations

> The only constant factor which remains from before the War is that of economic competition. Both the United Kingdom and Japan are in the position that they must export to live, and this state of affairs is unlikely to alter at any time in the foreseeable future. Thus Anglo-Japanese relations must be considered on the basis that the two countries will remain competitors in the economic field, and that great care will have to be taken to ensure that economic competition is so regulated as to avoid undue damage to either side.[12]

In an era where British industry still had the edge over Japan at least in third markets Dening pressed the British cabinets of the 1950s to accept the realities of trade competition. Dening argued that this was 'unavoidable', a stance that he had long taken and he maintained Japanese competition 'is only to be met by improving our skills, by increased productivity and better marketing, and not by tariffs and restrictions upon Japanese trade in order to protect industries in which the Japanese are able to compete successfully'.[13] Dening, returning to views that he had shared with Ernest Bevin, stated bluntly that Lancashire could no longer dodge the Japanese onslaught. He admitted that this 'is an unpleasant truth, but nothing to my mind will be achieved by refusing indefinitely to recognize it'.[14]

To reinforce his case that trade friction was better tackled than ducked, Dening widened his perspective and incorporated regional and global factors to buttress his survey. He told Eden that 'if Japan were to range herself on the side of our opponents, the whole position of the Western world in the Far East would be threatened and might prove untenable' and he added, for good measure, the powerful argument that strains between London and Tokyo would upset Anglo-American relations, since US 'energies and resources are directed towards keeping Japan in the western camp'.[15] The paper was a characteristically broad and well-reasoned piece of work, but Dening, for all his advocacy, was out of luck. Relations between Britain and Japan continued to deteriorate throughout the decade.

Anglo-Japanese tension clearly intensified during the Dening years. He found it increasingly hard even to begin to explain the Japanese position as the British governments of the 1950s came under strong political pressure to restrict Japanese products and prevent Japan's accession to international organizations. Dening's difficulties were not helped by the stronger showing now made by the Board of Trade within Whitehall and, therefore, in cabinet submissions. The Foreign Office could no longer count on dominating policy. Public opinion was no longer dormant and both Fleet Street and paperback publishers tended to fuel antagonism. Russell Braddon's bestseller *The Naked Island* kept Japanese wartime brutalities alive.[16]

Dening was surely correct to state in his annual report for 1953 that 'there is a growing feeling of coldness and of an unsympathetic attitude on the part of the United Kingdom towards Japan'. Yet by April 1956 little had changed and Dening was obliged to point out once again that Japan's proffered olive branch had still to be accepted by London. He was too experienced a diplomat to endorse suggestions from some Japanese quarters that things might finally be improving; he warned instead that Japanese goodwill was 'tempered by considerable caution as to the prospective response in the United Kingdom to any Japanese advances'.[17] Even the long-anticipated visit of a British minister to Tokyo was something of a disappointment in the autumn of 1956 as the Japanese felt slighted that a more senior figure than the chancellor of the Duchy of Lancaster ought to have been selected. For Japan to have to wait so long and then to have to welcome a minister whose functions were impossible to explain was to invite trouble.

Even the figure sent, Lord Selkirk, admitted to Selwyn Lloyd that he was 'uncertain' whether the visit had accomplished much. Selkirk underlined what Dening had long been pressing on London that the Japanese 'considered they were worthy of a visit from a very senior member of the Government'. He told Lloyd that 'ultimately the Japanese will, however, only respect either strength or real marks of friendship'; pointing out that 'We cannot produce the first, and I am very doubtful whether public opinion is prepared to consider the second.'[18]

Epitomizing Dening's problems was the cabinet's refusal to withdraw British qualifications to Japan's membership of GATT. The cabinet's rejection of the most-favoured-rights clause (Article 35) left his hopes of improving Anglo-Japanese commercial relations without much foundation; it would take more than a decade before the Japanese bureaucracy began to forget this quite intentional slap in the face. What Tokyo found particularly hurtful was the fact that British action was then followed by others within western Europe and the Commonwealth. Selkirk pointed out that the Japanese 'regard the use of waiver as a form of Asiatic discrimination and are, I understand, prepared to pay almost any price in order to get it withdrawn. The fact that it has no practical disadvantage to them at present is irrelevant compared with the question of prestige.'[19] Yet the British public's fears of Japanese export competitiveness in the 1950s were well founded as industry lost ground throughout the decade to renewed Japanese (and West German) manufactured goods, initially in third markets but then also domestically as the post-war battery of import controls and protective mechanisms were scrapped.[20] It may be that the restrictions on Japan's GATT accession did little to stem the economic tide, while doing much to make the diplomats' job in the Tokyo Embassy a daunting task.

Clearly Dening was on a hiding to nothing in matters of trade. Decisions were being taken (or avoided) in London within Whitehall over which he could do precious little. The difficulties and slowness of improving British commercial and financial links would be a headache for his successors in Tokyo. It was after all not until 1962 that a final Anglo-Japanese commercial treaty could be signed and some of the bitterness felt by both sides could gradually subside. Yet making for additional complications was the state of overall political ties between Britain and Japan; here Dening did have a larger role and his record was a mixed one. His pre-war experiences of Japan and his doubts over its post-war behaviour must have irked the Japanese. It is not surprising, for example, that the foreign minister, Shigemitsu, was seen by Dening as 'out of touch with world events' and initially at least not 'sufficiently aware of the present day facts of life to make him an effective Foreign Minister'.[21] Dening's own account to the Foreign Office of his attempts to produce, rather abruptly, an agenda of debating topics for Anglo-Japanese affairs suggests a heavy-handed bid to press Japanese diplomats to accept his views. If, as Dening reports, Shigemitsu was taken aback, then he had good reason.[22] Just occasionally there was a whiff of the nineteenth-century treaty port approach to Japan in Dening's behaviour. By the mid-1950s, and particularly after the Suez fiasco, the hectoring style ought to have been redundant. Indeed, at times Dening's annual reviews read more like a school report on a delinquent pupil than on a nation which could no longer be ignored or casually rebuffed.[23]

Still, most of the time Dening tried to be fair and he was clearly not given all the support that he expected from the cabinet. He had to acknowledge that 'the Japanese, who have found us unexpectedly tough in negotiation, look as a rule in vain for any indications that the United Kingdom is friendly towards Japan'.[24] All he could announce in his annual review for 1955 was that relations 'did not deteriorate quite as much as might have been expected, but there is nothing at present to indicate that they are likely to take a turn for the better in 1956. Indeed, with nationalism and particularly economic nationalism increasing in this country, they might well deteriorate'.[25] The prose and thought was characteristic of the man.

Dening finally left Tokyo on 1 May 1957. He earned only the briefest of mentions in the subsequent despatch of his successor and after reluctantly undertaking a series of speaking engagements dropped quickly out of the limelight. He continued, fortunately, to follow events in East Asia through his own writings and as chairman in turn of the Japan Society and Royal Central Asian Society. Loaded with honours, including the Order of the Rising Sun, First Class, Esler Dening died at the age of 79 in January 1977.

22

SIR GEORGE SANSOM (1883–1965): HISTORIAN AND DIPLOMAT

Gordon Daniels

Among British historians whose minds and senses have engaged Japan's rich civilization Sir George Sansom remains pre-eminent. Sixty years after the publication of his *Japan A Short Cultural History* and a quarter of a century after the completion of his *History of Japan*, these works remain classics of grace and rigour which set exacting standards for each generation of western scholars.[1] Yet Sir George Sansom was far more than a historian of formidable and subtle powers. He was a long-serving diplomat, linguist and aesthete who overcame illness and disappointment with epic patience and resolve.

George Bailey Sansom was born in Limehouse on the eastern fringe of London on 23 November 1883. His father was a naval architect who lost most of his savings by investing, unwisely, in his employer's company. As a result Sansom was never to study at a British university and regretted this intellectual loss to the end of his life. Yet within these relatively straitened circumstances Sansom received an education which heightened his cultural sensitivity and refined his linguistic skills.[2] After graduating from Palmer's School, Grays, he moved to the Lycée Malherbe in Caen, and then spent over a year at the Universities of Giessen and Marburg in Germany.

After returning to England Sansom spent some months in purposeful cramming and soon passed the examinations for the Far Eastern Consular Service. In 1904 he sailed for Japan and on arrival immersed himself in a variety of Japanese cultural activities which are rarely embraced by British diplomats. At Nagasaki he joined a Nō chorus, began the study of painting and calligraphy; and, more conventionally, began to collect ceramics, screens and other works of art. In these years of diplomatic apprenticeship Sansom also devoted himself to a wide variety of physical pursuits, one of which brought unexpected dangers. Fly-fishing, riding, golf and tennis were conventional diversions from official duties but Sansom also undertook adventurous cross-country hikes. On one of these he was gashed by a poisonous shrub and only a new drug from Vienna saved his life.[3]

Between 1910 and 1914 Sansom served in Yokohama, Tokyo, Chemulpo in Korea and Hakodate, but with the outbreak of war he returned to London and was recruited into the recondite world of naval intelligence. As part of these duties he was despatched to Archangel, and discovered that Russian forces did not lack supplies, but simply the will and organization to remove them from the quayside.

In 1919 Sansom returned to Japan and served as acting Japanese counsellor before assuming a variety of posts in Tokyo and the provinces. The years which followed were to see his reputation rise high within the Tokyo Embassy and in 1925 the ambassador, Sir Charles Eliot, evaluated him as follows:

> For intellectual brilliance Mr Sansom is generally admitted to stand first in the Japanese Service. He is an extremely good Japanese scholar – he has also published several valuable linguistic papers and translations. He is a very good draftsman in English, is well informed on all political and social questions and has specially studied commerce and financial matters. At present he is greatly handicapped by ill health.[4]

At this evaluation it suggests Sansom's relationship with Sir Charles Eliot was close and friendly. What is more, it extended well beyond the narrow confines of professional diplomacy. Both men were committed scholars who were deeply interested in Japanese Buddhism and its rich and subtle intellectual heritage. From these shared interests stemmed a close rapport which continued after Eliot's retirement to Nara.

By 1926, Sansom had begun work on his first important historical work, a cultural history of Japan. In this he was aided by a diplomatic life which retained some of the relaxed ambience of Victorian days. During the summer long periods were spent in the hills near Lake Chuzenji, and weekends and evenings were rarely disturbed by diplomatic work. This regime was especially conducive to Sansom's method of historical research, which differed markedly from much library-based historical enquiry. Sansom visited temples and shrines in Kyoto, Nara and Ise, and even travelled to Korea to examine sites and museums which illuminated the origins of Japanese art and architecture. Even more important was his creation of a sophisticated network of Japanese informants whose help he always acknowledged in later years. This group included Professor Anesaki Masaru, the great authority on religious history; Professor Fukui Rikichiro, a renowned scholar of Japanese art; and Professor Yashiro Yukio, who possessed a deep knowledge of both Japanese and European art. Later Sansom recalled the preparation of his cultural history with great warmth and enthusiasm:

I was in a state of continuous excitement. I had spent a decade or more in the society of Japanese artists scholars, collectors, archaeologists, monks, museums, directors, actors, farmers and fishermen. There is very little mentioned in the book with which I was not familiar – paintings, sculptures, buildings, landscapes, mountains and rivers.[5]

Even before he completed this labour of love Sansom had published his first major book, which was in part a by-product of his historical enquiries. Though his *Historical Grammar of Japanese* was chiefly 'a work of reference' for advanced students of Japanese, it was also 'designed to provide material for study of the affiliations of the Japanese language – for inquiry into the origins of the Japanese race'.[6] This pioneering work continued to be reprinted for forty years after its publication in 1928.

Japan: A Short Cultural History was finally published in 1931.[7] Despite Sansom's later achievements this event may have marked the highpoint of his Japanese experience. The book's preface mentions Japan's 'brave and lovable people', a description which would have been unlikely in the years following the Manchurian Incident of September 1931. However, the Manchurian crisis focused western attention upon Japan to an unprecedented degree, and may have contributed much to the *Cultural History*'s success in Europe and the United States. Despite its scholarly strengths, the *Cultural History*'s reception was not uniformly enthusiastic. *The Times Literary Supplement* acknowledged the author's 'erudition and painstaking research' but continued:

> candour compels the observation that the general reader is likely to find it more instructive than stimulating. His procession moves in stately fashion through the eventful centuries, compelling our respect: but it compels our regrets also, in that it moves without banners or beating of drums, giving but little hint of those dramatic elements, of that romantic quality, persistent throughout the darkest periods of Japanese history.[8]

This was scarcely the view of discerning Japanologists.

Arguably, the writing of the *Cultural History* may have posed less difficulties for Sansom than his next scholarly undertaking, the preparation for publication of Sir Charles Eliot's unfinished manuscript 'Japanese Buddhism'. Not only was Eliot's manuscript a draft, but it lacked a section on the major Japanese Buddhist leader Nichiren. In 1935 Sansom completed a final chapter on Nichiren's life and thought, and the book was published; but as he later confessed, 'adding a chapter to a book written by a genius is a terrible job ... your heart sinks as you take the pen'.[9]

Although *Japan: A short Cultural History* may now appear the most lasting product of Sansom's pre-war years, his diplomatic writing and reporting was of great contemporary significance. From 1926 to 1939 his principal role was that of commercial counsellor, at a time when trade was a central issue in Anglo-Japanese relations.

Sansom later claimed that he had accepted this position as it permitted him remarkable freedom and independence, but this rationale never detracted from his commitment to the post or the professionalism which characterized his economic reporting. Indeed, Sansom's observations on Japanese economic development was often prescient and prophetic. He perceived Japan's transition from a pre-modern to a modern economy before many others, and in 1932 concluded 'Japan is rapidly passing out of the imitative phase and is developing into a powerful industrial and commercial state.'[10] Long before the British textile industry had recognized the true dimensions of Japan's competitive power, he was attempting to persuade Lancashire industrialists to 'look upon Japan as a modern industrial country. In fact an able competitor'.[11] Sansom's perceptive analyses of international trade also led him to note the negative influence which western protectionism could exert on Japanese foreign policy. Despite his antipathy towards Japan's Manchurian adventure in November 1932, he could still write

> the Japanese, if they find themselves, as they well may, driven out of one foreign market after another by tariff measures directed against them, are likely to be confirmed in their present mood of hostility. They can argue that the very Powers which reproach them for their conduct in Manchuria are forcing them to desperate measures by closing other markets against them. This argument is not without foundation, for the past few years Japan has had to contend with tariff increases – some of which were aimed specifically at her – in India, Australia, South Africa and the United Kingdom; while she is now confronted with the possibility of further increases in the United States, the Philippines, Java and India, at a time when she is suffering severely from the boycott and depressed condition in China.[12]

These cogent opinions failed to dissuade Britain and her Commonwealth partners from taking 'legitimate defensive measures against Japan but the notion that trade lay at the centre of most international relationships – including those between Tokyo and the West – was to form an important motif in Sansom's diplomatic thinking.

Despite Sansom's understanding of Japan's economic difficulties he had no sympathy for her continental expansionism or the populist chauvinism which shaped her politics in the 1930s. His detestation of ultra-nationalist fanaticism was a natural product of his humane values but it was further deepened by his loss of close Japanese friends in the political assassinations of the time.[13]

In these years of increasingly exacting work Sansom still retained his broad cultural and intellectual vitality. In 1929 the Indian 'poet-sage' Tagore visited Tokyo, and Sansom and his wife Katharine met him to discuss 'literature and language'. Four years later George Bernard Shaw spent some days in Japan and Sansom escorted him to the Nō, to meet Prime Minister Saito and, more improbably, to confront the ultra-nationalist Araki Sadao, a bizarre battle of wits. Sansom's meetings with Tagore and Shaw probably helped him to keep abreast of recent literary trends, as did his encounters with Peter Fleming, W.H. Auden and Christopher Isherwood, all of whom visited Tokyo on literary pilgrimages to the Far East. Sansom's intellectual vitality was also apparent in his next ambitious plan for historical research. In 1934 he began active work on a major study of the impact of western thought on Japan. However, the final manuscript *The Western World and Japan* would not be published for a further sixteen years.[14]

By 1934 Sansom's reputation as a historian was so well established that he was invited to give a series of lectures on Japanese culture at Columbia University in New York. He happily accepted this invitation and arrived in New York in September 1935. To his surprise he was greeted like a Japanese scholar returning from distant lands. Dr Evarts Green, the head of the Japanese department at Columbia and Tsunoda Ryusaku, professor and librarian, waited at the quayside, accompanied by two students, who were to act as porters. In New York and Boston the Sansoms were honoured and feted in ways which would have been unimaginable in Tokyo. Perhaps the highlight of Sansom's stay was an invitation to speak at the prestigious Pilgrims dinner. He chose this occasion to advocate the expansion of oriental studies in American universities and concluded,

> All over the Far East important movements are shaping, which will presently affect our own lives in one way or another. The least we can do is to study them and I am convinced that all such study must be based upon a foundation of pure learning. Great progress has been made of late in Oriental Studies in this country – less in my own I am ashamed to say – but I wish to plead for still greater effort.[15]

Soon after Sansom rejected the offer of a permanent post at Columbia, but his exhilarating stay in New York had persuaded him that a stay in an American university would form an agreeable postscript to retirement.

In 1936 Sansom returned to Japan to find its politics more violent and volatile than before. These developments not only depressed him, they brought many practical difficulties to his work. As xenophobia suffused Japanese ministries, officials increasingly restricted foreign diplomats' access to information. This inevitably slowed the compilation of Sansom's annual economic reports.[16]

In 1937 overwork and the outbreak of the undeclared Sino–Japanese War further deepened Sansom's depression and an ulcerated stomach now added to his anxieties. Even worse, the new British ambassador, Sir Robert Craigie, knew little of East Asia or Japan and took scant notice of Sansom's expert knowledge and advice.[17] Craigie's indifference did allow Sansom more time to relax at his summer house in Kita Kamakura, but this was little consolation when Japan's government seemed set upon a course of authoritarian rule and military expansionism.

By 1939 these many depressing circumstances had persuaded Sansom to leave the Foreign Office and accept a new invitation to spend a term teaching at Columbia. In May he left Japan for London and on arrival quickly handed in his resignation.[18] Unfortunately, events moved too quickly for Sansom to escape easily to academic pastures. The outbreak of the war with Germany increased the Foreign Office's world-wide burdens and Sansom was recalled to official service. After some months working in London he was again despatched to Tokyo to work alongside his less-than-favourite ambassador, Sir Robert Craigie.

In Tokyo Sansom reflected on the complacency which had characterized British policy in the previous year. Recalling his own historical research he lamented the 'steady if almost imperceptible deterioration which overcomes a society or a class which will not accept or adjust itself to change'.[19] He continued, 'That has been our trouble. The defence of the status quo isn't necessarily immoral or mistaken but it always tends to be a losing battle unless it is conducted along with a more positive aim.' The condition of Japan in 1940 gave further cause for lamentation as many of its day-to-day felicities were giving way to coarseness and petty crime. On 27 July 1940 he wrote, 'It is infuriating to see the rude, tough kind of Japanese in the ascendant and to know that all the time in this country there are immense reserves of decency and kindliness and the essential things of civilization.'[20]

Having completed his temporary mission to Tokyo Sansom was free to spend the winter semester at Columbia. As before, his lectures on Japanese history were warmly received, and American friends, Louis and Jean Ledoux, provided generous hospitality at Cornwall-on-Hudson. Unfortunately, the harsh realities of Britain's position soon interrupted Sansom's academic idyll. On a visit to Washington he offered his services to the British ambassador Lord Halifax, who suggested creating a post which would permit Sansom to do 'Far Eastern things'. Unfortunately, before such a post materialized the Far Eastern crisis worsened, and Sansom was needed in Singapore.

In the spring of 1941 Sansom sailed from Los Angeles to take up his new position as advisor to the Far Eastern Mission of the Ministry of Economic Warfare. Despite its title this post involved political rather than economic duties; more specifically the collection of information concerning 'events and psychological movements in Malaya, South China, Thailand, Burma and . . . Singapore Island'.[21] Sansom was also appointed to be the civilian representative on the Singapore War Council and appears to have shocked his superiors by clearly stating that a Japanese attack was inevitable. Indeed, Sansom's forecast, that the war would begin 'about the end of November' was extremely accurate, for the attack on Pearl Harbor came a mere week later. Sansom also transmitted a message to Washington warning that Japanese forces in Indo-China were preparing to advance into Thailand and Malaya.[22]

By January 1942 it was clear that the fall of Singapore was inevitable and Sansom was ordered to Java to join General Wavell at his new head-quarters. At Bandung he acted as political and diplomatic advisor to General Headquarters and provided news and information to British and foreign journalists. On 15 February Singapore finally fell to Japanese forces and the Sansoms escaped from Batavia to Melbourne on a Dutch liner. After these months of stress and exhaustion in the tropics Sansom was again weak and ill and was compelled to spend some weeks convalescing in Australia.

In the late spring of 1942 the Sansoms recrossed the Pacific, and in May arrived in New York. During the summer they recuperated in the cool air of the Catskills, and in September the scholar-diplomat accepted a specially created post in the British Embassy in Washington. Sansom now became minister to deal with Far Eastern questions, a position which left him free to visit many colleges and universities to lecture on British policy and Far Eastern problems.

Seven months later Sansom was appointed to a new position in the British Embassy – liaison officer between the Foreign Office and the Combined Chiefs of Staff. In this capacity he was to liaise with American leaders regarding the shaping of policy towards defeated Japan. The Foreign Office hoped that Sansom would monitor and perhaps influence American thinking, but Sansom's views were often at variance with those of American planners.[23] These differences are hardly surprising for they stemmed from profound cultural and philosophical differences. Sansom always found American academic life and hospitality highly congenial, but his political views were very different from those which dominated Roosevelt's America. In short Sansom was a self-confessed 'old Tory' while New Deal conceptions of active government and social engineering increasingly dominated plans for the occupation of Japan. These differences were clearly apparent in a triangular conversation between Sansom, Hugh Borton and George Blakeslee on 28 July 1943. On this occasion Sanson lent his support to notions of economic recovery and an early peace, but showed himself hostile to ideas of radical reform. Hugh Borton summarized these elements in Sansom's thinking as follows:

In general Sir George was opposed to the enforcement by the United Nations of changes in the Japanese Constitution and Government as such enforcement would be practically impossible if the Japanese themselves were not convinced of the need for these changes. Specifically, he felt it extremely inadvisable to depose the emperor. The supervision from the outside of the Japanese educational system would be quite impossible. The enforced adoption by Japan of a bill of rights would have little meaning as the ordinary Japanese is little aware of the real significance of personal liberties.

Sir George believed that the military occupation of Japan, unless it came about as a result of hostilities, was both unnecessary and unwise. He believed that the future air strength of the United Nations would be sufficient to protect any disarmament commissions that might be sent to Japan to supervise the enforcement of the terms of surrender.[24]

No-one can doubt the sincerity of Sansom's views for they were consistently held throughout the war, but they were a significant obstacle to close Anglo-American co-operation. Furthermore, Sansom's conservatism may have contributed to the British government's tardiness in beginning discussion of Japan's future. In fact, Whitehall did not turn its formulated attention to these issues until May 1945 by which time most American policies had been formulated. On 28 May an official in the Department of State showed Sansom a draft of its plans for occupied Japan which envisaged a first phase of severe American military administration. Not only was this concept contrary to Sansom's non-interventionist views but 'the United States Government did not intend as yet to inform other Governments of their views or invite participation'.[25]

Soon after Sansom returned to London and drafted a critique of American policy which emphasized Japan's economic weakness and rejected the need for 'a costly machinery of *internal* controls'. Despite their realism and practicality, Sansom's views were not accepted by the foreign secretary, Anthony Eden, who feared any friction with Washington. Yet in one important respect Sansom's views anticipated the realities of the Occupation which was to come: he always favoured working through the Japanese government rather than attempting the complexities of direct military administration.

Despite Sansom's presence in London in these crucial weeks, his role was surprisingly restricted. He was not selected to accompany the British delegation to Potsdam and he attacked the Potsdam Declaration as 'really a poor document'. In a letter dated 30 July he sadly lamented his situation:

I have been seeing various old friends who all think I should have gone to Potsdam, and I thought so myself. But ... it would have been churlish to object. Also they all feel I should have been Ambassador to Japan before the war and think even now that I should be. But I have no ambition of that kind.[26]

Despite these morose reflections Sansom was selected to represent Britain on the Far Eastern Commission, the Allied body established to 'oversee' the Occupation of Japan from Washington. Before the Commission established itself in the American capital, it paid an exploratory visit to Japan in January and February 1946. Sansom took this opportunity to renew links up with many of his long-standing Japanese friends.

As before Sansom was critical of many aspects of American policy, in particular the notion of destroying the major industrial and financial groups, the *zaibatsu*. He also exhibited a disdain for aspects of American society which had been elevated to the status of blueprints for the new Japan. After a meeting with members of MacArthur's Civil Information and Education Section, he wrote acidly, 'education in the United States today is not of such a quality as to encourage one in feeling that it provides a model for any other country'.[27]

Yet for all his dislike of the radicalism and inexperience of many of MacArthur's aides, he recognized the Supreme Commander's own charisma and the overwhelming nature of American power. Before meeting any of his old Japanese friends, he felt it necessary to ask the Supreme Commander's permission. Even more striking was his tactful rejection of an invitation to meet the emperor after consulting General McCoy the American chairman of the Far Eastern Commission.[28]

Following his return to London Sansom's knowledge and judgement appear to have been more highly regarded by the new foreign secretary, Ernest Bevin, than by his predecessor Anthony Eden. He was frequently consulted on important issues of Far Eastern policy, and received the KBE 'in recognition of the valuable services' he had 'rendered to the state'.[29]

From May 1946 to October 1947 Sansom spent much of his time in Washington serving as both minister in the Embassy and United Kingdom representative on the Far Eastern Commission. In view of his long experience as commercial counsellor it was perhaps natural that he was now appointed chairman of the Commission's Committee on Economic and Financial Affairs. In this capacity Sansom saw uncertainty as a major threat to Japan's economic recovery, and repeatedly emphasized the importance of setting levels of industrial production which Japan would be permitted to achieve. Unfortunately American power and obstructionism left little scope for British diplomats to assert their influence, and Sansom could achieve little during his time in Washington.[30]

In the autumn of 1947 Sansom finally left the Foreign Office and satisfied his long-held desire to return to academic life. Twelve years after his first lectures at Columbia he became the first director of its Far Eastern Institute. Sansom was now 63 and had little appetite for university administration; however, most routine tasks could be safely left to his assistant, Hugh Borton. Freed from day-to-day duties Sansom had ample time for reflection and research.

Despite his fragile health Sansom still continued his transatlantic journeys and spent his summers at his home, Chandos Lodge at Eye in Suffolk. During these stays he strengthened his friendships with British writers on Asia such as Victor Purcell and Guy Wint, and consulted G.C. Allen on aspects of Japan's social and economic history. In particular, Sansom was troubled by an American tendency to apply the epithet 'feudal' to Tokugawa and modern Japanese society. In a letter to G.C. Allen he wrote:

> I think you would agree that many of Japan's troubles which are now attributed to feudal ideology, are in reality quite ordinary phenomena in a modern capitalist state, and may well in many cases represent a departure from feudal standards, thus being more Western than Eastern.[31]

Yet despite Sansom's advanced interpretation of Japan's economic development, he remained sceptical of American policies of democratization. He saw democracy as an essentially western phenomenon and in 1949 wrote of the Japanese: 'Why . . . should it be expected that a people whose social and political history has not prepared them for such a process, can be induced – spontaneously and indigenously? – to depart from the own tradition by precept or even by example, offered by their conquerors?'[32]

Despite his obvious dislike of aspects of American thought and action Sansom found Columbia a sympathetic and creative environment. In 1950 he completed *The Western World and Japan*, his first major book since 1931. This not only analysed the history of Europe's impact on Japan from the sixteenth to the nineteenth century, but anticipated much later scholarship. Sansom's new work clearly focused on the theme of 'westernization' or 'modernization', which was to preoccupy both American and Japanese scholars in the 1960s and 1970s.[33] Furthermore, Sansom's assertion that 'some at least of the causes that produced the industrial revolution had been operating . . . in parts of Asia, particularly Japan, long before the ships of the foreigners came to Japanese shores' unconsciously anticipated T.C. Smith's later analysis of the 'agrarian origins' of Japan's modern development.[34]

In October 1950 Sansom set off on his Far Eastern travels again. His first destination was Lucknow where he attended the Institute of Pacific Relations conference and met Prime Minister Nehru. Of greater interest was his subsequent visit to Japan where he met the emperor and lectured at the University of Tokyo. These lectures, later published as *Japan in World History*, demonstrated a generosity of spirit which was rare among contemporary visitors to Japan. In contrast to many Occupation personnel Sansom showed a deep admiration for Japanese culture and scholarship which must have impressed his Japanese hosts. In his first lecture he declared, 'I have no right to pose . . . as an authority upon Japanese history and no foreigner can hope to achieve the depth of knowledge and understanding which we expect from Japanese scholars. . . . We must regard ourselves as pupils not as teachers.'[35] Yet more impressive was Sansom's emphasis on Japan's broad significance in 'the history of the aggregate of human societies' – particularly at a time when many westerners saw Japanese as a uniquely delinquent people; of little relevance to the history of western or Asian humanity.

Despite the beginnings of Japan's economic recovery, life in Tokyo in 1950 was still harsh and austere. Weakened by cold and discomfort Sansom succumbed to double pneumonia and was unable to leave Japan for several weeks. He finally returned to Suffolk after convalescing in the dry, warm climate of the American west.

Sansom remained at Columbia until his retirement in 1954. During these years he lectured *twice* each week to undergraduates and, with the support of the Rockefeller Foundation, embarked upon another major project, a three-volume *History of Japan*. For a man who was physically frail and already 71 this was a vast heroic enterprise.

At this time the cold and humidity of New York and Suffolk winters increasingly threatened Sansom's health and he sought a drier and milder refuge for his retirement. Fortunately two friends from Singapore days now enabled him to settle in California. Two Australians, John Galvin and Stanley Smith, had worked with Sansom in 1942 and offered to build him a house on the campus of Stanford University. In this calm and exquisite setting Sansom was able to consult the Oriental Collection of the Hoover Institution, and meet distinguished Japanese scholars who were invited to Stanford. Among these was his old friend from the 1920s, Yashiro Yukio.

At Stanford Sansom confessed to being 'less given to enthusiasm, less capable of sustained effort and more cynical' than in earlier times, but within four years he completed the first volume of his new *History*.[36] Although Sansom made little use of post-war Marxist writing, he drew upon many original documents to describe the history and eclipse of the Heian Court. Even more striking was his fastidious account of Heian aesthetics and sensibilities, which was based upon a profound knowledge of literary sources.[37]

In preparing the second volume of his History, which analysed the years from 1334 to 1615, Sansom again drew upon many original sources as well as the knowledge of distinguished Japanese historians. For several months he worked 'at the same desk side by side' with Professor Toyoda Takeshi, and also corresponded with Fukui Rikichiro.[38] By 1961 the new volume was complete, and within four years Sansom published the third and final section of his History. Although John Whitney Hall regretted the 'modest proportions' of this concluding volume he acclaimed it as the work of a 'master craftsman', which succeeded in 'capturing the interplay between the [Tokugawa] system and its enemies'.[39]

In these final productive years Sansom received a series of well-merited academic honours and distinctions. In 1954 Columbia awarded him the honorary degree of Doctor of Laws. Soon after he became Honorary Consulting Professor at Stanford. In the 1960s Mills College and Leeds University added further honorary degrees.

Sir George Sansom died on 8 March 1965 in Tucson, Arizona. His ashes were laid in a mountain canyon.

Sansom's greatest achievements were those of a historian who combined courage, humanity and scholarly refinement. As a diplomat he pioneered the serious study of the Japanese economy – when few westerners understood its modernity or its crucial significance. Ironically the achievements of this remarkable Englishman owe most to friends and institutions beyond the seas. Without John Galvin and Stanley Smith, Stanford and Columbia, his health and creativity would have been much impaired.

23

CHRONOLOGY OF ANGLO-JAPANESE RELATIONS, 1858–1990

Valerie Hamilton

1859 Arrival of Sir Rutherford Alcock in Japan as British consul-general (to 1864)
Arrival in Nagasaki of Thomas Blake Glover
William Keswick of Jardine Matheson first British merchant to establish himself in Yokohama

1861 *Nagasaki Shipping List & Advertiser* launched by Albert W. Hansard
Attack on the British Legation in Tokyo
Thomas Blakiston to Hakodate
Dr William Willis to Japan

1862 'Richardson Affair' (*Namamugi jiken*): attack on British subjects by Satsuma retainers
Visit to London by *bakufu* mission led by Takeuchi Yasunori and Matsudaira Yasunao, including Fukuzawa Yūkichi
Japan Punch launched by Charles Wirgman

1863 Kagoshima bombardment: exchange of cannon fire between a British naval squadron and the Satsuma domain
Itō Hirobumi, Inoue Kaoru and three others (the Chōshū five) to Britain
Publication of Alcock's *Capital of the Tycoon*

1865 Sir Harry Parkes British minister in Japan (to 1881)
Satsuma Mission to London, including Mori Arinori

1866 Establishment of Japan's first modern textile mill, equipped by seven British technicians
Publication of Ernest Satow's *English Policy* (*Eikoku Sakuron*)

1867 First female ascent of Fujisan by Lady Parkes
Naval training mission to Japan led by Commander R.E. Tracey

1868 Arrival in Japan of Richard Henry Brunton with two assistants to set up lighthouse and telegraph systems

1869 Visit of Duke of Edinburgh (second son of Queen Victoria) to Emperor Meiji

1870 Samejima Hisanobu appointed envoy to Court of St James (but resident in Paris)

1871 Twelve Japanese students including Tōgō Heihachirō to Britain as naval cadets for training

Samuel Smiles's *Self Help*, the best-selling book in Japan

1872 Arrival of Iwakura Mission in Liverpool to begin a four-month tour of Great Britain; leaders received by Queen Victoria

Opening of the Yokohama to Tokyo railway, chief engineer Edward Morrell

Terajima Munenori first resident envoy to Court of St James

1873 Arrival in Japan of 33-strong party led by Commander Archibald Douglas to establish the Imperial Naval College

Arrival of Henry Dyer to become Principal of the Imperial College of Engineering (Kōbu Daigakkō)

Arrival of Basil Hall Chamberlain, later Professor of Japanese at Tokyo Imperial University

1874 Opening of Okura & Co in London: first overseas office of a Japanese commercial house

1875 *Hamlet* first translated into Japanese

1876 John Milne to Japan, 'father of seismology', to lecture at Imperial College of Technology

John Batchelor to Hakodate

Josiah Conder to Japan as Professor of Architecture at Imperial College of Technology

Visit to Japan by Christopher Dresser, promoter of Japanese arts and crafts

1878 Visit to Japan by Isabella Bird (Bishop)

1879 Visit of Liberal MP E.J. Reed to Japan

1881 Visit of the Prince of Wales (later George V) as a young naval officer aboard HMS *Bacchante*

First edition of Murray's *Handbook for Travellers in Japan*

1883 Opening of Rokumeikan, western-style ballroom

1885 First performance of Gilbert & Sullivan's *Mikado*

First Japanese Shakespeare performance, *Merchant of Venice* in Osaka by kabuki actors

'Japanese village' exhibition in London

1886 Sinking of the *Normanton* off Kyushu; anti-British riots over 'unequal treaties'

1888 Frank Piggott to Japan to advise in drafting of the Meiji Constitution

1891 Founding of the Japan Society of London Publication of Chamberlain's *Things Japanese*

1894 Conclusion of the Anglo-Japanese Commercial Treaty (revision of the 1858 Anglo-Japanese treaty)

1895 Ernest Satow, British minister in Japan (to 1900)

1897 Visit to Britain of delegation headed by Prince Takehito to Queen Victoria's Diamond Jubilee

Makino Yoshino (Yoshio Markino) to Britain (to 1942)

1900 Natsume Sōseki to London (to 1903) as a Japanese government scholar

1902 Conclusion of the Anglo-Japanese Alliance in London

1903 Establishment of School of Japanese at the University of London by W. Shand

1905 British and Japanese legations elevated to embassies: Hayashi Tadasu, first Japanese ambassador to London; Sir Claude MacDonald first British ambassador to Japan

First performance of Puccini's *Madame Butterfly* at Covent Garden

1906 Order of the Garter conferred on Emperor Meiji by Prince Arthur of Connaught

1907 Visit to Japan by Keir Hardie

1909 Bernard Leach to Japan

J.H. Gubbins, lecturer in Japanese at Balliol College, Oxford

1910 Great Japan–British exhibition at White City, London

1911 Japan represented by Prince Higashi-Fushimi at the Coronation of George V

1912 Funeral of Emperor Meiji attended by Prince Arthur

1918 Visit by Prince Arthur to Emperor Taishō

Return visit by Prince Higashi-Fushimi

1920 Hamada Shōji to Britain with Bernard Leach

1921 Three-week visit of Crown Prince Hirohito to Britain

1922 Visit of Prince of Wales to Japan

1926 Prince Chichibu to study at Magdalen College, Oxford

1929 Visit of Duke of Gloucester to Japan

1930 Visit of Prince Takamatsu to Britain

1934 Anglo-Japanese discussions in London regarding the cotton trade

Unveiling of memorial to William Adams in Gillingham

1935 Sir Frederick Leith-Ross to Japan to discuss China's financial problems

1936 Japanese withdrawal from London Naval Conference

1937 Visit of Prince Chichibu to Britain for Coronation of George VI

World speed record flight by Japanese aeroplane *Kamikaze* from Tokyo to London

1941 Japanese attacks on British territories in the Far East

1943 Launch of the BBC World Service Japanese language service

1947 Edmund Blunden to Japan as Cultural Liaison Officer to the British Mission

1948 Establishment of the British Chamber of Commerce in Japan

1950 Founding of the Japan Association

1952 Entry into force of the Peace Treaty with Japan signed at San Francisco in 1951. Resumption of diplomatic relations

1952 Air Service Agreement
      Establishment of the British Council representative office in Tokyo
1953 Visit of Crown Prince Akihito to Britain for the Coronation of Queen
      Elizabeth II
1954 Visit of Prime Minister Yoshida Shigeru to London
1956 Release of Akira Kurosawa's film *Throne of Blood*, based on *Macbeth*
1959 Establishment of the Japanese Chamber of Commerce in the United
      Kingdom
1960 Anglo-Japanese cultural agreement concluded: led to establishment of
      the Japan–United Kingdom Mixed Commission Founding of the
      Nippon Club, London
1961 First British post-war trade mission to Japan
      Founding of the Anglo-Japanese Economic Institute
      Establishment of the British–Japanese Parliamentary Group
1962 Anglo-Japanese Commerce Establishment and Navigation Treaty con-
      cluded; reciprocal waiving of passport visas agreement
      Visit of Prime Minister Ikeda Hayato to London
1963 First Regular Ministerial Consultation between Japanese Minister for
      Foreign Affairs and British Foreign Secretary
1964 London Symphony Orchestra to Japan
1966 Concert by *The Beatles* at the Tokyo Budōkan
1967 First British Nō performance at Aldwych Theatre, London
1968 New British Council Library in Tokyo opened by Iris Murdoch
      London Shakespeare Group tour of over thirty Japanese universities
1969 British Week in Japan, including Henry Moore exhibition and per-
      formances by the London Philarmonic Orchestra and London
      Festival Ballet
      British Book Display Centre in Tokyo launched
1970 Expo70, attended by Prince of Wales
      Two major art exhibitions in Japan at National Museum of Western
      Art and Hakone Open Air Museum
      Visit to Japan by the Royal Shakespeare Company: first by a British
      national theatre company
      First *Gagaku* performance in London by the Japanese Imperial Court
      Musicians
      National Film Theatre Japanese film season
1971 Visit to Britain by Emperor Shōwa, first Imperial state visit
      Agreement between Japan Academy and Royal Society to promote
      scientific exchanges
      Keidanren mission to Britain
1972 Visit by Prime Minister Edward Heath to Japan: first visit by a British
      prime minister
      Establishment of the Japan Foundation
      Opening of the YKK zip factory at Runcorn

First UK kabuki performance at Sadlers Wells
1973 Visit to Britain of Prime Minister Tanaka Kakuei
1982 Visit by Prime Minister Margaret Thatcher to Japan
1983 Prince Naruhito (Hiro) to Merton College, Oxford
1984 Inauguration of the UK–Japan 2000 Group
Visit of PM Nakasone Yasuhiro to Britain
Opening of Sōseki Museum in London
First UK 'Japan Week' organized by the Japanese Embassy, held in Glasgow
1985 Japanese version of *Macbeth* at the Edinburgh Festival directed by Ninagawa Yukio
Japan Exhibition at the Barbican
First meeting of the UK–Japan 2000 Group
First Anglo-Japanese Summer Festival in Battersea Park
1986 Opening of Nissan Motor Company plant at Washington, Tyne and Wear
Japanese Festival at Washington and Sunderland
Visit to Japan by Prince and Princess of Wales
Prime Minister Margaret Thatcher to Tokyo Summit
First Japanese float in the London Lord Mayor's Show entered by Nomura
1987 First Anglo-Japanese space venture: launch of satellite carrying major X-ray sensor
Channel 4 Japan Season
1988 Prime Minister Takeshita Noboru official visit to Britain
Opening of replica of Shakepeare's Globe Theatre in Tokyo
1989 Funeral of Emperor Shōwa attended by Duke of Edinburgh
British School in Tokyo opened
1990 Visit by Prime Minister Kaifu Toshiki to London
Opening of the British Museum's new suite of Japanese galleries by Prince Fumihito
UK 90 Festival in Japan
Formal announcement of the Japan Festival 1991

NOTES

1. THE JAPAN SOCIETY

1 He had been appointed medical doctor to the Naval Medical College in Tokyo in 1873 and had become medical officer to the British Legation in 1874. He died on 25 October 1898.

2 The term 'Jap' in the late nineteenth century was a familiar abbreviation, not a term of abuse or contempt.

3 It was presumably from this group that the Japan branch of the Japan Society of London grew and from which the present Japan–British Society developed. The *Japan Weekly Mail* for 7 November 1908 recorded that on 20 October a meeting was held at the Peers Club in Tokyo to consider the organization of a Society 'which shall be to the Japanese capital what the Japan Society is to London'. Among the Japanese present were several who had 'received their education at Oxford, Cambridge or other well-known seats of British learning'. Count Hayashi was appointed chairman of the meeting by acclamation. The British ambassador proposed that the Society should be called the 'Japanese and British Society' but the meeting preferred the name 'The British Society' which the *Japan Weekly Mail* declared was 'a good deal better than the flagrantly ungrammatical "Japan Society"'. The British ambassador was elected the president of the Society, whose objectives were declared to be: 'to encourage the study of things English [*sic*], and also to promote cordial relations between the people of Great Britain and Japan'. The inaugural meeting of the Society was held at the Imperial Hotel on 27 November 1908 to bid farewell to their Excellencies Mr and Mrs Kato, who were about to leave for London to represent Japan at the Court of St James. Among the toasts was one to the 'English Society' proposed by Captain Brinkley. His Imperial Highness Prince Fishimi became patron of the Society in November 1910. Unfortunately the records of the Japan–British Society were almost entirely lost as a result of the wartime air raids on Tokyo, but the Society's name was changed to the Japan–British Society at some date after 1910.

4 King Edward VII conferred the Grand Cross of the Order of the Bath on the Marquis during his stay in London.

5 Sir Laurence Alma-Tadema RA (1836–1912) was famous for his paintings of classical themes.

6 Prince Takehito Arisugawa was the younger brother and adopted son of Prince Taruhito Arisugawa who in turn had been adopted as a son by the Emperor Ninko (1800–46, reigned 1817–46), grandfather of the Emperor Meiji. Prince Taruhito Arisugawa (1835–95) commanded imperial forces in the Boshin war of 1868 and against the forces of Saigo Takamori in the Seinan war of 1877. Prince Takehito Arisugawa's career had been in the Japanese navy, having received his

early training in the Royal Navy. Princess Arisugawa came from the Maeda family (the former Daimyo of Kaga). She had been active in support of the Japan Red Cross during the Russo-Japanese War.

7 This lecture was reprinted and published in *A Tragedy in Stone and Other Papers* (London 1913), together with other lectures given by Lord Redesdale to the Japan Society.

8 *The Times*, 23 December 1909

9 An account of the exhibits in the section allocated to the Society is contained in *Transactions and Proceedings of the Japan Society* (1909–11), vol. IX, pp. 131–6.

10 A lecture on 'Japanese Wrestling' was given to the Society on 24 April 1912 by Iemasa Tokugawa, then an attaché at the Japanese Embassy in London.

11 The Prince Higashi-Fushimi is not to be confused with Prince Fushimi: the Fushimi and Higashi-Fushimi families were separate branches of the Imperial Family.

12 The Maeda had been *daimyō* of Kaga, which in Tokugawa times had had an annual income of over one million *koku* of rice.

13 An account of the visit to Japan of Prince Albert and Prince George of Wales (i.e. King George V) is given in *The Cruise of HMS Bacchante, 1879–1882* (2 vols), London: Macmillan, 1986. It was compiled from the private journals, letters and notebooks of Prince Albert Victor and Prince George of Wales with additions by John N. Dalton. Extracts are quoted in Hugh Cortazzi, *Victorians in Japan* (London 1987), pp. 124–7.

14 Duncan Macfarlane has drawn the writer's attention to a book published in Yokohama in 1923 entitled *Inaka or Reminiscences of Rokkosan and Other Rocks*, collected and compiled by The Bell Goat, Member of the Alpine Club, Member of the Ancient Order of Mountain Goats, Etc. Volume XVI. Chapter XI consists of some verses entitled 'The Golf of the Rising Sun' by 'Hari-Kari', allegedly reproduced from *Golfing* (London, March 1922). These verses begin:

They have troubles St Andrews never knew on the courses of old Japan;
You play on the top of a mountain peak at Kobe on Rokkosan
The holes are found on the higher ground, and the chasms lie in between,
And your drives all slide down the mountain side if you fail to hit
them clean.

The pitching too to the casual view, will move your heart to mirth;
The greens look more like bunkers there, than anything else on earth.
For you have to play upon greens of clay which are so uncommonly keen
That to give a chance to a decent approach, there's a ditch all round
the green.

15 This description is to be found in her book *Japanese Lady in Europe*, published in London in 1937 with an introduction by William Plomer. The dinner was presumably the one held at the Mayfair Hotel on 21 June 1933.

16 Both Mr Ichiro Matsudaira and Mr Yoshitomo Tokugawa became active members of the post-war Japan–British Society in Tokyo.

17 Mrs Aso was made an honorary DBE for her services to Anglo-Japanese relations after the Second World War.

2. CHARLES WIRGMAN

1 This article is based on my previous work which can be found in *Japanese–British Exchanges in Art 1850s–1930s*, published as a mimeo with grants from the Japan

Foundation, London office, and The Great Britain – Sasakawa Foundation in 1989, and the paper 'Charles Wirgman (1832–1891), recent discoveries and re-evaluations', to be found in the *Proceedings of the British Library Colloquium on Resources in Japanese Studies* (1988), London, The British Library, 1990. To obviate extensive footnoting here, I refer the reader to the first work in particular for bibliographical references and a detailed chronology. The only major additional material which has since come to light, to my present knowledge, is the series of early drawings by Wirgman from his 1857 voyage out to Hong Kong, and subsequent work in 1859 and 1859, which were sold in 1989. They are well illustrated in *Fine Chinatrade Paintings and Printed Material*, 26 September 1989, Hong Kong, Christies' Swire. I am also grateful to Mr Richard D. Martin for information about another group of works by Charles Wirgman in The Peabody Museum, Salem, Massachusetts, which were not covered in my earlier research.

2 His Japanese language manual has since been found in Stockholm. It has passages written by his teacher with annotations in roman letters by Wirgman and is dated 1867. This was together with a copy of the Japanese children's primer by Kawasari Sodaifu, *Yagen Doyu* (A Collection of Sayings and Metaphors), of 1844 marked 'C. Wirgman, his book, no. 137', and is in the Library of the Ostasiatiska Museet, in Stockholm. I am grateful to Dr Peter Kornicki and Mr Nakamura Mamoru for informing me of their existence and sending copies.

3. WILLIAM GEORGE ASTON

1 W.G. Aston, 'Japan', *Macmillan's Magazine* 26 (1872), p. 493.

2 ibid., p. 497.

3 W.G. Aston, 'Takamagahara', *Transactions of the Asiatic Society of Japan* 38 (1911) 3, unnumbered page at beginning of issue.

4 J.C. Hall, 'Eulogy upon W.G. Aston, C.M.G., D. Litt.', *Transactions of the Asiatic Society of Japan* 38 (1911), no. 5, p. v.

5 W.G. Aston, *A Short Grammar of the Japanese Spoken Language*, 3rd edn, London: Trübner & Co., 1873, p. 83; *A Grammar of the Japanese Spoken Language*, 4th edn, Yokohama: Lane, Crawford & Co., 1888, p. 188. (Note that the word 'Short' was dropped from the title on the 4th edition).

6 W.G. Aston, *A Short Grammar of the Japanese Spoken Language*, 1st edn, Nagasaki: F. Walsh, 1869, p. 6.

7 *A Short Grammar*, 3rd edn, p. 3.

8 ibid., Preface (unpaginated).

9 *A Grammar of the Japanese Spoken Language*, 4th edn. Preface (unpaginated).

10 W.G. Aston, *A Grammar of the Japanese Written Language with a Short Chrestomathy* (London: printed for the author at the office of *The Phoenix*, 1872), Preface (unpaginated).

11 B.H. Chamberlain, *A Handbook of Colloquial Japanese*, 4th edn, London: Crosby, Lockwood & Son, 1907, p. ii.

12 W.G. Aston, in *The Phoenix* 2 (1871–2), pp. 131–2.

13 W.G. Aston, 'Memorandum on the Loochooan and Aino languages', *Church Missionary Intelligencer and Record* 4 (1879) 8, pp. 490–1.

14 W.G. Aston, 'Hideyoshi's Invasion of Korea', *Transactions of the Asiatic Society of Japan* 6 (1878) to 11 (1883).

15 British Parliamentary Papers 1883/LXXV [C.3455]: *Despatch from Her Majesty's Minister in Japan Forwarding a Report on Corea*, 'Mr Aston to Sir Harry Parkes', p. 9.

16 W.G. Aston, 'A comparative study of the Japanese and Korean languages', *Journal*

of the Royal Asiatic Society 11 (1879), 317–64; Bruno Lewin, 'Japanese and Korean: the problems and history of a linguistic comparison', *Journal of Japanese Studies* 2 (1976), p. 391.

17 W.G. Aston, 'An ancient Japanese classic (The *Tosa Nikki*, or Tosa Diary)', *Transactions of the Asiatic Society of Japan* 3 (1875), 2, pp. 121–30.

18 W.G. Aston, *Nihongi: Chronicles of Japan from the Earliest Times to* A.D. *697*, 2 vols, Transactions and Proceedings of the Japan Society Supplement 1, London: Kegan Paul, Trench, Trübner & Co., 1896, p. ix.

19 W.G. Aston, *A History of Japanese Literature*, London: Heinemann, 1899, p. 401.

20 ibid., p. 386.

21 ibid., p. 378.

22 ibid., p. 269.

23 ibid., p. 294.

24 ibid., pp. 96–7.

25 W.G. Aston, *Shinto (The Way of the Gods)*, London: Longmans, Green & Co., 1905, p. i.

26 W.G. Aston, 'Kaempfer as an Authority on Shinto', *Man* 2 (1902), 182–4.

27 *Shinto*, pp. i, 376–7.

28 ibid., pp. 376–7.

29 *T'oung Pao* 12 (1911), p. 740.

30 George Sansom, 'Address delivered by Sir George Sansom at the Annual Ceremony [SOAS] 1956', *Journal of Asian Studies* 24 (1964–5), p. 566.

4. ERNEST MASON SATOW

1 E.M. Satow, *A Diplomat in Japan*, London: Seeley, Service & Co., 1921, p. 58.

2 ibid., p. 154.

3 Quoted in Grace Fox, *Britain and Japan, 1858–1883*, Oxford: Clarendon Press, 1969, p. 423.

4 Satow, p. 281.

5 B.M. Allen, *The Rt Hon. Sir Ernest Satow G.C.M.G: A Memoir*, London: Kegan Paul, Trench, Trübner & Co., 1933, p. 73.

6 ibid, p. 79.

7 Public Record Office PRO 30/33(11), Satow to Aston 18 January 1882.

8 Allen, p. 87.

9 E.M. Satow, 'Essay towards a bibliography of Siam', *Journal of the Straits Branch of the Royal Asiatic Society* 17 (1886), pp. 1–85; and 18 (1886), pp. 163–89.

10 Allen, p. 89.

11 ibid., pp. 96–7.

12 ibid., p. 110.

13 ibid., p. 132.

14 ibid., p. 134.

15 E.M. Satow, *Kuaiwa-hen, Twenty-five Exercises in the Yedo Colloquial*, Yokohama: Lane, Crawford & Co., 1873, p. iii.

5. JOSEPH CONDER

1 The best account of the exotic interests of the mid-Victorian architectural world is probably to be found in J. Mordaunt Crook, *William Burges and the High Victorian Dream*, London: John Murray, 1981.

2 See, for example, the Elephant Inkstand illustrated in J. Moraunt Crook, *The*

Strange Genius of William Burges, Cardiff: National Museum of Wales and the Victoria and Albert Museum, 1981, p. 115.

3 See in Crook, plates 64 and 76.

4 Louis Marie Julien Viaud (Pierre Loti), *Japoneries d'Automne*, Paris: Calmann-Levy, 1889, p. 83.

5 Wilhelm Boeckmann, *Reise nach Japan*, Berlin, 1886, pp. 59–63.

6 The baroness describes her visit to the house accompanied by long-time British advisor to Mitsubishi, Thomas Glover, in E. Mary d'Anethan, *Fourteen Years of Diplomatic Life in Japan*, London: Stanley Paul & Co., 1912.

7 Josiah Conder, *Kenchikuzumenshi*, Tokyo: Chuokoron Bijutsushuppan, 1981.

6. WALTER WESTON

1 Walter Weston, *Mountaineering and Explorations in the Japanese Alps*, London: John Murray, 1896; *The Playground of the Far East*, London: John Murray, 1918; *A Wayfarer in Unfamiliar Japan*, London: Methuen & Co., 1925; *Japan*, London: A. & C. Black, 1926.

2 'Obituary. The Reverend Walter Weston', *Geographical Journal* (hereafter *GJ*), XCV (January–June 1940), p. 478.

3 Maeda Tsukara, 'Nihon Arupusu no "hakken", Nihon kindai tozan shi ni okeru Wesuton', in Yosida Mitsukuni (ed.), *Jukyu Seiki Nihon no Joho to Shakai Hendo*, Kyoto: Kyoto Daigaku Jinbun Kagaku Kenkyujo Kenkyu Hokoku, 1986, p. 308.

4 Entry for Walter Weston in *Who's Who in Japan*, 1914.

5 Maeda, p. 309.

6 Nihon Seikokai rekishi hensan iin kai, *Nihon Seikokai Hyakunenshi*, Tokyo: Nihon Seikokai Kyokai Kyomuin Bunshokyoku, 1959, p. 280.

7 'Obituary', p. 479.

8 Maeda, p. 309.

9 'Obituary. Mrs Frances Emily Weston', *GJ*, XC (July–December 1937), p. 288.

10 'Mission reports: St Andrew's, Yokohama', *South Tokyo Diocesan Magazine* IX (April 1905) 26, pp. 13–16.

11 ibid., p. 17.

12 IX (December 1904) 25, p. 98.

13 ibid., XII (March 1908) 35, p. 16.

14 ibid., (April 1904) 23, p. 26.

15 Weston, *Playground of the Far East*, pp. 167, 237.

16 'Obituary. The Reverend Walter Weston', p. 479.

17 President's introduction before Walter Weston's paper on 'Exploration in the Northern Japanese Alps', *GJ*, XLVI (July–December 1915), p. 198.

18 *GJ*, L (July–December 1917), p. 80

19 ibid., p. 18.

20 See, for instance: John Batchelor, *Ainu Life and Lore: Echoes of a Departing Race*, Tokyo: Kyobunkwan, n.d; Batchelor, *The Ainu of Japan: The Religion, Superstitions, and General History of the Hairy Aborigines of Japan*, New York and Chicago: Fleming II. Revell, n.d.; Lionel Berners Cholmondeley, *The History of the Bonin Islands from the Year 1827 to the Year 1876 and of Nathaniel Savory, One of the Original Settlers: to Which is Added a Short Supplement Dealing with the Islands After Their Occupation by the Japanese*, London: Constable, 1915; Arthur Lloyd, *The Wheat Among the Tares: Studies of Buddhism in Japan: A Collection of Essays and Lectures, Giving an Unsystematic Exposition of Certain Missionary Problems of the Far East, with a Plea for*

More Systematic Research, London: Macmillan and Co., Limited, 1908; Lloyd, *Every-day Japan Written After Twenty-Five Years' Residence and Work in the Country*, London: Cassell and Company, Limited, 1909; Lloyd, *The Creed of Half-Japan: Historical Sketches of Japanese Buddhism*, London: Smith, Elder & Co., 1911.

21 Lloyd, *Every-day Japan*.
22 Cyril Hamilton Powles, *Victorian Missionaries in Meiji Japan: The Shiba Sect*: 1873–1900, Toronto: University of Toronto–York University Joint Centre on Modern East Asia, 1987, p. 51.
23 Lloyd, *Every-day Japan*, pp. 347–8.
24 Weston, *Unfamiliar Japan*, p. 29.
25 ibid., pp. 18–19.
26 Walter Weston, 'Explorations in the Japanese Alps, 1891–1894', *GJ*, VII (February 1896), p. 2.
27 Basil Hall Chamberlain, *Japanese Things: Being Notes on Various Subjects Connected for the Use of Travellers and Others*, Rutland, Vermont, and Tokyo: Charles E. Tuttle 1987 reprint of 1904 edition of *Things Japanese*, p. 70. See also, *The Japanese Alps*, p. 1. In the Preface to *Every-day Japan* Arthur Lloyd wrote: 'Professor Chamberlain I may describe as having been the good genius of my work; without his encouragement I should not have undertaken it.'
28 See Ota Yuzo, *B.H. Chenbaren: Nichio Aida no Ofuku Undo ni Ikita Seiyo Jin*, Tokyo: Riburopoto, 1990, pp. 36, 268. In a conversation with the author, Professor Ota indicated that Chamberlain last had contact with Weston in 1926.
29 Maeda, p. 317.
30 Weston, *Playground of the Far East*, p. 90.
31 ibid., p. vi.
32 ibid., pp. 52, 53.
33 Comment by Sir Claude Macdonald following Walter Weston's paper on 'Exploration in the Northern Japanese Alps', *GJ*, XLVI (July–December 1915), 199.
34 Weston, *The Japan Alps*, pp. 219–220.
35 *Japan*, p. 118.
36 Maeda, pp. 327–8.
37 ibid., p. 328.
38 Weston, *Playground of the Far East*, p. ix.
39 ibid., pp. 319–20.
40 *GJ*, LXIII (January–June 1924), pp. 462–3.
41 Weston, *The Japanese Alps*, p. 320.
42 ibid., p. vii.
43 ibid., p. 16.
44 Weston, *Playground of the Far East*, p. 111. See also, Walter Weston, 'Travel and exploration in the Southern Japanese Alps', *GJ*, XXVII (January–June 1906), pp. 24–6. In this paper, Weston called the mountain Huzan, the 'Phoenix' peak.
45 ibid., p. 120.
46 Weston, *The Japanese Alps*, p. 293.
47 Weston, 'Explorations in the Northern Alps', pp. 197–8.
48 ibid., p. 198.
49 Weston, *The Japanese Alps*, p. 322.
50 ibid., pp. 71–72.
51 ibid., p. 320.
52 Weston, *Playground of the Far East*, p. 158.
53 ibid., p. 158.
54 Walter Weston, 'Influence of nature on Japanese character', *GJ*, LXIII (January–June 1924), p. 111.

55 Weston, *Japan*, pp. 183–4.
56 ibid., p. 183.
57 ibid., p. 154.
58 ibid., p. 175.
59 ibid., pp. 235–6.
60 Weston, 'Influence of nature in Japanese character', p. 106.
61 Alun Hawkins has argued in terms of England that 'a strain emerged within English politics and ideas in the 1800s which linked the rural to a general crisis in urban society. That this in turn produced a cultural response from the 1890s and 1900s which, by 1914, had spread far across English art and letters, music and architecture, producing a ruralist version of a specifically English culture'. Alun Hawkins, 'The discovery of rural England', in Robert Colls and Philip Dodd (eds), *Englishness, Politics and Culture 1880–1920*, London: Croom Helm, 1987, pp. 62–88, 63. It is reasonable to assume that Weston's view of England was influenced by this ruralist strain, and it, in turn, helped to influence his view of Japan.

7. BABA TATSUI

1 Arthur Diosy, 'Introduction to the Third Edition of *An Elementary Grammar of the Japanese Language*', London, 1904, in *Baba Tatsui zenshū (BTZ)*, IV (Tokyo, 1988), 22. Arthur Diosy, a founding member of the Japan Society, knew Baba, and this introduction also tells how they met.
2 'The life of Tatui Baba', in *BTZ*, III (Tokyo, 1988), 135. This was written in English, in the third person, and completed mainly in 1885.
3 'The English in Japan: What a Japanese thought and thinks about them', in *BTZ*, I (Tokyo, 1987), pp. 111–12.
4 'The life of Tatui Baba', p. 163.
5 For this last period of his life, see Sugiyama Shinya, 'Amerika ni okeru Baba Tatsui', *Fukuzawa Yukichi nenkan*, 15 (1988), pp. 107–29.
6 See the entry for Wednesday, 25 January 1871, in William Plomer (ed.), *Kilvert's Diary: Selections from the Diary of the Reverend Francis Kilvert, 1870–1879*, abridged edn, London, 1944, p. 107; *Warminster Herald*, 4 March 1871; *Wiltshire Independent*, 30 March 1871.
7 'The life of Tatui Baba', p. 163.
8 Entry for Monday, 30 April, 1877, in *BTZ*, III (Tokyo, 1988), p. 218.
9 'The life of Tatui Baba', pp. 159–60.
10 ibid., p. 167.
11 Moncure Daniel Conway, *Autobiography: Memories and Experiences*, London, 1904, p. 356.
12 'The life of Tatui Baba', p. 157.
13 ibid., p. 163.
14 See, for example, Herbert Spencer, *First Principles*, 3rd edn, London, 1875, and Walter Bagehot, *Physics and Politics*, 2nd edn, London, 1872.
15 Katō Hiroyuki, *Jinken shinsetsu* (Tokyo, 1882).
16 'Honron', Part 6, *Jiyū shinbun*, 9 July 1882, in *BTZ*, II (Tokyo, 1988), pp. 20–3.
17 'Nairan no gai wa kakumei no ka ni arazu', *Jiyū shinbun*, 22 July 1882, in *BTZ*, II, pp. 63–8.
18 *Tenpu jinkenron* (1883), in *BTZ*, II, p. 88.
19 'Shinka bunri no niryoku', Parts 2 and 3, *Kyōson zasshi*, 22 October, 19 November 1879, in *BTZ*, I, pp. 79–84.
20 *Tenpu jinkenron*, pp. 114–15.
21 'Heikinryoku no setsu', *Kyōson zasshi*, 19 March, 1879, in *BTZ*, I, pp. 45–6.

22 'Gaikōron', *Ōmei zasshi*, 25 December 1880, in *BTZ*, I, pp. 200–2.
23 'Honron', Part 15, *Jiyū shinbun*, 10 August 1883; Part 16, 18 August 1883, in *BTZ*, II, pp. 45–8, 52.
24 'Preface', *An Elementary Grammar of the Japanese Language*, London, 1873, in *BTZ*, I, pp. 13–14.
25 *Tenpu jinkenron*, pp. 109–10.
26 'The English in Japan', pp. 111–29; 'The Treaty between Japan and England' (London, 1876), in *BTZ*, I, pp. 133–64.
27 'The English in Japan', pp. 112–13.
28 'The Treaty between Japan and England', p. 137.
29 ibid., p. 142.
30 From Baba's diary and the Trübner archives, it would seem that at least 150 copies of 'The English in Japan' were produced. See diary entry for 2 November 1875, p. 195 and the Trübner Publication Account Books, vol. 5, p. 17, Archives of Kegan Paul, Trench, Trübner and Henry S. King, British Library.
31 J.T. Dexter, 'The English in Japan', *Aesthetic Review*, January 1876, in *BTZ*, IV, pp. 44–5.
32 Yasunaga Gorō, *Baba Tatsui*, (Tokyo, 1897; reprinted 1987), pp. 228–9.
33 Entry for Friday 30 March 1877, p. 214.
34 Entry for Wednesday 23 May 1877, p. 221.

8. TWO PIGGOTTS

1 His autobiography was entitled *Broken Thread*, Aldershot, 1950. He had hoped when he started to write the memoir, that he could call it *Unbroken Thread*; the war forced him to change the title.
2 ibid., pp. 1–9.
3 See H.J. Jones, *Live Machines: Hired Foreigners in Meiji Japan*, Vancouver 1980. Also B.H. Chamberlain, 'Foreign employees in Japan', in *Things Japanese*, 5th edn London and Yokohama 1905, pp. 181–5. For the experiences of a *yatoi* civil engineer employed to build railways and bridges in Japan, see E.J. Holtham, *Eight Years in Japan, 1873–1881*, London 1883.
4 F.T. Piggott, 'The Ito legend: personal recollections of Prince Ito', *Nineteenth Century and After*, 67 (1910), pp. 173–6.
5 Takeda Kiyoko, 'The emperor system in modern Japan', Richard Storry Memorial Lecture No. 3, Oxford 1990, says that all documents in the Gaimushō re FTP are marked *kimits* secret.
    An interesting example of the questions to which FT refers together with his draft answers, is to be found in the Library of the Japan Society. In 1933 FSG presented to the Society a handsome black morocco document case containing the original proof copies of the Japanese Constitution, with corrections in red, which had belonged to his father. Loose in one of the folios is the following letter dated 27 March 1889:

Dear Mr Piggott,
    Mr Inoue Kowashi requests your kind information and opinion on the following questions:
1. The Constitition of the Empire says: the Emperor orders amnesty, pardon, commutation of punishments and the rehabilitation (Art. XI). And the Law of Election says: those who have been sentenced to confinement, when full three years have not yet elapsed since the completion or pardon of their sentences . . . shall be disqualified as elector or as eligible person (Art. XI-44).

Does this disqualification extend to those who have received the royal act of grace and rehabilitation?

2. If this disqualification is made to extend to those pardoned and rehabilited, then is it not the gross violation of royal prerogative of mercy?

3. How is it in England? K.H.

On the back of the letters are notes in pencil on *Rehabilitation*, 'pardon – sha men, great pardon – tai sha, special pardon – toku'. Another loose paper reveals FT's draft reply to the question on Article 67. 'You see, the thing is decidedly complicated. Read by a Japanese, it would be interpreted as three sentences rolled into one.'

I am grateful to Professor Ian Nish and Dr Kenneth Gardiner drawing my attention to these papers.

6 This album was acquired by Sir Hugh Cortazzi from FT's granddaughter, Juliet Piggott (Mrs H.F. Wood), and later presented on behalf of the Society to the Diet Library. See Sir Hugh Cortazzi, 'A Piggott album', *Proceedings of the Japan Society*, 105 (December 1986), pp. 55–9.

7 F.T. Piggott, Kt, MA, Ll.M., *The Music and Musical Instruments of Japan*, London: Batsford, 1893; 2nd edn 1909.

8 ibid., pp. 7, 31, 40.

9 F.T. Piggott, *The Decorative Art of Japan*, London: Batsford, 1910. Printed at the Box of Curios Press, Yokohama.

10 F.S.G. Piggott, *Broken Thread*, pp. 29–30, 63.

11 F.S.G. Piggott, *The Elements of Sōsho*, Yokohama: Kelly & Walsh, 1912.

12 *Transactions of the Asiatic Society of Japan*, XLI (1913), I, p. 187.

13 F.S.G. Piggott, *Broken Thread*, pp. 44–8. See also his address to the Japan Society in 1955, 'Return to Japan', in the *Bulletin of the Japan Society of London*, 17 (October 1955), pp. 9–12.

14 Talk on the BBC Home Service, reprinted in ibid., p. 13.

15 F.S.G. Piggott, *Broken Thread*, pp. 137–49, and *Bulletin*, 17 (October 1955), p. 13.

16 Personal communication from Juliet Piggott (Mrs H.F. Wood).

17 F.S.G. Piggott, *Broken Thread*, p. 335.

18 A full account of the wartime teaching of Japanese at SOAS may be found in Oba Sadao's *Senchū Rondon Nihongo Gakkō*, Tokyo, Chūō Kōronsha 1988. General Piggott is described on pp. 34–7.

19 Louis Allen, 'The General and Translators V', as yet unpublished. My thanks are due to Louis Allen for these special reminiscences.

20 F.S.G. Piggott, 'Return to Japan', *Bulletin* 17 (October 1955), pp. 9–12.

21 F.S.G. Piggott, *Broken Thread*, p. 338.

9. BASIL HALL CHAMBERLAIN

1 Quoted in Kusuya Shigetoshi, *Nezumi wa mada ikite iru – Chenbaren no denki*, Tokyo: Yūshōdō, 1986, p. 226

2 *The Language, Mythology, and Geographical Nomenclature of Japan, Viewed in the Light of Aino Studies*, Memoirs of the Literature College, Imperial University of Japan 1, Tokyo, 1887, pp. 74–5.

3 Kazuo Koizumi, ed., *Letters from Basil Hall Chamberlain to Lafcadio Hearn*, Tokyo: Hokuseidō, 1936, pp. 157–8.

4 *The Classical Poetry of the Japanese*, London: Trübner and Co., 1880, pp. 27–8. My emphasis.

5 ibid., pp. 117 and 124–5.

6 Kazuo Koizumi, ed., *More Letters from Basil Hall Chamberlain to Lafcadio Hearn*, Tokyo: Hokuseidō, 1937, p. 108.

10. KIKUCHI KYŌZŌ

1 Information on the College of Engineering comes from O. Checkland, *Britain's Encounter with Meiji Japan, 1868–1912*, Basingstoke and London: Macmillan, 1989; H. Dyer, *Dai Nippon, the Britain of the East*, London, 1904; J.E. Hunter, 'The development of technical education in Japan – foreign teachers at the Imperial College of Engineering, 1872–1885', BA dissertation, University of Sheffield, 1971; Kyū Kōbu Daigakkō Shiryō Hensankai (ed.), *Kyū Kōbu Daigakkō Shiryō*, Tokyo, 1931.

2 Sources used here for Kikuchi's life are Chūgai Sangyō Chōsa Kai (ed.), *Jinteki Jigyō Taikei*, vol. 12, *Sen'i Kōgyō Hen* (Tokyo, 1943); Kinugawa Tai'ichi, *Honpo Menshi Boseki Shi*, vol. 4 (Tokyo: Nihon Mengyō Kurabu, 1939); Nichibō Shashi Hensan Iinkai (ed.), *Nichibō Nanajūgonen Shi* (Osaka: Nichitō Kabushiki Gaisha, 1956).

3 It should be noted that an ability in English was the major prerequisite for entry to the college, since all classes were initially conducted in the English language.

4 Engineers' careers are commented on in H. Morikawa, 'The education of engineers in modern Japan: an historical perspective', and H. Uchida, 'Japanese technical manpower in industry 1880–1930', both papers presented at the Second Anglo-Japanese Conference on Business History, LSE, September, 1988; T. Yui, 'Development and organization of large industrial Enterprises in Japan' *Bulletin of the Institute of Social Sciences, Meiji University* 25 (1987), p. 1.

5 He served as adviser to at least one other company temporarily.

11. HAYASHI TADASU

1 T. Hayashi, *The Secret Memoirs of Count Tadasu Hayashi, G.C.V.O.*, edited by A.M. Pooley, London: Eveleigh Nash, 1915, pp. 1–7.

2 S.D. Brown and A. Hirota (eds), *The Diary of Kido Takayoshi*, 2 vols, Tokyo: University Press, 1985, vol. II, pp. 119–20.

3 G.M. Berger (ed.), *Kenkenroku: A Diplomatic Record of the Sino-Japanese War, 1894–5*, Tokyo: University Press, 1977, p. xvii (hereafter cited as *Kenkenroku*).

4 Hayashi, *Secret Memoirs*, pp. 8–9; Berges (ed.), *Kenkenroku*, pp. 50–3, 121.

5 Berger (ed.), *Kenkenroku*, pp. 203–5.

6 Diary of Dr G.E. Morrison (Mitchell Library, Sydney, NSW), 312/60, 8 March 1900, But see J.H. Gubbins, *The Making of Modern Japan*, London: Seeley Services, 1922, p. 247, who dates Hayashi's interest in the Alliance rather earlier.

7 Hayashi, *Secret Memoirs*, p. 110.

8 I.H. Nish, *The Anglo-Japanese Alliance, 1894–1907*, London: Athlone Press, 1966, pp. 127–34.

9 Hayashi, *Secret Memoirs*, pp. 135–7. 'Nichi-Ei dōmei to Itō Hirobumi' in *Gaimushō no 100-nen*, 2 vols, Tokyo: Hara Shobō, 1969, vol. I, pp. 415–29.

10 T. Hayashi, 'Nichi-Ei dōmei no shinsō', *Nihon Gaikō Bunsho*, Tokyo: Gannandō, Meiji 35, no. 25.

11 ibid.

12 ibid.

13 Ishii Kikujiro, *Gaikō Yoroku*, Tokyo: Iwanami Shoten, 1930, pp. 53–60.

14 Annual Report for the Tokyo Embassy by Rumbold 1913, p. 3 in *British Documents on Foreign Affairs*, Part I, Asian series: I.H. Nish (ed.), Japan, vol. 9. University Publications of America, 1990.

15 Cf. O.K. Falt and A. Kujala (eds), *Rakka Ryūsui: Colonel Akashi's Report on His Secret Cooperation with the Russian Revolutionary Parties During the Russo-Japanese War*, Helsinki: Societas Historica Finlandiae, 1988, pp. 56–60, 72, 93.

16 Hayashi, *Secret Memoirs*, pp. 8 and 236–41.
17 [British] Foreign Office records, 800/68 (Public Record Office, London), Mac-Donald to Grey, 19 February 1908: 'The Count is terribly heckled and harried in the Diet just now and being somewhat hot-tempered by nature the heckling is having a bad effect. He has several times told me that he sighs for peaceful times in England'. Also MacDonald to Grey, 13 July 1908: 'From personal experience I have found him lazy and forgetful and this has been the experience of my French, German and American colleagues. . . . Indeed he has made no secret of the fact that the work is too much for him, and he wants to get back to London'.
18 Hayashi, *Secret Memoirs*, p. 240.
19 Foreign Office 800/68, Greene to Grey, 31 August 1913.
20 Hayashi, *Secret Memoirs*, pp. 30–1.
21 Annual Report for the Tokyo Embassy by Rumbold 1913, p. 3 in *British Documents on Foreign Affairs*, Part I, Asian series: I.H. Nish (ed.), Japan, vol. 9. University Publications of America, 1990.
22 Hayashi, *Secret Memoirs*, pp. 31–4.
23 Hayashi, *Secret Memoirs*, pp. 57
24 F.H. Conroy, *The Japanese Seizure of Korea, 1868–1910*, Philadelphia: University of Pennsylvania Press, 1960, p. 514.
25 Foreign Office 800/68, Greene to Grey, 31 August 1913: 'The reason for the publication is probably to be found, in part at any rate, in the pique which Count Hayashi felt at the way in which he was treated when he retired from office. It seems that when the Cabinet fell in which he was Foreign Minister, he was not awarded any solatium in the way of a seat in the House of Lords, Privy Councillorship or pension, so much so, in fact, that he was reduced to straightened circumstances, and had to retire to a small villa by the sea.'
26 FO 800/68, MacDonald to Grey, 13 July 1908: 'Denison who is foreign adviser to the Foreign Office here tells me he is disliked in the Office being very indolent and also very hot-tempered'.
27 T. Hayashi, 'Jiji Shimpo', in I.H. Nish, *Alliance in Decline*, London: Athlone Press, 1972, p. 76.
28 Hayashi in the Preface to Arthur Lloyd, *Every-day Japan*, London: Cassell, 1909, p. xv.
29 Annual Report for the Tokyo Embassy by Rumbold 1913, p. 3 in *British Documents on Foreign Affairs*, Part I, Asian series: I.H. Nish (ed.), Japan, vol. 9. University Publications of America, 1990.
30 Sidney Webb and Beatrice Webb, 'Asian Travel Diary, 1911–12' (British Library of Political and Economic Science), p.f. 2863.

12. MARIE STOPES

1 There are three biographies of Marie Stopes: Aylmer Maude's *Authorized Life of Marie Stopes*, London: Williams and Norgate, 1924, Keith Brandt's *Marie Stopes: a Biography*, London: Hogarth Press, 1962, and Ruth Hall's *Marie Stopes*, London: André Deutsch, 1977. Only the last makes use of the voluminous Marie Stopes Papers, which were deposited in the British Library after her death and which were said to fill a 3-ton lorry.
2 Marie Stopes, *Love Letters of a Japanese*, edited by G.N. Mortlake, London: Stanley Paul and Co., 1911, p. 62.
3 The seven letters in the British Library, 58470, Vol. XXXV, date from July 1904 to November 1905. The further series is dated 1925–6. A printed invitation dated 1936 requests her to contribute to an album commemorating Professor Fujii's seventieth birthday. His last letter, dated 25 April 1949, thanks her for the guinea which she

sent ten years before, for the 'expense of album preparation', he has thought of her almost every day, though he has not written. The printed version of Fujii's last letter of course reads 'Dear Miss Meredith' and 'Yours sincerely, K. Watanabe'.

4 It is possible that the *Finis* printed at the end of the published letters was not so final as it would have us believe. The *Journal* records sessions of fossil-cutting with him in the laboratory, and her horror that he may have been exposed to leprosy. There is also an article published in the *Transactions of the Royal Society* 201 (1910), which claims to have been written with Professor K. Fujii. Even more curious is the draft of a letter to Professor Weiss in Manchester, dated 21 May 1908, in which she confesses herself in love, wanting to marry, that 'it is Professor Fujii', but that he is ill; she wants to know whether she would be dismissed from her lectureship if she married him.

5 Marie Stopes, *A Journal from Japan: A Daily Record of Life as Seen by a Scientist*, London 1910.

6 *Nature*, 5 August 1939. Obituary of Baron Joji Sakurai by Professor F.G. Donnan. Marie Stopes added a tribute on 9 September to his 'spiritual and literary sensibilities' revealed by his proficiency in the 'profound medieval religious plays, the Nō'. I am deeply grateful to Professor Ishibashi Hiro for material relating to Professor Sakurai and to Marie Stopes.

7 The play *Vectia* portrayed the situation she had undergone during her first marriage, an annulment of which she claimed after six years as a *virgo intacta*. The play was ready for performance in 1926, but banned at the last moment by the censor. She published the text under the title *A Banned Play and a Preface on the Censorship*, and wrote another play in six hours, *Our Ostriches*, as a substitute for the theatre first night.

8 Printed in *Transactions of the Royal Society of Literature*, 129 (1909). 'The Sumida River' was further produced as an opera, music by Clarence Raybould, in Birmingham and Glasgow in 1916.

9 Marie Stopes, *plays of Old Japan: The Nō*, London: William Heinemann, 1913; facsimile edn, London: Eclipse Press, 1927.

10 Marie Stopes 'Value and interest of Japanese fossils', *Transactions and Proceedings of the Japan Society of London*, 9 (1912).

11 ibid., p. 17 (1920).

13. SIDNEY WEBB AND BEATRICE WEBB

1 M. Cole, *The Webbs and Their Work*, London, 1969.

2 N. Mackenzie (ed.), *The Letters of Sidney and Beatrice Webb, Vol. II, Partnership 1892–1912*, Cambridge, 1978, p. 371.

3 All from ibid.

4 E. Wilkinson, *Japan versus Europe: A History of Misunderstanding*, Harmondsworth: Penguin, 1983), p. 43

5 J. Pemble, *The Mediterranean Passion: Victorians and Edwardians in the South*, Oxford, 1987, p. 1.

6 T.W.H. Crosland, *The Truth about Japan*, London, 1904, p. 9.

7 T. Yokoyama, *Japan in the Victorian Mind: A Study of Stereotyped Images of a Nation 1850–80*, London, 1987, p. 170.

8 Wilkinson, *Japan versus Europe*, p. 57.

9 C. Holmes and A.H. Ion, 'Bushidō and the samurai: images in British public opinion, 1894–1914', *Modern Asian Studies*, 14 (1980), pp. 317–19.

10 Pemble, *The Mediterranean Passion*, p. 260.

11 N. Mackenzie and J. Mackenzie (eds), *The Diary of Beatrice Webb. Vol. 3. 1905–1924 The Power to Alter Things*, London, 1984, pp. 164–5.

12 B. Webb, Diaries, MS, vol. 19 (1898), p. 10.
13 B. Webb, Diaries, MS, vol. 30 (1911–12), p. 90.
14 ibid.
15 ibid.
16 ibid., pp. 127e,f.
17 ibid., pp. 127f.
18 B. Webb, Diaries, MS, vol. 31 (1912), p. 101.
19 B. Webb, Diaries, MS, vol. 33 (1915–16), p. 87, letter of 5 October
20 S. and B. Webb, 'The social crisis in Japan', *The Crusade* III (January 1912), 26(9).
21 ibid., p. 26(9).
22 B. Webb, Diaries, MS, vol. 35 (1918–20), p. 97.
23 ibid., p. 132.
24 B. Webb, Diaries, MS, vol. 49 (1935), pp. 91–3.
25 B. Webb, Diaries, MS, vol. 51 (1937), pp. 101, 114.
26 ibid., p. 101.
27 J.P. Lehmann, *The Image of Japan: From Feudal Isolation to World Power 1850–1905*, London, 1978, p. 15.
28 Pemble, *The Mediterrenean Passion*, p. 274.
29 Sir Charles Eliot, *Letters from the Far East*, London, 1907, p. 140.
30 G. Moorhouse in a review of S. and B. Webb, *Indian Diary*, ed. Niraja Gopal Jayal (Oxford, 1988), in *The Times*, 5 November 1988.
31 Y. Okakura, *The Japanese Spirit*, London, 1905.
32 A. Stead, *The Great Japan: A Study of National Efficiency*, London, 1906, pp. 38, 42, 57.
33 B. Webb, *Our Partnership*, ed. B. Drake and M.I. Cole, London, 1948, p. 400.
34 Sir Oliver Lodge, *Public Service versus Private Expenditure*, Fabian Tract No. 121, London, 1907, pp. 10, 11.
35 J.M. Winter, 'The Webbs and the non-white world: a case of socialist racialism', *Journal of Contemporary History*, IX (1974), 188. See also A.M. McBriar, *Fabian Socialism and English Politics 1884–1918*, Cambridge, 1962, p. 337n; S. and B. Webb, *Soviet Communism: A New Civilization?* 2 vols, London, 1935.
36 Winter, 'The Webbs'.
37 B. Webb, Diaries, MS, vol. 14 (1891–4), p. 29.
38 B. Webb, Diaries, MS, vol. 30 (1911–12), p. 108.
39 S. and B. Webb, 'China in Revolution', *The Crusade*, III (March 1912), 27(6).
40 Winter, 'The Webbs', pp. 191–2.
41 M.D. Biddiss, 'Myths of the blood', *Patterns of Prejudice*, IX (Sept–Oct. 1975), pp. 11–19.
42 M. Harris, *The Rise of Anthropological Theory*, London, 1968, p. 130.
43 All from Winter, 'The Webbs', *op. cit.*, p. 185.
44 G. Watson, *The English Ideology*, London, 1973, p. 210.
45 Quoted in G.R. Searle, *The Quest for National Efficiency. A Study in British Politics and Political Thought 1899–1914*, Oxford, 1971, p. 57.
46 V. Chirol, *The Far Eastern Question*, London, 1896, p. 225.

14. MALCOLM KENNEDY

1 Kennedy Diary, Wednesday 27 November 1918.
2 ibid., Thursday 22nd July 1920.
3 ibid., 23 June 1920.
4 ibid., 17 August 1932. Important news items were sent to Reuters Far Eastern Office in Shanghai and thence to Reuters' head office in London by telegram;

other items were sent by mail. When the news items appeared in the newspapers those sent by telegram would usually carry the previous day's date: the other items, sent by mail, would carry a much earlier date. There was always the temptation for news agencies to redate mail items so that they would appear to have been sent by telegram and thus have more appeal to the newspapers, eager for the latest news.

5 *Punch*, 25 December 1935.

15. SIR CHARLES ELIOT

1 Major-General F.S.G. Piggott, *Broken Thread*, Aldershot, 1950, p. 204.
2 Sir Harold Parlett, 'In Piam Memoriam', in Sir Charles Eliot, *Japanese Buddhism*, London, 1935, xvii. Parlett's affectionate memoir is the fullest account of Eliot's personal life, although it says little of his activities as ambassador.
3 Thomas Preston, *Before the Curtain*, London, 1950, pp. 123–4.
4 Ian H. Nish, *Alliance in Decline: A Study in Anglo-Japanese Relations 1908–1923*, London, 1972, pp. 310 and 312–13, Eliot's first dispatch is Eliot to Curzon, 17 June 1920, *Documents on British Foreign Policy 1919–1939* (hereafter cited as *DBFP*), XIV (52).
5 Curzon to Eliot, 28 July 1921, *DBFP*, 1, XIV (350), note 1.
6 Eliot to Curzon, 13 January 1922, *DBFP*, 1, XIV (548).
7 The suggestion that Eliot thought of resigning but was persuaded to stay on to ease the transition in Anglo-Japanese relations is found in Captain M.D. Kennedy, *The Estrangement of Great Britain and Japan 1917–35*, Manchester, 1969, p. 66.
8 Eliot to A.J. Balfour, 29 June 1922, F.O. 371/8052 (F 2493/2493/23).
9 Curzon to Eliot, 17 February 1922, F.O. 371/8042 (F 654/1/23).
10 Eliot to Curzon, 1 May 1922, Lloyd George papers, F/56/4/3.
11 *The Times*, 17 March 1931.
12 Eliot to Balfour, 30 July 1922, F.O. 371/8047 (F 2800/426/23).
13 Eliot to Balfour, 29 June 1922, F.O. 371/8052 (F 2493/2493/23).
14 Eliot to Austen Chamberlain, 14 November 1924, F.O. 371/10961 (F 28/28/23).
15 Eliot to J. Ramsay MacDonald, 3 May 1924, F.O. 371/10391 (F 1968/1968/23).
16 See Dennis Smith, 'The end of Japan's Siberian adventure: withdrawal from the maritime province, 1921–1922', *Proceedings of the British Association for Japanese Studies* 11 (1986), pp. 13–19.
17 Eliot to MacDonald, 3 May 1924, F.O. 371/10391 (F 1968/1968/23).
18 Eliot to Balfour, 30 July 1922, F.O. 371/8047 (F 2800/426/23).
19 Eliot to MacDonald, 17 July 1924, F.O. 371/10303 (F 2435/14/23).
20 Eliot to MacDonald, 8 February 1924, MacDonald Papers, F.O. 800/219.
21 Dennis Smith, 'The Royal Navy and Japan in the aftermath of the Washington Conference 1922–1926', *Proceedings of the British Association for Japanese Studies*, 3 (1978), 2, pp. 69–86.
22 Eliot to MacDonald, 3 May 1924, F.O. 371/10319 (F 1968/1968/23).
23 Eliot to Austen Chamberlain, 14 November 1924, Austen Chamberlain Papers (Public Records Office), F.O. 800/256.
24 Eliot to Chamberlain, 3 September 1925, F.O. 371/10939 (F 4370/190/10).
25 Minute by V.A.A.H. Wellesley, 13 September 1924, F.O. 371/10244 (F 3099/19/10).
26 Eliot to Chamberlain, 15 January 1925, Eliot to Sir E. Crowe, 29 January 1925 and Eliot to Chamberlain, 4 April 1925, F.O. 800/257; Eliot to Chamberlain, 20 October 1925 and Chamberlain to Eliot, 24 November 1925, F.O. 800/258.
27 Katharine Sansom, *Sir George Sansom and Japan: A Memoir*, Tallahassee 1972, especially p. 77.
28 *DBFP*, 1A, II, pp. 953–4.

29 Sir F. Lindley to Arthur Henderson, 23 July 1931, *DBFP*, 2, VIII (495). Lindley was troubled by the deteriorating status of cricket in Japan.

16. ADMIRAL YAMANASHI KATSUNOSHIN

1 Yamanashi Katsunoshin, *Rekishi to Meisho*, Tokyo: Mainichi Shinbunsha, 1981.
2 Stephen Howarth, *Morning Glory*, London: Hamish Hamilton, 1983, p. 45.
3 Letter from Yamanashi to S.H. Mumford, President of Shell Oil Co. Ltd, Japan dated 1 August 1961.
4 Howarth, *Morning Glory*, p. 54.
5 This was the only time the British and other foreign navies fought under Japanese command.
6 Howarth, *Morning Glory*, p. 126.
7 Edwin O. Reischauer, *My Life between Japan and America*, New York: Harper & Row, 1986.
8 Yamanashi Shinichi 'Memoirs of my father', *Hatou Journal of the Naval Defence College*, 1976, pp. 85–91.
9 See Hashiguchi Isamu, *Jozetsu to Kamoku*, Tokyo: Simul Publications, 1976; Hirakawa Sukehirō, 'R.H. Blyth and Hirohito's denial of the divine character of the Tenno', *British Association for Japanese Studies, Proceedings*, 1985, pp. 33–41. Hirakawa Sukehiro, *Heiwa no Umi to Tatakai no Umi*, Tokyo: Shinchosha, 1983, pp. 33–41.
10 William P. Woodard, *The Allied Occupation of Japan 1945–1952 and Japanese Religions*, Leiden: E.J. Brill, 1972.
11 Elizabeth Gray Vining, *Quiet Pilgrimage*, Philadelphia: J.B. Lippincott, 1970.
12 In the late 1940s and early 1950s Yamanashi was the head of the Sendai Dormitory in Tokyo, where university students from Sendai lived.

17. ARTHUR WALEY

1 Alison Waley, *A Half of Two Lives*, London: Weidenfeld & Nicolson, 1982; and Marian Ury, 'Some notes toward a life of Beryl de Zoete', *The Journal of the Rutgers University Libraries*, XLVIII, 1 (June 1986).
2 Cyril Connolly, *The Modern Movement*, London: André Deutsch and Hamish Hamilton, 1965, p. 7.
3 Kenneth Allott (ed.), *The Penguin Book of Contemporary Verse*, Harmondsworth: Penguin, 1962, p. 109
4 Arthur Waley, *A Hundred and Seventy Chinese Poems*, London: Constable, 1962, p. 8.
5 Arthur Waley, *Japanese Poetry: The Uta*, Oxford: Clarendon Press, 1919; reprinted, London: George Allen & Unwin, 1976, p. 12.
6 Arther Waley, 'Notes on the "Lute Girl's Song", *The New China Review*, 2 (1920), p. 596.
7 *Times Literary Supplement*, 19 November, 1919, p. 646.
8 From *An Essay on Translated Verse* (1684) by the Earl of Roscommon.
9 Ivan Morris, *Madly Singing in the Mountains*, London: George Allen & Unwin, 1970, p. 118.
10 Morris, *Madly Singing*, p. 155.
11 Arthur Waley, *The Nō Plays of Japan*, London: George Allen & Unwin, 1921, p. 5.
12 Earl Miner, *The Japanese Tradition in British and American Literature*, Princeton University Press, 1958, p. 137.

13 Koyama Hiroshi *et al.* (eds), *Yōkyokushū*, vol. 2, in *Nihon koten bungaku zenshū*, Tokyo Shōgakkan, p. 262.

14 Ezra Pound, *The Translations of Ezra Pound*, London: Faber & Faber, 1953, p. 316.

15 Waley, *The Nō Plays of Japan*, p. 124.

16 Suyematz Kenchi'o (Suematsu Kenchō, in modern transliteration), *Genji Monogatari*, London: Trübner & Co., 1882).

17 See, for instance, the opening sentences of each; also Marian Ury, 'The imaginary kingdom and the translator's art: notes on re-reading Waley's *Genji*', *Journal of Japanese Studies*, 2 (1976), 2, pp. 267–70.

18 *The Times*, 19 May 1933, p. 8.

19 *Times Literary Supplement*, 18 March 1926, p. 206.

20 *Vogue*, 66 (July 1925), 2, pp. 53 and 80.

21 Ralph Freedman, *The Lyrical Novel*, Princeton University Press, 1963.

22 Edward Seidensticker (trans.), *The Tale of Genji*, New York: Alfred A. Knopf, 1976. For a useful list of Waley's inaccuracies see Richard Bowring, *Murasaki Shikibu, The Tale of Genji*, Cambridge University Press, 1988, p. 78.

23 Arthur Waley, *The Originality of Japanese Civilization*, Oxford University Press, 1929.

24 *Vogue*, 66 (July 1925), 2, p. 53.

18. TSUBOUCHI SHŌYŌ

1 Kawatake Shigetoshi, *Tsubouchi Shōyō* (Dai-ichi Shobō, 1988; reproduction of book first published in 1939), p. 194.

2 Collected in Odagiri Hideo *et al.* (eds), *Nihon Puroretaria Bungaku Taikei*, San'ichi Shobō, 1955, introductory vol., pp. 333–44, and vol. 1, pp. 293–304.

3 Tsubouchi Shōyō, 'Minshū kyōka to engeki' (published July 1919), in Ōmura Hirotake and Date Yutaka (eds), *Shōyō Senshū* (Shun'yōdō, 1926–7), IX (1926), pp. 47–8.

4 For assessments of Tsubouchi's work in literary theory, see Marleigh Ryan, *Japan's First Modern Novel*, New York: Columbia University Press, 1967; Peter Kornicki, *The Reform of Fiction in Meiji Japan*, New York: Ithaca Press, 1982, and Richard Bowring, *Mori Ōgai and the Modernization of Japanese Culture*, Cambridge University Press, 1979.

5 Kawatake, *Tsubouchi*, pp. 731–4.

6 Kinoshita Junji, *Nihongo no Sekai*, XII, Chūō Kōronsha, 1982, pp. 143–57.

7 Peter Milward, 'Shakespeare in Japanese translation', in Joseph Roggendorf (ed.), *Studies in Japanese Culture*, Tokyo: Sophia University Press, p. 191. For further comment in English on Tsubocuhi's Shakespeare translations, see Hisae Niki, *Shakespeare Translation in Japanese Culture*, Tokyo: Kenseisha, 1984.

8 Odagiri Susumu, Nihon Kindai Bungakkan (eds), *Nihon Kindai Bungaku Daijiten*, vol. 2, Tokyo: Kōdansha, 1977, p. 409.

9 Kawatake, *Tsubouchi*, p. 612.

10 ibid., pp. 613–14.

11 Robert Withington, *English Pageantry*, vol. 2, Cambridge, Mass.: Harvard University Press, 1920, p. 193.

12 ibid., p. 192.

13 ibid., p. 195.

14 Quoted in ibid., p. 195.

15 ibid., p. 202.

16 Tsubouchi Shōyo, 'Pe-jento no tekiyō han'i', *Senshū*, IX, p. 287.

17 Tsubouchi Shōyō, 'Shinminshūgeki o okosan to suru riyū', *Senshū*, IX, pp. 208–17.
18 Tsubouchi, 'Pe-jento', *Senshū*, IX, p. 288.
19 ibid., pp. 289–93.
20 For example, Tsubouchi Shōyō, 'Minshū hon'i to wagageki no zento' (published 1919), *Senshū*, IX, pp. 93–102.
21 In the grounds of the Army School at Toyama. Ōmura Hirotake, 'Pe-jento jōen ryakki', *Saku to Hyōron* II (10), reprinted in *Senshū*, IX, Appendix, p. 25.
22 Ōzaki Kōji, *Tsubouchi Shōyō*, Miraisha, 1965, p. 168.

19. WILLIAM PLOMER

1 Peter F. Alexander, *William Plomer: A Biography*, Oxford: 1989, p. 83.
2 Alexander, *William Plomer*, p. 113.
3 William Plomer, *Double Lives: An Autobiography*, London: 1943, p. 175.
4 ibid., p. 176.
5 ibid., p. 177.
6 ibid.
7 ibid., p. 181.
8 William Plomer, *Paper Houses*, 1942, p. 149.
9 Alexander, *William Plomer*, p. 144.
10 Plomer, *Paper Houses* (1942), pp. xiii–xiv.
11 Plomer, *Paper Houses*, Harmondsworth: Penguin, 1943, p. 9.
12 ibid., p. 10.
13 ibid., p. 12.
14 ibid., p. 21.
15 ibid., p. 31.
16 ibid., pp. 89–90.
17 William Plomer, *Four Countries*, London: Cape, 1949, p. 226. (The story was written in 1946.)
18 Plomer, *Double Lives*, p. 187.
19 ibid.
20 ibid., p. 207.
21 Alexander, *William Plomer*, p. 175.
22 William Plomer, *Sado*, London: 1931, p. 103.
23 ibid., p. 141.
24 ibid.
25 ibid.
26 ibid., p. 143.
27 ibid., p. 144.
28 ibid., p. 145.
29 ibid., p. 146.
30 ibid., p. 147.
31 ibid., p. 148.
32 ibid., p. 149.
33 ibid., p. 150.
34 ibid., p. 150.
35 ibid., pp. 154–5.
36 ibid., p. 155.
37 Alexander, *William Plomer*, p. 178.
38 Plomer, *Double Lives*, p. 208.
39 ibid., p. 209.
40 Plomer, *Sado*, p. 241.

41 William Plomer, *At Home*: Memoirs, London: 1958, pp. 11–12.

42 William Plomer, *Collected Poems*, London: Cape, 1960.

43 A clear allusion to van der Post's dream of Mori.

44 Correspondence in the Plomer Manuscripts, Durham University Library Archives, Captain K. Mori to William Plomer, 8 November 1956.

45 Alexander, *William Plomer*, p. 378, n. 56.

46 ibid., pp. 300–1.

47 ibid., p. 301.

48 ibid., p. 303.

49 Curlew River, *A Parable for Church Performance*, London: Faber and Faber, 1964, p. 31.

50 Alexander, *William Plomer*, p. 306.

51 Plomer, *Double Lives*, pp. 199–200.

52 ibid., p. 202.

53 ibid., p. 216.

20. G.C. ALLEN

1 M.M. Gowing, 'George Cyril Allen, 1900–1982', *Proceedings of the British Academy*, 71 (1985), p. 475.

2 See *Mirror to a Mermaid: Pictorial reminiscences of Mason College and the University of Birmingham. 1875–1975*, University of Birmingham, 1975, pp. 46–7. On p. 77 is to be found a further photograph of the 1918–19 Faculty of Commerce, showing George Allen – then in his first year – towards the rear of the group.

3 The original manuscript of this was entitled *Japan Yesterday and Tomorrow*. It is rather surprising to find that the earlier version was turned down by a number of publishers at the beginning of the 1970s on the grounds that it consisted too largely of 'personal reminiscences' and would not find a market. As *Appointment in Japan*, it was finally published by The Athlone Press, London, in 1983.

4 These comments, handwritten on the original reunion cards, are to be found among the collected papers of G.C. Allen, stored in the manuscript division of University College Library, London.

5 Gowing, 'Allen', p. 474.

6 This is the opening to Chamberlain's memoirs of nearly two decades in Japan, *Things Japanese*, Kegan Paul, Trench Trübner & Co. Ltd., London, 1891, p. 1.

7 The two books were published by Allen and Unwin (in 1928) and Longmans, respectively. For a comprehensive bibliography of George Allen's published works, see Gowing, 'Allen', pp. 488–91.

8 Published by The Athlone Press, London, in the early part of 1990.

9 *A Short Economic History of Modern Japan, 1867–1937* was published by George Allen & Unwin in 1946.

10 The phrase is Sydney Checkland's, in an unpublished letter to Margaret Gowing in which he looked back with considerable perception over George Allen's career.

11 Allen, *Appointment in Japan*, p. 11.

12 ibid., p. 66.

13 This is ably summarized by M.M. Gowing in her British Academy memoir, 'Allen', pp. 480–2. In an interview given at the end of his life, in September 1980, George Allen himself provided a vigorous and not always flattering account of his BOT experiences.

14 For a fuller account, see George Allen's own 'retrospective' in 'Britain's Perception of Japan's Post-War Economic Prospects', *Proceedings of the British Association for Japanese Studies*, Sheffield: Centre for Japanese Studies, 1977.

15 See G.C. Allen and A.G. Donnithorne, *Western Enterprise in Far Eastern Economic Development: China and Japan*, Allen & Unwin, London 1954, p. 188.

21. SIR ESLER DENING

1 Reference to separate parts of his career can be found in Philip Ziegler, *Mountbatten*, London, 1985; Peter Dennis, *Troubled Days of Peace*, Manchester, 1987; Christopher Thorne, *Allies of a Kind*, London, 1978; Alan Bullock, *Ernest Bevin*: Foreign Secretary, London, 1983; Roger Buckley, *Occupation Diplomacy: Britain, the United States and Japan, 1945–1951*, Cambridge, 1982; Peter Lowe, *The Origins of the Korean War*, London, 1986. On the Tokyo Embassy years, see Buckley 'From San Francisco to Suez and beyond: Anglo-Japanese relations, 1952–1960', in Warren Cohen and Akira Iriye (eds), *The Great Powers in East Asia* (New York, forthcoming).
2 The phrase is the title of D.C.M. Platt's work, *The Cinderella Service: British Consuls since 1825*, London, 1971. Nothing comparable to P.D. Coates's splendid work, *The China Consuls: British Consular Officers, 1843–1943*, Hong Kong, 1988, yet exists for its Japan counterpart.
3 Thorne, *Allies of a Kind*, p. 548n.
4 See Buckley, 'Responsibility without power: Britain and Indonesia, August 1945 to September 1946', in Ian Nish (ed.), *Indonesian Experience: The Role of Japan and Britain, 1943–1948* London: LSE, 1979. A falling out with Australia's Macmahon Ball precluded Dening from winning the job of head of the UK Liaison Mission to occupied Japan. Ball was the Commonwealth's representative on the Allied Council for Japan and the two men had clashed over Indonesian policies.
5 Bullock, *Ernest Bevin*, p. 153.
6 I am grateful to Lord Henniker for discussions on the professionalism of Dening and Bevin's trust in his work.
7 Morrison to Yoshida, 8 September 1951, in Morrison papers, FO 800/639.
8 Chancellor of the Duchy of Lancaster (Lord Selkirk) to Selwyn Lloyd, 24 October 1956, FJ 1054/45A (FO 371/121048).
9 Records from official Japanese sources are beginning to trickle out for this period. For information on abortive Japanese attempts to join international organizations and the negative British response, see the *Japan Times*, 16 October 1989.
10 Dening to Eden, 24 March 1953, FJ 1051/21 (FO 371/105374).
11 Dening was not immune from such attitudes. In the same despatch he wrote, 'the Japanese, physically unprepossessing and lacking the superficial charm of many other oriental nations, are, in my experience, if no better certainly no worse than many other Asians with whom we have to deal. Provided they do not once again come under the direction of a totalitarian regime, they are at least as likely to honour obligations into which they have freely entered – and this is an important qualification – as other oriental countries'. Dening to Eden ibid.
12 ibid.
13 ibid.
14 ibid. Dening, deploying his usual bluntness, wrote that it has 'been obvious for the last 25 years to my knowledge that, even without dumping or commercial malpractices or sweated labour, the Japanese cotton industry can compete successfully with Lancashire'.
15 ibid.
16 Braddon's article in the *Daily Express* for 25 November 1955 was headlined, 'They'll Get You Yet! Beware those Japs'. Commentary on Emperor Shōwa's death and funeral suggests that the approach still continues.

17 Dening to Foreign Office, 18 April 1956 FJ 1052/3 (FO 371/121046). Dening clearly endorsed the Japanese doubts that the visit to London by Japanese Dietmen had made any substantial difference to British thinking.

18 Selkirk to Lloyd, 24 October 1956.

19 ibid. See also CAB 128/29 (1955) and CAB 129/77 (1955).

20 For discussion of the worsening trade picture, see A.R. Prest and D.J. Coppock (eds), *The UK Economy: A Manual of Applied Economics*, London, 1974, ch. 3.

21 Dening to W.D. Allen, 25 January 1955, FJ 1051/4 (FO 371/11523).

22 ibid. Dening's suggestion 'seemed rather to alarm him, and he said that was a very serious subject, to which I retorted that we need not discuss it as seriously as all that'. After Dening had made his pitch he felt the 'response to what I said was virtually nil'. This might have had something to do with Dening's approach and the lack of preparation from a nation that likes to come prepared.

23 Dening's remarks on American foreign policy in the region were equally harsh. He had more than a few differences with US officials, including Dulles, though his relations with the US ambassador, Allison, in Tokyo were cordial.

24 Dening to Selwyn Lloyd, 'Japan: Annual review for 1955', FJ 1011/1 (FO 371/121030).

25 ibid.

22. SIR GEORGE SANSOM

1 G.B. Sansom, *Japan: A Short Cultural History* was first published by the Cresset Press, London in 1931, and remains in print. G.B. Sansom, *A History of Japan to 1334*, *A History of Japan 1334–1615* and *A History of Japan, 1615–1867* were also published by the Cresset Press, in 1959, 1961 and 1964 respectively. They remain in print.

2 For Sansom's early life see Katharine Sansom, *Sir George Sansom and Japan: A Memoir*, Tallahassee, Florida, 1972, pp. 1–3. *The Reminiscences of Sir George Sansom*, New York: Oral History Research Office, Columbia University, 1957, pp. 1–4; E.T. Williams and C.S. Nicholls (eds), *Dictionary of National Biography, 1961–1970*, Oxford 1981), pp. 922–3, and his Obituary in *The Times*, 10 March 1965.

3 K. Sansom, *Sir George Sansom*, pp. 6–7.

4 Sir Charles Eliot's official assessments of Sansom's qualities are reprinted in K. Sansom, *Sir George Sansom*, pp. 12–13.

5 Letter from Sir George Sansom to Professor Marius Jansen, 1 September 1959. (Kindly supplied to the author by Professor Jansen.)

6 G.B. Sansom, *An Historical Grammar of Japanese*, Oxford, 1928, p. vii.

7 G.B. Sansom, *Japan: A Short Cultural History*, 1st edn, p. vii.

8 *Times Literary Supplement*, 7 April 1932.

9 G.B. Sansom, *Reminiscences*, p. 17.

10 Memorandum by Sansom, enclosed in Lindley to Simon, No. 574, 28 October 1932 (F 8307/39/23), FO 371/16242 cited in W.R. Louis, *British Strategy in the Far East 1919–1939*, Oxford, 1971, p. 218.

11 K. Sansom, *Sir George Sansom*, p. 32.

12 Memorandum by Sansom, 11 November 1932, enclosed in Lindley to Simon, No. 603, 11 November 1932 (A 8174/53/45), cited in Louis, *British Strategy in the Far East*, p. 219.

13 K. Sansom, *Sir George Sansom*, p. 95; G.B. Sansom, *Reminiscences*, p. 36.

14 K. Sansom, *Sir George Sansom*, pp. 36, 56–68 and 77. G.B. Sansom's, *The Western World and Japan: A Study in the Interaction of European and Asiatic Cultures* was finally published by the Cresset Press, London in 1950.

15 K. Sansom, *Sir George Sansom*, p. 89.
16 ibid., p. 92.
17 ibid., pp. 94–7.
18 Sansom later recounted his resignation as follows: 'I had said to the permanent Under Secretary, I really don't see why I should stay. I'm not going back to Japan. I hate your ambassador there. He's a fool', *Reminiscences*, p. 57.
19 K. Sansom, *Sir George Sansom*, p. 110.
20 ibid., p. 114.
21 ibid., p. 120.
22 ibid., p. 123–4.
23 Sansom's work in wartime Washington is well summarized in Roger Buckley, *Occupation Diplomacy, Britain, the United States & Japan, 1945–1952*, Cambridge, 1982, pp. 10–13.
24 'Sir George Sansom's views of postwar Japan', Memorandum of Conversation, 28 July 1943. Participants, G. Sansom, G.H. Blakeslee, H. Borton, Drafted by H. Borton, reprinted in Ōkurasho Zaiseishishitsu (ed.), *Shōwa Zaiseishi, Shūsen Kara Kōwa made. Vol. 20 Eibun Shiryō*, Tokyo, 1982, pp. 6–7.
25 Llewellyn Woodward, *British Foreign Policy in the Second World War, Vol. 5*, London, 1976, pp. 519–21. Sansom's role at this time is also summarized in Chihiro Hosoya, 'George Sansom, Diplomat & Historian', in I.H. Nish and C. Dunn (eds), *European Studies on Japan*, Tenterden, Kent, 1979, pp. 116–18.
26 K. Sansom, *Sir George Sansom*, p. 141.
27 ibid., p. 154.
28 ibid., p. 146.
29 ibid., p. 161.
30 For the official history of the Commission, see G.H. Blakeslee, *The Far Eastern Commission: A Study in International Co-operation 1945 to 1952*, Washington, DC, 1953). For Sansom's role see Buckley, *Occupation Diplomacy*, pp. 76–9.
31 Letter from Sir George Sansom to G.C. Allen (undated). MS Add. 247/2/0 (G.C. Allen Papers, University College, London).
32 G.B. Sansom, 'Can Japan be reformed?', *Far Eastern Survey*, 2 November 2949, p. 258.
33 This preoccupation was most evident in the five volumes of the 'modernization' series published by Princeton University Press.
34 G.B. Sansom, *The Western World and Japan*, p. 223; see also T.C. Smith, *The Agrarian Origins of Modern Japan*, Stanford University Press, 1959.
35 G.B. Sansom, *Japan in World History*, London, 1952, p. 1.
36 Letter from Sir George Sansom to Professor Marius Jansen, 1 September 1959.
37 Marius Jansen, 'Review of G.B. Sansom, *A History of Japan to 1334*', *Journal of Asian Studies*, 18 (1958–9), pp. 501–3.
38 G.B. Sansom, *A History of Japan, 1334–1615*, p. vii.
39 John Whitney Hall, 'Review of G.B. Sansom, *A History of Japan, 1615–1867*', *Journal of Asian Studies*, 23 (1963–4), pp. 615–17.

INDEX